North American Homeland Security

North American Homeland Security

Back to Bilateralism?

Imtiaz Hussain,
Satya R. Pattnayak, and
Anil Hira

PSI Reports

PRAEGER SECURITY INTERNATIONAL
Westport, Connecticut · London

Library of Congress Cataloging-in-Publication Data

Hussain, A. Imtiaz, 1953–
North American homeland security : back to bilateralism? / Imtiaz Hussain, Satya R. Pattnayak, and Anil Hira.
p. cm.
Includes bibliographical references and index.
ISBN 978–0–313–35686–5 (alk. paper)
1. Free trade—North America. 2. National security—Economic aspects—North America. 3. National security—United States. 4. United States—Defenses—Economic aspects. I. Pattnayak, Satya R. II. Hira, Anil. III. Title.
HF1746.H87 2008
363.34'56—dc22 2008022564

British Library Cataloguing in Publication Data is available.

Library of Congress Catalog Card Number: 2008022564
ISBN-13: 978–0–313–35686–5

First published in 2008

Praeger Security International, 88 Post Road West, Westport, CT 06881
An imprint of Greenwood Publishing Group, Inc.
www.praeger.com

Printed in the United States of America

The paper used in this book complies with the Permanent Paper Standard issued by the National Information Standards Organization (Z39.48–1984).

10 9 8 7 6 5 4 3 2 1

Contents

Preface vii

Abbreviations xi

1 North America's 9/11 Dilemma: Puzzles, Payoffs, and the Institutional/ Procedural Matrix 1

2 U.S. Homeland Security and Post–9/11 North American Integration: The Homeland Era 30

3 Asymmetry Squeezing Out Trilateralism? Canadian Ambivalence on U.S. Strategic Primacy 56

4 Mexico and Homeland Security: Revolving Doors and Transient Interests 103

5 Canada–U.S. Relations Since 9/11: Putting Humpty-Dumpty Back Together? 131

6 Post–9/11 Mexico–U.S. Relations: Green Pastures, Rough Patches, Muddled Outcomes 159

7 Canada, Mexico, and Homeland Security: Oddballs 198

8 9/11, Theory, and the *North America* Idea: Trilateralism on Trial? 226

9 Conclusions: North American Tango—Only For Two 241

Notes 253

Appendix: Investigative Questions 291

Bibliography 293

Index 313

Preface

When the world's largest economy shuttered its borders on 9/12 for the first time in the modern era, its top two trading partners, Canada and Mexico, were not only directly and brutally impacted, but also faced increasing security filters thereafter. Had a different era in cross-border North American relations begun? On the one hand, the DHS (Department of Homeland Security) was established as the central agency in the largest administrative overhaul since World War II to keep not only the United States safe, but also revive a wider security community. On the other hand, based on the Washington Consensus, free trade movement in the Western Hemisphere independently reached its own crossroads: As the United States looked beyond NAFTA (North American Free Trade Agreement) toward a CAFTA (Central American Free Trade Agreement) in 2003, the FTAA (Free Trade Area of the Americas) initiative grinded almost to a halt. Were trade thrusts impeded by 9/11 restrictions, if not directly, then indirectly? Canada and Mexico were left with fewer options *vis-à-vis* their giant neighbor: Under a neoliberalist drive, Canada proposed free-trade to the United States in 1985, with Mexico following suit in 1990, only to have a post–Cold War security threat suddenly haunting them both. It was not so much a question of whether they would join their overwhelmingly largest trading partner in securing common frontiers, but whether regional commitments would continue with sincerity and priority or become superficial.

How Canada and Mexico responded to the DHS establishment leads first to a country-specific study of 9/11 policy responses across North America, then to appraising the region's three bilateral relations, highlighting security and intelligence, before exploring trilateral possibilities. Driven by theoretical tenets from integration, interdependence, and realism, the volume examines North America's guns-butter trade-off under full theoretical light.

Stemming from a PIERAN (*El Programa Interinstitucional de Estudios sobre la Región de América del Norte*) fellowship, the research and writing profited from three seminars. In chronological order, these were at UIA (*Universidad Iberoamericana*), Mexico City, during April 2006, VU (Villanova University), Pennsylvania, in October that year, and SFU (Simon Fraser University), Burnaby, BC, in Canada, during March 2007—our respective home institutions. We remain indebted, and extend our appreciation, to the following reviewers: Edward D. Mansfield and María Pía Taracena Gout at Ibero, David Barrett, Jorge Nowalski, and Lowell Gustafson at Villanova, and Emmanuel Brunet-Jailly and Eric Hershberg at SFU, not to mention other erudite participants.

Each of us profited from comments to several papers presented in various scholarly conferences: Imtiaz Hussain at the AMEI (Mexican Association of International Studies) in 2002 and 2005, the 2003 International Studies Association annual convention, University of Toronto's Munk Center, University of Victoria, British Columbia, and the Latin American Studies Association, all in 2004, and the World International Studies Committee meeting in Bilgi University, Turkey in 2005; Satya Pattnayak at the Comparative Social Science Research Conference in Tokyo's Sophia University during July 2006; and Anil Hira at the BCPSA (British Columbia Political Science Association) and the ACSUS (Association of Canadian Studies of the United States) annual conventions. Again we graciously acknowledge reviewer comments and audience inquiries at these fora.

As a uniquely structured North American resource-base, PIERAN requires one scholarly institution from each of the three North American countries to engage in any of its funded research. Our debts, gratitude, and acknowledgements accordingly assumed a triangular trajectory. SFU's Hira, replacing George Melnyk from the University of Calgary who withdrew for health reasons, was commendably supplemented/complemented by Douglas Ross, thanks Alex Leger of PSEPC (Public Safety and Emergency Preparedness Canada) and Aaron Hywarren of Canada's DND (Department of National Defence) for their kind assistance in arranging some of the field research interviews. His appreciation for Brunet-Jailly and Hershberg also extends to Alex Leger, Peter Avis, Margaret Purdy, Francis Furtado, Hussain, Mansfield, and Taracena Gout for valuable editorial comments.

Pattnayak similarly extends his gratitude to several observers of the border dynamics for having donated generous time for interviews in Austin, TX, San Diego, CA, Madison, WI, Seattle, WA, and Bellingham, WA. He is especially indebted to Hugh Conroy of the Whatcom Council of Governments in Bellingham, Washington, for willingly sharing his valuable time and information.

In coordinating the project, Hussain acknowledges continued support of Blanca Torres, PIERAN's coordinator at COLMEX (*El Colegio de México*), her committee colleagues, in particular David Mena Aleman and her successive program assistants, Mari Carmen Muñoz and Alejandro Garcia Buenrostro. He also appreciates direct support from his own research assistants—Mario Ivan Coronel Sanchez, Hilda Patricia Gutíerrez Chávez, and Jonathan Gilbert Acosta—Alejandro Anaya Muñoz for managing the seminars as department director, and Juan Francisco Zuleta Godínez for coordinating the finance. He is most grateful to six other individuals: Gustavo Acua Popocatel for company on several field-trips to, and through, the Mexico–U.S. borders, support for research in Houston, Philadelphia, and Mexico City, and travels to New York and Washington; Ken Fleuriet, his former University of Pennsylvania student and subsequently a Texan legislator, for introduction to the Texan border; Geri Fleuriet who eased navigating the perilous Brownsville-Matamoros and McAllen-Reynosa border cross-points; Randy Fleuriet, who gave several interview leads and numerous tips in Harlingen, McAllen, and Edinburg, all in Texas; Blanca Martínez, another former student now happily launching a teaching career in her own right, while serving as Stephen Clarkson's research assistant; and Mansfield for a Visiting Professor stay at the Christopher Browne Center of International Politics, which he directs, at the University of Pennsylvania, during 2006–07.

All three of us acknowledge the very useful comments from two PIERAN reviewers twice; and appreciate the enormous support and guidance Adam Kane at Praeger and BeaconPMG's Manohari Thayuman gave us, especially through a number of bumpy moments and through many of their colleagues. Hussain gratefully acknowledges colleagues, editors, and publishers where portions of this manuscript have been or will be published for their permission. These include: David Mena Alemán and Emma R. Norman, editors of *Politics and Policy,* and Michael Streeter of Blackwell/Wiley (vol. 36, no. 1, February 2008, pp. 108–31); Richard R. Valcourt, editor of *Journal of Intelligence and Counterintelligence* (where an article is forthcoming); and Stuart Farson, Peter Gill, Mark Pythian, and Shlomo Shpiro who edited the PSI Handbook *Global Security and Intelligence, National Approaches,* vol. 1: *The Americas and Asia* (Westport, CT: Praeger, 2008), 67–92, in the Praeger Security Series, Suzanne Paris at Praeger for promptly issuing the permission. Needless to say, none of them are responsible for any omissions or commissions. We alone are responsible for them.

In the final analysis, none of the work would have been smoothly concluded without the support of competent secretarial staff members and research associates. Hussain is indebted to Amalia Miguel Cruz and Patricia Garcia Espinosa (both department secretaries); and Pattnayak to Dana Moss (his research associate).

Abbreviations

ABM	Antiballistic missile
ACLU	American Civil Liberties Union
AFL-CIO	American Federation of Labor-Confederation of Industrial Organizations
APEC	Asia Pacific Economic Cooperation
APIS	Advanced Passenger Information System
ASAT	Antisatellite (weapons)
ASC	Amalgamated security community
ASEAN	Association of Southeast Asian Nations
BCC	Border Crossing Card (Mexico–United States)
BEA	Bureau of Economic Analysis (United States)
BEW	Board of Economic Welfare (United States)
BIF	Border Infrastructure Fund (Canada–United States)
BIP	Border Industrialization Program (*Maquiladoras,* 1965)
C4ISR	Command, Control, Communications, Computers, Intelligence, Surveillance, and Reconnaissance
CAFTA	Central American Free Trade Agreement
CATSA	Canadian Air Transport Security Authority
CBCF	Cross-border Crime Forum
CBNRC	Communications Branch of the National Research Council (Canada)
CBP	Customs and Border Protection (United States)
CBSA	Canadian Border Service Agency
CDAI	Conference of Defence Association Institute (Canada)
CF	Canadian Forces
CFIA	Canadian Food Inspection Agency
CFR	Council on Foreign Relations (New York)
CIA	Central Intelligence Agency

CIB	Criminal Investigation Bureau (Canada)
CIC	Citizen and Immigration Canada
CIG	Central Intelligence Group (United States)
CINCNORAD	Commander-in-Chief North American Aerospace Defence Command
CINCNORTHCOM	Commander-in-Chief Northern Command
CIPAC	Critical Infrastructure Partnership Advisory Council
CISEN	*Centro de Inteligencia y Seguridad Nacional*
CMR	Civilian-military relationship
COFAA	Conference of the Armies of the Americas
COMINT	Communications intelligence
CORBOR	Coordinated Border Infrastructural Program
CPIC	Canadian Police Information Centre (Canada)
CSBMs	Confidence and Security Building Measures
CSI	Container Security Initiative (United States)
CSE	Communications Security Establishment (Canada)
CSIS	Canadian Security and Intelligence Service
CTC	Counter Terrorism Center (United States)
C-TPAT	Customs-Trade Partnership Against Terrorism
CUFTA	Canadian–U.S. Free Trade Agreement
CUSP	Canada–U.S. Partnership
DCI	Director of Central Intelligence (United States)
DCI	Department of Citizenship and Immigration (Canada)
DDCI	Deputy Director of Central Intelligence (United States)
DEA	Drug Enforcement Agency (United States)
DFA	Department of Foreign Affairs (Canada)
DFAIT	Department of Foreign Affairs and International Trade (Canada)
DFS	*Dirección Federal de Seguridad*
DHS	Department of Homeland Security (United States)
DIA	Defence Intelligence Agency (United States)
DMA	Defence Ministerial of the Americas
DND	Department of National Defence (Canada)
DNI	Director of National Intelligence (United States)
DOD	Department of Defence (United States)
DON	Department of the Navy (Canada)
DOS	Department of State (United States)
DOT	Department of Transportation (United States)
DP	Dominion Police (Canada)
EAI	Enterprise for the Americas Initiative (June 27, 1990, United States)
EC	European Community
ECSC	European Coal and Steel Community
EDIG	Executive Directorate of the Inspector General (Canada)
EII	Enforcement Information Index
EO	Executive Order (United States)
EPIC	El Paso Intelligence Center
EU	European Union

FAST	Fast and Secure Trade
FBI	Federal Bureau of Investigation (United States)
FDA	Food and Drug Administration (United States)
FDI	Foreign direct investment
FDR	Franklin Delano Roosevelt
FEMA	Federal Emergency Measures Act (United States)
FEMD	Federal Emergency Management Directorate (United States)
FHWA	Federal Highway Works Administration (United States)
FIRA	Foreign Investment Review Agency (Canada)
FISA	Foreign Intelligence Surveillance Act (United States)
FLQ	*Front de Liberación du Québec*
FOLs	Forward Operating Locations
FTA	Free Trade Agreement
FTAA	Free Trade Area of the Americas
GDP	Gross domestic product
GSA	General Services Administration (Canada)
GWB	George W. Bush
HSAC	Homeland Security Advisory Council
HSC	Homeland Security Council (United States)
HSSTAC	Homeland Security Science and Technology Advisory Committee
HUMINT	Human intelligence
IADB	Inter-American Defence Board
IAEA	International Atomic Energy Agency
IANC	Inter-American Naval Conference
IBETs	Integrated Border Enforcement Teams (Canada)
IC	Intelligence Community
IC	Interinstitutional Council (Mexico)
ICBM	Intercontinental ballistic missile
ICC	Immigration and Customs Canada
ICE	Immigration and Customs Enforcement (United States)
ID	Implementation duties
IEDs	Improvised Explosive Devices
IG	Inspector General (Canada)
IPC	Intelligence producers committee
IPFSC	International Port Facility Security Trade (Canada–United States)
IRCA	Immigration Reform and Control Act (United States, 1986)
IRTPA	Intelligence Reform and Terrorism Prevention Act (United States)
ISAF	International Security Assistance Force
ITAR	International Traffic in Arms Regulations
JIB	Joint Intelligence Bureau (Canada and United States)
JTTF	Joint Terrorism Task Force
LAWs	Legalized Agricultural Workers (United States)
MC	McDonald Commission
MID	Military Intelligence Division (United States)

MPI	Migration Policy Institute
MRC	Mackenzie Royal Commission
NACC	North American Competitive Council
NAFTA	North American Free Trade Agreement
NATO	North Atlantic Treaty Organization
NEP	National Energy Policy (Canada)
NEXUS	North American Expedited U.S. border clearance program (United States–Canada border)
NFIB	National Foreign Intelligence Board
NIAC	National Infrastructure Advisory Council
NIC	National Intelligence Council (United States)
NORAD	North American Aerospace Defence Command
NORTHCOM	Northern Command
NSA	National Security Advisor (United States)
NSC	National Security Council (United States)
NPT	Non-proliferation Treaty (1968)
NSRB	National Security Resources Board (United States)
NSS	National Security Strategy (United States)
OAG	Office of the Attorney General (Canada)
OAS	Organization of American States
OASSIS	Operation Against Smugglers and Traffickers in the Safety and Security Initiative
OEM	Office of Emergency Management (United States)
OHS	Office of Homeland Security (United States)
OMLA	Office of Mexicans Living Abroad (Mexico)
ONI	Office of Naval Intelligence (United States)
OSS	Office of Strategic Services
OTMs	Other than Mexicans
OWI	Office of War Information (United States)
PAN	*Partido Acción Nacional*
PAPS	Pre-Arrival Processing System (Canada)
PAS	Performance Advancement System
PATRIOT	Providing Appropriate Tools Required to Intercept and Obstruct Terror (Act)
PCO	Privy Council Office (Canada)
PFP	*Policícia Federal Preventiva* (Mexican)
PGR	*Procuraduría General de la República* (Mexican)
PHF	Personal history files
PMR	Policy-making responsibility
PRI	*Partido Revolucionario Institucional*
PRD	*Partido de la Revolución Democrática*
PRN	*Partido Revolucionario Nacional*
PSC	Pluralistic security community
PSEPC	Public Safety and Emergency Preparedness Canada
QDR	Quadrennial Defence Review (United States)
RAWs	Regionalized Agricultural Workers
RCMP	Royal Canadian Mounted Police

REI	Regional Economic Integration
RFDs	Radio frequency identification devices
RIA	Revolution in intelligence affairs
RMA	Revolution in military affairs
RNWMP	Royal North West Mounted Police
RRT	Rapid Response Team
SAGARPA	*Secretaria de Agricultura, Ganaderia, Desorollo Rural, Pesca y Alimentación*
SAWs	Specialized Agricultural Workers
SBP	Shared Border Process (Canada–United States)
SDI	Strategic Defence Initiative
SEDENA	*Secretaría de Defensa Nacional*
SENTRI	Secure Electronic Network for Travelers Rapid Inspection
SFU	Simon Fraser University (Burnaby, BC, Canada)
SG	Solicitor General (Canada)
SG	*Secretaría de Gobernación*
SHIP	Strategic Highway Infrastructure Program (Canada–United States)
SIGINT	Signals intelligence
SIRC	Security Intelligence Review Committee (Canada)
SOA	Summit of the Americas
SPP	Security and Prosperity Partnerships
SSP	*Secretaría de Seguridad Pública*
START	Strategic Arms Reduction Talks
TAU	Threat Assessment Unit (United States)
TBWG	Transportation Border Working Group (Canada–United States)
TC	Transportation Canada
TSA	Transportation Security Administration (United States)
TTIC	Terrorist Threat Integration Center (United States)
UIA	*Universidad Iberoamericana* (Mexico City)
UNCTAD	United Nations Conference on Trade and Development
USCG	United States Coast Guard
USCIS	United States Citizen and Immigration Service
USDA	United States Department of Agriculture
USSS	United States Security Service
VACIS	Vehicle and Cargo Inspection System (Canada-United States)
VISIT	Visitor and Immigration Status Indicator System (United States)
VU	Villanova University (Pennsylvania, U.S.A.)
WCG	Whatcom Council of Governments (Canada–United States)
WHTI	Western Hemisphere Travel Initiative
WMD	Weapons of mass destruction

1

North America's 9/11 Dilemma: Puzzles, Payoffs, and the Institutional/ Procedural Matrix

STAKES AND STAKEHOLDERS

As the 9/11 dust continues to settle in 2008,[1] North America—consisting of the United States, Canada, and Mexico—faces at least four trade-offs:[2] (a) security-economy; (b) collective versus state interests; (c) a post–9/11 security regime confronting pre–9/11 trade integration; and (d) adjusting cross-country comparisons to embedded country-specific values. North America's new concerns may actually be revitalizing some old behavioral patterns.

Turning to the first puzzle, economic-security trade-offs get to the heart of the *North America* idea spawned by economic integration. They are neither new across North America nor exclusively dependent on formal institutions. Informal activities, or what Guadalupe González González and Stephan Haggard call cross-border externalities,[3] also influence policy outcomes. We refer to both legitimate and illegitimate activities of the kind as *procedures,* capable of acquiring *institutional* claims over time. Grain embargoes against the Soviet Union during the early 1970s illustrated a formal Cold War trade-off; while several strategies of containment were pursued under the institutional guidance of the NSC (National Security Council).[4] Also impacting outcomes, however, were attitudes, like the *better-dead-than-red* U.S. mentality of the 1950s, actions like Cuban refugees receiving automatic U.S. residency upon landing in Florida, as well as unanticipated developments, such as the 1980s East European democratic surge ending the Cold War. Though the Cold War did not speak for North America in one voice, it entwined Canada and the United States, through NATO (North Atlantic Treaty Organization), perhaps not in a linear love affair, but guided by explicit common purposes. On the other hand, through most of the Cold War, Mexico was not penalized for its Cuban (though not communist) sympathy, indicating U.S. intolerance levels to be a variable. How did Mexico's pre–9/11 NAFTA (North American Free Trade Agreement) enthusiasm adjust to post–9/11 war-on-terrorism indifference? What impact will this have on North American integration? Will it connect as well with Canada under a security imperative as it did under economic integration, or could 9/11 provide the United States the occasion to shift attention back to Canada from Mexico just as NAFTA shifted greater U.S. attention to Mexico from Canada? Indeed, how will regional economic integrative efforts adjust to security imperatives Cold War type?[5]

Choosing between collective action and self-help involves another trade-off. During the 1950s, for example, economic pursuits were more sharply defined and determined by military considerations than in the 1960s,[6] when a Cold War thaw sparked economically driven regional integrative measures in the Western Hemisphere.[7] Security considerations still had the last laugh, especially across Latin America where military dictators or authoritarian governments, with U.S. support, prevailed over democratic demands, as in Chile during the 1970s. When Cold War atmospherics resurged in the 1980s, U.S. trade preferences were reduced to no more than bilateral FTAs (free trade agreements).[8] Interestingly, Canada and Mexico proposed free trade to the United States only when the Cold War was waning,[9] in 1985 and 1990, respectively, prompting the United States to open several flanks of trade agreements—bilateral, plurilateral, multilateral, and so forth, in the 1990s.[10] Will this shift toward collective action survive a one-track, U.S.-driven security onslaught? Or is the 2002 U.S. NSS (National Security Strategy),[11] or the Bush Doctrine,[12] becoming the counterpart of George F. Kennan's 1947 *Long Telegram* and the Cold War, opening a "long-term, patient but firm and vigilant" approach toward terrorism?[13] More importantly, since 9/11 was an attack on U.S. soil, how deep will Canada and Mexico engage in any U.S. homeland security? Will, in fact, the homeland be prioritized by *security* or *defence* imperatives, options clarified subsequently?[14]

Derived from both trade-offs, the third puzzle asks if a security regime can be built upon pre–9/11 U.S. interests in economic regimes. Regional economic integration in the 1990s depended on aggressive U.S. marketing of free-trade, from "Alaska to Tierra del Fuego," as George H.W. Bush envisioned with his EAI (Enterprise for America Initiative) on June 27, 1990. Beginning with the 1994 Miami SOA (Summit of the Americas), continuing with the FTAA (Free Trade Area of the Americas) from 1998, and persisting after 9/11 in George W. Bush's competitive liberalism,[15] establishing a trading regime crossed many hurdles, exposed a pattern of cooperation, and generated more hopes than concerns. Yet, with the DHS (Department of Homeland Security) and a war in Iraq reinserting security imperatives,[16] all three North American countries must not only face a welfare-warfare trade-off, highlighted by the first puzzle, but reconfigure past regimes to fulfill contemporary security needs. In facing new challenges, will state-centricism prove more efficient than regime coordination? If intentions and actions remain positive, how will they adjust their institutions, then redirect them against opening sociological gateways to terrorism: not just home-grown Muslims shifting loyalties to *jihadi* causes within the United States, but also capitalizing on porous U.S. borders, either directly or through *coyotes*?[17]

On a different track of the third puzzle, North America's pre–9/11 threats also emanated from the phenomenal growth of emerging Asian economies, led by China and India,[18] as well as nuclear proliferation and the resort to WMD (weapons of mass destruction). Since all of these received more U.S. time, attention, and resources,[19] terrorism as a U.S. threat hypothetically carries symptoms of expanding cooperation.

In addition, with all three countries deeply dependent on each other for trade and investment—some more so than others—institutionalizing a common security interest depends, in part, on how the homeland is defined. Does it mean only the United States or North America? Even more pertinent, does the approach adopted reflect *homeland security*, defined as "civilian-led measures to protect the people, property, and systems of a country," or *homeland defence*, meaning "military-led measures to defend a national territory."[20] In short, will they bring North America full circle: upgrading security amid expanding economic flows; institutionalizing responses amid ever-growing cross-border societal linkages; and adding unilateralism to the bilateral, trilateral, and multilateral agendas Canada and Mexico have with the United States?

If further institutionalization results, what new principles, norms, rules, and decision-making procedures do we expect;[21] yet if informal actions and behaviors continue, how will they be regulated? In fact, whether there is interpretational symmetry or not between the three countries—not just over events and developments, but also concepts—opens up the fourth question: How to streamline the oftentimes dissimilar sociocultural and political economy values of the three countries, and thereby, how to forge a sustainable common security outlook against the new security threat without sacrificing advantages of economic integration? In addition to visible borders, invisible value-based barriers also distinguish countries. Taking security as an example, Canada has long advocated human security, as opposed to the military security the United States prioritizes; and Mexico, particularly during regional economic integration, faced greater security threats from within rather than outside, in direct contrast to the United States. Can the values bred by these different orientations be sufficiently blended? Taking the role of intelligence, for example, how will the internationalist orientation of the U.S. CIA (Central Intelligence Agency) be streamlined with the largely domestic orientation of both the CSIS (Canadian Security and Intelligence Services) and Mexico's CISEN (*Centro de Inteligencia y Seguridad Nacional*)?

From another angle, during World War II, Canada and the United States not only developed mutual interests over security values, but were also able to embed these within an Anglo-Saxon intelligence context;[22] yet, by the same account, even though Mexico's military collaboration with the United States also dates back to World War II, Mexico is seen today as some form of a "Hispanic challenge."[23] Will the contrast between Canadian–U.S. institutional cooperation and Mexican–U.S. institutional suspicion reflect, or boil down to, an Anglo-Saxon set of values developed since World War II and distinguished from any Hispanic values?

Although ours is not a comparative study of culture, it is hard to ignore cultural impacts on security imperatives, especially when stereotyping not only runs deep but, in scattered cases, also explains reality better than analysis. The "Hispanic" reference carries with it images of poverty, laziness, and petty crime, for example, while "Anglo-Saxon," from at least the time of Max Weber, portrays thrift, industriousness, and a progressive work ethic.[24] Whether these caricatures represent reality or not, it is not hard to bump into them when traveling from the northern U.S. border to the southern.

Two narrow questions demand attention under the North American microscope: What did the 2002 U.S. HSA (Homeland Security Act) entail? How did the two neighbors respond? Whereas HSA provides the institutional principles, norms, rules, and decision-making procedures, our inquiry if these were absorbed in Canada and Mexico leads to an analysis of how they were regionally institutionalized in the first place, and what adjustments were needed, if any. Whether any new Canadian–Mexican comparative light is shed, the analytically least developed bilateral relation across North America gets unusually full treatment.

TWO CONTEXTS AND THREE COUNTRIES

Since neither security community nor economic integration lacks a comprehensible architecture, we begin by placing ground-level observations into security community theoretical constructs. We turn first to the security trenches, that is, the nature of the HSA, and the Canadian and Mexican responses. Since the events behind North American economic integration have been thoroughly examined in the literature,[25] and are not the direct subject of our own investigation, we restrain our discussions to merely interpreting theoretical applications. Relaxing both integrative theories (security community and neofunctionalism) to include hybrids (interdependence itself and the neorealism), we not only investigate the relevance of these paradigms under the drastically changed post–9/11 order, but also if there exists anything like a "best fit."

Defence Abandonment and Security Homecoming: 9/11 Policy Responses

How did the three North American countries specifically respond to 9/11? We begin with the United States before assessing the two neighbors, in alphabetical order.

The United States

Neither security nor restructuring the administration for security reasons constitutes new U.S. imperatives. As Howard C. Relyea observes, John Jay had talked about *national safety* in *Federalist Papers #3* and Alexander Hamilton of *national security* in *Federalist Papers #70* in the 1790s; while Theodore Roosevelt in peacetime, rather than Abraham Lincoln during war, first authorized an administrative reorganization, creating the Department of Commerce and Labor and the Committee on Organization of Government Work, in 1903.[26] However, the most sweeping reorganization was under his nephew, Franklin Delano Roosevelt (FDR), driven first by a "world in depression,"[27] then a global war. His 1939 Reorganization Act created the Executive Office of the President, consisting of the White House Office, the

Bureau of the Budget, the National Resources Planning Board, the Office of Government Reports, the Liaison Office for Personnel Management, and a provision to establish an emergency management office as and when required.[28]

As matters transpired, the OEM (Office for Emergency Management) was created on May 25, 1940, while the Reorganization Act was renewed in 1941, 1945, 1949, 1953, 1955, 1957, 1961, 1964, 1965, 1969, 1971, 1977, and 1984. Authorized by an earlier War Powers Act, on December 18, 1941, FDR also created the Office of Production Management, Office of Price Administration and Civilian Supply, Office of the Coordinator of Inter-American Affairs, Office of Scientific Research and Development, Office of Lend-Lease Administration, and the Office of Facts and Figures. The cream organizations, however, were left to his successor, Harry S Truman,[29] whose July 1947 National Security Act established the CIA, the NSC, and the NSRB (National Security Resources Board).

Thus, when George W. Bush proposed an OHS (Office of Homeland Security) to both congressional chambers on September 20, 2001, then utilized EO (Executive Order) 13228 to establish it, followed by creating the HSC (Homeland Security Council) on October 8, he undertook a more fundamental reorganization than FDR: In signing the HSA in 2002, Bush created DHS on November 25,[30] which opened for business on March 1, 2003. FDR was not only on a faster track with his reorganization and in finding lesser opposition than Bush, but he also faced unpredictability and imponderables on fewer occasions than Bush. Even though it amalgamated the Coast Guard, INS (Immigration and Naturalization Service), TSA (Transportation Security Administration), FEMA (Federal Emergency Measures Act), and the Agricultural Department's Animal and Health Inspection Service, the DHS still left out the intelligence agencies—suggesting the wider range of perceived threats than FDR faced in the 1940s. Both resorted to sprawling bureaucracies to confront their threats, and though the 1980s Reagan Revolution sought to dismantle the New Deal, Bush, who is often dubbed Reagan II, put into motion one of the largest administrative expansions in U.S. history. Just to begin with, DHS commanded 170,000–180,000 workers.[31]

At stake, on the one hand, was the distinction between *homeland security* and *homeland defence:* Whereas responsibility after the Pearl Harbor attacks was entrusted to such central agencies as the DOD (Department of Defence) and CIA, thus prioritizing defence, post–9/11 responsibility falls at multiple levels of decision-making—federal, state, and local; whereas *homeland defence* is reactive, *homeland security* is proactive.[32] On the other hand is a clash between Article I, Section 8 and Article II, Section 2 of the constitution. Whereas the former authorizes Congress to enact laws to create offices and appoint officers, Article II, Section 2 of the constitution authorizes the president to make appointments, regardless of consultation with or advise from the Senate—a conundrum also affecting Canada and Mexico—as evident later. A climate of enhancing executive powers, at the expense of legislative, was fully exploited after 9/11, in turn breeding, as Relyea observes for the United States, potential confusion from overlapping authorities, duplication, and a disregard for the constitutionally mandated balance of domestic powers.[33]

Headed initially by Tom Ridge, DHS was led by Michael Chertoff during most of our research calendar (2004–08). At a slightly lower level is a group including the vice president, attorney general, secretaries of defence, health and human services, and transportation, and the directors of CIA, FBI (Federal Bureau of Investigation), and FEMA, among others—a body too overloaded to deal with emergencies, and without a clear-cut division of labor. Be these as they may, the relationship with the NSC is not established, and indeed no definition of homeland security has even been attempted.[34] EO 13228 authorized OHS "to lead, oversee, and coordinate a comprehensive national strategy to safeguard [the USA] against terrorism and respond to any attacks that may come,"[35] and HSC was made responsible "for advising and assisting the President with respect to all aspects of homeland security," serving "as the mechanism for ensuring coordination of homeland security-related activities of executive departments and agencies and effective development and implementation of homeland security policies."[36] Such open-ended mandates were not only inconsistent with what the founding fathers had in mind, even against emergencies, but also predicted chaos, confusion, and incoherence by encouraging intrusion, arrogance, and a bureaucratic hierarchy.

Even five years after establishing OHS and HSC, "a significant [security] gap" still exists. Bruce Berkowitz ascribes this to inadequate intelligence.[37] Creating the TTIC (Terrorist Threat Integration Center) narrowed this gap but invited interagency hostility: DHS did not want it, and since it is authorized to operate within the United States and against U.S. citizens, the CIA and FBI also remain reluctant hosts. The "wall" Kate Martin sees between intelligence gathering and law enforcement not only predicts, but also increases, interagency incompetence.[38] One victim is individual liberty. For example, the October 2001 PATRIOT Act allows the CIA to utilize the FISA (Foreign Intelligence Surveillance Act) to wiretap, conduct private searches, and eavesdrop on foreigners within the United States operating on behalf of other countries or groups.[39] The Kean Commission even proposed creating a domestic intelligence agency.[40] In arguing for *transforming* operations rather than *reforming* them,[41] Deborah C. Barger proposes the first task to be to identify "what intelligence is," then "to tackle the greater question of what intelligence should do."[42] A debate on RIA (revolution in intelligence affairs), she argues, is also currently needed, just as the post–Cold War RMA (revolution in military affairs) entailed two decades of debates before 9/11.

EO 13228 posed many organizational problems, raised infinite constitutional inconsistencies, and jeopardized foreign policy, albeit indiscriminately. In spite of Bush's post–9/11 clarion call for other countries to be with the United States or against it, EO 13228 treated *all* countries with circumspect and suspicion, beginning with the very U.S. neighbors—Canada and Mexico.

To recall, Canada's May 1985 proposal to establish a FTA with the United States was not only accepted—and implemented from January 1, 1989—but also expanded into the NAFTA following a similar proposal from Mexico in February 1990,[43] and implemented from January 1, 1994. Thus, by the time of 9/11, NAFTA-based transactions between Canada, Mexico, and the United States had both expanded and diversified. When the United States first closed its borders on the heels of 9/11, NAFTA relations faced an unforeseen impediment. Seven years later, as this manuscript is being completed, NAFTA-based transactions face a crossroads at which, interestingly, security imperatives appear much less deterministic than other emerging trade developments and cross-border externalities. To what extent were the administrative U.S. reorganizations mirrored in Canada and Mexico, if at all; and how influential was the United States in bringing about those changes, if any?

Because of the gravity of the issues and stakes involved, but also owing to a simultaneous deterioration of Canadian–U.S. relations just when Mexico–U.S. relations were scaling new heights,[44] those questions find North American relations at another turning-point. George W. Bush dispensed with a U.S. tradition of making the maiden presidential visit to Canada, and even immediately after 9/11 in what Andrew Cohen calls "the great snub,"[45] Canada was not initially mentioned as the special friend with which the United States shared the largest unprotected boundary in the world, not to mention the largest bilateral trade relationship. In fact, even Great Britain did not rank high on Bush's initial list of special friends. Smitten by Vicente Fox Quesada, the new Mexican president, Bush engaged in unprecedented parleys with his southern counterpart, all reflecting *rancho* politics, as two landowners sought to extend their mutually reinforcing philosophies of a market economy and deeper integration. At some point or another, the sour side of Mexico–U.S. relations was bound to intervene, a dimension filled with incompatible positions on immigration, drugs, and the prickly asymmetrical context, all representing externalities of trade integration.[46] Fox became the first Mexican president to propose treating transboundary human flows as in the then European Union—very much like commodities, and all a part of economic integration. No matter how much he sympathized with at least the principle behind the proposal, Bush was trapped between a Congress unwilling to make any far-reaching immigration deal of the sort and a southern counterpart who had become his most exclusive friend. It was not only cast on the bilateral relationship one week before 9/11, but also became an immediate victim of 9/11. When 9/11 events dominated world news for quite a few days thereafter, Fox took a low profile for long enough to be noticed by White House staff-members. When his call came, in addition to being too late, it offered little comfort, and proved inadequate of the leader of the second largest U.S. trading partner then. Every day since rebounds off that single disconnection.[47]

Canada

Canada had its own U.S. disconnections. In part due to its post–Cold War shift from the NATO-based *collective security* to a more multilaterally shaped *cooperative security*,[48] Canada's initial 9/11 responses did not fall in line with U.S. expectations. According to Jill Sinclair, cooperative security *a la* Canada emphasizes (a) contact and dialogue among countries; (b) democratic development; (c) human rights; and (d) economic development.[49] To defeat the continued action–reaction spiral of foreign policies, she continues, Canada sought a security architecture defined by (a) multilateralism; (b) reassurance rather than deterrence; (c) complementing, coexisting, or replacing bilateral security arrangements; (d) promoting military and non-military security; (e) flexibility and adaptability; and (f) norms, principles, and practices of transparency.

Clearly these were not at all suitable to the post–9/11 security view in Washington. Also inchoate was a personality clash between Jean Chrétien, Canada's prime minister, and George W. Bush, reflecting ideologically contrasting positions on the political spectrum. Neither sought to dissolve or correct this. Even though the two countries share 8,000 kilometer of an unprotected border, Roger Gibbins observes "they share it in very different ways":[50] 75 percent of Canada's population lives in the 150-mile belt from the border, thus adding border population dependency and the more unsettled consequences over issues such as national integration and national sovereignty, to extant power asymmetry, as a source of potential friction. As Paul Ganster and Alan Sweedler posit, the Mexican–U.S. border differs conceptually and substantively from the Canadian–U.S. counterpart. Whereas the former reflects (a) a passively shared security community; (b) economic interdependence; (c) relatively easy transboundary labor flows; (d) a shared cultural environment; and (e) a shared remoteness of the border regions from the centers of economic and political powers,[51] the latter conveys (a) a more robustly shared security community; (b) a lesser border population dependency; and (c) labor-flows not necessarily constituting a border industry; especially now Mexican *maquiladoras* seem to be migrating to the south of the country or abroad. Prevailing cultural commonalities along the Canadian–U.S. frontier, Gibbins argues, prevents a sense of border remoteness from growing.[52]

After the Cold War, Canada experienced a RIA but not a RMA. In addressing domestic security, Bill C-9 elevated the CSIS over the RCMP (Royal Canadian Mounted Police), from June 21, 1984. Though CSIS evaluates terrorist threats through the TAU (Threat Assessment Unit), keeps in contact with community leaders of expected problems, combines functions with ICC (Immigration and Customs Canada) to feed the EII (Enforcement Information Index), and streamlines government agencies at various policy-making levels, almost all of its work is more counterintelligence than counterterrorism. Many argue police and intelligence functions do not go well together.[53] In the wake of 9/11, CSIS–RCMP coordination increased since the RCMP does not have sufficient funds to fulfill localized antiterrorism tasks, and especially because terrorism falls under Canada's Criminal Code penal jurisdiction, whose responsibility is local, not federal.[54] Even with the SIRC (Security and Intelligence Review Committee) and EDIG (Executive Directorate of the Inspector General) as CSIS watchdogs, 9/11 pushed Canada to raise the intelligence ante in keeping with U.S. expectations, but by the same token, also running afoul of the public at large. Rather than reflect Canadian priorities, these changes exposed Canadian divisions: Chrétien kept his distance from Bush, Paul Martin's attitudes fluctuated, and Steve Harper's hopes of deepening commitments straddle over buried hatchets, for example, over the Arctic Ocean sovereignty issue.

Peter Chalk and William Rosenau point to CSIS's inability to penetrate terrorist cells, weakness in channeling intelligence across various levels, and coordination problems with local and provincial officials.[55] As if compensating for these, Justice Minister Anne McClellan's Bill C-36 of October 15, 2001, "was designed to enhance the federal government's capacity to protect Canada," and "contribute more effectively to international efforts aimed at combating global terrorism."[56] This is very consistent with the cooperative security philosophy: It ratified two UN documents—the International Convention for the Suppression of the Financing of Terrorism, and the International Convention for the Suppression of Terrorist Bombings. Ronald J. Daniels and others, however, remain concerned how enhancing federal powers reduces Canadian liberties and weakens profederation feelings. The bill defines terrorism for the first time and specifies various offenses and penalties, in addition to permitting the police to judicially supervise investigations and apply sanctions as and when required. It also elevates electronic surveillance, provides power to suppress critical information from the public, and authorizes arrest based on reasonable suspicion regardless of a tradition respecting the innocence of every person until proven guilty.

Gary T. Trotter explains how McClellan's claim of Bill C-36 being *Charter-proof*,[57] captures the honest helplessness: "Individually, most of these changes are small. Cumulatively, they claim significant liberty in an insidious way. The legislative style of Bill C-36, apparently fashionable these days, is to graft onto existing provisions terminology, nuances and new categories, designed to cover the latest emergency situation. This triage style of legislations creates for law that is confusing and unwieldy."[58] The key term, *triage,* used by medical personnel to distinguish between life and death, raises the question if 9/11 events, or U.S. responses to 9/11, became Canada's damoclean predicament.

The answer may still be up in the air. While applauding "the increasingly robust democratic process that has surrounded the introduction of the bill," Kent Roach still chastises the entire notion of *Charter-proofing* for at least three reasons:[59] (a) "citizens and elected representatives may be too quick to accept as wise or necessary what the government's lawyers conclude is permissible to do";[60] (b) 9/11 is interpreted as if "law enforcement and coordination, including intelligence gathering, was inadequate," not because "the criminal law was inadequate," thus "creating many new offices, increasing the investigative powers of the police and increasing punishments for terrorist offenses," and in the process, "routinely ratchet[ing] upon already broad and severe criminal law in response to horrific crimes";[61] and (c) given the above, the resultant "criminalization of politics" distinguishes "old political case" pitting the accused against the state, from "new political case," including "the accused and the state, but also the victim, potential or actual."[62]

Fearing a "more repressive" state, "with increased emphasis on the investigation and punishment of crime" rather than exploring the case,[63] Roach (a) streamlines the U.S. approach; (b) echoes concerns of Sujit Choudhry about how Bill C-36 is silent over "one of the central issues in the public debate...ethnic and racial profiling...";[64] and (c) complicates what Audrey Macklin calls "the immigration-as-security-threat leitmotif," whereby "the functionality of borders is being eroded even as—or perhaps because—the demand to fortify them is reaching new levels of fervour [*sic*]."[65]

Mexico

Just as Canada's 9/11 concerns rally around individual rights and liberties, Mexico's concerns overlap extant measures against narcotrafficking into the United States, how it converges with especially illegal emigration, and thereby an unavoidable U.S. Mexican intrusion against which Canada is relatively more insulated. With borders eliciting such different connotations, the merging of domestic-international policy preferences dramatized by 9/11, produces quite different results. By elevating legal concerns over social consequences, Canada is able to keep foreign policy considerations at bay, whereas Mexico, regardless of whether it elevates legal or social concerns over each other, must inevitably do so in terms of its foreign policy relations with the United States at any given time. When reflecting consonance, those relations go deeper than between Canada and the United States; but if they become incongruous, more friction awaits the United States in the south than in the north. We argue 9/11 accents the incongruity portion of the bilateral equation: It does so in part by feeding into existing policy incompatibilities—over drugs, for example—and in turn, dramatizing cultural incompatibilities, especially as they relate to legal practices.

Just as Canada confidently sought institutional/orientational changes through procedural changes, Mexico's prioritization of institutional/orientational shift under Fox was stifled by incompatible or confusing procedures. With the CISEN established in 1989 to replace the disbanded DFS (*Dirección Federal de Seguridad*), and a specific intelligence agency emphasizing HUMINT (human intelligence), SIGNIT (signals intelligence), and COMINT (communications intelligence), CISEN continues to be thwarted by precisely the DFS ailments: extortion, torture, corruption, and a weak institutional setting. Christopher Leroy gallantly argues, although Mexico's democratization from 2000 constrained some of these excesses, CISEN nevertheless succumbed to the inevitable turf-fighting every newly created agency faces,[66] as previously observed with both the U.S. DHS creation and Canada's Bill C-36. Placed directly under the Mexican Interior Ministry, CISEN is responsible to the inter-institutional council, comprising of the interior secretary, attorney general, secretaries of public security, defence, navy, finance, and public administration through a National Security Threat Assessment report. It does not make policy and controls no budget. Upon taking office, Vicente Fox Quesada created a NSA (National Security Advisor), and appointed Adolfo Aguilar Zinser to that post until he was made Mexican Permanent Envoy to the United Nations in January 2002. Amidst inter-agency rivalry, the NSA post was abolished. CISEN's low-profile positioning in the executive branch (by remaining under the Interior Ministry rather than under the NSA) means it must also compete with other intelligence agencies—SEDENA (controlled by the Defence Secretariat), SEMAR (controlled by the Navy), PGR, SSP (Public Security), and FPP (Police), just like the CSIS and RCMP in Canada, as well as DHS, CIA, and FBI in the United States.

Even more diversionary is the connection between intelligence and narcotics. Though a vitally needed relationship, and especially under the watchful eyes of counterpart U.S. agencies, Mexico's IC (intelligence community) remains exposed to corruption and narcotrafficking penetration.

In the aftermath of 9/11, both the PRI (*Partido Revolucionario Institucional*) and PRD (*Partido de la Revolución Democrática*) sought to bring intelligence under congressional control. Article 73, Paragraph 28 of the constitution was amended to facilitate this in 2003, although Article 89, Paragraph 6 also authorizes the president to manage security. By sloughing off its tainted reputation and assuming more responsible postures, CISEN could fit and facilitate 9/11 needs, but as in the United States and Canada, distinguishing the extent of executive power from the open-endedness of legislative oversight, bedevils the new Mexico. Unlike the United States and Canada, where checks and balances reflect a deeper tradition of the rule of law prevailing over the resort to force, Mexico still needs to work out in practice the proper and constitutionally more commensurate interbranch power equation. In sum, as in the United States and Canada, the IC faces a reorganization deficit, but unlike the United States and Canada, 9/11 may be imposing harsher conditions for an unconvincing Mexico to iron out. Could domestic political differences more than intelligence-driven convergences undermine each North American country in its responses to terrorism? Whereas all three agree on the urgency to do something, and the sooner the better, the motivations and methods remain too far apart to produce a coherent singular strategy.

Comparative Context

In summarizing and further developing the comparative context, table 1.1 also explores the immediate backdrop to the 9/11 demands, as previously discussed, and plays on the institutional-procedural tendencies of policy interests, serving as either inputs or outcomes. Under the *nature of responses* dimension, Canada's and Mexico's remain a function of U.S. responses, yet from the *prior intelligence experiences* dimension, we notice how both Canada and Mexico were shaking the security tree from the 1980s, very much like the United States but completely independently in Canada and largely independently for Mexico. Consequently, whereas prior experiences fed directly into 9/11 responses for the United States, they were more indirect for both Canada and Mexico.

In turn, the second dimension of table 1.1, relating to *institutional/procedural tendencies,* shows the United States adopting an institution-driven 9/11 response, although ad hoc procedural responses were not uncommon, especially when perceived security threats increase, while neither Canada and Mexico institutionalized the security threat quite as explicitly and wholeheartedly: Whereas Canada will not, owing to the nature of its constitution, federation, and twenty-first-century vital interests, Mexico cannot because of the peculiarities of belated democratization generating greater gaps between the written word (constitution) and everyday governance (including neglect of the checks-and-balance imperative, impunity tendencies,

Table 1.1 9/11 Demands: Backdrop, Institutional/Procedural Tendencies, and Interests

Dimension	United States	Canada	Mexico
1. Immediate 9/11 responses	HSA, DHS, PATRIOT Act	Bill C-36	Delayed countermeasures
2. Nature of responses	Unilateral, stakes pushed higher through sanctions, explicit strengthening of decision-making hierarchy (federal over state, executive over legislature)	Mixed, both independent and multilateral; stakes pushed higher through implicit and explicit sanctions; federalism-based hierarchy promoted	Supplied upon U.S. demand, not spontaneously; tepid rather than robust in tone; hierarchy in flux (executive vs. legislature)
3. Prior intelligence experiences	NSS originated in 1986 Goldwater-Nichols Act, and 1992 Presidential Directive	RCMP faced CSIS competition from 1984	CISEN created 1989
4. Nature of prior experiences relating to 9/11 responses	Direct and incremental	Indirect and unexpected, shift from local to federal	Indirect and unexpected, shift from combating drugs, domestic insurgency
5. Institutional/procedural tendencies	Institutions determine procedures	Greater emphasis on procedural approach to institutional modifications	Institutions emphasized by tyranny of procedures, too many agencies, unavoidable U.S. influence; U.S. influence most effective at decentralized level, and over procedures than over institutions
6. Interests	Preempt threats: immigration and terrorism belong to same family of concerns	Preventive approach	Immigration and terrorism represent two different issues

and so forth). Thus, in terms of *interests,* whereas the United States embraces preemption, Canada and Mexico do not, but in different ways: Canada goes to the other extreme of prevention, placing antiterror concerns high on its agenda, and thereby antagonizing the United States less than Mexico, where neither preemption nor prevention commands as much priority as the more homegrown issues of emigration and narcotrafficking. Mexico sees these issues as being very different from security imperatives, but the United States packs them all into one ball of potential threat.

9/11 RESPONSES IN THEORETICAL LIGHT

As indicated, we rely on two major clusters of theories, the integrative (security and neofunctionalist) and hybrid (interdependence and neorealism), with intelligence paradigms thrown in between them. If anything, 9/11 raised the need for greater intelligence, and since a thriving intelligence theoretical industry was brewing since the end of the Cold War, we turn to this literature to capture nuances traditionally omitted by integrative and interdependent theories.

Security Community

Popular in the first decade of the Cold War, security community resurfaced as an explanatory framework after the Cold War ended. Under the Bush Doctrine, however, given the emphasis on preemption, security community arguments remain arguably incomplete without the inclusion of intelligence paradigms. Accordingly, a treatment of the tenets of security community is followed by a two-dimensional appraisal of intelligence principles, contexts, and institutional norms. The first exposes some of the components of the very definition of regimes, as described previously: principles, norms, rules, and decision-making procedures. The second paves the way for comparative analyses of intelligence across North America.

Does North America constitute a security community? In moving from the trenches to the theoretical front, we can fortunately draw upon previous works by others addressing similar questions. Karl Deutsch and others who developed the security community thesis at the height of the Cold War,[67] that is, the mid-1950s, also distinguished between the amalgamated and pluralistic varieties. Although the 50 states of the United States constitute what they labeled ASC (amalgamated security community), thus becoming a synonym of domestic political integration, their more interesting type, between sovereign countries and labeled PSC (pluralistic security community), was illustrated by Canada–United States, among others. Since the end of the Cold War, Jorge Dominguez and Rafael Fernandez de Castro led an adventurous group of scholars who saw Mexico belonging not only to a security community with its northern neighbor, but also different types of a PSC prevailing.[68] We need not be detained by the merits and disadvantages behind each claim, since the literature is replete with them,[69] but reassessing the very tenets under different 9/11 light helps answer the lead question. What are they? How relevant are they post–9/11? Why should not their relevance be subordinated to the more underlying broader currents of commerce influencing intercountry relations in the region?

Navigating these lesser questions, we strip the two integrative theories (security community and neofunctionalism), and two hybrids (interdependence and neorealism) to their essential features for comparisons, and add intelligence paradigms here and there since 9/11 went beyond the sum of the parts of integration and interdependence by reaffirming values (borrowed from security community),[70] demanding canons of cooperation (borrowed from both security community and neofunctionalism), stoutly demonstrating statist peculiarities (interdependence), and responding to an invisible global threat (neorealism) through a priori information (intelligence). Tables 1.2 and 1.3 identify and elaborate the catalyzers, varieties, and tenets/characteristics of security community, in that order.

Table 1.2 traces catalyzers of a politically integrated community in the three North American countries. The overall picture exposes integrative wrinkles, but also reaffirms no single wrinkle can prevent the emergence of a broader community.

The purposeful orientation shift taking place was bipartisan in all three countries, meaning the dominant two parties generally believe in a North American security community, but only in the United States can any single political party reverse this: Canada and Mexico may be too relatively small to reverse North American integrative efforts, but also domestic parties have too many other issues to spar over to make this shift a matter of do-or-die. Consequently, institutionalizing this shift, the second catalyzer, bears the same trait: It is underway in all three countries, and though reversible in all three, Canada's and Mexico's low-intensity security imperatives make it unimportant, and thus reduces any reversibility concern, but high-intensity U.S. security imperatives makes reversibility a critical consideration. The quality of leadership becomes all the more important, while in Mexico reversibility is more likely given the single-term presidential tenure.

Do negative instincts alienate positive counterparts? This is more likely in Mexico and the United States than in Canada owing to how rules are treated: Canada places a high degree of respect on rules, Mexico is more flexible, while the United States subordinates them to force, resulting in better chances of compromise in Canada than in Mexico and the United States. If asymmetry raises its head here, it does so more conspicuously with the fourth catalyzer: safeguarding against external shocks. Canada and Mexico can do little to safeguard against the United States, but can free-ride the U.S. security system against any other external threats; by contrast, the United States permanently prioritized such safeguards since Pearl Harbor.

Given the inherent North American asymmetry, exploring new avenues of collaboration has not and cannot become perpetually vibrant: collaboration seeks either symmetrical outcomes or the reduction of asymmetries, both unlikely North American expectations. Thus, this catalyzer is perpetually undersupplied. The last catalyzer, compatible leadership, is perpetually unpredictable owing to the United States: Canadian and Mexican leaders do not have many other options than to go with the U.S. flow; yet U.S. leaders have the habit of taking Canada or Mexico too much

Table 1.2 North American Political Integration: Catalyzers

Catalysts	Canada	Mexico	United States
1. Occurrence of purposeful orientation shift?	Yes, it is bipartisan, and no reversion seen as yet	Yes, it is bipartisan, and no reversion seen as yet	Yes, it is bipartisan, but is reversible (for at least exogenous reasons)
2. Institutionalization of orientation shift?	Has been initiated, no reversal fears as yet, leadership has been critical	Has been initiated, no reversal fears as yet, leadership has been critical	Has been initiated, but remains reversible, leadership is critical
3. Gresham's law in integrative instincts (bad instincts driving out good ones)?	Probability is lower, disagreements have been rules-respecting	Probability is higher, disagreements can be and have been rules-defying	Probability is higher, disagreements can be and have been rules-defying
4. Safeguarding against external shocks?	Less need, impossible to do so against United States	Less need, impossible to do so against United States	Greater need, would produce Pareto suboptimal results
5. Exploring new avenues of collaboration?	Consistently missed opportunity	Consistently missed opportunity	Consistently missed opportunity
6. Compatible leadership?	Present, necessity-driven	Present, necessity-driven, but with a wildcard possibility	Present, but potential not fully utilized, carries wildcard possibility

Adapted from Karl W. Deutsch, et al., *Political Community and the North Atlantic Area: International Organization in the Light of Historical Experience* (Princeton, NJ: Princeton University Press, 1957), chap. 2; and Joseph S. Nye, "Comparing Common Markets: A Revised Neofunctionalist Model," in *Regional Integration: Theory and Research,* eds., Leon N. Lindberg and Stuart A. Scheingold (Cambridge, MA: Harvard University Press, 1971), chap. 5.

for granted, as Bush did with Canada in his first term and Mexico in the second, thus sowing seeds of suspicions.

What do the tenets and characteristics say? Table 1.3 lists twelve security community characteristics, the first three stemming from a PSC, the remaining nine to an ASC. If NAFTA seriously sought to integrate the three countries, the nine amalgamated features would show signs of convergences (dimensions 4 through 12), but significantly, 9/11 was not the only reason why this has not happened: Dimension 11, for example, calls for decreasing barriers to mobility across political boundaries, meaning Mexicans would be as free to move to the United States as U.S. citizens would be to relocate to Mexico; and this has never been possible, with Fox's most concerted effort to make it happen being shot down one week before 9/11 as the most promising instance. Even Canada and the United States, with open pre–9/11 borders, could not become one amalgamated community: With so many regional and cultural differences plaguing Canada alone, U.S. amalgamation complicates relations rather than clarifies them.

Table 1.3 Conditions of Pluralistic and Amalgamated Security Communities: The 9/11 Difference

Dimension	The 9/11 difference
1. Value compatibility	Increasing pre–9/11 convergences, tendency of some values to diverge after 9/11, especially as to how preemptive responses should be
2. Behavioral predictability	High before 9/11, diminishing thereafter, but not to critically low levels
3. Mutual responsiveness	High before 9/11, still remains high, but clouded somewhat by mutual suspicion
4. Value complementarity	High before 9/11, still very high but propensity to diverge exposed
5. Distinctiveness in lifestyles	High before 9/11, but showing tendencies to converge, still high post–9/11, but slow evaporation of those tendencies
6. Reward expectations before burden sharing	Described pre–9/11 relations well, but becoming less of a post–9/11 factor
7. Increasing political and administrative functions	High before 9/11, with NAFTA creating many of these, not expanded or utilized sufficiently after 9/11
8. Economic growth distinguishing core areas from peripheral	Clearly evident in all three countries before 9/11, continues to still characterize each country
9. Geographical and social communications linkages	Proved to be areas of growth pre–9/11, continue to be important growth areas post–9/11, though facing more hurdles
10. Multiplication of communications and transactions	Very high pre–9/11, continues to be high post–9/11, though facing hurdles
11. Decreasing barriers to mobility across political boundaries	Not a significant pre–9/11 concern, though barriers remained, increasing source of post–9/11 concerns, with boundaries being strengthening to the point of challenging the integrative spirit
12. Increasing political elites	From being key pre–9/11 players of integration, elites serve less as agents after 9/11

Adapted from Karl W. Deutsch, et al., *Political Community and the North Atlantic Area: International Organization in the Light of Historical Experience* (Princeton, NJ: Princeton University Press, 1957), chap. 2; and Joseph S. Nye, "Comparing Common Markets: A Revised Neofunctionalist Model," in *Regional Integration: Theory and Research,* eds., Leon N. Lindberg and Stuart A. Scheingold (Cambridge, MA: Harvard University Press, 1971), chap. 5.

Compared to other bilateral relations, nevertheless, Canada, Mexico, and the United States show greater value compatibility (belief in regionalized trade, for example), behavior predictability (eventually aligning with George Bush's "with us" camp), and mutual responsiveness (e.g., the periodical NAFTA-based summits). Of course, on all three counts, there were larger and deeper examples before 9/11 than after, just as not all three North American bilateral relations supply symmetrical responses simultaneously.

Yet, 9/11 raised some other values, related more with life-death than welfare-enhancing issues showing considerable incompatibilities. As a discussion of intelligence below shows, Canada–United States and Mexico–United States relations shift in opposite directions in discussing military-related values.

Progressing from these three PSC tenets toward the nine ASC counterparts was difficult even before 9/11, though 9/11 does not make ultimate integration impossible. Many values continue to complement or mirror those across nationalistic boundaries in North America (respect for private property and fundamental human rights, for example), while others do not (selected protectionist attitudes over some commodities of trade while upholding the principle of free trade; unilateralist behavior while broadly seeking reciprocity). Unconnected values reaffirm the tenet of lifestyle distinctiveness (Canada's treatment of cultural industries under NAFTA, Mexico's reluctance to privatize electricity under NAFTA given its traditional public sector treatment, and the United States treating minimum wage standards so exclusively as to keep its own lifestyles one step ahead of the others).

All three countries sought integrative rewards, but asymmetrical fears also spiked after 9/11. In turn, both asymmetry and growing burdens have prevented political and administrative functions from expanding and working effectively: If they did work effectively, immigration would not be a growing Mexico–U.S. problem, for example, and in the Canada–U.S. relations, "studs and suds, hogs and logs" would not continue as unresolved dispute areas.[71]

NAFTA certainly distinguished growth areas from nongrowth counterparts, with proximity to the United States being one of the yardsticks: Thus the north of Mexico benefited more than the south. It also penalized separatists or localists, like the indigenous groups in Mexico's south. Even in Canada, Montréal, and Québec, compared to Toronto or Vancouver during the NAFTA years, saw more corporations migrate out than in, at least initially; and the entire eastern Canadian region did less well than the western. Clearly these distinctions directed or reflected greater social communications unequally, and with them overall communications and transactions, as well as lower barriers, also unequally.

In all three countries, more elites travel across national boundaries, suggesting the growth in this area. However, that does not mean they all agree or think alike.

Do the first three PSC dimensions show more North American optimism? The Canada–U.S. dyad increasingly reflected these characteristics after World War II, while Mexico passionately embraced them in the 1990s. Thus, at least two PSCs existed in North America before 9/11, since Canada and Mexico barely sustained a relationship before the 1990s, and both were too driven by low-politics (nonmilitary) issues in the 1990s. Was 9/11 a dividing line, that is, a force behind combining the two existing PSCs into one North American community, or eliminating them for other nationalistically driven forms of community? We posit two interrelated responses? First, just because multiple integrative threads depict the two dyads even after 9/11, we often end up neglecting differences and divergences, but by the same token, when we highlight those incompatibilities, we do not convey disintegration. Whether clouded by ideology, personality, or culture, or glowing through streamlined policies, complementarities, or a vast number of identities whose key unpredictable feature is how many of them, both dyads lay greater claim than many others reflecting the three PSC features just as they also show the highest degree of that fundamental incompatibility of asymmetry than any other dyad. Based on given tenets, both were, are, and for as long as the broad brushstrokes of today's international system remain, will be able to reflect this conditioning of simultaneous integration and asymmetry. In turn, a second consideration demands greater attention: Are the tenets too broad in an increasingly cluttered world and too bland to be able to usefully distinguish country propensities, especially after 9/11 changed the protagonism ballgame by facing invisible nonstate actors for the first time?

Adding all the nuances and finesses, warts and beauty spots without advancing farther, we may find subjective interpretations filling some of the missing blanks. For example, the three PSC types forwarded by Domínguez and Fernandez de Castro—balancing, abnegation, and bandwagoning—explain specific policies, though not structures. Aggregating policies to define an epoch, as Domínguez and Fernandez de Castro do, expose inconsistencies, nonstate dynamics, such as societal groups like Greenpeace, and more reasons to move out of familiar theoretical loops. The idea of a PSC is not fatalistically injured, but even in its crippled form, unless a more convincing model emerges, it still commands analytical respect by default.

Intelligence Offshoots

Building security communities and preserving values could produce contradictory results. By bringing principles, norms, rules, and decision-making procedures into the equation, tables 1.4, 1.5, and 1.6 challenge the purity or impurity of security community tenets. At the same time, the 9/11 difference is gleaned both by comparing the various elements across the three countries as well as through pre– and post–9/11 perspectives. Even before addressing them, one notices, how during the age of neoliberalism (when NAFTA was produced), references to intelligence was minimal, and only if the subject matter was military security. Not only has the pre–9/11 political economy outlook adopted a deeper cultural strain after 9/11, but paradigm tenets also face greater vulnerability unless modified—all cluttering the analytical plane. Intelligence paradigms offer no solution to this predicament, but fill missing blanks.

Of the six principles in table 1.4, only the first and last carry a country-centric tone; but since these are the critical principles, capable of vetoing the many principles reflecting similarities, we get a sense of both security community angulations and

Table 1.4 Intelligence Principles

Principles	Country responses	The 9/11 differences
1. Intelligence derives from international conflict or rivalry	Clearly true of the United States since 1947, somewhat less so for Canada, considerably less so for Mexico	Greater Canadian interest, but less so for Mexico
2. Conduct or use of intelligence involves secrecy	True for all countries	Even more true after 9/11
3. Clandestine collection of information is the fundamental activity of intelligence	True for all countries	Even more true after 9/11
4. Truth must be the basis of good intelligence	True for all countries, but the principle does not exclude false information	Even more true after 9/11
5. Intelligence in a vacuum is of no value, tardy intelligence is of little value	True for all countries	Even more true after 9/11
6. Special activities must involve native knowledge of the national groups toward which they are directed	Given the first principle (of United States being very external, Canada both external and domestic, and Mexico domestic), only the United States seeks native knowledge abroad, Canada relies largely on U.S. information (through NATO), and Mexico has little or no experience on this	As true a principle before 9/11 as after

Adapted from Winn L. Taplin, "Six General Principles of Intelligence," *International Journal of Intelligence and Counterintelligence* 3, no. 4 (1989): 475–91.

limitations. Both these principles shape institution-building, the other four principles belong to a menu of procedures.

With the external environment projected in the first principle, the sixth elevates the need for native knowledge. As the third column spells out, the United States has had plenty of experiences with both since the 1947 creation of the CIA, thus giving its intelligence apparatus more of an external bent than domestic; Canadian intelligence during both World Wars (RCMP), the Cold War (CSIS), and after 9/11, though relying on the United States for external knowledge, adopted an introverted orientation, especially keeping tabs on suspected migrants; and Mexico's intelligence has historically been fully stretched just keeping abreast of internal threats, whether from revolutionaries before World War II or increasingly drug traffickers after World War II.

Historical experiences, geographical positioning, and cultural characteristics compound these orientations, widening the country differences. The largely affect attitudes and behaviors more than institutions. Table 1.5 identifies them as background/conditioning forces behind intelligence, and illustrates them as possible areas of North American incompatibilities.

Turning to the first element, a sense of shared security history speaks more for Canada and the United States than for Mexico–United States. For example, both Canada and the United States belonged to NATO (Canada proposed it, United States adopted it reluctantly in the 1940s), Mexico did not. However, both Canada and Mexico share critical geographical peculiarities, the second element: next-door location to a military, economic, and industrial superpower. With the third element, the differences become conspicuous: Canada and the United States share an Anglo-Saxon background as influential in the shaping of its institutions as in daily activities, such as the language spoken, diet, clothing, and so forth; but while Mexico and the United States also share a Hispanic overlap, there is more friction than accommodation in their relationship; and a Canada–Mexico cultural heritage is yet to evolve.

The seven elements in table 1.5 bounce off the three orientations depicted in table 1.4 (United States being largely external, Canada mixed, and Mexico largely domestic). The United States is more interested in promoting democracy abroad (first element), but in none of the three countries have domestic democratic institutions impacted intelligence. Similarly, the media are kept at a safe distance from intelligence pursuits in all three countries (second), while suspicion toward the government/military (third) again reflects the external U.S. orientation and the domestic Canadian and Mexican orientation. Mobilization-demobilization (fourth), much like the notion of invincibility (fifth), or preference for total wars (sixth), relates with war and reflect experiences only of the United States, again reiterating its external orientation. On the other hand, a tradition of citizen-soldier (seventh) speaks only of Mexico, that too before World War II, reinforcing Mexico's domestic intelligence orientation.

What impact did 9/11 have on these? Perhaps the salient observation was to sharpen and spike their impacts on only the United States: establishing democracy abroad received greater urgency, keeping the media at bay was pursued more religiously, suspicion of government/military increased, while the fourth, fifth, and sixth elements exposed more mobilization–demobilization, as well as greater demonstration of, and preference for, total war. Yet, even these revealed limits.

The seven factors directly impacting strategic culture, also from table 1.5, are more of a variable within and between countries, emphasizing patterns of uninstitutionalized behavior (preference for total war, for example), procedures (such as the mobilization-demobilization cycle), and in some cases institutions (democracy, for instance). Here too we notice how security considerations summon values from the deep recesses of the past, very unlike their economic counterparts which place more of a premium on the present and the future.

Institutional norms behind intelligence, listed in table 1.6, depict more similarities, or at least a predictable range of outcomes. Almost all the 14 norms, if not all, show North American similarities, differing only in degree. Yet, 9/11 makes this degree critical, as in the "with us or against us" George W. Bush dictum. Although Michael A. Turner developed the fourteen norms based on a study of only

Table 1.5 Elements of Strategic Culture

Categories	Country implications	The 9/11 differences
Background influences:		
1. Sense of history	1. Runs incompatibly deep in each country	1. 9/11 overrides historical orientations/experiences
2. Geographical endowment	2. Contiguity exposes asymmetry	2. Not affected by 9/11, in fact security tightened more
3. Cultural heritage	3. Greater Canada–United States overlap than Mexico–United States	3. 9/11 accents past history of shared experiences (Canada–United States) over mixed experiences (Mexico–United States)
Factors directly affecting strategic culture:		
1. Democratic institutions	1. Promoting democracy abroad characterizes U.S. intelligence; not a robust Canadian or Mexican factor	1. Democracy promotion yielding diminishing returns (especially in Iraq)
2. Role of media	2. Keeping media in the dark was the preferred intelligence target	2. Media penetration of intelligence, and polarization increasing
3. Suspicion of government/military	3. Reflects attitude of intelligence agencies toward other countries in all three countries: Canada's RCMP, Mexico's CISEN, and U.S. DHS/CIA/FBI	3. Same attitude spreading among citizens, especially "persons of interest"
4. Mobilization–demobilization pattern	4. Relevant only during/after war: more relevant for United States than Canada or Mexico	4. Increasing limits on mobilization, but demobilizing increasingly difficult
5. Notion of invincibility	5. Relevant only for United States	5. Even United States made to feel ordinary
6. Preference for total wars	6. Relevant only for United States	6. Growing needs for lesser wars
7. Tradition of citizen-soldier	7. Relevant only in pre–World War II Mexico	7. Not impacted

Source: Donald Snow, *National Security: Defence Policy for a New International Era* (New York, NY: St. Martin's Press, 1995), 42–65.

U.S. intelligence, a North American comparative study profits by applying them to Canada and Mexico. By and large, 12 of them show similar patterns in all three countries, leaving only the first and twelfth differentiating those countries. Institutional survival, the first of the 14, characterizes only the United States, where both the CIA and FBI have persisted in their original formats. Canada's RCMP and CSIS have been under pressure constantly, especially with accountability under greater demand than in the United States; while in Mexico, every presidential turnover predicts a change. In the same way, primacy of intelligence analysis (twelfth) echoes the orientations in table 1.4 (U.S. external orientation, Canadian mixed, and Mexican exclusively domestic): Only the United States gives intelligence analysis this primacy, whether it is wrong or correct (Saddam's WMD as a wrong intelligence information; the early 1960s Soviet nuclear missile installation in Cuba as a correct counterpart), and its external orientation permits security community construction; but Canadian and Mexican introversion not only reduces the impact of intelligence analysis, but also prevents security community construction. If anything, 9/11 sharpened and spiked each of these elements with the result of deepening differences—more so with Mexico than with Canada.

Integration through security community tenets is clearly not enough without invoking the intelligence paradigm. Invoking intelligence owing to the emergence of an invisible threat like terrorism, on the other hand, cuts deep into the heart of

Table 1.6 Intelligence and Institutionalized Norms

Institutional norms	Country comparisons	9/11 differences
1. Institutional survival	Greater survivability in United States than in Canada, Mexico has least	Sharpened, spiked difference
2. Secrecy	Roughly similar	Sharpened, spiked difference
3. Intelligence exceptionalism	Roughly similar	Sharpened, spiked difference
4. Ambiguous mandate	Roughly similar	Sharpened, spiked difference
5. Confederal structure	Roughly similar	Sharpened, spiked difference
6. Flexible accountability	Roughly similar	Sharpened, spiked difference
7. Separation of intelligence from law enforcement (police)	Roughly similar	Sharpened, spiked difference
8. Competitive intelligence	Roughly similar	Sharpened, spiked difference
9. Separation of intelligence from policy	Roughly similar	Sharpened, spiked difference
10. Policy support	Roughly similar	Sharpened, spiked difference
11. Can-do attitude	Roughly similar	Sharpened, spiked difference
12. Primacy of intelligence análisis	True in United States, less so in Canada, even less in Mexico	Sharpened, spiked difference
13. Emphasis on current intelligence	Roughly similar	Sharpened, spiked difference
14. Provision for accurate, timely, and relevant intelligence	Roughly similar	Sharpened, spiked difference

Source: Michael A. Turner, "A Distinctive U.S. Intelligence Identity," *International Journal of Intelligence and Counterintelligence* 17, no. 1 (2004): 49; but see 42–61.

integrative theories in general: A weak security community undermines neofunctionalist expectations.

Economic Integration: Leaving the Heart at Home Again?

Regional economic integration became the star North American model of the 1990s, reviving and enhancing neofunctionalism. Table 1.7 shows how neofunctionalist prerequisites (first four dimensions), process mechanisms (next seven), and perceptual frameworks (last three) were more robust before 9/11, indicating greater economic integration, though not eliminated, survives in a less rigid post–9/11 form. In short, 9/11 only dented their armor; how long the injury remains and whether individual pieces may atrophy without threatening the larger edifice, we do not know for sure. In the absence of another 9/11, we argue they will all plod along, as muddling in the international system may be more normal than abnormal; since the first lesson of simply surviving is self-defence, bilateral arrangements hypothetically offer greater safety than trilateral, plurilateral, and multilateral counterparts.

Where then are we left? By all accounts, 9/11 was a cataclysmic moment, but equally conspicuous is how routine life, the return to business, and the picking up of threads did not cave in: For them to do so would really necessitate a paradigm shift. By not doing so, though, does not mean a paradigm shift is not due. Whether it is or is not, we need to first sort out the prevalent paradigms: Must they be replaced wholesale, or by parts, or at all? Just by hanging on without direction, the 12 security community and 14 neofunctionalist tenets enhance interdependent relations of sorts. It is to those two sets of theories we turn next.

Interdependence: Interpretational Safety

A third variety is often applied to North America, or at least cannot be dismissed from contention: interdependence. Whichever interpretation we take, the end-product remains the same: It is so generic, it will absorb any and every dynamic, and offer some creditable explanation of each. Interpretational *safety* precedes *precision* or *sufficiency*. Modifying the pathfinding treatment of Robert O. Keohane and Joseph S. Nye,[72] and borrowing from Henry Nau's work,[73] table 1.8 distinguishes between interdependence and integration. The first three dimensions belong to Keohane and Nye, the next three to Nau. Echoing prior discussions, the *integration* column could easily be labeled pre–9/11, and *interdependence* post–9/11. Clearly integrative efforts cannot be dismissed even though they explain post–9/11 dynamics less robustly; and since a PSC assumes a degree of coordination we do not always find after 9/11, interdependence may appeal more, even though we must dispense of some of the characterization and colorings.

The first three dimensions in table 1.8 of the Keohane/Nye complex interdependence model find greater meaning with the addition of Nau's interdependence-integration comparative categories in the last three table 1.5 dimensions. We not only find the characteristics of interdependence but can also place them on

Table 1.7 Neofunctionalist Prerequisites, Processes, and Perceptions: Any 9/11 Difference?

Dimension	Any 9/11 difference?
1. Economic symmetry among units	Never existed before 9/11, not in existence after 9/11, yet integration was still pursued pre–9/11 and not abandoned post–9/11
2. Elite complementarity	Strongly present pre–9/11, still exists after 9/11 but more difficult to convene and harmonize
3. Pluralism	Very robustly evident in Canada and United States before 9/11, and embraces Mexico after 9/11 too (actually after 2000)
4. Capacity to adapt	Increasing pre–9/11 tendency, but diminishing thereafter
5. Spillover	Very robust before 9/11 and after 9/11: States may no longer effectively serve as gatekeepers, apparently even armed with 9/11 imperatives
6. Growing transactions	Increasingly so before 9/11 with Mexico, constantly evident with Canada; still important today
7. Growth in intergovernmentalism	True both before 9/11 and after
8. Transnational growth	True both before 9/11 and after
9. Elite socialization	True both before 9/11 and after
10. Growth in ideological identity	True both before 9/11 and after, but after 9/11 different ideological identities simultaneously adopted by various countries
11. Increasing interaction with external actors	True both before 9/11 and after, but individually so more than collectively
12. Benefit distribution higher and more equitable	Not really: Canada and Mexico enjoy trade surpluses increasingly, both before and after 9/11, but these have not reduced asymmetry with United States
13. Converging perceptions of external problems	Very possible before 9/11, almost impossible after
14. Integration as cost free	Possibility before 9/11, questionable thereafter

Adapted from Joseph S. Nye, "Comparing Common Markets: A Revised Neofunctionalist Model," in *Regional Integration: Theory and Research,* eds., Leon N. Lindberg and Stuart A. Scheingold (Cambridge, MA: Harvard University Press, 1971), chap. 5.

a continuum with integration. Extant works in the literature generally position Canada–U.S. relations closer to the integration end of the continuum and Mexico–U.S. relations, in spite of the brief Fox–Bush honeymoon, closer to the interdependence end. Robert Gilpin, for example, found more integrative than disintegrative features in the Canada–U.S. dyad before Pierre Trudeau's nationalistic outbursts in the

Table 1.8 Interdependence Versus Integration: Insights

Dimension	Interdependence	Integration
1. Channels of communication	Multiple, but security most important	Multiple, but economic most important
2. Hierarchy of issues	Not necessarily, but military ever-present as dominant priority	Yes, economic definitively at the top
3. Subordination of military	Yes, conditionally (in crisis)	Yes, unconditionally
4. Nature of institutional membership	Voluntary and involuntary, emphasizing all institutions	Involuntary, emphasizing only central institutions
5. Catalyst	New knowledge	Competitive markets
6. Placement of regionalism along levels of policy-making analysis	Less important to globalization and nationalism	More important than globalization and nationalism

Sources: Robert O. Keohane and Joseph S. Nye, *Power and Interdependence: World Politics in Transition* (Boston: Little, Brown, 1997), chap. 1–2; and Henry Nau, "From Integration to Interdependence: Gains, Losses, and Continuing Gaps," *International Organization* 33, no. 1 (Winter 1979): 119–47.

1970s:[74] The 1965 Canada–U.S. Auto Pact reiterated a sectoral approach to regional economic integration largely ignored by latter-day neofunctionalists,[75] even though the phenomenon giving neofunctionalism birth—the ECSC (European Coal and Steel Community)—was itself sectoral.[76] Trudeau's Third Option, NEP (National Energy Policy), and FIRA (Foreign Investment Review Agency) all sought to either deprive the United States of economic opportunities, to say the least, or punish his southern neighbor, to say the most.[77] Whichever, they produced a cost-price squeeze, Canadian uncompetitiveness, and a MacDonald Report proposal to return to the United States. Banishing the golden historical lesson, of Sir Wilfrid Laurier losing the 1911 elections after proposing a FTA to the United States, Brian Mulroney proposed the seed of NAFTA to Ronald Reagan at the Shamrock Summit in May 1985.[78] Integrative efforts more than disintegrative once again ruled the day.

For as long as Mexico relied on ISI (import-substitution industrialization), it remained both figuratively and literally independent of the United States; but when ISI was exhausted by the mid-1970s, Mexico sputtered more often than embraced its colossus of the north. Even amidst embrace, Jorge Chabat, among others, sees more interdependence than integration.[79]

The Realism Family

Famous for its parsimony and lack of analytical ambition, the realism family mirrors existing conditions, profiles past history sharply, and unlike its contending paradigms, ignores nonconflictual alternatives. The only claim to a strategic dialectic is between state interests and systemic influences over policy-making: Hans J. Morgenthau's

Table 1.9 The Realism Family: Achilles Heel?

Dimension	Features
1. State as a dominant actor?	This is the star actor in the family, the be-all and end-all of every power distribution, where from all other nonpolitical activity springs
2. Policy reflecting internal or international competitiveness?	Realists from Carr and Morgenthau emphasize the state level of analysis, with greater dependence on internal mobilization of resources; neorealists like Waltz find their state driven by external power distribution changes, taking the domestic context more for granted
3. Is international competitiveness orderly or anarchic?	Orderliness is dictated more by stability between the great powers: the fewer there are, the more stability, according to Waltz; but Deutsch and Singer find stability even from multiple powers. Anarchy results when dominance (by one power or many) begins to evaporate, encouraging adventurous states to stake a claim

Source: Kenneth N. Waltz, *Theory of International Politics* (Menlo Park, CA: Addison-Wesley, 1979), chap. 5.

state interests were defined in terms of power, Kenneth Waltz's market analogy characterizes systemic interpretations, but both realism and neorealism remain anchored in the self-help instinct. Table 1.9 extracts three features from Waltz's classic neorealist thesis: The belief in the state being the dominant and exclusive actor shaping policy outcomes; policies juggling either state interests or external influence; and anarchy becoming a permanent feature.

Both history and geography help explain why realism is not a satisfactory nor a sufficient paradigm explaining North America. In the final analysis, the United States never really had the kind of hostile neighbors Europe was replete with throughout history, and given, on the one hand, a shared born-free upbringing with Canada, and on the other, a Manifest Destiny relationship with Mexico, realist underpinnings either were inherently absent or embarrassingly irrelevant. If this was the fate of the dominant North American country, Alexis de Tocqueville's mid-nineteenth-century predictions of the United States eventually becoming a superpower echoed apprehensively in both Canada and Mexico, relegating the military option with their common neighbor. With Canada and Mexico fitting the realist theoretical profile even less, when the United States did become a superpower, Canada replaced isolation with integration far earlier than Mexico, in part due to more shared values, in part through greater strategic considerations.

If an anarchic North American situation does not prevail in its fullest meaning (illegal Mexican emigrants to the United States do not constitute anarchy), the first realist trait, of the state as the central and exclusive actor, is very much a North American reality: It is what holds Canada together, the basis of identity under isolationism for Mexico and much of U.S. history, and the pivot of U.S. superpowerdom. That does not necessarily predict the first realist feature of state interests will always prevail in policy-making, preferences, and orientations: external influences remain increasingly potent.

ARGUMENTS AND HYPOTHESIS

Contemporary North American experiments may not be far different from West European experiences of the 1950s: Just as significant external developments, like the 1971 Bretton Woods breakdown and the post–1973 oil price-hikes altered the rosy initiation of the ECSC in the 1950s, so too may external developments shift North America from interdependence toward integration, or from regional integration toward hemispheric or global integration. For example, if China becomes the top U.S. trading partner, Canada and Mexico may swallow U.S. asymmetry and seek more meaningful regionalized arrangements, or if U.S. indebtedness soars or the dollar collapses, regional arrangements to thwart market vulnerabilities may be reinforced. On the other hand, spiraling Mexican wages may shift U.S. production to Central America or beyond the Western Hemisphere, just as Canada's immigrants from China and India might diversify interests from North America toward Asia. Of course, another 9/11 would drive the nail into the regionalization box more forcefully, though not in unpredictable directions.

Exploring how each U.S. neighbor responded to 9/11, the comparisons and contrasts between them, and where the United States is headed, the North American architecture cannot be ignored. We fasten our safety belts with the following three arguments.

First, any coexistence of security and regional economic integration imperatives will benefit the former against the latter. Subsets of this argument include (a) FTAs will gradually be displaced by strategic trade considerations and (b) security imperatives will themselves prioritize hierarchy over community.

Second, any retreat from regional economic integration toward security imperatives will ultimately show the characteristics of interdependence or mutual dependence. Camouflaged by this trend will be two other paradoxical tendencies toward (a) trade diversification and (b) security free-ridership.

Third, interdependence in a region with a past history of formal regional economic integration is more likely to produce state-society fissures than not. Among the subset arguments, the region will face more disagreements/conflicts between (a) the states; (b) societies across state boundaries; and (c) societal groups themselves.

Behind these arguments lies our underlying hypothesis: North American dynamics will shift from trilateralist explorations to bilateralism.

We test these in the next seven chapters. Whereas chapters 2, 3, and 4 examine the country-specific cases of the United States, Canada, and Mexico, in that order, chapters 5, 6, and 7, assess the Canada–United States, Mexico–United States, and Canada–Mexico bilateral relations, respectively. Chapter 8 reconsiders bilateral findings in a trilateral setting, and Chapter 9 draws conclusions and projects implications.

Chapter 2 was written largely by Satya Pattnayak, chapter 3 by Douglas Ross and Anil Hira, and chapters 4 and 8 by Imtiaz Hussain. All three collaborated, to varying degrees, over chapters 1, 5, 6, 7, and 9.

METHODS, TECHNIQUES, AND SOURCES

As with any research, the questions of validity and reliability of our analysis loom large. The importance of knowing whether or not we indeed measured what we sought out to measure is paramount. Methodologists have argued that a single scale measurement of the dependent and independent variables can run into potential problems of reliability.[80] The level of confidence in the measurement increases with the number of items used to measure the variables of interest. For example, Bohrnstedt[81] and Curtis and Jackson[82] have argued that the average of multiple measurements is a better estimate of the true value of the variables of interest than any single one, since it is assumed that errors in measurement will be random, and will cancel each other out.

The issue of validity has of course a different interpretation than reliability. Validity indicates the degree to which an instrument measures what it is supposed to measure in the model. In our research, it deals with the central research question: To what extent our presentations of data and trends indeed measure the real economic-security trade-off? Keeping in mind the issues of reliability and validity, we carefully sorted through multiple trends and data, and cross-checked these with information from multiple sources, including aggregate, contextual, and interview-based.

Several sources of information were used. First, in addition to the printed material circulated by the various U.S. government agencies, research papers, journal articles, and books written by analysts, journalists, and scholars were consulted. Hard data were collected from the Bureau of Economic Analysis, UNCTAD's World Investment Report, Survey of Current Business, and the Institute of International Education sources.

Second, several arguments developed in chapter 2 were tested in two research conferences held in San Diego, California (March 2006), and Madison, Wisconsin (April 2006). In the first, at the ISA (International Studies Association) annual conference in San Diego, interrelationships between security and the trade issues were disentangled by attending four panels that addressed these issues. In the second conference at Madison, the National Title VI Fulbright-hays Outreach Conference, held in April 27–29, 2006, the importance of cultural differences in deciphering intercountry relationships was the main focus. Two such panels were visited at the Madison conference, and questions on the North American cultural differences were presented to the panelists. The responses of the panelists formed the basis of cross-checking of the reliability of trends detected by us.

Third, a limited content analysis of media coverage of the U.S.–Canadian relations, cross-border dynamics in particular, was done during a Vancouver visit in March 2006. Similar content analyses were conducted in Mexico City, during December 2006 and August 2007. During these visits, television commentaries and newspaper and popular articles on the U.S.–Mexican relations were analyzed, and to the extent that these divulged from or corroborated our analysis of the aggregate trends were duly noted in the respective chapters.

Finally, aggregate trends detected from the ecological data also needed to be corroborated in contextual and personal terms. The persons originally scheduled to be interviewed had been replaced with new personnel by the time our project schedule became finalized to conduct interviews. This required inevitable changes to be made. Instead, interviews were conducted with experts in the area of border dynamics on both the U.S.–Canadian and the U.S.–Mexican borders.

Researching U.S.–Canadian border dynamics in chapter 3, five interviews were conducted in June 22–25, 2006 with researchers at the Border Policy Research Institute at the Western Washington University and border project supervisors at WCG (Whatcom Council of Governments) in the Seattle-Bellingham area. For survey research related confidentiality reasons, names could not be divulged. However, frank and honest open-ended questions were presented to them. The interviews lasted between 30 and 50 minutes. No recording of the interviews was made but notes were taken. The questions in general were geared toward generating nuanced insights into our key hypothesis: "By promoting bilateralism over trilateralism in North America, the U.S. DHS undermines regional integration." Of course, the answers mainly targeted the U.S.–Canadian border dynamics.

Turning to the U.S.–Mexican border issues in chapter 4, five in-depth interviews were conducted with researchers engaged in studying the border dynamics. The interviews were conducted in Austin, Texas in June 9–12, 2006. Since the questions were open-ended, interviewees were encouraged to say as much over as many issues as possible. No recording was made but notes were taken. As with the U.S.–Canada border region interviews, each lasted between 30 and 50 minutes. At the request of the interviewees, their names remain confidential. These interviews were open-ended, and the main focus was to gain insights into the new U.S.–Mexico border dynamics in the post–9/11 period. A list of the questions on both borders is provided in the Appendix.

Furthermore, an additional visit was undertaken to the Blaine, Washington checkpoint on the U.S.–Canadian border in June 2006 in conjunction with the interviews conducted in the Seattle-Bellingham area, as mentioned earlier. The visits were intended to get a personal sense of the security implications by observing the flow of traffic at the checkpoints on the U.S. side. Brief conversations were made with visa and customs inspectors in the checkpoint area during their breaks. Each conversation lasted under five minutes. Only those agents willing to speak to us were included in the conversation. Altogether, eight such brief conversations were made. The main thrust of the conversation was on the increased securitization of the border, and what might that mean for the flow of goods, services, and people across the border. To the extent that ideas discussed during the interviews collided or extended the main arguments discussed in chapters 2, 5, and 6, they have been mentioned in these chapters. Since multiple sources amply testify to the increased militarization of the U.S.–Mexico border, no such trip was made to any check-points on the U.S.–Mexico border.

All observations and analyses adopt Alexander George's structured-focused in both case and comparative studies. In testing theories, for example, specific tenets provide the structure, upon which focused comparisons of all three countries follow.[83]

2

U.S. Security and Post–9/11 North American Integration: The Homeland Era

INTRODUCTION

The terrorist events on September 11, 2001 in the United States resulted in the loss of about 3,000 innocent lives. But a confident superpower's psyche was damaged for the long haul. It was a day that would live in infamy as it perceptibly changed the U.S. view of the world for the foreseeable future. Not since Pearl Harbor in December 1941 had the country seen such devastating attacks on its soil with so many casualties.

Adopting a social science theoretical perspective, this chapter examines the repercussions of these catastrophic events on U.S. policy, homeland security organization, and North American integration. It is organized into five sections. Section I introduces the policy response, Section II analyzes the organizational structure of the new DHS and its relationship with other security agencies, Section III examines the effects of the new security policy on selected economic and social indicators at the aggregate level, Section IV broadly assesses the impact of securitization on North American integration, and in Section V the theoretical tenets are discussed.

POLICY RESPONSE

After the initial shock and disbelief, a new security regime was swiftly installed, requiring behavioral changes for both citizens of the United States and the rest of the world. In September 2002, the first official NSS document was circulated.[1] Sensing the dangers lurking within and beyond the borders of the United States, the document called for better defences for the homeland. In articulating the multifaceted dangers, it states:

> . . . The gravest danger our Nation [*sic*] faces lies at the crossroads of radicalism and technology. Our enemies have openly declared that they are seeking weapons of mass destruction. . . . The United States will not allow these efforts to succeed. We will build defenses. . . . We will cooperate with other nations to deny, contain, and curtail our enemies' efforts to acquire dangerous technologies. . . . As a matter of common sense and self defense, America will act against such emerging threats before they are fully formed.[2]

Observers have noted that the tone of the security strategy is short on the use of soft power to produce a safer world.[3] For example, Joseph Nye argues that although international terrorism provoked such a security-oriented posture, it would be better to use soft power to elicit greater cooperation from states suspected of fomenting terrorism. Countries may decide to cooperate under the fear of hard power targeted against them but up to a point, beyond which incentives have to be in their interests.[4]

Appealing to all countries to unite in the face of common dangers of terrorist violence and chaos, the U.S. administration threatened action against hostile countries supporting terrorists, even as it committed itself to expanding trade and investment. The response harped much on the importance of weak links in the form of governments unable or unwilling to control terrorist activities within their legally recognized borders.[5] Identifying less capable governments as being more likely to succumb to terrorist networks and drug cartels from within their borders, it was a veiled warning to Mexico, as well as to Colombia and other Andean countries to not engage in such activities or face consequences if they do. The document stated:

> ...For most of the twentieth century, the world was divided by a great struggle over ideas: destructive totalitarian visions versus freedom and equality. That great struggle is over....America is now threatened less by conquering states than by failing states. We are menaced less by fleets and armies than by catastrophic technologies in the hands of the embittered few. We must defeat these threats to our nation [*sic*], allies, and friends.[6]

A clear emphasis was put on other countries' responsibility in the fight against common terrorism. For example, the document stated:

> ...Nations [*sic*] that enjoy freedom must actively fight terror. Nations that depend on international stability must help prevent the spread of weapons of mass destruction. Nations that seek international aid must govern themselves wisely, so that aid is well spent. For freedom to strive, accountability must be expected and required.[7]

Such projections of U.S. intentions have come at a time of high levels of anti-Americanism overseas. For example, in the same year that the war in Iraq started and the installation of DHS was fairly complete, a Eurobarometer poll found that the United States plays a negative role in fighting global poverty, protecting the environment, and maintaining peace in the world, according to the majority of Europeans.[8] A Pew Global Attitude Poll also found similar sentiments among 22 of the 42 countries surveyed that year. The high unpopularity in the Pew Poll apparently stemmed from the unfavorable rating of the U.S. foreign policies.[9]

Although many have drawn parallels with the aftermath of Pearl Harbor in December of 1941, the 9/11 events created qualitatively different multilateral alliances. Unlike a world of divided major powers in the days following the Japanese attack on Pearl Harbor, the contemporary major powers at least were united in their condemnation of the attacks of 2001, and all had promised cooperation to combat international terrorism.[10] Many argued that in an age of globalized information networks, instead of the older strategies of using strong conventional defences to deter nonstate enemies, an emphasis on sharing information and cooperative activities would produce a better outcome.[11] Still others have lobbied in favor of using greater amount of hard power to pursue the terrorists. Robert Kaplan and William Kristol, for example, have advocated a much more vigorous pursuit of foreign security policy objectives in light of the decisive edge in hard power for the United States.[12]

The events could not have been more ironic. It is worth noting that the Bush administration had assumed power in January of 2001 with an initial agenda of not to engage in nation-building, but the events in September later that year obligated it to change course with regard to the tone of its foreign policy.[13] George W. Bush's realist bent first emphasized great powers, such as Russia and China, but uncontrollable external events forced him to elevate problems faced by weak governments around the world.[14]

The terrorist events of September indeed changed U.S. policy and tone, and introduced a new form of U.S. internationalism. The new internationalism focused, in general, on how to make the world safer for greater political and economic freedoms, peaceful relations with other states, and respect for human dignity. In order to achieve these goals, the strategy called for: (a) collaborating with other states to defuse regional conflicts; (b) preventing enemies from threatening the United States or its allies and friends with WMD; (c) promoting greater economic growth worldwide through free markets and free trade; (d) expanding the circle of development by opening societies and building the infrastructure of democracy; (e) developing cooperative agendas of action with other main centers of global power; and (f) transforming America's national security institutions to meet the challenges and opportunities of the twenty-first century.[15]

Table 2.1 illustrates the strategies and goals as delineated in the 2002 and 2006 NSS documents. Each document elaborates on the security, political, economic, and organizational strategies to achieve the immediate and ultimate goals. The 2002 document did not emphasize the challenges of globalization in the areas of health, human and drug trafficking, and natural disaster management, whereas the 2006 document contains an entirely new section on such challenges, which indicates an expanding notion of national security, and willingness to use instruments of both hard and soft power.

In recent years, the processes of globalization have reduced barriers that used to limit the flow of ideas, information, humans, capital, and technology across the national borders. The risks of not attending to common threats of diseases, illegal drugs-trade, human trafficking, and environmental degradation would jeopardize the security of the hemisphere. In that regard, the tone in the 2006 document called for greater collaboration among countries in the areas of economic, health, and environmental development, and in better managing natural disasters.[16]

Contrary to the big wars in the twentieth century, the war against terrorism has been increasingly "privatized."[17] While the previous wars were between states or

Table 2.1 Strategies and Goals as Embodied in the 2002 and 2006 National Security Strategies

2002–06	Security strategy	Political strategy	Economic strategy	Organizational strategy	Challenges of globalization	Immediate goal	Ultimate goal
NSS, 2002	Preemption, prevent enemies from acquiring WMD	Work with other countries to defuse regional conflict	Promote development, free markets, free trade, and build infrastructure	Agenda for multilateral collaboration with other centers of global power	Not developed	Transform national security institutions to meet the challenges of twenty-first century	Defeat global terrorism, champion aspirations of human dignity
NSS, 2006	Same strategy continued	Same strategy continued	Same strategy continued	Same strategy continued	Public health pandemics, illicit trade in drugs, human beings, environmental degradation, and natural disaster requiring international response	Same goals	Same goals

Source: The White House, *The National Security Strategy of the United States of America, 2002 and 2006.*

governments, the current animosity with the United States entices transnational terrorist organization to seek WMD from vulnerable governments. Under this scenario, a comprehensive strategy would only succeed if sustained by the cooperation of other countries. While in the past governments declared war on other governments, the new war on terrorism is against nonstate enemies, and largely against invisible or privatized groups of people. Increasingly, it has become clear that terrorist cells operate independently of states and move around rather rapidly and freely of state regulations. Many of these micro group-actors operate on the basis of support from communities because of various commonalities in interest.[18]

In that respect, the State Department's Report to the 109th Congress on Global Terrorism is important. This 2006 document reports a significant decline in state-sponsored terrorist acts while it cites a noted increase in state-supported antiterrorist cooperation.[19] The report admits that there is considerable overlapping of terrorism and other crimes, and the fact that there are multiple micro level actors may make it difficult to combat security-related problems.

If micro actors are now expected to instigate small-scale acts of terrorism with grave implications for the economy and security of the United States, the antiterror strategy is likely to include a greater emphasis on law enforcement. By creating the new DHS, the U.S. government thus took an important step in organizational innovation.

HOMELAND SECURITY ORGANIZATION

Immediately following the 9/11 attacks, an OHS was created within the White House to develop a comprehensive national strategy to secure the country from terrorist threats and attacks, and coordinate all executive efforts to achieve this goal.[20]

The DHS, which succeeded the OHS, was officially established by the HSA of 2002. By virtue of the creation of DHS, the Bush administration undertook a radical reorganization of government agencies, not seen since the Truman administration created the NSC and the DOD in 1947. Administratively, the new Department deals with 87,000 different governmental jurisdictions at the federal, state, and local levels, and is the third largest bureaucratic entity within the federal government.[21] Figure 2.1 profiles the various DHS directorates.

DHS is managed by a cabinet level secretary, and this office is supported by several other offices characterized by a functional division of labor: The Privacy Office is to minimize the amount of intrusion into individual privacy; the Office of Civil Rights and Civil Liberties is to provide departmental policy advice on such issues; the Office of Inspector General is to conduct and supervise audits, investigate and inspect the departmental programs; the Citizenship and Immigration Services Ombudsman is to recommend problem resolution between individuals and employers and increase efficiency of the immigration system; the Office of Legislative and Intergovernmental Affairs is to function as primary liaison to members of Congress and their staff, the White House and the Executive Branch, and other federal agencies in the area of

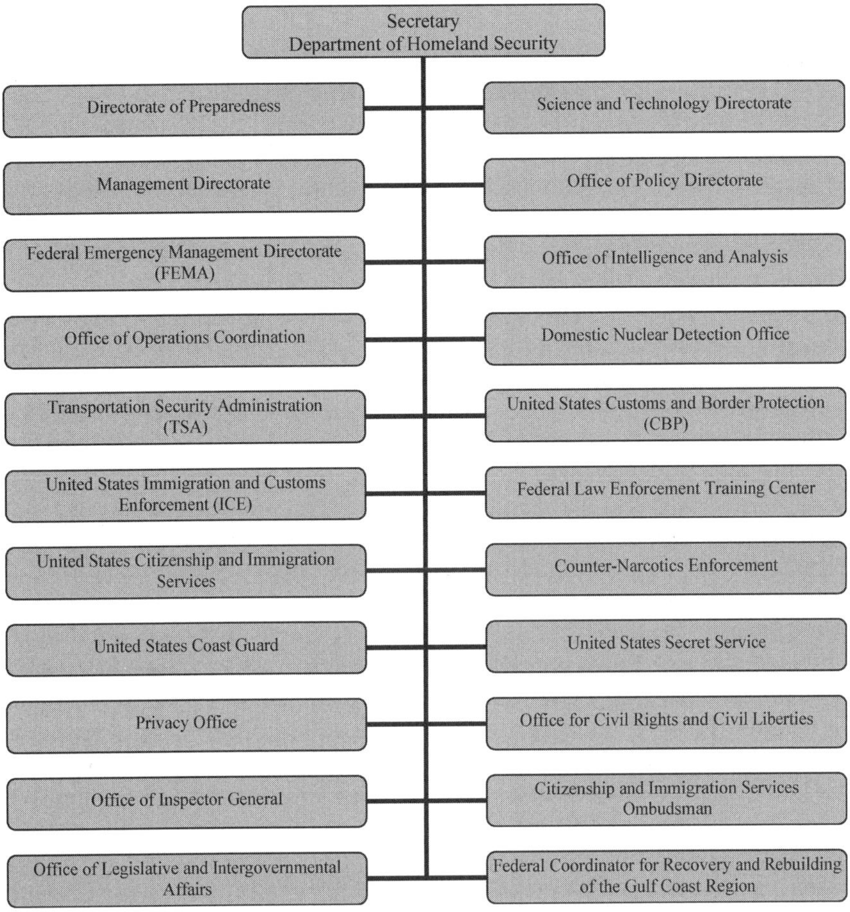

Figure 2.1 DHS Organizational Chart.
Source: www.dhs.gov/xabout/structure/index/shtm.

national security; and the Office of the Federal Coordinator for Recovery and Rebuilding of the Gulf Coast Region is to assist in long-term planning and coordinate the federal government's response to rebuild the Gulf Coast region following the devastations by hurricanes Katrina and Rita.

Whereas the Directorate of Preparedness is expected to coordinate with state, local, and private sector organizations to identify threats, determine vulnerabilities, and allocate resources toward high-risk areas, the Science and Technology Directorate is the primary research and development wing of the new department, formed to provide capabilities to federal, state, and local officials to protect the United States. The budget appropriations, expenditures, accounting and finance, procurement, human resources, information technology systems, facilities and equipment, and performance measurement fall under the Management Directorate purview.

Similarly, the Office of Policy Directorate formulates policy, coordinates among the various components of the new Department, and provides a centralized system of long-range planning and coordination to protect the United States.

The FEMD (Federal Emergency Management Directorate) manages natural disasters and federal response and recovery efforts following any national incident, while the Office of Intelligence Analysis procures and analyzes information from multiple sources to engage in both current and future assessment of threats to the United States. The security situation for the United States on a daily basis, is monitored by the Office of Operations Coordination, which also coordinates required activities within DHS and with state governors, advisors, law enforcement partners, and critical infrastructure partners in all 50 states and 50 largest metropolitan areas.

Nuclear detection efforts with federal, state, local, tribal, and private sector organizations to ensure a coordinated response to any nuclear threat, on the other hand, becomes the responsibility of the Domestic Nuclear Detection Office, while the TSA protects the nationwide transportation network to ensure the freedom of people and commerce. Similar responsibilities along U.S. frontiers fall upon the United States CBP (Customs and Border Protection), including facilitating flows of legitimate trade and travel, and preventing terrorists and weapons from entering the United States.

The largest investigative arm of DHS is the United States ICE (Immigration and Customs Enforcement), responsible for identifying and shutting down vulnerabilities at the country's borders, economic, transportation, and infrastructure security. On the other hand, the USCIS (United States Citizenship and Immigration Services) administers immigration and naturalization functions and establishes immigration services and priorities, while the USCG (United States Coast Guard) protects the environment and national economic interests in the ports and waterways, on international waters, or any maritime region required to support national security. Furthermore, the USSS (United States Secret Service) protects the president and senior government officials, investigates counterfeiting and financial crimes, and identifies theft, computer fraud, and cyber attacks on financial, banking, and telecommunications infrastructures. Finally, the Federal Law Enforcement Training Center provides career-long training to law enforcement officials to safely and proficiently fulfill their responsibilities.

The department also consists of at least five advisory panels. In no particular order, first is the HSAC (Homeland Security Advisory Council), created to provide advice and recommendations to DHS Secretary on matters related to homeland security. The Council consists of leaders from state and local levels, first responder communities, the private sector and academia. Second, the NIAC (National Infrastructure Advisory Council) advises the secretary of DHS and the president on security of the information systems of the public and private institutions. Third, the HSSTAC (Homeland Security Science and Technology Advisory Committee) is responsible for independent, scientific, and technical planning advice for the Under Secretary for Science and Technology within DHS. Fourth, the CIPAC (Critical Infrastructure

Partnership Advisory Council) is designated to facilitate effective coordination between federal infrastructure protection programs and the infrastructure protection activities of the private sector and of state, local, territorial, and tribal governments. Finally, the Interagency Coordinating Council on Emergency Preparedness and individuals with disabilities is created to ensure that the federal government appropriately supports safety and security of individuals with disabilities in disaster situations.[22]

As listed earlier, DHS is a huge structure and, as with any massive organizational creation, it took time to organize, reorganize, and take shape. With an annual budget of about $US40 billion and over 180,000 employees, DHS began its task of protecting the United States in early 2003.[23]

Thus far, the DHS mandate to ensure connectivity across the various components within the Department and between DHS and other federal, state, and local agencies has not been easy. The Department's own inspector of information technology has testified before Congress that in trying to facilitate an effective intergovernmental connectivity, DHS has failed to clearly define the relationship between existing systems of information used in other agencies and the new system in place at the Department. Furthermore, the guidelines to use the new system of information have been deficient, resulting in underused facilities by clients. DHS also has not established performance yardsticks using which an assessment may be made to gauge its coordinating performance.[24]

The self-evaluation report of the Department has pointed to a number of challenges and limitations faced by the organization. Because of resource limitations, DHS has been less than effective in the sharing of security information across levels of government agencies. In particular, the connectivity with state officials has been less than adequate.[25]

Subsequent federal legislation has established new goals and authorities that have impeded the performance of DHS as well. For example, although the HSA of 2002 gave DHS the responsibility to coordinate and share information related to threats of terrorism with other agencies, the subsequent IRTPA (Intelligence Reform and Terrorism Prevention Act) of 2004 superseded that by establishing the Office of the DNI (Director of National Intelligence).[26] The Office of DNI remains external to DHS, and coordinating with DNI requires a new set of information sharing procedures, policies, and technologies.[27]

Another major problem faced by DHS is its weak authority to require state and local governments to use its information network and share information. Since state laws vary widely, it has been difficult to facilitate effective coordination across levels of governmental agencies. A foremost obstacle has been the culture of inertia among many law enforcement agencies that are averse to information sharing with a new agency.[28]

DHS has also faced significant challenges in building an effective acquisition of management infrastructure to facilitate contracting activities with the Department. In particular, ethics training has been insufficient to better facilitate partnership arrangements with the private sector. In addition, the standards of program management within the Department have varied widely attesting to significant problems in building an organizational and oversight capacity.[29]

These problems notwithstanding, the relationship between DHS and other important federal agencies that were kept out of the bureaucratic reorganization must be further analyzed.

CIA and FBI

The main argument of the 9/11 Commission Report was based on the narrative that the dispersed parts of the U.S. government did not communicate with each other adequately and effectively.[30] The creation of DHS was designed to address the deficiencies of the previously demarcated division of labor between two well-known agencies: CIA and FBI. Much of the criticism about intelligence failure to detect the 9/11 attacks has focused on the CIA and the FBI. The 9/11 Commission was of the opinion that the attacks could have been prevented had the agencies responsible for intelligence and law enforcement communicated effectively about their suspects.[31] It is true that both organizations did not extensively interact prior to 9/11. They were mandated to be that way.[32] Since its inception, the CIA was prevented from law enforcement and domestic intelligence gathering. The agency was only responsible for foreign intelligence and overseas operations. The FBI, on the other hand, was responsible for domestic law enforcement, and intelligence gathering was never its main mission. These distinctions between intelligence gathering and law enforcement seemed to have worked fairly well during the Cold War.[33] However, in an era of franchised terrorist activities and sleeper cells, the distinction worked to the disadvantage of the United States.

Both the CIA and the FBI operate with vastly distinct missions, under different codes, and standards. Generally speaking, evidence that is good enough for CIA to frame its analysis is not good enough for the FBI, as the standards of prosecution are higher in a federal court of law.[34] The Cold War had maintained a sharp distinction between home and abroad. These sharp distinctions had kept the agencies from communicating with each other as well as with the now defunct INS regarding the possible apprehension of several 9/11 hijackers.

The creation of DHS is meant to bridge these distinctions. DHS is expected to have its own intelligence analysis capacity, and bridge the law enforcement and intelligence gathering functions within one department. It is also expected to provide a window not only to the policy-makers but also to other agencies to voluntarily share their critical intelligence. In that sense, DHS, in addition to creating its own intelligence analysis wing, will also need information from CIA and FBI.

At the time of the creation of DHS, no agency systematically was reviewing all pertinent domestic information for intelligence and warning purposes. DHS thereby becomes the first agency to link the domestic with the foreign, intelligence with law enforcement, and intelligence analysis with warning and policy. But the expectations are bound to be affected by interagency rivalry.[35] For example, the CTC (Counter Terrorism Center) is located within the CIA, and has mostly done foreign terrorism.

The FBI has never done intelligence prior to 9/11. DHS is expected to bridge this gap and provide its analysis on the basis of the information collected by both the CIA and the FBI.[36]

As mentioned earlier, the 2004 IRTPA created the DNI position to facilitate the transition from the Cold War oriented IC to a new effective system of intelligence direction and management. But the DNI was never given the kind of control over the IC as was expected. Furthermore, DNI remains outside of DHS.

Security scholars have observed that the creation of DHS and DNI has not really solved the problem of intelligence coordination and effective policy formation. The DOD intelligence apparatus has not been mandated by the president to cooperate with the DNI. The DOD currently gets 70 percent of the total intelligence gathering budget of the federal government, so it would make sense to bring DOD's intelligence analysis wing under the DNI.[37] But no such presidential directive currently exists.

With the new bureaucratic realignment, the CIA seems to have been downgraded, and has lost its direct access to the White House. But the expectation is that its views with regard to terrorism and other threats will be integrated with that of DOD's intelligence analysis, and will be circulated by DNI to other agencies, such as DHS and FBI. In that regard, there is some attempt to centralize the information clearing house. The TTIC was converted into NCTC (National Counter Terrorist Center), moved into the White House, and kept directly under the DNI. Even under a highly neutral setting, this bureaucratic realignment is difficult to produce effective results.[38]

In the meantime, the FBI has set up JTTF (Joint Terrorism Task Forces) in most major cities to provide early warning of terrorism and assistance to local and state police with regard to terrorism-related activities. In theory, JTTF is supposed to include representatives from the CIA and DHS, but little record exists so far as to the extent of their success.[39] The idea of joint intelligence centers has been used successfully in the past. For example, James Marchio argues that joint intelligence centers were successfully employed during the first Gulf War in 1991, and may have a greater relevance in the post–9/11 context.[40] Importantly, how effective the new arrangements both within DHS and without have been can only be answered definitively in the event of another terrorist attack. Because of the complex nature of the alignments described earlier, it is difficult to predict that the new warning paradigm is likely to come from DHS.

In a country visited by more than a million persons daily, whose economy accounts for about 28 percent of the global economy, and where foreign trade represents about 22 percent of the national economy, implementing the goals of homeland security means seeking to change the way the entire world works.[41] In the first place, such a massive administrative reorganization is utterly complex and time consuming in trying to just make each component participate in order to satisfy the overriding new goal of homeland security.

Other notable legislations have also empowered the law enforcement wings of the federal government. For example, The U.S. PATRIOT Act of 2001 has enhanced considerably the powers of the administrative authorities to intercept electronic communications, detain noncitizens considered threats to national security, and limit the judicial review of the alleged.[42] The office of the U.S. Attorney General has also been empowered to overrule judicial decisions releasing illegal arrivals on bond. Besides, unilateral ordinances have been passed in many smaller townships across the country, which forbids employment of illegal residents.[43]

Scholars have been concerned with the constitutional issues of privacy and individual rights and liberties in the United States in light of the new securitization of the federal government.[44] Violations have been recorded in the prosecution of detainees rounded up in the many sweeps of suspected terrorists since 9/11. Hundreds of detainees have been denied legal rights to representation, and court hearings have been held in secret. Such actions create conditions tantamount to violating the principles that the U.S. Constitution characterizes as sacred to sustain a democratic way of life.

The PATRIOT Act of 2001, passed in the wake of the terrorist attacks, and renewed in 2006, has given the law enforcement agencies broad powers to arrest and implement antiterrorist policies, and prosecute much of it in secrecy.[45] Many of the PATRIOT Act provisions have been interpreted as contradictory to the Civil Rights Act of 1964, and as amended in 1967, which barred discrimination on the basis of race, color, and national origin.[46] Emphasizing this point, the Center for Constitutional Rights summarizes:

> Perhaps the most disturbing aspect of the government's actions has been its attack on the Bill of Rights, the very cornerstone of our American democracy. The War on Terror has seriously compromised the First, Fourth, Fifth, and Sixth Amendment rights of citizens and non-citizens alike. From the USA Patriot Act's over-broad definition of domestic terrorism, the FBI's new powers of search and surveillance, to the indefinite detention of both citizens and non-citizens without formal charges, the principles of free speech, due process, and equal protection under the law have been seriously undermined.[47]

The processes discussed above indicate the potential implications for the U.S. economy, and those of others, of the sweeping mandate given to DHS and other security agencies. But how have the economy and society fared since 9/11? We now turn to an examination of several key indicators.

EMPIRICAL TRENDS

With so much bureaucratic organization and realignment of agencies in the federal government, has there been any significant impact on the country's economic and social life? In the following section, we analyze selected indicators.

As table 2.2 illustrates, total U.S. exports to the rest of the world have recovered by 2002 from the shocks of 2001, and by 2005 they have registered an increase of over 35 percent. Total U.S. imports have also followed a similar pattern, and by 2005

Table 2.2 U.S. International Transactions (in $US billion)

	2000	2001	2002	2003	2004	2005	2001–05 (percent change)
Total exports	1,422	1,293	1,245	1,319	1,527	1,750	+35.3
Total imports	1,778	1,631	1,654	1,777	2,111	2,455	+49.8

Source: Bureau of Economic Analysis Data, 2000–2005, released 2006.

have increased by 49 percent over 2001. Such increases demonstrate the overall attractiveness of the U.S. economy, and the fact that the extent of its involvement with the rest of the world in matters of foreign trade has not been affected insofar as total volumes are concerned.

In matters of direct foreign investment, tables 2.3 and 2.4 illustrate interesting trends. The average annual U.S. FDI inflow during 1990–2000 constituted, on average, about 22 percent of the total world inward flow. But by 2005, the share of the inward flow of FDI had declined to 10.8 percent of the total world inflow. In matters of outflow, U.S. FDI flow constituted on average 18.6 percent of the 1990–2000 world outflow, but following the 2001 attacks, this share increased to 25 percent in 2002, 23 percent in 2003, and 27 percent in 2004, before taking a negative turn in 2005.

As table 2.5 illustrates, the share of inward FDI stock as a proportion of GDP has increased from 12.9 percent in 2000 to 13 percent in 2005, but the share of outward FDI stock as a proportion of GDP has increased considerably more, from 13.5 percent to 16.4 percent. Both these figures are considerably smaller than the total FDI inward and outward stocks as a ratio of world GDP, indicating perhaps greater opportunities for higher returns outside of the U.S. economy. But on the whole, the investment figures do not indicate any consistent downward economic trend in the years following the 9/11 attacks.

After 9/11, many of the stringent restrictions and delays were incurred in the travel sector. As table 2.5 illustrates, the tourism sector was indeed badly hurt by the attacks with negative growth rate in real output in 2001. Subsequently, however, the recovery has been evident in the growth rate of real output. From 2002 until 2005, the sector consistently registered positive real output growth rates, ranging

Table 2.3 Foreign Direct Investment (FDI): Flows Overviewed ($US million)

FDI flows	1990–2000 (annual average)	2002	2003	2004	2005
United States-inward	109,513	74,457	53,146	122,377	99,443
United States-outward	92,010	134,946	129,352	222,437	−12,714
World-inward	495,391	617,732	557,869	710,755	916,277
World-outward	492,566	539,540	561,104	813,068	778,725

Source: UNCTAD, World Investment Report 2006; www.unctad.org/fdistatistics.

Table 2.4 Foreign Direct Investment Stocks (selected years, $US million, percent GDP in parentheses)

FDI stocks	1990	2000	2004	2005
United States-inward (%GDP)	394,911 (6.9)	1,256,867 (12.9)	1,526,306 (13.0)	1,625,749 (13.0)
United States-outward (%GDP)	430,521 (7.5)	1,316,247 (13.5)	2,063,998 (17.6)	2,051,284 (16.4)
World-inward (%GDP)	1,789,303 (8.5)	5,802,293 (18.3)	9,544,887 (23.3)	10,129,739 (22.7)
World-outward (%GDP)	1,791,092 (8.6)	6,471,435 (20.5)	10,325,240 (25.2)	10,671,889 (23.9)

Source: UNCTAD, *World Investment Report, 2006,* www.unctad.org/fdistatistics.

from 0.7 percent in 2002 to 6.7 percent in 2004 and 4.9 percent in 2005. Air transportation was affected in the immediate aftermath of 9/11, which is shown in table 2.5. The total air passenger transportation sector experienced negative growth rate in 2001, but since that year it has registered positive annual growth rates consistently. The domestic air passenger services have grown by over 6 percent annually since 2002. The international air passenger services, however, continued to experience negative growth rate until 2003, after which the growth rate has become positive. These upward trends indicate that the air transportation subsector within the travel industry has factored in the additional security provisions put in place after 9/11.

The real output in the tourism sector has continued to grow in dollar terms since 2001. As illustrated in table 2.6, after the decline in 2001, the total tourism related goods and services have grown 16.3 percent since 2001. During 2001–05, domestic air passenger services have grown by 25 percent while the international passenger transportation services have registered increases of over 14 percent.

Similar upswings have been recorded in international travel, both in and out of the United States, as illustrated in table 2.7. Total international travel and tourism services have registered a 15.8 percent increase in revenue between 2001 and 2005. In 2001, inbound travel and tourism accounted for 52.6 percent of the total

Table 2.5 Annual Growth in Real Output by Tourism Commodity, 2000–05 (percent change from preceding year)

Commodity	2000	2001	2002	2003	2004	2005
All tourism goods and services	2.9	−5.1	0.7	3.3	6.7	4.9
Total passenger air transportation services	5.7	−9.3	−1.8	3.3	13.3	6.0
Domestic passenger air transportation services	6.0	−6.7	−0.6	6.9	10.4	6.6
International passenger air transportation services	5.1	−15.3	−4.7	−4.4	20.3	4.8

Source: The Survey of Current Business, U.S. Travel and Tourism Satellite Accounts, June 2006, 15.

Table 2.6 Real Output by Tourism Commodity, 2000–05 (in $US million)

Commodity	2000	2001	2002	2003	2004	2005	2001–05 percent growth rate
All tourism goods and services	516,532	489,961	493,518	509,614	543,508	570,159	+16.3
Total passenger air transportation services	100,479	91,129	89,517	92,496	104,822	111,118	+21.9
Domestic passenger air transportation services	72,308	67,464	67,090	71,745	79,239	84,435	+25.2
International passenger air transportation services	28,171	23,860	22,730	21,730	26,135	27,379	+14.7

Source: The Survey of Current Business, U.S. Travel and Tourism Satellite Accounts, June 2006, 16.

Table 2.7 U.S. International Travel and Tourism, 2000–05 ($US billion)

	2000	2001	2002	2003	2004	2005	2001–05 (percent change)
Total international travel and tourism	188.1	168.9	158.4	154.8	178.8	195.6	+15.8
Inbound travel and tourism	102.3	88.9	82.6	79.1	92.4	104.7	+17.7
Outbound travel and tourism	85.8	80.0	75.8	75.7	86.3	90.9	+13.6

Source: The Survey of Current Business, U.S. Travel and Tourism Satellite Accounts, June 2006, 18.

international travel and tourism services. But by 2005, this share has increased to 53.5 percent. This is remarkable since the outbound domestic travel from the United States has also increased since 2003. In total amounts, the inbound travel and tourism services generate more revenue than the outbound international travel and tourism from the United States, both of which have registered double-digit growth rates during 2001–05. Such figures indicate that the restrictions in security have largely been factored in by the agencies and travelers, and the United States is still a major destination for international travelers.

Internal U.S. travel also made a big comeback. As can be seen in table 2.8, the 85 percent share of U.S. residents in total internal travel, of all internal travel, in 2001, increased to 86.5 percent by 2005. Such data indicate that the travel and tourism industry overall has indeed recovered from the initial downturn after 9/11.

As illustrated in table 2.9, although the total revenue has increased, the rate of employment growth in the overall tourism sector has been dismal. The total number of people directly employed by the tourism industry barely moved during 2001–05. In total, there were 5.636 million people directly employed by the industry in 2001, while in 2005 this number had only moved by 9,000 to about 5.645 million, far below its 2000 peak of over 5.7 million. The air transportation services have also experienced reduced number of employment. This decline may have been caused

Table 2.8 Internal Travel and Tourism in the United States by Residents and Nonresidents, 2000–04

Year	Residents ($US billion)	Nonresidents (inbound; $US billion)	Total ($US billion)	Residents (percent share)	Nonresidents (inbound; percent share)
2000	412.8	81.6	494.4	83.5	16.5
2001	402.4	71.2	473.6	85.0	15.0
2002	410.6	65.8	476.4	86.2	13.8
2003	441.3	63.7	505.0	87.4	12.6
2004	475.3	73.9	549.2	86.5	13.5

Source: The Survey of Current Business, U.S. Travel and Tourism Satellite Accounts, June 2006, 18.

Table 2.9 Direct Employment by Tourism Industry, 2000–05 (in 000s)

Industry	2000	2001	2002	2003	2004	2005
All tourism industries	5,712	5,636	5,474	5,452	5,560	5,645
Food and drinking places	1,625	1,611	1,640	1,698	1,760	1,805
Air transportation services	600	596	518	477	496	495
Rail transportation services	10	10	11	12	14	14
Water transportation services	27	28	27	28	30	31

Source: The Survey of Current Business, U.S. Travel and Tourism Satellite Accounts, June 2006, 20.

by innovation and labor-saving use of technology as well, so it is difficult to say how much the security restrictions imposed in the post–9/11 period contributed to this particular decline in employment. However, the employment has increased in the food (12.0 percent), rail transportation (40.0 percent), and water transportation services (10.7 percent) during 2001–05.

One of the main sources of tension has been visa issuance to foreigners, including foreign students. It is public knowledge that several of the 9/11 hijackers had overstayed their legal visas, which led to a tighter scrutiny of student visas. As can be seen from table 2.10, the total number of undergraduate foreign students has consistently declined since 2000. Similar decline has taken place in the total number of foreign students at U.S. colleges and universities. The number of foreign graduate students increased between 2000–01 and 2003–04, but has since been declining. Such decline may be explained in light of tighter visa restrictions as well as expanding opportunities in other countries, such as the United Kingdom and Australia, for higher education.[48]

NORTH AMERICAN INTEGRATION

The data analyzed in the previous section, although aggregate in nature, indicate that the overall recovery has been well underway since 2002 in the U.S. economy, travel, and higher education. But how have the changes in U.S. policy and the reorganization of its security apparatus affected North American integration?

Since 1994, United States, Canada, and Mexico have worked together to sustain the NAFTA. In the almost eight years prior to 9/11, the North American continent

Table 2.10 Foreign Student Enrollment (in 000s) in U.S. Higher Education, 2005–06 (total numbers include students not pursuing degrees)

Years	2000–01	2001–02	2002–03	2003–04	2004–05	2005–06
Undergraduate	260	255	254	250	240	236
Graduate	245	260	265	270	265	260
Total	550	580	580	570	565	564

Source: Institute of International Education, *Open Doors: Report on International Educational Exchange* (New York, 2006).

had become the world's largest economic bloc. On the positive side, all three countries experienced impressive increases in the volume of economic transactions with each other. However, with increased trade, investment, and movement of people and other services, many problems, or what scholars have called "negative externalities," also became more prominent.[49] Aside from the sensitive issue of "national sovereignty," the NAFTA years before September 2001 saw an increase in illegal drug shipments, human trafficking, and migration across the Mexico–U.S. border, and the smuggling of drugs, cigarettes, migrants, and arms across the Canada–U.S. border.[50] Many of these negative externalities predate 9/11 but, as we shall see later, they were merged into the security paradigm in the post–9/11 time period. It is true, however, that the United States frequently chastised Mexico for such increases while relative political silence permeated the air on the Canadian transgressions.[51]

Despite these increases in cross-border activities, each country continued to maintain largely separate policies toward refugees, border, immigration, screening of goods entering each other's territories, and intelligence gathering.[52] Such differences can be attributed to the U.S. fear over the possible loss of national sovereignty in decision-making by the less powerful partners in Canada and Mexico. Undoubtedly these differences have created much of the tensions faced by Canada and Mexico in light of the policy changes announced by the United States after 9/11.

In the regional scheme of things, both Mexico and Canada have exhibited characteristics that label them as weak governments from the U.S. point of view. The weakness has been primarily defined by United States in terms of deeds, and not necessarily in terms of the potential to be helpful.

In the case of Mexico, the pervasiveness of drug-cartels, in particular in the northern parts of the country has raised the red flag for the U.S. administrators. The issue of illegal drugs has overlapped into illegal immigration, since many reports underline the importance of drug-runners as agents of human trafficking as well.[53] The overarching problems of high poverty and lack of widespread economic development have made the problems of drugs and illegal immigration only that much worse. The Mexican border has already become militarized in a post–9/11 world, thus making it the most inspected of the two U.S. land borders.[54] Together, these deficiencies, both structural and behavioral, have made Mexico a target of much political and media-based fury in the United States.

Canada, on the other hand, has been branded as soft on terrorism, largely based on how it has proceeded to deal with the issues of multiculturalism, treatment of asylum seekers, and for being too lenient on the deviant expression of human cacophony of behaviors. Canada has often been portrayed as a haven for terrorists in U.S. media because of its liberal refugee and immigration system.[55] In 2001–02 alone, the Canadian border saw an increase of border security personnel by 300 percent.[56] The negative attention given to the U.S.–Canada border post–9/11 by the U.S. officials was largely echoed in the interviews conducted near the U.S.–Canada border. From practically no attention in the pre–9/11 period to negative attention in the post–9/11 period has caused much resentment in Canadian circles.

Both Canada and Mexico have figured prominently in the U.S. assessment of a possible North American security perimeter.[57] The new security paradigm envisioned by the U.S. government has promoted the two border countries into the crucial frontline in the new war against international terrorism. Notably, this has transformed the geopolitics of the region, perhaps irrevocably, with implications for the economic development and well-being of Canadian and Mexican societies.[58]

As noted earlier, a key component of DHS plan is the security of borders and all modes of transportation including land, air, and maritime routes. Simply put, the very meaning of borders has been broadened. The overseas strategy of homeland security covers many major initiatives: to create *smart borders;* combat fraudulent travel documents; increase the security of international shipping containers; intensify international law enforcement cooperation; help foreign countries fight terrorism; expand the protection of transnational critical infrastructure; amplify international cooperation on security science and technology; improve cooperation in response to attacks; and review obligations to international treaties and law. In that respect, the Western Hemisphere as a whole has become a prime area of international cooperation; Mexico and Canada along with the rest of Latin America and the Caribbean are being identified as the regions of importance for the overseas reach of DHS.

Since its inception, DHS has taken the lead in a number of activities including preclearance inspection, CSI (container security initiative), appointing DHS attachés at U.S. embassies, and adjudicating refugee and immigration applications overseas. The new Department has also stationed security inspectors at the world's major ports, mostly in West Asia and Europe but also in the Caribbean, to enhance the security of all modes of transportation against terrorists.[59] As will be elaborated in the subsequent chapters, the United States has entered into new border agreements with both Canada and Mexico in order to establish secure flows of people and goods, and protect cross-border critical infrastructure.[60]

The smart borders program has shifted the focus from the security of physical borderlines toward a layered management across air, sea, and land transportation system involving the prescreening and prevention of undesirable goods and people destined for United States, Canada, and Mexico.[61] This entails a massive reorganization of border business, and the new policies have affected the entire supply chain around the world. The effectiveness of these policies, however, depends on host countries to put in place compatible rules and mechanisms, including limiting the freedom of their own citizens.

The imperatives of U.S. homeland security have in effect obliterated the distinction between the traditional and nontraditional dimensions of security. Traditional areas of North American exchange, such as immigration, trade and investment, trafficking in narcotics, arms and people, money-laundering, law enforcement, and intelligence gathering, have become the subjects of increased scrutiny. In other words, most issues between the United States and its two immediate neighbors have come under the securitization process. The asymmetry in the regional relationships has always been there, as will be elaborated in the subsequent chapters, but as a consequence of the additional security measures both borders have to live with the new assertiveness in U.S. posture.

Do Mexico and Canada have the political will and, above all, the capability to live with such U.S. imperatives? In the immediate aftermath of 9/11, many such measures, including the closing of all transportation exchanges were implemented unilaterally; six years later, the two countries are still struggling to integrate their respective systems with the new security measures.

Historically, Mexico has always been sensitive to U.S. policy changes that may imply intervention in its internal affairs. Canada has also had a long history of maintaining a strong emphasis on multilateralism in international affairs. Under the new security paradigm, the United States now expects potential attacks from both Mexico and Canada.[62] Considered particularly prone are the U.S. assets in the region. The sensitive issue of national sovereignty has indeed appeared in the Mexican and Canadian discourse. The sentiments are particularly strong when these countries are being asked to comply with the seemingly intrusive measures of U.S. homeland security, as discussed extensively in other chapters.[63]

THEORETICAL TENETS

Much has been written about the preponderance of security in the post–9/11 setting. Dire predictions have been made about the United States shutting down its borders that would negatively affect North American economic integration. In the following paragraphs, we discuss a number of possible scenarios in a general way in light of the theoretical paradigms discussed and typified in chapter 1.

The first exercise wrestles with the tenets of neofunctionalism and seeks to explain the extent to which 9/11 and the policy changes since have made a difference to the tenets of the theory. Table 2.11 guides the relevant discussions.

Economic asymmetry was structurally much prominent between the United States and Canada although on cultural matters, the differences were glossed over. It was of course more apparent in the relationship between United States and Mexico in the pre–9/11 days. In the five years since 9/11, the extent of economic asymmetry has widened, more so between the United States and Mexico. That is partly because the United States has been able to grow faster than Mexico despite its massive amounts of budget deficit and external debt. Mexico's per capita GDP grew by 2.9 percent during 2003–04, compared to Canada's 2 percent and the U.S. growth rate of 3.4 percent during the same time period.[64] The overall economic asymmetry between the United States and Canada and between the United States and Mexico has grown further.

In the immediate aftermath of 9/11, the empathy factor contributed to a high level of elite complementarity during 2002–03. Since late 2003, however, the United States elites have increasingly grown apart, largely due to how the threat has been respectively perceived by the Republican and Democratic leaderships. With the ascension of Howard Dean as the Chair of the Democratic National Committee in 2005, the top level complementarity has indeed been ruptured. This rupture has

Table 2.11 Neofunctionalist Attributes: Pre– and Post–9/11

Dimension	Pre–9/11	Post–9/11
1. Economic asymmetry among units	Much asymmetry existed with both Canada and Mexico; more *vis-à-vis* Mexico than Canada	Extent of economic and military asymmetry has grown with both Mexico and Canada; much more with Mexico than with Canada
2. Elite complementarity	Existed with regard to United States–Canada and United States–Mexico policies	Rupture with both Mexico and Canada; signs of amends with Canada under Harper; possible amends with Mexico under Calderōn
3. Pluralism	Limited disagreement on major issues	Extent of disagreement has widened, more with Mexico on immigration and Canada on "toxic rain" and "common North American" defence
4. Capacity to adapt	Slow since bureaucratic reorganization was not in order	In the immediate aftermath, massive reorganization of DHS showed capacity to adapt; with the passage of time the danger is complacency
5. Spillover	Robust pre–9/11	Huge spillover in the immediate aftermath of 9/11; five years after, the spill-over has created major bifurcation of popular sentiments
6. Growing transactions	Canada and Mexico were two of the top three trading partners	The extent of economic transaction declined in the immediate aftermath; since it has recovered and exceeded the level of pre–9/11 transactions with Canada; is recovering with Mexico
7. Growth in intergovernmentalism	Existed pre–9/11	Continues to exist post–9/11
8. Transnational growth	Was already growing	Five years after 9/11, economic growth has been sustained; some growth has occurred in security matters as well
9. Elite socialization	Existed pre–9/11	It has always been there
10. Growth in ideological identity	Existed in a general way	But with political polarization within the United States, a sector or issue-specific identity is more likely to be pursued with both Canada and Mexico

11. Increasing interaction with external actors	The trend was already present	Since 9/11, greater interaction in technology, security, and patents has occurred with both Mexico and Canada
12. Benefit distribution higher and more equitable	Did not exist	Has increased the cost of transactions with Mexico with regard to border fence and militarization; increasing tensions with Canada as well, thus increasing the transaction cost
13. Converging perceptions of external problems	Was potentially possible	Issue-specific convergence on North Korea and possibly Iran but on other issues specific divergence with both Mexico and Canada
14. Integration as cost free	Potentially possible before 9/11	Generally possible in the security arena but on bilateral issues of immigration, trade, and drug-trafficking much disagreement among groups in larger society has increased the cost of possible integration

affected the level of elite complementarity with the Canadian and Mexican elites as well, with partisanship coloring complementarity.

In the case of the United States at least, pluralism is more a function of domestic events and the new dynamics these may unravel. Not until the 2006 November Congressional elections did some semblance of pluralism return to the U.S. legislature. Several domestic events have since widened the dissenting voices of President George W. Bush's official policy on terrorism and the Mexican and Canadian border dynamics. Increasingly, many Republican and Democratic leaders have shown their disagreements over the official initiatives in border security, illegal migration, in particular from Mexico, and free trade. Immediately after 9/11, much effort was put into the reorganization of the homeland security structure and fine-tuning of the policy-praxis dynamics. However, as more and more time elapses between 9/11 and the setting up of the subsequent political and economic processes, there has been a tendency to fall back to a level of normalcy that is comparable with the pre–9/11 context.

The Bush administration has repeatedly failed after 9/11 to sustain a sense of unified populace in the face of rapidly changing situation in Iraq, domestic tragedies in the South (e.g., disaster relief management problems in the aftermath of Katrina and other hurricanes), and varying interpretations of the border dynamics with the two neighbors, in particular Mexico. The federal government has been unable to serve as the main gatekeeper as other political and cultural groups (e.g., *La Raza,* ACLU, and others) with large followings interpret events of consequence differently as and when they occur. In recent months, the AFL-CIO has joined forces opposing the president's tough anti-illegal immigration crackdown initiative.[65]

Intergovernmentalism has always been true in pre–9/11 days; it has remained so since 9/11 but with changes in priorities across the issues of bilateral importance with Mexico and Canada. This is the preferred mode of diplomatic exchanges, preferable to supranationalism. Undoubtedly, North America's borders have been smartened and intergovernmental bilateralism has increased since 9/11. But as Stephen Clarkson maintains, the three states exercise considerable autonomy, so much so that even though Mexico and Canada share the virtues of multilateralism in international affairs, they both seek to compete with each other more than cooperate while attempting to curry favor with the United States.[66] Even then, intergovernmentalism seems to be favoring Canada over Mexico, given the greater number of institutions established with the former over the latter.

During the disagreements over the U.S. war efforts in Iraq in 2003, U.S. diplomacy was less than stellar. Since Condoleezza Rice took over as the Secretary of State, more channels of socialization have been open to the elites of both Mexico and Canada. With Canada, it is likely to increase even further with the Conservative-led government of Stephen Harper in power after the 2006 parliamentary elections. The same is hoped for with the new Mexican government under Felipe Calderón, who took the reigns of presidency in December 2006. In areas such as antinarcotics law enforcement, much cooperation has been initiated.

As ideological differences within the U.S. political circles gather momentum with each new cycle of elections, it would be difficult to hypothesize how this would eventually turn out. Identity is a fluid concept and its construction is mostly a perceptual game played by the United States elites and the reaction to such utterances in Canada and Mexico may not be correctly predicted. We argue that diverging ideological identities would persist but the depth of such differences would depend not only on which sector or area of contention but also how the positions are articulated by U.S. leaders.

Diplomatic interactions in the areas of free trade, technology transfer, border control, migration, and hemispheric security have increased after a rather unilateral freeze of such efforts in the immediate aftermath of 9/11. We predict that such interactions would continue to increase.

As discussed in other chapters, increased militarization of the Mexican border has heightened the costs for Mexico. The United States has suffered as well since the number of return migrants to Mexico has declined significantly.[67] This has contributed to a swelling of the number of undocumented Mexican migrants in the country which has generated an emotional debate about border security and migration. No comparable militarization has occurred on the Canadian border as of yet, thus contributing to an unequal distribution of anticipated benefits for the respective populations.

With regard to gathering threats from surging violence and criminality in the border areas, an issue-specific convergence may not be ruled out between United States and Mexico on how to address such common issues. The same goes for immigrants from countries that are on the U.S. watch list. But divergence is expected to continue on other bilateral issues affecting the United States and its neighbors.

Integration entails anticipated costs for societal groups largely in terms of how such efforts are perceived by its members. Various interest groups in the United States have different agendas, and so the costs can be minimized only in the event that alliances are formed across multiple interest groups. For example, *La Raza* is unequivocally opposed to any border control that might affect the flow of illegal and legal migration from Latin America to the United States. Similarly, many organized labor groups have shown support for undocumented workers with the hope that it would bolster unions. In the area of homeland security, such overarching alliances are more feasible than on trade, immigration, and environmental issues. The calculation of the total cost would depend on how such alliances develop across major issue areas.

Turning to the relationship between integration and interdependence, following table 2.12, in the post–9/11 period, multiple channels of communication between the United States and its neighbors have opened up. These have been at both the state and nonstate levels, although a visible shift has been noted in favor of "security." In contrast, in the pre–9/11 period, the emphasis in the multiple channels of

Table 2.12 Interdependence Versus Integration: Insights

Dimension	Interdependence	Integration
1. Channels of communication	Less in economic matters; but more in security-related issues since 9/11	Pre–9/11 channels favored general integration
2. Hierarchy of issues	The immediate reaction after 9/11 has contributed to greater interdependence	More integration has occurred in the security arena with both Mexico and Canada
3. Subordination of the military	U.S. military is subordinated to civilian authority	Much more integrated security-economic combo approach has been pursued since 9/11
4. Nature of institutional membership	Preponderance of security post–9/11 precluded interdependence	Security affected integration as well; but since limited integration efforts on specific issues has returned
5. Catalyst	New security dynamics has potential to facilitate greater interdependence	Economic force of markets may withstand efforts to segregate the three North American markets
6. Placement of regionalism along levels of policy-making analysis	Greater interdependence talks were in vogue pre–9/11 but since global concerns on terrorism has dwarfed specific forces of interdependence	Regional integration was dead in the immediate aftermath of 9/11, but since it has made limited comeback on issues affecting environment, pharmaceutical collaboration, and security coordination

communication among the three countries had favored "economic integration," at least since 1994.

Economic issues were undoubtedly in the forefront of all binational deliberations before 9/11 while security issues are dominant in the immediate aftermath of 9/11. But in recent years, a bundling of the security and economic issues has been emphasized. The expansion of private sector companies in the security sector has been stellar since 9/11. Over time, it is entirely possible to have security and economic considerations reinforce, not mutually exclude, each other.[68]

Since 9/11, in the case of the United States, the military continues to be subordinated to the civilian authorities. The security dynamics are as much military as they are nonmilitary.

Since 9/11, the involuntary security restrictions imposed on all institutions and actors have precluded greater integration with the Mexican and Canadian counterparts. A greater sense of North American security can be achieved only through a common integrated security perimeter that stretches from southern Mexico near the Guatemalan border to the Northern Canadian frontiers in the Arctic. As the years pass without another terrorist attack on U.S. soil, the imperatives of global competitive markets are expected to dwarf anticompetitive regional forces.

Regional economic considerations were paramount in the pre–9/11 days, whereas since 9/11 broader hemispheric or global considerations have undoubtedly superseded the regional North American consideration. However, since the beginning of George W. Bush's second term as president, regional considerations have been given greater consideration. For example, migration issues have become more salient in the 2007 Congress where the Democrat Party has regained power.

Realist considerations, profiled in table 2.13, remain dominant in the nature of the state: It is the dominant actor in all three countries, especially the United States and Mexico, though Canada's decentralized federal system contrasts the U.S. counterpart. Abroad, where realism is mostly relevant, only the United States seems

Table 2.13 The Realist Concerns: Insights

Dimension	Features
1. State as dominant actor	In the immediate aftermath of 9/11, the federal state dominated, but since then gradual opposition has emerged from factions within the Democratic and Republican parties. State continues as a dominant actor but with much greater appeasement to the private sector
2. Policy reflecting internal or external competitiveness?	In the immediate aftermath of 9/11, policy essentially reacted to external dynamics; since then, it has become more interactive with acknowledgements of the limits of reactive approach
3. Is international competitiveness orderly or chaotic?	Since the end of the Cold War, the international order was relatively chaotic with one superpower; more so since the war in Iraq as the United States is unable to define or chart a concerted course of action with much international legitimacy

to be a conscious and purposive actor, with Canada entering the global arena mostly for economic pursuits, or under collective security organizations. Mexico stays away from this arena.

Undoubtedly, the executive branch at the federal level has taken much of the initiative since 9/11. But over time, political opposition manifested through popular sector groups and factional differences within the Democratic Party as well as the Libertarian wing of the Republican Party has challenged the unilateral supremacy of the federal government in all security- or economy-related transactions.[69]

In the immediate aftermath of 9/11, the U.S. reaction was primarily reactive to external events. However, over time it has become more interactive. The 2006 controversy over the possibility of Dubai Port World managing six major U.S. ports clearly shows an interaction between the external and domestic dynamics. U.S. reaction to the Mexican President Vicente Fox's migration-related statements has contributed to much emotional reaction toward illegal immigration across the southern border. Under the Republican president, with regard to Canada the cultural issues related to gay marriage and health care clearly create a dividing line which may have some spill-over effect on economic integration or regional security.

In the post–Cold War era, the international order has been unstable largely because the United States has been unable to propose a coherent foreign policy paradigm. Piece-meal foreign policy reactions toward countries that it considers evil, such as Iran and North Korea, has added much uncertainty to the stability of the international system. It seems more chaotic since 9/11, largely because the United States has chosen to act alone (mostly) in Iraq during the war campaign (but less so since the occupation began) and it has frequently refused to work within the parameters of existing international treaties. Such international chaos may diminish with a change in the political party in power in Washington. Such disregard for international conventions and treaties has not proved helpful in generally resuscitating the NAFTA-based forces in the region. Such resurgence has only happened partially.

Overall, the sense thus far is that although the security dynamics have indeed dwarfed several of the North American integrative processes since 9/11, these by no means have happened along all major dimensions of the triadic relationship between the United States, Canada, and Mexico.

CONCLUSIONS

The events of 9/11 in the United States have produced significant changes in the security strategy and the most radical level of bureaucratic reorganization since the late 1940s. Although DHS was been created to implement the new security policy, the problems of interorganizational coordination have continued to persist. Only a future incident would help us evaluate the effectiveness of the new organizational structure.

Generally speaking, these changes have not negatively impacted the macro economic growth and stability of the United States. In the years since the disruption due to 9/11, the aggregate indicators of trade, investment, travel, and employment have generally performed well, and have indeed surpassed their pre–9/11 peaks.

But Canada and Mexico have continued to face an increase in transaction costs due to the new security measures in place on the U.S. side of the border. NAFTA, although facilitated tremendous growth in economic transactions between the three countries, did not really create many institutions that would oversee the harmonization of policies in security matters. That gap has been addressed by both countries at the bilateral levels. But no North American security institution has yet been created to coordinate such issues among the three partners. National politics, sensitivities about sovereignty, and perceived cultural differences, among others, have been the obstacles to that possible creation. In that sense at least, the central hypothesis of this project that 9/11 has prompted the bilateral security imperatives to supersede the issues of unfettered free trade in North America generally bears truth.

3

Asymmetry Squeezing Out Trilateralism? Canadian Ambivalence on U.S. Strategic Primacy

Douglas A. Ross and Anil Hira

INTRODUCTION[1]

This chapter examines the Canadian response to the 9/11 terrorist attacks on the United States and to other U.S. policy and institutional changes that ensued as well. These changes are profound in terms of both domestic and regional governance and in terms of their potential impact on economic prosperity in Canada. Thus far, much of the literature on Canada after 9/11 has been reactive about what such changes may portend for the future of Canadian–U.S. relations in long-term perspective.[2] This chapter systematically examines what changes have occurred with respect to foreign policy, domestic security, economic and immigration policy, as well as the institutional adaptations that have flowed from these 9/11-induced policy shifts.

There is a structurally grave tension at the heart of contemporary Canadian governance. Because continentally integrationist forces in the economy remain very powerful, a formerly broad trend toward diverging Canadian and U.S. identities as expressed through foreign policy, domestic laws, immigration policy, and social attitudes may now have been thrown into reverse.[3] Furthermore, a decade-long window for forging a new era of trilateral cooperation with the United States and Mexico during the 1990s may now be closed completely—and perhaps obliterated forever—by greatly increased U.S. demands for historically unprecedented bilateral cooperation in both military operations and national security surveillance and enforcement. To the extent that Canadians have begun to share fears about a decline in world order and global security as well as a decline in relative U.S. power, the willingness to align Canadian foreign and defence policies more closely with Washington actually may increase. More importantly, Canadian desires to appease Washington's need for more security in order to assure continued economic flows appears to be developing without any clear plan, analysis, or long-term strategy.[4] The analysis here is aimed at a wide international audience, thus necessitating the provision of placing material on Canadian history and foreign policy in context. Some background discussions among Canadian intellectuals and nongovernmental groups are also assessed, as these reflect the wider ongoing debate that concerns the policy reforms and adjustments Canada can and should make in response to 9/11. Finally, a brief analysis of the Harper government's response to the changed security environment is also included, as well as discussion about the possibilities for managing the now divergent perspectives on international security issues in Ottawa and Washington.

The chapter is based on an analysis of primary and secondary sources, as well as off-the-record interviews with over a dozen Canadian officials across a variety of ministries, conducted over a two-week period by Anil Hira in Ottawa in summer 2006 and updated in early November 2007 by Douglas Ross. In order to elicit the utmost frankness, the comments of all interview sources have been kept anonymous.

With respect to foreign policy, there has been a marked divergence in Canadian thinking and behavior from the global strategy developed by the Bush administration post–9/11. In June 2003 over 70 percent of Canadians rejected the U.S.-organized invasion and occupation of Iraq.[5] In the wake of the failed U.S. occupation strategy and the humanitarian disaster that has unfolded in Iraq over the past four years, Canadian sentiments about the wisdom of Prime Minister Jean Chrétien's avoidance of involvement have only strengthened. By October 2006, 79 percent of Canadians felt that staying out of Iraq was the correct decision.[6] Yet Canadian decision-makers also recognize the "free rider" label that Canada has long worn due to low defence expenditures could produce major economic costs with declining U.S. confidence in Canadian security.[7]

As a result, a small, temporary Canadian role in the military stabilization of Afghanistan was initiated in late 2001 to show support for the United States "war on terror" by deploying Canadian "special forces" to eastern Afghanistan. A far larger longer-term deployment after mid-2003 was accepted by Canadians only because that deployment enjoyed unanimous support from NATO, and latterly significant support from the United Nations as well. Arguably, from Ottawa's vantage point, the larger deployment also committed the country's limited resources to the Afghan theatre and thereby precluded any possible U.S. overtures to help with the occupation and rebuilding of Iraq. But when Canadian casualties in Afghanistan rose in 2006 and 2007, public support for the mission fell steadily, although at the time of writing, support for, and opposition to, the mission have been roughly comparable for over one year.[8] The Afghan deployment remains, as one pollster termed it, a "highly divisive issue" with considerable potential for volatility in voter responses if *Taliban* and "foreign fighter" insurgents continue to improve their skills with improvised explosive devices—and kill or maim a significant number of Canadian soldiers, whether they are in reinforced light armored vehicles or even tanks (via "stacked," cell-phone-detonated antitank mines) or just victims of suicide bombers on crowded city streets. Ambiguity in Canadian foreign policy in part reflects a lack of consensus within Canada itself, with a wide spectrum of ideological, political, and regionally based (Quebec) differences in public opinion on foreign policy, as well as a lack of clarity about how to best promote Canadian interests, which are largely ignored, in U.S. halls of power.[9] J.L. Granatstein states:

> For Canada, the object has always been to provide just enough military capacity to be able to tell Washington that it need have not fear about its northern border and to oblige the United States to plan the defence of the continent. . . . Most times, this claims was not wholly accurate, but Canada provided sufficient military resources and cooperated closely enough with the Pentagon that the U.S. military felt more or less reassured. . . . But (after the Cold War) Canada cut budgets and personnel deeper and faster than the Americans did. . . . The Chrétien government (cuts) amounted to one-third of defence spending, and the Canadian Forces' strength, equipment, and capabilities collapsed.[10]

Thus the Afghan mission represents a resolve to assuage U.S. fears in the post–9/11 climate. Recent research into the origins of the Canadian deployment in Afghanistan has highlighted the apparently decisive role of officials in both DND (Department of National Defence) and DFA (Department of Foreign Affairs) in convincing the last two liberal governments to embark on the Afghan mission in anticipatory deference to U.S. strategic goals.[11] Withholding support for the Anglo-American-led invasion and occupation of Iraq was thought to require some compensatory combat deployment elsewhere to sustain Canada's position as a supportive U.S. ally. With troops in Afghanistan but none in Iraq, Canadian audiences could be told that Ottawa was standing up against U.S. pressures while U.S. officials could be mollified by the sacrifice of money and lives in Afghanistan. To several foreign policy commentators, this stance was seen as rather "duplicitous."[12] With casualties an ever-present political concern, the Harper government announced that the mission's future would be determined by a parliamentary vote in early 2009, while the government's thinking would be strongly shaped by the report of a special advisory task force on Afghanistan composed of former officials and politicians, all of whom are experts in relations with the United States but who are totally lacking in any sort of experience in military affairs and counterinsurgency warfare.

The very peculiar composition of the panel (to report by January 31, 2008), in this respect, reflects the fundamental fact that Canada's Afghan mission is seen as necessary for maintaining the health of the Canadian–U.S. security relationship—in addition to whatever tangible contribution participation in the ISAF (International Security Assistance Force) makes to international security through increasing stability in Afghanistan itself.[13] From DND's perspective, doors long closed to Canadians in the Pentagon reopened after the commitment of CF (Canadian Forces) to a combat role. Very rapid procurement of the long-range Boeing C-17 transport aircraft was a direct result of Canada's Afghan military commitment in Kandahar province. Rapid procurement of $20 billion in additional capital equipment, including new tactical air transport, heavy lift helicopters, supply ships, tanks, and army trucks for the military has also been smoothed by the newly reestablished operational rapport with the Pentagon.[14] Finally, success in finding a solution to the dual-nationality problem posed by U.S. ITAR (International Traffic in Arms Regulations) regulations for Canadian defence industries' bidding on Pentagon contracts was also thought to have been made possible by Canada's Afghan commitment (confidential source).

In a broader strategic context, Ottawa rejected U.S. pressures to support its ABM (antiballistic missile) defence vision from 2003 to 2005, although it did agree to amend operational procedures in NORAD (North American Aerospace Defence command) in August 2004 so as to facilitate ABM activities by the U.S. NORTH-COM (Northern Command). Under Liberal Party leadership, it also rejected the U.S. approach to nuclear strategy, which, in the Bush era, has entailed the attainment of complete nuclear "primacy" over all other nuclear rivals, preferring to continue to support the core goal of eventual global denuclearization that is at the heart of the Nuclear NPT (Non-Proliferation Treaty) regime.

In the wake of the Canadian "no" on ABM collaboration, the Pentagon after some irritation moved on, but its attitude toward NORAD's future is at best very skeptical. NORTHCOM as a combatant command is now tasked with continental missile defence, and its Commander-in-Chief (CINCNORTHCOM), is also CINC-NORAD under a "two-hatted" posting arrangement. Washington's initial reaction to the Martin Government's "no" on full ABM cooperation in early 2005 was to consider ending the binational air defence relationship during the Donald Rumsfeld-Admiral Keating tenure of office (then-secretary of defence and CINCNORTHCOM, respectively). But under subsequent chiefs, U.S. Secretary of Defence Robert Gates and Canadian General Gene Renuart, as of early 2007 the new CINCNORAD/CINCNORTHCOM, U.S. officials apparently have been working hard to extend binational operations into jurisdictions that were hitherto always domestic. The steady growth in size and capacity of NORTHCOM is creating ever broader pressures on Canadian government civilian departments to extend liaison/cooperation activities to NORTHCOM with little or no central coordinating management of these contacts on the Canadian side. DND's new Canada Command has thus far had too few human and financial resources to be able to provide such a coordinating point of contact with the Canadian government, and staff at NORTHCOM have seemingly indicated that they are not especially interested in working through Canada Command. This development has some officials quite concerned. The developing relationship is thus posing the challenge of a new era of "defence against help,"[15] for both policy-makers in DND and the Canadian government more broadly.

Whether Canada's twin rejection of strategic nuclear primacy and ABM deep cooperation holds in the Stephen Harper era remains to be seen. Both Prime Minister Harper and his two ministers of National Defence have indicated that they are very much open to greater collaboration in continental missile defence than were their liberal predecessors. Harper and his Minister of the Environment have brought Canadian policy on climate change issues and the Kyoto Protocol targets much closer to that of the Bush administration. They have also commenced a series of major defence initiatives in the Arctic, ostensibly to strengthen Canadian sovereignty over the Northwest Passage and reinforce Canadian claims to the immense territory of the Canadian Arctic archipelago and its putatively vast subsurface energy resources. But these actions may not necessarily lead to any further intensification of disputes with Washington over Canada's Arctic sovereignty. Indeed some critics think the Harper government is simply trying to improve the national capacity for resisting

Russian resource expansionism in the Arctic basin in conjunction with an enhanced U.S. presence in the far north.

Regarding issues of domestic security and border security, there was initially much more congruence in the two national approaches post–9/11, but from 2004 onward differences in concept and actions have been manifested. With respect to immigration and refugee policy, both countries have clearly tightened their frontiers over the past five years, but on this issue the U.S. government and many politicians in Congress continue to see Canada as a seriously weak link in the U.S. security perimeter.[16] As border security issues gained rising prominence in the U.S. Congress and especially within the Republican presidential primary campaign through 2007, Canadian officials became alarmed by the unwillingness of the DHS to postpone and compromise its plan for passport identification of all travelers crossing the U.S.–Canada border under its WHTI (Western Hemisphere Travel Initiative). Heightened security on the U.S. side of the border generated a 34 percent fall in the number of American visitors from 2000 to 2006, and with a steady rise in the value of the Canadian dollar compounding the effects of tighter U.S. security screening, tourist visits from the United States fell a further 10 percent from January to September 2007.[17]

Under both Liberal and Conservative governments spending on the Canadian military and on internal security improvements rose considerably post–9/11. But while the Canadian public service understood the depth of U.S. security fears and advocated still greater spending, at the political level, successive Canadian governments simply have not been prepared to commit sufficient resources, financial and human, to strengthen the Canadian security perimeter to the degree sought by American leadership. Without additional major investments in the Coast Guard, the RCMP, port supervision and port personnel screening, the CSIS and the CBSA (Canadian Border Services Agency), one cannot say that border surveillance and enforcement will credibly apprehend or deter would-be terrorists aiming to harm Canadian or U.S. citizens. Accordingly, the U.S. side of the common border is becoming harder to cross to the point where trade and commerce has been impaired. By August 2007, one commentator suggested that the DHS had "completely hijacked Canadian–American relations" by backing out of preclearance negotiations.[18] The era of "smart border" technological fixes to ensure continued high volume of trade flows even in crisis may be drawing to a close.

The politically constrained Canadian response has been due partly to the recognition that no amount of spending will guarantee perimeter and internal security, nor, more practically, will it be able to ensure a moderate U.S. border response in the event of a transborder attack coming from or through Canadian territory. Partly Canadian reluctance to spend at the political level may be due to the conviction that U.S. insecurity has been worsened immeasurably by the U.S. intervention in Iraq, and a related but publicly unspoken hope that Canada's nonparticipation in the Iraq occupation may make Canada much less of a target for radical Islamists. Finally, the perception that Washington policy-makers may never be able to find sufficient unity and political will to control their southern border also may have led to Canadian skepticism about the security value of vastly greater spending on the Canadian perimeter. Paradoxically, despite the catastrophically adverse economic effects of possible future border closures following another 9/11-scale attack in the United States, some Canadian politicians may privately welcome U.S. perceptions of Canadian security deficiencies in the belief that it will cause U.S. authorities to be more vigilant and foster tighter U.S. screening all along the common frontier. Neither Canadian nor U.S. border authorities check outgoing traffic from their countries; it is up to each country's entry screening personnel to identify and neutralize incoming threats—as did the Port Angeles agent who caught Ahmed Ressam in 1999 as he attempted to drive south to bomb Los Angeles airport.

Thus, serious differences of opinion about long-term security planning and short-term organizational responses to the immediate threat of terrorism complicate Canadians' bilateral relations with U.S. counterparts. Despite growing apprehension about the ability of NATO's relatively small force to prevail in Afghanistan against the Taliban (see the warning of looming defeat from the Senlis Council),[19] Ottawa's role in the Afghan war is unlikely to end any time soon, regardless of which federal party forms the next government. But additional very deep differences of opinion are almost certain to arise should the Bush administration launch its long-prepared bombing campaign against Iranian nuclear facilities. A second counterproliferation war of this type would likely have a poisonous impact on bilateral cooperation and raise the prospect of a dramatic spike in anti-U.S. sentiment all across Canada.

In complete contrast to the turmoil and uncertainty in the realm of national and international security policy, on the economic front there remains a deep and broad consensus in the business communities on both sides of the border about the necessity and desirability of maintaining a border that is as open as possible for trade, investment, and business travel. The considerable tension between the economic and security imperatives cannot be resolved any time soon, and is only too likely to become a major issue in Canadian federal politics—most especially so in an era of minority governments.

Historical Differences on International Security: Iraq and Prior Conflicts

Historically, Canadians have had mixed feelings about major directional shifts in U.S. international security policy, particularly when this led to intensified U.S. military intervention overseas. It is not at all surprising that Canadians are less than full-fledged allies in the "war on terrorism" as judged from a U.S. perspective, or that they have preferred to take a more pragmatic and case-by-case approach to instances of state-supported terror. Nor have Canadians supported the determinedly unilateralist U.S. approach to the challenges of nuclear proliferation. Canadian governments have seen a vital if not critical role for major international institutions such as the United Nations, the International Atomic Energy Administration and NATO. Some unilateralist supplementary actions from time to time may make it necessary for the United States or Europe to deal with specific threats, but in the long term, most Canadian policy-makers prefer to rely on multilateral responses to major international security challenges. With respect to the special challenges pertaining to the diffusion of nuclear weapons technology, for example, an issue area of major policy divergence from the current U.S. leadership, Canadian governments have consistently upheld the validity of the Nuclear NPT's ultimate Article 6 goals: negotiations in good faith by the nuclear weapon states toward complete nuclear disarmament, followed ultimately (and admittedly in the distant future) by the relinquishing of all weapons of war.[20] Current U.S. preferences for the indefinite retention of nuclear weapons, and for their further refinement and improvement as fighting instruments—sufficient perhaps to wage preventive nuclear first-strikes on Russia and China—are seen as deeply destabilizing and therefore quite unwise.[21] Unilateral deployment of layered strategic ABM defences are seen as especially problematic, although the Harper government has shown signs that it might try to alter this position if it were to attain a majority in the next federal election.

In this respect, Canadian leaders have supported a "transformation" of world politics—but one that is to be achieved through an incrementally built-up multilateral consensus and a patient elaboration of universally binding international treaties, conventions and norms. Simply trying to eliminate the "bad guys" in world politics, the declared policy of George W. Bush's administration, is seen as bellicose and corrosive to the effort to build and extend the reach of a global regime of arms control and disarmament. Many Canadian leaders may harbor hopes of an eventual global victory for democratic transformation, but they do not think democracy can be forced on other states. New democracies are more likely to endure if they spring from authentic domestic roots, rather than imposition through foreign military occupation and external fiat.

The conflict in Iraq is not the first time that fundamental differences have arisen between Ottawa and Washington about the merits of overseas intervention. During the Cold War, U.S. military interventions in Asia were viewed highly skeptically or critically. Ottawa reluctantly sent a small, symbolic Canadian contribution to Korea from 1950 to 1953 (only some 27,000 military personnel rotated through that conflict over three years of fighting in contrast to over 5.7 million U.S. citizens who saw duty there). Canadian governments chose to remain on the sidelines in a "truce supervisory role" throughout the U.S. intervention in Vietnam, Cambodia, and Laos from 1954 to 1975. In both of these "limited wars," Canadian governments aimed to restrain their superpower allies through persuasion and diplomacy—vainly at the tactical level for the most part.[22] Canadian leaders never found the domino "theory" credible, and they were totally opposed to hawkish elements in the United States who were inclined toward anticommunist "rollback" in Asia—in effect, war with (and advocacy of regime change in) communist China. Containment, multilateralism, and international institution building were at the heart of the Canadian approach to waging the Cold War.[23]

All U.S. direct and "overt" interventions in Central and South America and the Caribbean were viewed with considerable disfavor from the era of Louis St. Laurent through Jean Chrétien: The lengthy history of intervention in Guatemala (1954),

Cuba (1961–62), the Dominican Republic (1965), Chile (1970), El Salvador, Grenada, and Nicaragua in the early 1980s, and Panama (1991), were all criticized widely in the Canadian press and seen by the senior civil service and political levels of successive Canadian governments as strategically illogical and at times as quite an immoral use of U.S. "special forces" military or CIA personnel. The repeated interventions by the United States in effect kept Ottawa from joining the OAS until the Cold War was clearly drawing to an end in 1988–89—because of the certainty of a direct collision of views over Washington's Latin American policies prior to that time.

Canadian involvement in bilateral security measures was needed during the Cold War to set constraints on the intrusive and at times demanding presence of the United States.[24] More than a little of the intensity of Canadian economic nationalism during the Cold War stemmed from fears of a "silent surrender" of sovereignty through the progressive expansion of U.S. corporate control over key sectors of the Canadian economy. The integrating tendencies of geography, culture and the vision of an unimpeded continental division of labor, however, proved to be irresistible. When Pierre Trudeau's efforts to implement a NEP and to restrict and reduce levels of foreign (i.e., mostly the United States) investment collapsed in the early 1980s under pressure from the Reagan administration and grave regional anger over the projected redistributive costs that would be borne by oil-rich Western provinces, nationalist economic fervor was spent. Only four years after Trudeau's retirement, Canadians narrowly approved the regional free trade concept in the 1988 national elections. This turnaround was based on the hope that both the bilateral CUFTA (Canada–U.S. Free Trade Agreement, and later the NAFTA) would end problems with selectively protectionist behavior by Congress on behalf of U.S. special interests. Both agreements failed to achieve this goal entirely, although they did stimulate a rapid growth in bilateral trade overall. Nevertheless, many Canadians came to resent U.S. pressures on their country, which seem to have worsened since Mulroney and Chrétien backed free trade, first continentally, then throughout the hemisphere. On refugees and immigration, internal security, and public policies involving health care, pharmaceuticals, or different approaches to state regulation of private enterprise (as in the forest products industry, ranching or agriculture), U.S. political and economic pressures to conform to U.S. approaches have not been happily received.

Post–9/11, as noted, neither the Canadian government nor Canadian public opinion approved of the U.S. invasion and occupation of Iraq. That popular view remains very firm. As in most other countries, the U.S. intervention in Iraq is seen as having increased the risk of international terrorist acts, not diminished them (in Canada 69 percent think it has increased the risk, 22 percent think it has reduced it).[25] In 2005 a classified CSIS report concurred with that judgment, as did the head of CSIS, Jim Judd, in a public statement in October of that year.[26]

On the other hand, the far more authentically multilateral removal of the *Taliban* regime in late 2001, and the now NATO-led effort to stabilize Hamid Karzai's elected government in Kabul, enjoyed, until recently, substantial majority support from Canadians. Since Autumn 2001, Ottawa made a major commitment of both "special force" commandos (elements of the JTF2 unit) and, after August 2003, regular force troops first to Kabul (and parts of the eastern provinces), and after mid-2005 to Kandahar (polls indicated 66 percent support for a combat role in 2002, but only 52 percent in March 2006).[27] One early survey indicated that 62 percent of Canadians opposed sending troops to Afghanistan, and only 27 percent approved such a deployment.[28] To combat falling support for the mission the Chief of the Defence Staff, General Rick Hillier, waged an unusually active publicity campaign to promote the importance of Canada's Afghan role—so much so that Prime Minister Harper felt compelled to assert that the Canadian involvement would be determined by civilian leadership, not the senior officer corps.[29] Hillier's initial success led to Harper's March 2006 visit to Kandahar, Kabul, and Islamabad. Harper then gave what seemed to be unqualified and possibly indefinite support for the mission. But with a rapid increase in Canadian casualties from mid-2006 to mid-2007, the Prime Minister was forced to commit his government to ending the Canadian Afghan mission in January 2009 should any proposed extension at that time then fail to secure a clear parliamentary "consensus" that included significant opposition party support.[30] As of August 2007, polls indicated that deployment of Canadian soldiers to Afghanistan was opposed by a solid majority of English-speaking voters and over two-thirds of Quebec voters.[31] By July 2007, the liberal party, under new leader Stéphane Dion, was firmly committed to termination of the mission in 2009,[32] while Jack Layton's New Democrats have consistently called for immediate withdrawal. Somewhat perversely Gilles Duceppe's *Bloc Québecois,* however, refrained from endorsing any clear withdrawal date so long as humanitarian action remained the foremost part of the Canadian mission.

With respect to international security issues, many analysts have complained that there has been no clear Canadian national security framework, vision, or long-term strategy.[33] The first such policy statement was made in 2004, however it is too early to say if there is any consensus on the goals set out in that short document. This absence is natural enough for a middle power lacking grand strategy ambitions. In terms of foreign policy, as outlined later, Canada has traditionally relied upon an involuntary U.S. security guarantee to cope with potential threats from all third countries. From the U.S. perspective, this has often been a source of frustration because of perceived Canadian "free-riding" at the expense of the U.S. taxpayer—an American perception that has intensified since the last decade of the Cold War. Canadian governments, however, have simply accepted what they have perceived to be an involuntary commitment from Washington that the United States cannot avoid extending. The chief problem for Canadian security planners then, from this "free rider" perspective, is one of "defence against help" in those situations where Ottawa wants to protect its sovereign control over national territory and ocean approaches during peacetime.[34] Far too little time is spent actually scanning the international horizons for trends and events that may eventually threaten Canadians' welfare.

Up to 1968 Canadian governments tried to contribute usefully and responsibly to Western international security debates. But with Pierre Trudeau and popular

Canadian disillusionment with the U.S. intervention in Vietnam, came a progressive decline in Canadian international security activism. This decline had actually begun in the aftermath of the Cuban missile crisis when the U.S. government, from the Canadian perspective, failed to honor the NORAD agreement's obligation to "consult" meaningfully prior to imposing its air-naval blockade. The offense of this unacceptably unilateral behavior was compounded later when Washington assisted in the electoral demise of the Diefenbaker government via a well-timed press conference by a U.S. general and a still more calculated State Department press release.[35] The inability to influence U.S. actions with respect to either nuclear arms control issues or crisis decision-making, coupled with the steady escalation of violence in Vietnam during the 1960s, led to a retrenchment and disengagement from "high policy" security issues by Ottawa that was probably inevitable. It certainly fed impulses in the Canadian elite that can only be termed either "free-riding" or "functionally isolationist," or both.[36]

While Canadian differences with U.S. international security policies grew deeper in the decades of the 1970s and 1980s (the latter decade often referred to as the "second Cold War"), security cooperation with Western Europeans also became more difficult. As the peoples of Europe drew more together, Canadians were incrementally excluded from an active or effective role in NATO. Trudeau's cuts to Canada's force deployments in NATO in the early 1970s had exacerbated the country's waning influence with European leaders and had contributed to a fading of interest in a "North Atlantic Community" by Canadians. So too did the utter failure to secure any meaningful boost in trade and investment relations with Europe under a "contractual link" negotiated with the EU in 1976. While still an active, middle-ranking power on the international stage in the 1970s and 1980s, Canadian governments cultivated other venues for multilateral engagement such as the Commonwealth, *la francophonie,* and later the WTO (World Trade Organization). Canadian commitments to UN peacekeeping in the 1980s and early 1990s helped induce many Canadians to lose sight of the fact that their military forces were at root created for lethal defence or coercive diplomatic intervention. Peacekeeping came to be seen as a "better" way to use military force by many Canadians, and a further way to differentiate Canadian policies from more aggressive U.S. approaches to security threats.

During Lloyd Axworthy's tenure as Minister for Foreign Affairs, the Canadian government tried to "brand" itself not only through a greater rhetorical support for peacekeeping but also under a broader doctrine built on the notions of "human security" and "soft power" (a term developed by the U.S. international affairs analyst Joseph Nye alluding to a capacity to persuade and induce policy and behavioral emulation). Human security involved basic universal rights for safety and security of person and access to essential social services; as a policy it entailed an international responsibility to promote attainment of these goals wherever they were not being met—even to the point of engaging in humanitarian intervention as part of an international "responsibility to protect" (later referred to as "R2P"). As Foreign Minister, Axworthy led a "soft power" campaign to ban the use of land mines and secured a modest level of Canadian funding to help pay for their removal globally. The treaty was pronounced a success, although the United States, Russia, China, and India refused to endorse the treaty, citing overriding security needs for landmine use. Ten years after the conclusion of the treaty, it is not clear that the total number of buried mines has in fact been reduced to any significant degree, although progress in de-mining in several countries has been considerable, there are now 157 signatories compared to the original 122, and undoubtedly many civilian lives have been saved as a result of the convention.

In the wake of the Ottawa Land Mines Convention, Axworthy's Liberal successors went on to back international efforts to constrain the dissemination of small arms but with much less success. Under both Chrétien and Prime Minister Paul Martin, Liberal governments took pride in promoting "good governance," and sent jurists to China and RCMP officers to Haiti, Afghanistan, and elsewhere to try to foster improved respect for the rule of law and a more sensitive administration of justice and law enforcement. One of the most notable virtues of such human security initiatives were their very low cost: training judges or police is decidedly less costly than training armed forces—or equipping them, or dispatching them on "peace enforcement" missions. During the Chrétien-Martin years, spending on both defence and foreign aid fell sharply as a percentage of GDP from some 2.5 percent to less than 1.5 percent. In fact the elimination of the federal government's year-to-year deficits during Martin's tenure as finance minister was accomplished in large measure by sacrificing the country's international force projection and aid provision capacities.[37] According to Library of Parliament generated data for Canadian Senator Colin Kenny, defence spending per capita (in constant 2006 dollars) was some $Cdn625 when Trudeau left office and $525 when Mulroney left office. The figure bottomed out at $400 per capita under Chrétien in 1997, rose modestly to $475 per capita by the time Martin stepped down as prime minister, and has risen to almost $550 under the Harper government.

Canada's foreign policy responses after 9/11 had to be pursued both multilaterally and bilaterally with Washington. On some issues, mostly economic, one set of reactions was driven by the need to express solidarity with the United States to reduce potentially punitive action from Congress; on other issues, mostly related to international security, another pattern of advocacy demanded greater distance from U.S. policies that were perceived to be threatening international instability or simply were incompatible with Canadians' international values. Some business groups, such as the Conference Board of Canada and the Canadian Council of Chief Executives claimed that Canada could not afford to alienate its largest trading partners by indulging in an independent approach to international security issues. Their dream of greatly expanded security cooperation by Canadians in return for the final full ending of all trade obstacles from the U.S. Congress (labeled "deep integration") has thus far failed to gain traction in the face of U.S. security concerns.

Scholars are predictably divided ranging from historian Granatstein who suggested the need for greater solidarity with U.S. policies, including Iraq, to an array of critics such as Stephen Clarkson who criticized accommodation with the United

States.[38] Michael Ignatieff, a Canadian political theorist turned Liberal politician (Deputy Leader of his party at time of writing), pointed out that Ottawa's unwillingness to adequately fund military, peacekeeping, and aid activity left the Canadian government with little recourse for independent action, a stance that touched off considerable criticism inside the Liberal Party.[39] Though Canada's performance does not match its self-image as a peacekeeper (the country ranked 34th in terms of numbers of troops committed to UN peacekeeping in 2004 and 50th by 2006), Canada did provide very modest financial support for multilateral initiatives to fight AIDS in Africa.

Though willing to support the multilateral "stability operations" in Afghanistan with United States and European NATO forces, at least for a limited term, Prime Minister Chrétien pointedly refused to support the U.S. war in Iraq because it lacked the legal authority of a UN Security Council resolution.[40] Chrétien's preference for a commitment to Afghanistan over Iraq was highly controversial and prompted one senior Canadian army officer, General Cam Ross, to resign in protest because of the physical incapacity of the CF at that time.[41] Business groups feared, quite incorrectly as it turned out, that the United States might retaliate against Canadian economic interests,[42] while activist, academic, and policy-making groups enthusiastically supported the Canadian "no" to participation in the invasion and occupation of Iraq.

Liberal leaders were prepared to support the "war on terror" but only up to the limits allowed by the United Nations. They were not prepared to endorse George Bush's proposals for an open-ended and largely unilateral crusade against nuclear proliferation to arbitrarily identified "rogue" states. Bush's effort to deny the "world most dangerous weapons" to the world's most irresponsible governments was seen to fly in the face of Canadian efforts to build a stable structure of international law anchored by the United Nations and applied universally. The Canadian "no" with respect to Iraq was guided less by superior intelligence assessments about the absence of WMD in Saddam's Iraq than by a political determination that Bush's counter-proliferation unilateralism was likely to be deeply corrosive to international order.[43] Ottawa's analysts concluded that Saddam's regime probably did have small amounts of biological and chemical agents, but no nuclear weapons capacity.[44] Other Canadian officials thought the intervention in Iraq was likely to create more terrorists than it would eliminate.[45] The decision also played well in domestic politics, underscoring Canada's ability to say "no" to participate in U.S. interventions.

The Antiballistic Missile Debate

In recent years, one bilateral issue in particular has frustrated both Ottawa and Washington greatly: what to do about ABM defence cooperation? The evolving Canadian stance *vis-à-vis* participation in U.S. plans for a layered missile defence strategy for North America reflected both considerable ambivalence and a long history of discussion of the issue inside the Canadian government and a broader defence policy community. The Chrétien decade, 1993–2003, saw Ottawa reject U.S. calls for missile defence deployments and support the indefinite retention of the Soviet–U.S. (later Russo–U.S.) ABM Treaty that had banned extensive ABM deployments and highly constrained ABM technology development since 1972. The Clinton administration's effort to neutralize Congressional Republicans' advocacy of ABM deployments was applauded quietly in Ottawa, and Prime Minister Chrétien even went so far as to make his preference for Al Gore over Bush known in the run-up to the presidential elections in 2000.

Paul Martin, by contrast, took up the reins of the Liberal Party with an open mind on the subject of missile defence coupled with anxiety about the consequences of Chrétien's "no" on Iraq. Accordingly, with the support of three other members of his first Cabinet (John McCallum, Bill Graham, and David Pratt), Martin was ready to endorse specific arrangements for limited involvement in the summer of 2004 just after the election that had reduced his government to minority status. In August 2004, Martin's government approved the use of NORAD's infrastructure in Canada to facilitate the tracking and attack assessment of any missile reentry vehicles headed for North America from across the polar region. But this agreement, which was of considerable practical consequence to U.S. authorities, was coupled with an explicit statement that such cooperation did not constitute endorsement of U.S. plans to deploy a thick, multilayered area defence of North America against ballistic missile attack though Canada would be nonetheless partially covered by the system.[46] Under pressure from the Québec wing of the Liberal Party, Martin retreated from endorsement despite a visit to Ottawa by President Bush to try to extract such an open-ended commitment. Quebeckers were the most ardently opposed to missile defence of all provincial electorates, just as they were the most ardently opposed to Canadian support for intervention in both Iraq and Afghanistan.[47]

Canada has participated in the NORAD since 1958. But over the 50 years of cooperation in air defence and aerospace early warning, Canadian authorities have never agreed to participate in any U.S. plans for comprehensive strategic missile defence. In 1969, an ABM exclusion clause was written explicitly into the NORAD renewal agreement concluded that year. This clause was removed in 1981, when the Reagan administration pressed for its excision. But even a Conservative government under Brian Mulroney did not endorse the grand scheme for thick missile defences called for by President Reagan in his SDI (Strategic Defence Initiative) speech of March 23, 1983, when the president proposed rendering the ballistic missile threat "impotent and obsolete." Mulroney formally gave a "polite no" to a U.S. invitation to participate in SDI in 1986 with no adverse consequences for Canadian–U.S. relations—just as his Liberal predecessors had done 17 years earlier. NORAD cooperation in air defence and aerospace early warning remained undiminished despite these rejections of an important U.S. "grand strategy" preference.

Since 2002, the CF have developed a good working relationship with the new U.S. NORTHCOM and, under the auspices of a binational planning group, developed plans to add maritime security operations to NORAD's mandate in the 2006 renewal.[48] But the inherent indecisiveness of the Canadian government concerning U.S. requests for a broad "in principle" endorsement of missile defence continues to the present day.[49] Since January 2006 Prime Minister Harper and his first Minister of National Defence, Gordon O'Connor, indicated several times that they were willing to consider any new but specific proposals from the Pentagon. This marked a return to the interest expressed by Paul Martin's government in late 2003 and early 2004. But the Conservatives' invitation was still well short of the support, the Bush administration was hoping to elicit. There is no indication to date that the prime minister is prepared to give any sort of unqualified support to global ABM development plans that Washington might wish to adopt.[50] It is unlikely that the Pentagon will wish to reopen discussions until such time as there is a majority government in Ottawa.

During the June 2007 G8 summits, Harper expressed support for the U.S./NATO deployment of ABM sites in Poland and the Czech Republic, asserting that "there is no reason to interpret those actions as a threat against Russia." But his official spokesperson also noted that the Canadian government opposed a global ABM shield and that for any bilateral discussions to occur on further joint Canadian–U.S. ABM activities "the Americans would have to ask us, and that hasn't happened. It's not on our agenda."[51]

Since well before 2000, DFA officials were strongly opposed to the concept of comprehensive missile defences, fearing that that they would undermine strategic nuclear relationships between the United States and Russia and between the United States and China, and thereby resuscitate rivalries in nuclear arms deployments. The case on behalf of unconditional missile defence cooperation with the United States was made discreetly only by officials from DND during the 1990s and such expressions of support remained low-key even after 9/11. But DND's political influence was weak with Liberal Cabinets which were in no way disposed toward supporting "militarism" or "nuclear arms races"—or undercutting their own electoral appeal among strongly anti-ABM voters in Quebec.

Canadian supporters of missile defence do exist in both major federal parties. They have argued that defences built only against small-scale "rogue states" cannot be destabilizing *vis-à-vis* Russia and China now that both countries are deeply involved in global market economics. Second, Canadian opposition to U.S. plans just might lead to a severe marginalization or even termination of NORAD defence cooperation with very adverse and expensive implications for the Canadian government's ability to know what is happening in its own airspace in peacetime. Third, cooperation on the missile defence issue might help to soften Congressional attitudes on protectionist trade measures against Canadian softwood lumber and beef imports; and it certainly would help protect existing levels of Canadian aerospace export trade under the Defence Production Sharing Agreements. Fourth, Canadians need to be in on the design phase of any comprehensive layered ABM systems because intercept engagement may sooner or later take place over Canada. Fifth, a closer defence relationship with Washington would augment, not diminish, Canadian international standing (Ottawa's greater access to decision-making in Washington would give Canadian policy statements more credibility). Sixth, some level of layered ABM defences could save millions of lives in the event of an accidental or unauthorized launch of ballistic missiles (due to either technical malfunction, or events ensuing after civil war in some nuclear-armed country—Russia or in the future Pakistan might be cited). Seventh, modest ABM defences held multilaterally would undercut the feasibility of crisis scenarios of limited counterforce attacks to "show resolve," thus reducing the risk of great power nuclear-based "skirmishing." Lastly, weaponizing space would not mark a qualitatively huge jump in the international military exploitation of space: existing satellites are used for reconnaissance, surveillance, and targeting of fixed and moving targets on earth with the attacks launched from weapon systems on the ground or from aircraft. Would it really matter if space-to-space and space-to-earth strike capabilities were added to the great power arsenals, when the United States is already exploring the prospects for conventionally armed ICBM strikes and now that China has tested an ASAT (antisatellite weapon) comparable to the most advanced American ASAT?

Critics in Canada, including three generations of Foreign Affairs/External Affairs officials, have consistently argued that a two-dimensional race in offensive and defensive strategic nuclear arms will accelerate the arms race, block further reductions in nuclear stockpiles and deployed nuclear systems, and, worst of all, are likely to worsen crisis instability by creating perceived incentives to strike first in any developing confrontation. For the foreseeable future any U.S. rush into layered ABM defences cannot be matched by any other nuclear weapon state. No other state has the requisite economic resources or technological capabilities. But such a world would not be stable. A world with an asymmetrical ABM defence advantage held by the United States is only likely to stimulate further offsetting offensive deployments by Russia, China, and any other country that might feel threatened by an American capacity to engage in implicitly or explicitly nuclearized coercive diplomacy. This is all the more true when U.S. strategic analysts begin to predict reasonably confidently that the United States now possesses strategic nuclear primacy—that is to say, an ability to carry out a disarming first-strike—against the highly vulnerable nuclear arsenals in both China and Russia.[52]

As a result of the U.S. abrogation of the ABM Treaty in 2002, some 1500 to 2000 more Russian warheads remain in service targeted at North America than would have been the case had abrogation not occurred and had START III been implemented. Russian defence planners have accelerated the development of long-range nuclear capable cruise missiles, and they have already tested the world's first MaRVs (maneuvering reentry vehicles) for new ICBMs that have remained in serial production. In late May 2007, they tested an advanced MIRVed (six warheads per missile) replacement for SS-18 and SS-19 ICBMs that will be land-mobile in their deployment.[53] The Russian long-range bomber force has been refurbished rather than retired as seemed likely a decade ago, and long-range bomber patrols over the Arctic near Alaska were reinstituted several years ago. In 2007, President Putin, after failing to win over President Bush to an alternative ABM radar site in Azerbaijan both before and during the G8 Summit,[54] signaled his considerable displeasure concerning U.S. ABM deployments in Eastern Europe by confirming Moscow's abrogation of the CFE Treaty on European conventional force restraints,[55] and by authorizing additional regular bomber flights toward the United Kingdom, Canada, and Alaska, and U.S.

bases in the Pacific.[56] Additionally, Putin threatened that U.S. ABM deployments in Europe would necessitate retargeting European sites with both ballistic and cruise missiles with nuclear warheads.[57] Finally, the Russian government has continued to refuse to discuss its immense inventory of tactical nuclear weapons and the Cooperative Threat Reduction security measures that are needed to reduce the risk of stolen "loose nukes"[58]—largely because of fears of an emerging U.S. nuclear first-strike capacity.[59] It was thus not surprising when Putin and China's Hu Jintao attended a major joint military exercise by the Shanghai Cooperation Organization in August 2007 that was labeled as "anti-NATO" and "Warsaw Pact 2" in the Russian press. Iran's President Ahmedinejad also attended the event as a "guest of honor."[60]

U.S. ABM defences in space would, if they went ahead, pose special problems that threaten crisis stability and arms race stability simultaneously. A U.S. capacity to strike at other countries' satellites is likely to touch off a competition in ground-based antisatellite systems and later space-based ones as well. The Chinese successful test of a direct-ascent ASAT weapon on January 11, 2007 certainly suggests this is a palpable risk.[61] For any country fearing a U.S. disarming first strike, the temptation to strike first themselves possibly with nuclear weapons to destroy U.S. space-based assets and any vulnerable ground- or sea-based ABM facilities would be quite powerful. That risk in turn would increase the pressure on U.S. leaders to make sure that U.S. forces preempted any such efforts by destroying adversary ASAT or other ABM suppression systems before they could be used. The stage might then be set for a race across the threshold of nuclear use and an early end to the existing "taboo" on nuclear detonations.

In a less dramatic but still highly menacing scenario, Chinese leaders might be tempted to invade Taiwan after blinding what John Pike has called "the low hanging fruit" of U.S. imaging reconnaissance satellites.[62] In the face of stepped-up U.S. global ABM deployments, the Chinese military could also threaten to ruin the usability of space by destroying many satellites at various altitudes to create a vast debris cloud that would destroy all satellites in low or medium orbits—without resort to nuclear warheads. That step could be taken prior to any such global ABM system going operational.

The ABM file will not be an easy one for Prime Minister Harper to handle. Russian and Chinese actions over the past five years have strengthened anti-ABM sentiment in Canada considerably. The various arguments for and against are technically complex and filled with political uncertainty and are therefore not suited to public elaboration. Endorsing a globally ambitious U.S. ABM deployment without any sort of treaty-defined arrangement on a cap for interceptor deployments of the type that were embodied in the ABM treaty would be both strategically and politically hazardous. In addition to the concerns already noted, such endorsement could lead to Ottawa being ensnared in sharing the cost of a massively expanded air defence wall capable of handling new generations of stealth bombers and cruise missiles that sooner or later will be able to reach North America—if U.S. strategic relations with China and Russia continue to deteriorate. An ABM "roof" is quite pointless, after all, without capable air defence "walls."

Canadian Domestic Security Responses After 9/11: Security Culture Divergence?

While skepticism restrains Canadian participation in U.S. "draining the 'swamps'" efforts against international terrorism, on the domestic and bilateral front the response has been far more cooperative and positive. Canadians have long enjoyed the benefits of largely unconstrained economic access across "the world's longest undefended border." Cooperation with the new DHS has been considerable and it continues to grow as the frontier evolves from mere geographic marker into a mature "police border."

U.S. policy changes after 9/11 led to the creation of the DHS and a host of other legal and intelligence shifts. The DHS embodies the newly heightened concern about the potentially unlimited reach of terrorism, not only mixing domestic with international concerns but also including functional areas that were traditionally considered at arm's length from security. DHS's purview includes emergency relief; cyberterrorism and countermeasures; travel, transportation, and infrastructure security; and immigration and border security. DHS took over the former INS. DHS also sought to coordinate the work of various agencies across domestic/international and function lines, ranging from the Department of Energy to the FBI and CIA. This was in response to the major gaffes revealed in intelligence sharing as a result of 9/11. *Securing Our Homeland,* the DHS strategic plan for 2004, contained a wide panoply of objectives and concerns, along with a few of particular interest to this analysis.[63]

Objective 2.1 states that the DHS will create "smart borders," which will monitor and prevent the importation of drugs, terrorists, and "other illegal activity." Objective 6.4 states that the DHS will "facilitate the efficient movement of legitimate cargo and people." Furthermore, the document noted: "The border of the future must integrate actions to screen people and goods abroad prior to their arrival in sovereign U.S. territory to ensure compliance with entry and import regulations. Agreements with our Canadian and Mexican neighbors are central to this effort. America's borders will be made more efficient, posing little or no obstacle to legitimate travel and trade." The report stressed the vital importance of international cooperation to prevent future terrorist threats. This aspect is the central focus of the Canadian response to 9/11, namely the creation of a smart border agreement that would not threaten trade with the United States, as we discuss in the next section on migration issues. In pursuit of this goal of reassuring U.S. trading partners, Canada shook up its institutions and policies.

In fact, the Canadian security and intelligence apparatus has been under sustained scrutiny since the 1985 Air India bombing that killed 329 people on a flight from Toronto to London. The bombing was the worst single terrorist attack before 9/11 and has sparked a host of ongoing investigations. The bombing also led to stricter Canadian security in airports.

Canada's preoccupation with accommodating the United States without losing sight of its own independence led to the 2001 Anti-Terrorism Act (Bill C-23) passed on December 18, 2001. The Act was designed to facilitate domestic monitoring and actions against potential terrorists. It allowed the labeling of groups and individuals as terrorist in nature, and permitted investigative hearings to prevent potential acts of terrorism and terrorist activities. It also broadened the possibility for domestic monitoring of activities, including financial transactions and other communications. The Act, like the U.S. PATRIOT Act, has been highly controversial with domestic minority groups (especially Canadian Muslims) fearful that the legislation will erode their civil liberties. Kent Roach suggested that it may unduly target religious groups, and that its "preventive arrest" and investigative hearings provisions may impinge unduly on Canadian civil liberties. As in the United States, these provisions curtail privacy protection.[64] The Act underwent a regular five-year review which saw the opposition parties in parliament defeat Prime Minister Harper's late February 2007 effort to extend the preventive detention and judicially compelled testimony provisions by a further three years. Bill C-23 was not significant in helping to bring charges against eighteen young men in Toronto in the summer 2006 who allegedly conspired to attack parliament, behead MPs, and blow up landmarks with truck bombs. In fact, the lapsed provisions were never used at all from 2002 to 2007.[65]

Such fears were reinforced in 2002 with the case of Maher Arar. Arar, a Syrian Canadian, was deported by the United States back to Syria with Canadian bureaucratic complicity in response to U.S. concerns about potential terrorist activity. In January 2007, Arar received a formal apology from Prime Minister Harper and compensation of some $Cdn10.5 million plus legal costs because of RCMP actions that led to his torture. Three other individuals are also alleged to have been abused in Syria or Egypt because of requests for information by Canadian security personnel who, it is alleged, sought to have the suspects interrogated under torture.[66] As a result, the Act and RCMP behavior were placed under close scrutiny. The release of information that some 74 CIA flights had landed in Canada since 9/11 in February 2006 aroused public misgivings that Ottawa has been complicit in a good many instances of "extraordinary rendition"—a process that is widely acknowledged to be quite inconsistent with civil liberties attitudes in Canada. There is also some question about data on Canadian consumers which was being processed by U.S. companies, but was also vulnerable to U.S. DHS seizure and surveillance under the PATRIOT Act. At the same time, there are concerns among Canadian officials that the United States was not giving full intelligence from Iraqi-based sources that were relevant to threats at home, because of Canada's noninvolvement in that war. Such issues point to the seemingly out-of-date institutional and legal infrastructure that predates 9/11.

Notwithstanding the abuses that may have occurred, internal security spending has continued to rise. Canadian governments have begun to invest heavily on improving immigration screening to try to identify potential terrorists, on improved airport and air travel security, and on more thorough inspections of cargo at major ports. Transportation security spending increases have been a high priority. Canada's transport industries handle over $Cdn1 trillion in goods annually. One in fifteen jobs in Canada is in the transport business. Almost 80 million passenger trips are made on airlines, almost 40 million a year on ferry trips. Four million people a day use rapid transit or rail services. Of the $Cdn9 billion allocated for better transportation security since 9/11, some $3 billion went to transportation security improvements. A May 2007 report for TC (Transport Canada) estimated that Canadian and U.S. security tightening also cost the Canadian shipping industry some $Cdn2.6 billion since 9/11. The report found that 86 percent of the new costs were generated by tougher U.S. security requirements.[67]

Despite many new internal procedural reforms and a considerable infusion of new money, the 2007 report by the Auditor General found that the CBSA was still lagging badly in its implementation strategy. Some $525 million spent on new technology over the previous three years "had not been guided by a strategic plan." Border guards still did not trust the information systems with which they were provided, while many individuals who had been placed by CBSA's risk assessment system on "lookout" watch lists were still entering the country without scrutiny.[68] CBSA must scrutinize some 96 million people entering Canada at 1,269 ports of entry by land, sea and air traffic (roughly half are returning Canadians). Over $Cdn400 billion in goods must be screened. With a staff of 12,800 and a budget of $1.5 billion per year, CBSA managers have not yet come to the point where they can provide border guards with timely intelligence and current investigation information as well as past compliance behavior by given individuals (as is now done in the United States). Inexplicably, hundreds of commercial containers are shipped out of Canada each year across the U.S.–Canada border even though they have been tagged "Do Not Load," while CBSA studies indicate that about 37 percent of the information it receives from airlines about passengers is inaccurate.[69]

There has been considerable consolidation and change in Canada in regard to agencies related to security. The PCO (Privy Council Office) is the key advisory organization on security for the prime minister. Within the PCO is the office of the National Security Advisor. Public Safety Canada, formerly the Department of Public Safety and Emergency Preparedness, is responsible for the RCMP, CSIS, CBSA, and Correctional Services Canada. While CSIS covers both domestic and international intelligence, the RCMP remains the police force, with some intelligence capabilities. The DCI (Department of Citizenship and Immigration) covers migration issues, while CBSA, created in a 2003 interdepartmental restructuring, is involved with customs and security at border crossings. The CSE (Communications Security Establishment), which monitors electronic communications, reports to the DND. Foreign Affairs Canada and International Trade Canada cover diplomatic relations and international economic affairs. Besides being home to Canada's military, DND is also the administrative home to CSE, the provider of electronic intelligence and information protection. TC covers security threats in that area. Since 9/11, Canadian agencies have been meeting on a regular basis with their U.S. counterparts. A binational Planning Group has coordinating efforts to match Canadian DND with the U.S. DOD. DND also set up Canada Com, which is a liaison and policy group that specifically responds to requests for DND help by PSEPC (Public Safety and Emergency Preparedness Canada) for domestic natural disasters or security threats.

In the months after 9/11, the then-Canadian Foreign Minister, John Manley, worked hard to complete a series of "smart border" improvements that would ensure sustained movement of goods and services across the border—even in crisis circumstances. The agreement, while marking a significant step forward, did not presage substantive improvements in the physical security of key border crossing points that have been identified as points of exceptional vulnerability, but it did establish preclearance and notification procedures that helped to speed up commercial transits at the border. In this area, in particular, it is easy to see the nexus between economic and security interests in the new global war on terror. For instance, in a statement to the Canadian Standing Senate Committee on National Security and Defence in 2003, an aviation corporation owner stated:

> There is a huge amount of money for everyone if the public is placated and huge losses if people believe that anything bad might happen.... Everyone makes money selling fuel and it is all predicated on an illusion. In one sense, we know it is not safe....[70]

The 2004 Senate report on airport security concluded that coordination remained a serious problem. "The RCMP does not have overall responsibility for security at airports. Right now, no one is in charge." The report goes on to note that the CATSA (Canadian Air Transport Security Authority) is the delivery agency for preboarding screening of passengers, baggage, and personnel, but does not report to the RCMP. CATSA follows guidelines set by TC. Meanwhile, local airport authorities actually deliver the physical security services at airports.[71] Three years later, the same Senate investigative committee deplored the lack of governmental reform, reiterating their main finding that "security at Canadian airports is largely an illusion."[72] The RCMP still has not been given central control, nor has any other agency. CATSA still does not receive security intelligence directly. Airport employee background checks are inadequate. Restricted areas do not have adequate control. Flight and ground crews are not checked effectively. Baggage screening is poor and air cargo and air mail shipments are very vulnerable to terrorist exploitation. The dangers posed by armed marshals on flights could be dispensed with completely, if only the government had required double doors into all aircraft cockpits. The "known shipper" system is inherently insecure, while aircraft from small airports or float planes get into larger airports on "air-side" without full screening of passengers and crew. Government officials, however, attempt to hide all these gaps behind official secrecy. The Chair of the Senate Committee told the Air India inquiry in June 2007: "We believe that every time an individual is going air-side to work around aircraft, they should be searched in the way a passenger was searched."[73]

Port security is another zone of gravely deficient capability. Since the early 1980s TC has gone through a dramatic organizational retrenchment. With the privatization of many functions, market-driven imperatives asserted themselves across the country's transportation grid. The department workforce shrank from 25,000 to 5,000. Departmental staff no longer ran security operations at airports or ports. The federal government's port police force was dismantled and private port operators were tasked with providing security. The main focus of the scaled back department became one of regulating standards of security, licensing and certifying pilots, certifying airlines for safety, conducting inspections to ensure timely compliance and so forth. Port security deteriorated as a result.

Over four million cargo containers enter Canada each year. About 30 percent eventually are forwarded on to the United States.[74] Up to 2004, around 4 percent (national rate) are screened lightly,[75] and of those, only a small fraction are actually "destuffed" and searched thoroughly. Few ports have an ability to X-ray significant numbers of containers while simultaneously checking for radiation emissions. There are only fifteen VACIS (Vehicle and Cargo Inspection Systems) for the entire country in CBSA hands, and they are used only intermittently.[76] This extremely low level of screening is unlikely to improve in the foreseeable future. Customs and Excise union employees told the senators that "ghost cans" (containers without identifying origins that are not empty) regularly enter and leave major Canadian ports.[77] In the Senate Committee's view "every single container entering the United States via Canadian ports [should] be screened." Screening should include complete documentation every time, weigh-ins upon arrival in Canada and at time of departure, density checks for detection of contents at variance with bills of lading, radiation emission checks, and mandatory use of tamper-recording seals that use radio frequency identification devices. But there is little likelihood that these recommendations will be acted upon without a major incident to provoke their adoption.

With respect to the control of Canada's territorial waters, the situation is even worse than the gaps in coverage in port security. As noted above, the 2003 Standing Senate Committee on National Security and Defence found that Canada's coasts have been "virtually undefended."[78] The Canadian Coast Guard has been seriously underfunded for decades and it would take a major infusion of capital to rectify the inadequate number of ships and personnel with which they are expected to control Canadian coastal regions. The land-based law enforcement backup to the Coast Guard is even less capable. While in 2003, only 13 RCMP personnel were available for law enforcement along 7,400 kilometer of Nova Scotia coastline, in 2007 the situation was no better—only 14 officers were available. Ships less than 300 tons do not need to have identifying transponders. As a Senate Report stated, "The Coast Guard does not have a constabulary function, it is not armed and it reports to the Department of Fisheries and Oceans, all of which contribute to a focus away from coastal security. Despite its name, the Coast Guard doesn't play a serious role in guarding our coasts."[79] Exacerbating this situation are questions about coordination between the Coast Guard, the RCMP, and local authorities.[80]

The Harper government has moved to address this criticism by establishing Marine Security Operations centers, on each coast, where the different agencies will have a physical location in order to share information. However, it is not clear how information will be shared and how decisions will be made in crisis situations. There is also a new bilateral initiative to patrol the Great Lakes with U.S. counterparts, yet, here again, there seems to be no clear jurisdiction, protocols, or institutional chains of command across the different binational institutions.

As of 2007, little progress has been made on either coastal or inland waters security. According to the Senate Committee, the Coast Guard remains "toothless," lacks any institutional mandate for security enforcement, and has received no significant retasking and budget in the five years since 9/11. Canadian coasts remain "undefended" despite the Harper government's pledge to frame its approach to security in terms of "Canada First."[81] Any security concerns are reported to the RCMP, but the number of police officers available is woefully inadequate. The Coast Guard is a generation away from capable enforcement, even if there was a will to buy and arm the new aircraft and new helicopter-equipped littoral cutters the Coast Guard would require—which there is not.[82] Meanwhile organized crime elements remain present in Canada's three major ports (Vancouver, Montreal, and Halifax). Employee screening remains unreliable; six of Canada's 19 largest ports have no background checks on personnel at all.[83] "To our knowledge," the senators write, "no Canadian ports have waterside fencing or 24/7 waterside police patrols."[84] They note that the port of Rotterdam has over 420 police; Canada has only 24 RCMP for all 19 major ports—and all 24 have been stationed in Vancouver, Montreal, and Halifax only. The contributions of local police forces to port security are very few and where they occur it is primarily to promote boater safety and search and rescue. No level of government is taking proper care to protect and regulate the security measures for large ferry boats and cruise ships. Overall, the picture remains very "bleak" indeed.

With respect to the Arctic and the Harper government's expressed determination to protect Canadian sovereign claims over the Northwest passage, the situation is marginally better. In July 2007, Prime Minister Harper announced plans to spend $Cdn3 billion on six to eight new "ice-strengthened" ships to patrol Arctic waters. The ships, however, will not be heavy icebreakers. Their operations will exclude winter months in the thick ice regions of the Northwest Passage. The announcement was said to make good on the Conservative Party's "Canada First Defence Strategy" that was announced in 2006.[85] In August 2007, the prime minister went on to announce the creation of a $Cdn100 million deep-water port at Nanisivik (at the northern end of Baffin Island) as well as an Arctic military training base at Resolute Bay, Nunavut. Initial operational capability for the port is projected for 2015. Meanwhile the Canadian Rangers will be modestly increased in numbers and their equipment and training markedly improved.[86]

While the steps to improve the Canadian security presence in the Arctic may be well worthwhile from a sovereignty enhancement perspective, they do nothing at all to cope with the very serious security threats facing the vast majority of Canadians living south of the 55th parallel. Developing new spending plans for Arctic ships when Canadian seaports, airports and coastal approaches remain highly vulnerable seems strategically illogical if not irresponsibly negligent. Perimeter defence is simply not Harper's consideration anymore than it was his Liberal predecessor's.

Organizational Considerations

9/11 required a rethinking of both domestic and international institutions in terms of the nexus between security and economics. Concerns for domestic civil society protection, sovereignty, and an independent foreign policy need to be balanced with concerns regarding terrorism, smooth economic commerce, and security cooperation. Thus far, institutional changes have included ad hoc efforts with no particular level of organizational coordination between Canada and the United States, reflecting the lack of coordination on the regional (e.g., there is no security counterpart to NAFTA) and international level (NATO separate from WTO) despite the new reality of security-economic linkage. These efforts are occurring on the federal level through interagency coordination, joint teams, and task forces, and attempts to streamline security measures. They are also occurring on the provincial, regional, and municipal levels, and between, public, private, and nonprofit organizations and with individuals. It is interesting to note ongoing subnational activity, for example, annual summits engaging Quebec and New York officials since 1983.[87] One of the primary challenges is the problem of information sharing and coordination of various efforts.

Despite the strong efforts to centralize management under Public Safety Canada—the spitting image of the U.S. DHS—the same problems that DHS faces lurk around the corner for Canadian officials. PSEPC is a coordinating agency covering a wide gamut of different partners, from the RCMP to emergency management to health threats to CSIS in terms of intelligence sharing. In theory, centralization should ease information flow and make coordination easier. In practice, however, PSEPC is dealing with long-standing agencies that have a naturally strong sense of bureaucratic turf protection. Our interviews with public officials revealed a great deal of trepidation and uncertainty in regard to what information could be shared without violating privacy protection in Canada. As a result, the individual pieces of information from diverse sources may never be "fused," just as important information from the FBI, the CIA, and the Pentagon prior to 9/11 was never synthesized in the United States. Moreover, PSEPC as a purely policy advisory and coordinating agency, covers so many different areas that it lacks a clear sense of mission, objectives, prioritization, as well as an ability to measure progress.

As in the case of DHS, PSEPC does not have either carrots or sticks to get agencies to work together. Most interviewees in Ottawa noted that PSEPC was overwhelmed, understaffed (and suffering from turnover), and underresourced for such a monumental task. This is compounded by the muddling of the security mission with economic agencies' concerns, both domestic and international. In a crisis situation, there is no clear set of protocols or guidelines to establish a clear chain of command. In a situation such as an unusual ship on the high seas, the Coast Guard which scans domestic waters would have to report back to the RCMP, the RCMP would then need a warrant, and then the RCMP would have to use the Coast Guard vessels to intercept the vessel. If the ship by then were to have moved back to international waters, DND would now have to be brought in to summon a naval vessel. This is a recipe for disaster in the minute-by-minute world of terrorist threats, such as the U.S. military's inability to launch jets to protect either New York or the White House and Pentagon during 9/11. It is also a recipe for triggering massive help from the U.S. NORTHCOM, whether Canadian authorities wish it or not.

Similar scenarios, such as Canadian citizens linked to terrorist activities abroad, or foreign citizens attacking a domestic military base, bring into further relief the inadequacy of the new institutional relationships. The problem is compounded when one considers the need to coordinate across provincial lines and down to the provincial and municipal levels, where, as one interviewee put it, there is not much political capital in spending on security rather than road and other local priority projects. A couple of interviewees in the Canadian public service suggested that, within particular issue areas, communication across geographical levels is competent, however, across issues and within the federal government across agencies, it is still problematic.

In sum, while the new working groups bring together different individuals from across agencies, and while the idea of a coordinating agency in PSEPC may seem logical, these are only interim steps without any proven or even probable competence for dealing with major crises. In some future crisis involving a terrorist attack, it will be very difficult for PSEPC and DND to establish a clear center of authority if that has not been done in "peacetime." It is unlikely that the PCO will be able to provide central coordination that is timely and effective without considerable advance planning and rehearsal. Efforts are underway to address these problems, but progress has not been visible.

These organizational communication and coordination problems are compounded by the lack of clear long-term thinking about the role of the military in the new age of terrorism. The CF leadership has been promoting "transformation" for a decade without much to show for it. It has only just begun to acquire new long-range, heavy-lift transport aircraft after coping with obsolete worn-out tactical aircraft for at least a generation. The military planners still think in terms of fighting conventional warfare, and hope to acquire new fighter aircraft and new ships that will permit the CF to project force to distant regions. The military officer class is not interested in training for "aid to the civil power" in the event of a major terrorist incident in Canada or the northern United States that might involve nuclear, radiological, biological, or chemical weapons. Neither do they think much about the tens of thousands of ground troops they would need to be able to impose quarantines quickly on major Canadian cities or at selected crisis points at the border. The CF officer elite seems convinced that NATO should attempt to stabilize the Karzai government, even if casualties continue indefinitely, and even if Afghan operations should begin to eat up a major share of DND's operating budget. In this respect they seem out of touch with both Canadian public opinion and Canadian security interests. "Nation building" on the cheap is not possible by NATO and the United States in Afghanistan, or by the United States and its shrinking "coalition of the willing" in Iraq.

In Afghanistan, Canada and its NATO allies face a protracted insurgency that is likely to remain ideologically committed, adaptable, and well supplied from secure rear areas. Pakistan is unlikely to be able to crush Afghan insurgent training sites near the Afghan border. With that risk in prospect, and with Pakistan's military in possession of some 60 atomic weapons (Federation of American Scientists estimate), does it make sense to attack insurgent forces on the Pakistani side of the border if such attacks threaten to topple General Pervez Musharraf or any elected successor?

A majority of the Afghan people depend on the cultivation of poppies and the sale of heroin. NATO governments have not come up with an alternative crop for Afghan farmers, or an alternative economy for the Afghan regional warlords. The lessons of Vietnam to win "hearts and minds" and the political nature of such struggles seem to have been ignored in both Iraq and Afghanistan. There is no clear mission and no way to gauge progress without thinking more clearly about these key contextual factors. NATO soldiers with little to no local language capability, no history or background in the region, and no understanding of the local politics have very little chance of long-term success.

When asked about this gap in training and "peacemaking" capability, one official said that since many Canadian soldiers are from small towns, they could relate to the issues faced by provincial leaders in Afghanistan. The clear lesson of the lack of timely and accurate HUMINT from 9/11 seems to have been lost so far in terms of CF's priorities and strategic planning. Building a new Afghan National Army under President Hamed Karzai's control will not solve the problem if there is no viable police force to protect villagers from Taliban intimidation and blackmail, and no viable solution to the problem of a heroin-based economy. Burning villagers' only cash crop is not going to build support for the government in Kabul. DND's current force projection mandate needs fundamental rethinking.

Clearly whether Liberals or Conservatives govern in Ottawa, the defence budget and the national security budget are both going to be very limited relative to the nature of the transnational terrorist threat. Should it be the priority of the CF to participate in nation-building on the other side of the planet or ensure security for the 2010 Vancouver Winter Olympics, or security for large ferries and giant cruise ships? Is the Canadian navy best used to protect the coasts if no federal party is willing to finance the upgrading and arming of the Coast Guard? Should scarce resources be spent on sovereignty over the Northwest Passage, when the country's airports and major sea and inland ports are woefully insecure? In an ideal world, the Canadian government would be able to fund all of these worthy missions, but in the real world of constrained budgets and minority governments that is not possible.

Economic and Trade Effects of 9/11 on the Canadian Economy

Differences in resource endowments and the geographic isolation of some areas have weakened Canadian unity. Claims of "Western alienation" in the Canadian prairies and British Columbia have been reinforced by Alberta's burgeoning oil- and gas-derived wealth and a sense of political disengagement by the people of these provinces from federal Liberal governments that have struggled to win seats for MPs in the West.

If any such inferiority is widespread, it would likely be the product of a sense of constrained economic opportunities. One cannot exclude from consideration the integrative impact of U.S. direct investment in Canada since the 1930s, which has accelerated the importation of additional economic, scientific, and technological processes originally developed south of the border. Primarily because of the highest levels of foreign ownership of any developed country, the Canadian economy has been (and remains) the weakest among the G7 countries in terms of private sector spending on research and development. Few if any United States or other foreign corporate subsidiaries have product development or global marketing mandates; such work is reserved for headquarters, somewhere in the United States. Given this persistent structural aspect of Canada's "branch plant economy" during the Cold War, and the failure of CUFTA and NAFTA to reduce in any significant way the levels of U.S. ownership of the leading sectors of the economy, many talented and highly educated Canadians continue to feel they must leave for the United States if they are ever going to realize their full economic potential. Each year a considerable number of Canadians emigrate to the United States seeking greater economic opportunity, although not on a scale that provoked fears of a "brain drain" in the 1960s. Nevertheless the trend throughout the 1990s was for some 22,000 to 35,000 young, highly educated Canadians to leave for employment in the United States each year, about 0.1 percent of the adult population.[88]

Canada's population is heavily urbanized but, with the exception of Edmonton and St. John's, the larger urban centers are all located close to the U.S. border, a geographic reality that has contributed enormously to a pattern of north-south economic integration with the U.S. economy. The fact that four-fifths of the country's trade and investment with United States is facilitated by a common language and legal-business culture reinforced what geographic proximity had initiated. One analyst has speculated that some additional impetus favoring continental economic integration flowed from Canadians' chronic inferiority complex *vis-à-vis* U.S. society, a society that has been seen as consistently more prosperous and productive, and that has enjoyed a higher standard of living.[89]

The Canadian economy continues to have an interesting dualistic nature. While large parts of the economy, including parts of urban Ontario, Quebec, and British Columbia have well-diversified industrial and service sectors, other regions in Canada, including Alberta, Saskatchewan, Manitoba, British Columbia, and the Maritime provinces are dominated by traditional natural resource exports, ranging from fisheries to wheat and cattle to minerals, forest products and fuels. The Canadian economy originally revolved solely around these "staples," with all the incumbent problems of commodity price and earnings fluctuations. Canada is also highly trade dependent—by geography and infrastructure, the sparse population is oriented more along North-South rather than East-West corridors. The desire to lock in the dominant customer market, namely the United States, in order to avoid disturbances in economic growth was consummated, amidst great dispute with the NAFTA agreement in 1992 under the Conservative Mulroney Government. Since NAFTA, Canadian dependence upon U.S. trade and investment has only increased. In several sectors, such as mining, energy and automobiles, there are industrial clusters that overlap the border, with heavy U.S. investment in key companies.

The Canadian business sector's reaction to 9/11 was swift and certain. More than 40 business associations and individuals founded the Coalition for Secure and Trade-Efficient Borders to push Canadian policy-makers toward reassuring the

Table 3.1 Canada's Unchanged U.S. Dependency (in percent)

	1996	1997	1998	1999	2000	2001	2002	2003	2004	2005
United States	81	82	85	87	87	87	87	86	85	84
Others	19	18	15	13	13	13	13	14	15	16

Source: Author calculations from *Statistics Canada.*

United States on border security. This was backed up by several reports by the Conference Board and the Canadian Council for Chief Executives.

The Canadian relationship with the United States is easily clarified with some basic statistics. Table 3.1 shows the overwhelming Canadian dependence upon the United States as the major trading partner is virtually unchanged since 9/11.

Table 3.2 shows that this holds regardless of whether we look at exports or imports. It is interesting to note that dependency for exports is significantly greater than dependency for imports.

On the other hand, table 3.3 demonstrates a small dip in total value of both exports and imports from 2001–03, but the absolute amount of trade volume has resumed its positive trajectory from 2003–04 onwards.

Table 3.4 demonstrates the general product mix of Canadian U.S. exports remain the same. The most significant difference is the increasing value of oil exports, and to a lesser extent plastics derived from petroleum.

Table 3.2 Export–import Proportions by Partner (in percent)

Exports	**2000**	**2001**	**2002**	**2003**	**2004**	**2005**
United States[1]	83.6	83.7	83.8	82.6	81.7	81.4
Japan	2.6	2.4	2.5	2.4	2.3	2.3
United Kingdom	1.7	1.6	1.5	1.9	2.2	2.1
Other EEC	3.9	4.0	3.9	4.1	4.1	4.2
Other OECD[2]	2.8	2.9	3.0	3.2	3.4	3.4
Other countries[3]	5.3	5.4	5.3	5.8	6.3	6.5
Imports						
United States[1]	73.6	72.7	71.5	70.1	68.9	66.8
Japan	3.2	3.0	3.3	3.1	2.8	2.9
United Kingdom	3.4	3.4	2.9	2.7	2.6	2.4
Other EEC	5.8	6.6	7.2	7.6	7.4	7.6
Other OECD[2]	5.3	5.3	5.5	5.7	6.1	6.2
Other countries[3]	8.7	9.0	9.5	10.7	12.2	14.2

Source: Author calculations from *Statistics Canada.*

[1]Includes also Puerto Rico and Virgin Islands.

[2]Organization for Economic Co-operation and Development excluding the United States, Japan, United Kingdom, and the other European Economic Community.

[3]Countries not included in the European Economic Community or the OECD.

Table 3.3 Total Value of Canadian Exports and Imports by Partner

Exports	2000	2001	2002	2003	2004	2005
Total	429,372.20	420,730.40	414,056.00	400,175.40	429,134.20	453,600.20
United States[1]	359,021.20	352,165.00	347,072.10	330,468.30	350,769.30	369,284.10
Japan	11,297.40	10,120.80	10,146.90	9,770.30	9,958.00	10,488.10
United Kingdom	7,273.30	6,910.30	6,182.20	7,699.70	9,439.70	9,692.00
Other EEC	16,846.30	16,688.90	16,353.00	16,423.60	17,461.70	19,211.90
Other OECD[2]	12,059.00	12,172.50	12,460.50	12,679.60	14,394.40	15,238.40
Other countries[3]	22,875.10	22,672.90	21,841.30	23,134.00	27,111.00	29,685.70
Imports	362,336.70	350,071.20	356,758.60	342,608.00	363,075.80	386,906.90
United States[1]	266,511.10	254,330.70	255,259.70	240,291.90	250,064.40	258,430.00
Japan	11,729.80	10,571.90	11,732.60	10,644.90	10,018.90	11,182.60
United Kingdom	12,289.30	11,954.10	10,180.90	9,166.10	9,461.20	9,111.60
Other EEC	21,136.50	23,197.10	25,862.10	25,999.70	27,014.60	29,247.70
Other OECD[2]	19,067.60	18,649.80	19,685.60	19,692.00	22,217.10	24,115.20
Other countries[3]	31,602.50	31,367.60	34,037.60	36,813.40	44,299.60	54,819.80

Source: Author calculations from *Statistics Canada.*

[1]Includes also Puerto Rico and Virgin Islands.

[2]Organization for Economic Co-operation and Development excluding the United States, Japan, United Kingdom, and the other European Economic Community.

[3]Countries not included in the European Economic Community or the OECD.

Table 3.4 Top Canadian Exports to United States: Pre– Versus Post–9/11

	Average 1996–2000		Average 2001–2005
87—Motor vehicles, trailers, bicycles, motorcycles, and other similar vehicles	70,807	87—Motor vehicles, trailers, bicycles, motorcycles, and other similar vehicles	78,302
27—Mineral fuels, mineral oils, bituminous substances, and mineral waxes	31,695	27—Mineral fuels, mineral oils, bituminous substances, and mineral waxes	62,796
84—Nuclear reactors, boilers, machinery, and mechanical appliances	25,690	84—Nuclear reactors, boilers, machinery, and mechanical appliances	26,822
85—Electrical or electronic machinery and equipment	17,733	85—Electrical or electronic machinery and equipment	16,952
44—Wood and articles of wood (including wood charcoal)	15,057	44—Wood and articles of wood (including wood charcoal)	15,491
48—Paper, paperboard and articles made from these materials	13,275	48—Paper, paperboard and articles made from these materials	14,151
39—Plastics and articles thereof	7,816	39—Plastics and articles thereof	11,853
94—Furniture, and stuffed furnishings; lamps and illuminated signs; prefabricated buildings	6,354	94—Furniture, and stuffed furnishings; lamps and illuminated signs; prefabricated buildings	8,266
76—Aluminum and articles thereof	5,943	76—Aluminum and articles thereof	7,764
88—Aircrafts and spacecrafts	5,201	88—Aircrafts and spacecrafts	7,534

Source: Author calculations from *Industry Canada,* current $Cdn million.

Canadian imports from the United States again demonstrate remarkable stability in import product mix from before and after 9/11, as table 3.5 portrays. Together, tables 3.4 and 3.5 indicate much of Canadian–U.S. trade reflecting Lindert (like products) intraindustry features. This suggests a deep vertical integration (suppliers to buyers in the production process) of the two economies.

These tables reflect the deep economic dependency of Canada on the United States. Indeed, Canadian trade with non-U.S. partners, including Mexico, is insignificant. Nonetheless, Canada also has attempted at various times to follow a more multilateral route to reduce its dependence on possible political changes in U.S. economic policy. Canada was a leader in the creation of the WTO and participates in a variety of other multilateral groups, such as the Cairns group of

Table 3.5 Top Canadian Imports from the United States: Pre– Versus Post–9/11

	Average 1996–2000		Average 2001–05
87—Motor vehicles, trailers, bicycles, motorcycles, and other similar vehicles	44,106	87—Motor vehicles, trailers, bicycles, motorcycles, and other similar vehicles	48,962
84—Nuclear reactors, boilers, machinery, and mechanical appliances	39,129	84—Nuclear reactors, boilers, machinery, and mechanical appliances	38,157
85—Electrical or electronic machinery, and equipment	22,360	85—Electrical or electronic machinery and equipment	17,922
39—Plastics and articles thereof	8,310	39—Plastics and articles thereof	10,421
90—Optical, medical, photographic, scientific, and technical instrumentation	6,942	90—Optical, medical , photographic, scientific, and technical instrumentation	7,022
73—Articles of iron or steel	4,405	73—Articles of iron or steel	6,530
48—Paper, paperboard, and articles made from these materials	4,392	48—Paper, paperboard, and articles made from these materials	5,247
40—Rubber and articles thereof	3,358	40—Rubber and articles thereof	4,883
27—Mineral fuels, mineral oils, bituminous substances and mineral waxes	3,278	27—Mineral fuels, mineral oils, bituminous substances, and mineral waxes	3,688
94—Furniture and stuffed furnishings, lamps, and illuminated signs, prefabricated buildings	3,051	94—Furniture and stuffed furnishings, lamps, and illuminated signs, prefabricated buildings	3,581
29—Organic chemicals (including vitamins, alkaloids, and antibiotics)	2,880	29—Organic chemicals (including vitamins, alkaloids, and antibiotics)	3,536
88—Aircrafts and spacecrafts	2,716	88—Aircrafts and spacecrafts	3,501
76—Aluminum and articles thereof	2,704	76—Aluminum and articles thereof	3,067
49—Printed books, newspapers, pictures, manuscripts, and the like	2,697	30—Pharmaceutical products	3,066
72—Iron and steel	2,614	72—Iron and steel	2,922

Table 3.6 Truck Crossings by Border Station, 2000–04

		Millions					Percent				
Crossings	**Province**	**2000**	**2001**	**2002**	**2003**	**2004**	**2000**	**2001**	**2002**	**2003**	**2004**
Windsor–Ambassador Bridge	Ontario	3.54	3.38	3.48	3.41	3.49	26	25.6	25.9	25.8	26
Sarnia–Blue Water Bridge	Ontario	1.48	1.47	1.56	1.61	1.71	10.9	11.1	11.6	12.2	12.7
Fort Erie–Peace Bridge	Ontario	1.45	1.35	1.31	1.27	1.27	10.6	10.3	9.7	9.6	9.4
Niagara Falls–Queenston Br.	Ontario	1.04	1	1.05	1.01	1.01	7.7	7.6	7.8	7.7	7.5
Lacolle	Quebec	0.79	0.79	0.78	0.77	0.78	5.8	6	5.8	5.8	5.8
Pacific Highway/Douglas	British Columbia	0.87	0.79	0.78	0.75	0.75	6.4	6	5.8	5.7	5.6
Lansdowne	Ontario	0.53	0.5	0.53	0.49	0.49	3.9	3.8	3.9	3.7	3.6
Top 20 (trucks)		12.1	11.7	12	11.8	12	88.9	88.9	89	89.2	89.3
Other crossings (trucks)		1.51	1.47	1.48	1.43	1.44					
Total all border crossings (trucks)		13.6	13.2	13.5	13.2	13.5					

Source: Transport Canada.

agricultural-producing nations. Canada has also supported the floundering FTAA, and has signed a variety of bilateral FTAs outside of NAFTA, including with Chile. Canada has more recently sent and received diplomatic missions to and from China, seeking to become a "Pacific gateway" of resources and investment capital for that fast growing economy. Canada's attempts to diversify its trading partners have not reduced its vulnerability to U.S. pressure. In a sense, economic vulnerability gives the U.S. government enormous indirect leverage if it wishes to press Ottawa for compliance with its security policy wishes.

The data on physical crossings are quite limited. Table 3.6 shows that there was a roughly stable rate of truck crossings at the major Canada–U.S. border crossings, though some variation by crossing occurred. It is interesting to note, in contrast, that the number of cars and other vehicles crossing has gone down steadily over the same period.

However, a consultants report to TC, released in 2005, revealed that Canadian truckers found substantially increased costs as a result of U.S. post–9/11 security measures at crossings. Trucks haul 70 percent of trade with the United States, 57 percent of exports and 80 percent of imports. These measures include the need to gather information for the new pre-arrival processing system as well as FDA (Food and Drug Administration) information for agricultural shipments prior to arrival, and security compliance with the C-TPAT (Customs-Trade Partnership Against Terrorism), which is required for approval for fast border clearance. Additional costs were required for FAST (Free and Secure Trade) cards, driver training, upgrading information systems, and new security equipment. In addition, there are costly delays while awaiting FAST approval of shippers and drivers. The study also suggests that there likely has been an increase in waiting times at the border. The study estimates total costs at a minimum of $Cdn178.9 million per year.[90]

Canadian economic vulnerability has come to the forefront in recent years with the softwood lumber dispute, finally settled in 2006, with Canada surrendering a large proportion of U.S. duty charges, part of which went directly to the White House for "meritorious objectives." In addition, a major blow was suffered by cattle producers in the West when the U.S. banned imports because of concerns regarding BSE infestation. These disputes revealed as much about domestic U.S. politics as about foreign policy, as competing producers in the United States of lumber and cattle were better organized than importers. On the other hand, Canada has some cards in its hands in terms of negotiations. Fears of potential privatization of health care and of water have led to Canadian leaders reassuring the public on those fronts. Similarly, the unquenchable U.S. appetite for energy resources has it looking northward amidst its policy fiasco in the Middle East. Canada is now the largest supplier of petroleum to the United States. Unfortunately, the federal-provincial structure has prevented Canadian policy-makers from capitalizing on such possibilities. Alberta's strong policy independence and refusal to use the oil card to extract concessions for other areas in Canada's national interests, such as softwood lumber, has, in combination with the inherent split with Francophone Quebec, prevented the development of a consistent national trade and investment strategy.

Canadian Responses to Immigration, Refugees, and Border Security

As in Mexico, Canadian society has been strongly influenced by U.S. economic influences. But far more than in Mexico, Canadian popular and "high" culture have been greatly shaped by U.S. cultural trends. This cultural impact has been somewhat mitigated by strong regional identities and by provincial control over education. Canada's national (federal-level) commitment to bilingualism and biculturalism is supplemented by a de facto "multiculturalism" that is the product of continuing extraordinarily high levels of immigration (some 250,000 to 300,000 per year on a population base of some 30 million), with many of these people from Asia and only a small fraction coming from French-speaking countries of origin. Almost all such immigrants have preferred to integrate into an English-speaking society. Not surprisingly this has added to internal tensions between francophone Quebecers and the rest of the country and fed separatist sentiment in that province. Aboriginal communities in the Western provinces and the north also have expressed concern about the impact of such immigration on their position within the national community, despite a fairly flexible federal structure which has permitted a high degree of provincial autonomy and has even accommodated aboriginal self-government to an unusual degree by international standards.

The heavily Asian component of Canadian immigration and the equally heavy component of Latino emigrants to the United States have already produced significant cultural divergence between the two countries. It has also led to demands that the Canadian border with the United States be tightened up because of populist anti-Latino activists in southwestern U.S. states who managed to make illicit Latino immigration a major issue in congressional elections in the 2006 and 2008 congressional elections. In an effort to avoid charges of ethnic bias, U.S. immigration exclusionists have demanded a new wall along the Canadian border to keep out "illegals," even though estimates of the numbers of illicit entrants from Canada are fewer than 5 percent of the 400,000–500,000 illegal migrants per year who cross the southern border of the United States.[91]

For Canadian observers the most important aspect of the U.S. immigration debate is its massively negative impact on U.S. tourism and convention business in Canada. The imminent requirement (June 2008, or possibly June 2009) for all returning U.S. citizens (and visiting Canadians or Mexicans) to have passports or equally secure identifying documents is certain to damage Canadian tourist-related industries quite dramatically as it takes effect over the next two years. Northern U.S. states have resisted the WHTI scheme vociferously since it was first proposed in 2004. They too will suffer a further drop in tourism dollars from Canadian sources, and a major drop in consumer export sales. U.S. state governments have been very slow as well to embrace the "real ID" program for upgrading state-issued driver's licenses into secure documents, fearing the high cost of producing such documents.[92]

The hardening of the border in this respect has been treated as something of a national insult by some Canadians, and as a reflection of an unjustified U.S.

perception that Canada is a "weak link" in U.S. security. The hardening border may also be feeding the sense of inferiority in some quarters as well. While some Canadians may feel inferior to their U.S. neighbors, other Canadians have celebrated their commonalities—but often by differentiating themselves from U.S. methods and approaches to public institutions, values and foreign policy. Canadians strongly support their national health care system, even as they demand better service; they also have supported more generous welfare, social security, and educational benefits. Most Canadians strongly support the abolition of capital punishment and see its continuance in the United States as morally retrograde and racially discriminatory (see comments by Senator Celine Hervieux-Payette).[93] Because Canadians have experienced lower rates of crime and violence, and fewer problems with guns and narcotics, most Canadians feel they enjoy a more peaceful and equitable existence than do most Americans. For Canadians who share such sentiments, there is often an anti-U.S. subtext in political discussions, so much so that one senior political commentator noted during the run-up to the January 2006 national elections with respect to outgoing Prime Minister Martin's campaign that "dwelling on the failures of Americans is our favorite way of feeling accomplished and virtuous."[94]

Such attitudes have led many Canadians to oppose any strong dependence upon the United States. A good many nationalists in the centre and left of the political spectrum fear the "americanization" of societal values and thus resist any further acquisitions in Canada by U.S. corporations.[95] Stéphane Roussel summarized the situation as a "Triangular Contradiction," where Canadians feel they are pulled by three competing goals: security, sovereignty and prosperity.[96]

Regardless of these philosophical and cultural differences, with Canada's dependence on the U.S. economy, Ottawa naturally feels compelled to ensure the ease of cross-border traffic flow all along the border. More than 200 million people and 14 million vehicles cross the border every year. The Ambassador Bridge in the busiest corridor, Windsor-Detroit, home to the auto industry, witnessed more than 12 million vehicle crossings in 2000 alone.[97]

The main feature of Canadian and U.S. responses to 9/11 is to work toward "compatibility" and cooperation in terms of information sharing, screening, and enforcement measures along the border. Canada feels it suffers a "credibility gap" in terms of U.S. policy-makers, dating from the 1998 Ressam arrest at the Port Angeles, Washington border crossing, and false beliefs that many of the 9/11 hijackers came through Canada.[98]

The efforts at reassurance explain Canada's attempt to develop stricter border control measures to reassure the United States. The Ridge-Manley accord of December 2001 called for a "smart border," meaning one in which stricter security would not prevent the convenient flow of goods, services, and people. The implication is that with some greater investment in technology and border infrastructure, there would not be such a trade-off. The idea is to tighten inspection of goods and people before they arrive in North America ("the perimeter concept"), and to facilitate traffic of both within North America through preclearances. In the same month, a Joint Statement on Cooperation on Border Security and Regional Migration Issues followed.

The Joint Statement placed Canadians on the U.S. Foreign Terrorist Tracking Task Force, agreement to review visitor visas, agreement to develop common biometric identifiers for travel documents, increases in immigration officers overseas, and enhancement of Integrated Border Enforcement Teams. In 2002, Canada and the United States established the Binational Planning Group for enhancing cooperation among military, intelligence, emergency response, and maritime surveillance. The group has 50 staff members, including 20 Canadian military personnel, and one member of PSEPC and is located at NORAD headquarters in Colorado Springs. The mandate of this temporary group was extended until 2006, and there has been some discussion of making it permanent.[99] The group was however disbanded in 2006 when its work was judged to have been finished just prior to NORAD renewal.

In addition, the governments of Canada and the United States have agreed to pre-screen ships entering the St. Lawrence Seaway in the port of Montreal, and to coordinate marine security regimes. There are joint operations at major ports to screen shipments.[100] One major feature of smart borders is the NEXUS pass system, which allows for more rapid clearance by frequent border crossers. There is also the FAST program, a preclearance program for companies that frequently ship cargo across the border. Despite a few incidents and expressions of concern by U.S. officials over lax security, there has not been any major change in the basic nature of the border relationship thus far. This has led to criticism of under-funding and under-training of Canadian border agents as well as discussions around whether they should be armed. Moreover, a number of border posts continue to be manned by a single officer, and others do not have adequate access to security databanks.[101]

In more concrete terms, the United States has increased its security presence on the Canadian border. It has tripled agents on the border, and the Coast Guard now stops all boats and escorts oil and gas tankers in the Great Lakes. So far, efforts have been concentrated at the major commercial crossing points, such as Detroit-Windsor and Vancouver-Blaine.[102] The Windsor-Detroit crossing is by far the most important conduit, being the location where 23 percent of bilateral trade passes. For 2004, the total value of trade through that border crossing was $Cdn141.67 billion. The vital importance of this physical link has raised alarm about its possibility of becoming a target.[103] In turn, Canada has increased the border security budget by $Cdn280 million, including beefed-up border presence, additional security and intelligence personnel (including 2000 reassigned RCMP officers) and airport security measures. In addition, Canada further tightened its visa regime, requiring visas from Saudis and Malaysians. Canada also increased refugee screening, and detention and deportation capacity, and introduced a new tamper-resistant permanent resident card for new immigrants.[104] A variety of more under the radar changes have also ensued in terms of increasing cooperation with the U.S. security apparatus. Besides greater information sharing, the number of U.S. agents, including customs, FBI, and immigration officials operating in Canada has tripled.[105]

The possibility of more stringent U.S. enforcement of borders has disquieted some Canadians. The United States introduced the provisional idea that Canadians would need to carry passports to cross the border. Discussions have also centered on various digital voice, fingerprint, and iris recognition equipment for screening visitors. Former Canadian Ambassador to the United States, Allan Gotlieb, echoing the sentiments of several in the business community, has suggested in response the idea of forming a "common perimeter" and customs union, in other words a fully integrated border.[106] Again, nationalists such as Stephen Clarkson would see this as an end to the differentiating factors of Canada, including public rights to access to health care, lower crime and inequality, and greater public-private partnerships in production, a process which they fear has already begun under neoliberalism.[107]

On the domestic side, there are concerns that Canada is not living up to its self-image as a place for refugees, and that conditions for them may worsen with 9/11 fears. The 1976 Immigration Act was the principal guiding framework for immigration law before 9/11. The 1976 Act removed all explicit traces of discrimination against the physically and mentally handicapped and along the lines of sexual preference, however maintaining denial clauses for health, criminality, safety and national security reasons. The Act was touted as an excellent example of Canadian liberalism. Since 9/11, several important policy changes have taken place. CBSA was created in December 2003 as part of the new PSEPC portfolio. PSEPC was created as anew department in April 2005. The CBSA is designed to coordinate border security agencies, including) customs, the Intelligence, Interdiction, and Enforcement program of CIC (Citizenship and Immigration Canada) and the Import Inspection at Ports of Entry program from the CFIA (Canadian Food Inspection Agency). Further coordination occurs with the DND, the RCMP, the Department of Foreign Affairs and International Trade, and local public and infrastructure officials. These programs are now under the jurisdiction of the SG (solicitor general), who now has the titles of deputy prime minister and minister of public safety and emergency preparedness.[108] One way to understand the central challenge of the 9/11 failures is the failure of coordination, when intelligence clues were passed over, not passed along, or action upon them was simply delayed until it was too late. In the post–9/11 world, there is a need to coordinate action across economic and security lines, across geographic lines, and to integrate local, regional, national and international crisis planning in unprecedented ways. In the United States, the DHS experiment has received major critiques in terms of the capability of the agency to coordinate action, as well as the highly politicized nature of its budget expenditures. In Canada, the attempt to consolidate security under the Privy Council and the PSEPC has also received criticism. For instance, during Senate testimony regarding responsibility for security training for aircraft crew, there was a split between two branches of TC, security and civil aviation, over jurisdiction.[109] There is a high probability that the rather ad hoc bilateral coordination with the United States on security matters will become more institutionalized over time. It is unlikely that a unified "North U.S. Security Perimeter" that does away with borders between Canada and the United States will happen, for the various reasons stated in this analysis. However, the idea of a North U.S. "layer" of coordinated security seems likely and would follow traditional Canadian strategic reliance on the United States for its national security.[110] As one interviewee stated, it is not enough merely to create PSEPC. A major change in the culture of each organization in the public sector is also needed.

Canada's Stance Toward Mexico Post–9/11

Despite the existence of NAFTA, Canada's relationship with Mexico remains under-developed. Though there are obvious parallels in terms of reducing strategic dependence on the United States, these have yet to be developed. Canadian trade with Mexico remains a small fraction of total trade. Canada receives some Mexican migrants, however for a variety of reasons the nature of immigration is quite different in Canada than in the United States. First, Canada has no long-standing history of Mexican settlement, unlike the Southwestern United States, seized from Mexico in the nineteenth century. Second, with no border contiguity, distance makes reaching the Northern border more difficult and expensive. Third, Canadian immigration laws are enforced at the workplace, and the national health care system requires proof of citizenship for access. For all of these reasons, the family and institutional networks that facilitate Latin U.S. immigration are just beginning to spring up in Canada. Indeed, most experts note that the relationship with Mexico remains very much on the backburner. Canadian policy-makers are focused on the bilateral relationship with the United States, following the lead their economic interests dictate, despite Mexican efforts to forge a more trilateral relationship.[111] Since much of the Canadian left has a sense of nationalism (even if unrequited), there is a strong reluctance to consider the idea of entering into a North American U.S. citizenship, which they fear would lead to U.S. dominance.[112]

Nonetheless, in terms of strategic cooperation, trade and investment diversification, and Canada's interests in multilateral rules of law regarding NAFTA, Canadian policy-makers have recognized the desirability of greater cooperation with Mexico. In March 2007, there was discussion of a joint Mexican–Canadian WTO and NAFTA complaint regarding U.S. corn subsidies, which have devastated Mexican agriculture. There were also a number of issues set up for discussion in 2007 through the Canada–Mexico partnership. As Canada is presently experiencing a labor shortage, that is likely to be the issue of greatest prominence.

Yet, most of Canadian–Mexican interactions revolve around trilateral North American ones. Before September 11, in parallel with discussions around the FTAA, there was discussion of the creation of a "NAFTA plus" arrangement which would move toward a common market, allowing for the free movement of goods, services, investments and freedoms. Mexican President Vicente Fox Quesada even briefly suggested a common currency, though this idea does not have strong support in Canada. However, by 2002, the Canadian government had backed away from this idea, moving instead toward the idea of a bilateral customs union with the United States as a step forward. The idea did not gain much traction within the Bush administration.[113] In other words, Canadian policy-makers seem to recognize the strategic value of extending and strengthening trilateral relations and NAFTA regimes, but do not see this as feasible in the short-term given Washington's security concerns.[114]

Canadian and Mexican counterparts have participated in ongoing hemispheric security exercises, such as the Conference of American Armies, the System for Cooperation between the Air Forces of the Americas, the IANC (Inter-American Naval Conference), and the Inter-American Defence Board, but never with any explicit bi- or trilateral focus.[115] A renewed effort to shore up the security issues around NAFTA trade led to the SPP (Security and Prosperity Partnership) of North America, announced on March 23, 2005. The agreement covers cooperation in security, transportation, the environment, and public health, and in 2006 the Harper government pledged $Cdn1.4 billion toward security over the next two years, including $Cdn73 million toward securing the financial system; $Cdn202 million toward the border security components of SPP, and $Cdn101 million toward arming border officers and eliminating sole officer posts. For Canadian economic nationalists, the SPP is much feared because it is thought to be covertly planning for corporate-bureaucratic cooperation to rapidly expand extraction of oil from the Alberta tar sands as well as bulk water exports to the parched regions of the United States southwest and southeast. The SPP also contains coordinating commissions in the NACC (North American Competitiveness Council), geared toward coordinating regulatory policies, North U.S. Emergency Management, Avian and Human Pandemic Influenza, North U.S. Energy Security, and North U.S. Smart and Secure borders.

Harper's "New" Conservative Government

While the new Harper government was lauded in the United States as pro-American, there are not yet any signs of major changes in Canadian international security policy—certainly not with respect to Iraq. The Harper government has supported the Afghanistan mission, despite wavering public support and questions about the endgame similar to those facing the United States about Iraq. In February 2007, the government announced its commitment of an additional $Cdn100 million (on top of the existing $Cdn100 million) to Afghan reconstruction, to be spent over the following 10 years. On April 24, 2007, a Liberal motion to withdraw troops by 2009 was defeated 150-134, by the Conservatives and the NDP. The NDP wanted an immediate withdrawal of the troops. The then Defence Minister, Gordon O'Connor, stated that troops may be needed until 2010.

Prime Minister Harper's March 2006 visit to Afghanistan and Pakistan clearly cemented his government's support for the NATO ISAF mission for at least one year and possibly much longer. His second Minister of National Defence, Peter Mackay, was visiting Kandahar province in October 2007 when the base he was visiting was rocketed by Taliban rebels. While he escaped injury the attack was said to have demonstrated the improved intelligence capacity of the insurgent forces.[116] The Harper policy team seem to be navigating on the Afghan file with as little strategic awareness or vision as their Liberal predecessors. One must hope that the Manley panel will jolt them into a more serious appreciation of the risks they are running with an insurgency running rampant, an Afghan government administration that is entirely dependent on the corrupt practices of a narcoeconomy (with the sole credible plan of economic diversification vetoed by U.S. ideological preferences), and with an endless supply of recruits for the Taliban just across the border in nuclear-armed, politically unstable Pakistan.

The Harper government indicated that it will try to increase the strength of the regular forces from 60,000 to 75,000; that it will look seriously and with sympathy on any specific new proposals for cooperation on ABM defences. The government did renew NORAD with an expanded mandate to include the surveillance and control of all maritime approaches to North America,[117] and in this round of renewal both governments finally agreed to give the NORAD arrangement a formalized treaty foundation.

According to Margaret Purdy, Special Advisor to the Deputy Minister for TC (public lecture at Simon Fraser University, February 23, 2006), the new government has made a number of promises in regard to security. Their main focus has been on quelling Canadian fears about crime, including issues of drugs, organized crime, and gun violence. In terms of national security, the new government appointed a new National Security Commissioner to coordinate the activities of all relevant agencies through a National Security Review Committee, established a Canadian agency for foreign intelligence, began the reestablishment of port police, and ordered a new inquiry into the Air India bombing. Purdy noted that the Canadian Government continues to struggle to convince United States that "we are not a weak link." The "struggles" are likely to continue so long as Ottawa refuses to take border security issues sufficiently seriously. The Canadian problem is more than just one of "image" and perception.

During the January 2006 election campaign, the Conservatives pledged to issue firearms to Canadian border inspectors at all land crossings and end the practice of having single officers on duty at remote locations for long periods of time. The timetable for such reforms is, however, very long. Coast Guard ships are supposed to be replaced in a more timely fashion, but again no new spending has been committed for ship acquisition any time soon. The Harper government announced in 2006, that before 2016 all border guards will be equipped with weapons to track possible criminals, after controversy regarding whether they should be armed. Also, Harper promised to spend over $100 million to add extra staff to patrol borders, including 400 or more new officers.

In response to the need for better coordination among security branches, the Harper government set up a new 24-hour Government Operations Centre, as well as the Integrated Threat Assessment Centre. There is also an annual meeting and a permanent high-level forum among the ministers to coordinate action on emergencies, and the intention to create a national emergency response system. It also created a new Public Health Agency of Canada, in part to manage the risk of intentionally or naturally spread diseases. Partly in response to worries about the new intrusiveness into privacy, the Government set up a Cross-Cultural Roundtable on Security to encourage citizen input.[118]

The Harper Cabinet will be facing a major budgetary challenge to make good on its declared commitment to refurbish the capital equipment of the CF, but given the budgetary surplus position that his government has inherited it is in a far better position to contemplate major increases in defence spending than any other G7 country. Indeed, the Harper government announced a $Cdn1.1 billion increase in spending by the armed forces in 2006 over two years. From June 2006 to July 2007 the Harper government announced new defence equipment acquisitions worth some $Cdn24 billion.[119] On top of that, in the wake of Russian declaration that an immense portion of the Arctic basin belonged to Moscow in July 2007, Harper announced the intention to buildup CF in the region, including a new military port and new vessels. An international scramble for the Arctic now seems likely given its importance to shipping and, more importantly, a potential resource gold mine, including petroleum reserves opening up ironically due to global warming.[120] In addition to the new Arctic Offshore Patrol Ships called for in the Harper government's October 2007 budget, if new icebreakers are needed as well as new submarines with air-independent propulsion to shore up Canadian control over the Northwest Passage, the cost to Ottawa could mount into tens of billions over the next two decades.

The Harper government has continued the Counter-Terrorism Capacity Building Program, begun in 2004, to "share expertise" on security measures with the United Nations and other multilateral fora, and has participated in several international terrorism joint exercises, notably "triple play" with the United States and United Kingdom in 2005. In short, while the Harper government has achieved a significant rapprochement with the United States, certainly in comparison with previous Liberal Governments, there is no sign of a major shift in Canadian foreign policy in terms of support of multilateralism or support for the Iraq war. Rather, Harper seems to be using the "wiggle room" of terrorism to releverage new resources into Canadian foreign policy toward greater activism through renewal of the military, with a principal focus in Afghanistan, but also greater activism on other fronts such as attempts to increase (free) trade agreements (e.g., with Colombia and the Asia Pacific Gateway initiative) outside the NAFTA guise and to remain active in peacekeeping, such as providing financial support for Darfur and substantial support in Haiti. However, these new initiatives do not seem to be part of a coherent vision for Canada's role in the world, a problem we return to in our conclusion.

CONCLUSION

Ostensibly Canada's main concern following 9/11 remains to ensure steady unimpeded trade flows with the United States.[121] This is a reflection of the Canadian reality of deep economic dependence upon U.S. export markets (still over 80 percent of Canadian exports). Canadians continue to try to balance the desire to maintain their social and governance differences from the United States while reassuring their dominant partner. That ambivalence is illustrated by Canadian and U.S. defence headquarters' security arrangements. For example, Canada's DND headquarters, unlike the Pentagon, occupies a large office building in the middle of Ottawa, with a mass transit bus loop in front of the building and a shopping mall, the Rideau Centre, across the street. There are no metal detectors, although there are some security gates for guests. There is an underground garage and the parking lot is easily accessible without identification. The strangely lax security for these vital leadership buildings is in sharp contrast to the considerably tighter security at Canadian airports, or at key transit points for trade with the United States. But this state of affairs is perhaps symbolic of the overall ambivalence that the Canadian government has shown on questions of internal and frontier security.

After spending several billion dollars on border security improvements over the past six years, officials in Ottawa seem to have drawn the conclusion that there is little point in spending much more. Keeping the Canada–U.S. border open is certainly an extremely high priority but Canadian leaders are not yet convinced that it is essential to secure all ports of entry, build an effective territorial land-sea surveillance system on both coasts, create a Coast Guard (or territorial sea navy) that actually has a meaningful enforcement capability, or assist the Americans directly by providing comprehensive screening of all container traffic passing through Canadian territory toward American destinations. On this last point, some 30 percent of all containers arriving Canadian seaports are transshipped to U.S. destinations. Having Hong Kong style screening and inspection for all cargo should be an option with only a 1–2 percent increase in shipping costs.[122] Lacking such improvements, it is entirely conceivable that dangerous materials (fissile or biological in particular) or individuals could be moved through Canada and onwards to U.S. territory—with potentially calamitous subsequent effects on transborder trade flows after another damaging 9/11 style attack occurs.

This chapter has brought forward several issues that warrant further investigation, issues that apply not only to Canada but to all countries in the new security environment. 9/11 has begun to change the nexus between security and economic linkages in Canada and the United States (and in Mexico). In key sectors such as energy, migration, and transportation, 9/11 is forcing cooperation between security and economic institutions and coordination of policies within key sectors where these were previously separate. At this point, it does not seem to threaten commerce in Canada, yet fears of potential U.S. reactions following another attack are widespread. A relatively small incident (as compared to the damage, say of a natural disaster or highway fatalities) could have profound economic reverberations as the news spread and stoked fear throughout the population. The hugely magnified effect, a process illustrated well in the immediate aftermath of 9/11, which precipitated not only a new era of institutional governance, but two wars and a massive expenditure for non-economically productive security (except for those receiving such contracts), reversed the operation of the normal expectations of power in international relations. Overwhelming military power cannot be equated with immunity from attack. Thus, a handful of people with relatively low expense can create havoc at the largest levels, especially in an atmosphere in North America unaccustomed to such incidents.

The effect is akin to the herding effects of stock market crashes, such as the one that occurred in East Asia in 1999, where there was an emotional reaction to the loss of confidence by one significant asset holder that becomes magnified into a massive flight of capital. Such scenarios should push us to think more carefully about what we mean by terrorism and by security. Many U.S. analysts are worried about the grossly magnified impact that detonation of a containerized radiological dirty bomb would have on the U.S. economy as ports all across the United States scrambled to tighten container screening. Still more pessimistic analysts who are associated with the advisory network informing the Democratic Party, not the Bush administration, are convinced that American border security and internal security measures are simply incapable of preventing a fission bomb attack (or attacks) on U.S. territory.[123] It seems all too clear that officials in Canada charged with national security either reject these possible threats as too remote to warrant action by Ottawa or else see them as a uniquely U.S. problem.

In the new security environment, where any target is vulnerable, though higher profile targets are preferred, and where terrorists can be either foreign visitors (with or without visas) or "homegrown," what is the appropriate calculus for achieving adequate security at a reasonable cost? As one Canadian official put it, there is a danger that the threat of terrorism may overwhelm the ability to sort out and maintain other functions as well as our financial capabilities. This is especially true of the major threats (nuclear detonations or biological agent release) that can be labeled catastrophe terrorism. To our knowledge, there has been little real discussion of this issue thus far in either Ottawa or Mexico City, yet, it is not a purely existential question but one which must be engaged in order to set priorities and move from a reactive, fear-based milieu to one in which governments can act sensibly and proactively to address the gravest weaknesses that render Canada and the U.S. vulnerable. Our discussions with Canadian officials suggest that Canada probably cannot sufficiently reassure U.S. leaders so that the common border would not be closed immediately following another 9/11—or worse a fission bomb attack on an American city. Many U.S. officials and political leaders still fear that the "weak link" to the North may be endangering U.S. security, and they would almost certainly react in future to such an event in the same way that the border was closed on September 12, 2001. Canadian leaders, therefore, should think much more imaginatively about the potential costs of not working to build the world's most secure border.

Border security is not a core interest of U.S. citizens only. The security of the common border should weigh far more heavily in Ottawa's calculations (and Mexico City's) than it does at present. State of the art container screening can be built that would impose costs of little more than $Cdn20 per container shipment, according to estimates presented to Senator Colin Kenny's Committee on National Security and Defence. While it may also be true that even a perfect Canadian effort would still see border traffic interrupted for days or even weeks following another attack, clear evidence or even plausibly suspicious evidence that the attack had been planned, executed, funded, or even just facilitated by agents based in Canada could see the border closed for months and transborder commerce grievously reduced for years to come.

Notwithstanding the positive steps by the Harper government, we have also seen that there remains massive confusion about how to coordinate a public sector response to terrorism at the multilateral, bilateral, national, and provincial levels, and across functional lines. A more serious long-term plan based on protocols for action and a clear chain of command needs to be developed. This type of thinking is hard to come by in Ottawa and Washington, where timelines are short-term in response to the political climate. However, it is particularly important for Canada to further develop its institutional and policy priorities in order to coordinate with the United States from a strong base of self-confident action and clarity of thought and strategy. Such a foundation would provide for a more mutually beneficial relationship in the long-run. Canadian leaders need to avoid reactive, crisis-driven responses to American demands by anticipatory planning, coordination, and spending on tangible, crisis-accessible instruments—whether in the military, the police, the IC or public health management.

One interviewee noted that we cannot view every single event through the prism of terrorism. But it is also true that authorities on both sides of the border need to think more clearly about the most plausible and remediable vulnerabilities that now exist. To date, Canadian governments lack clear, integrated planning for coping with future acts of major terrorism. Emotionally and politically charged thinking explains Canada's mixed, incoherent and at times illogical if not negligent reactions thus far. Transcending partisan perspectives in Ottawa to foster a proactive, creative

Table 3.7 Catalyzers of Political/Security Integration Compared

Dimension	Pre–9/11	Post–9/11
1. Occurrence of purposeful orientation shift?	Yes, Canada sought to increase facility of economic access to United States	Yes, appeasement of United States sought in new security measures to ensure economic access
2. Institutionalization of orientation shift?	Yes, e.g., SAGITS and new trade institutions	Yes, new security consolidation and institutions
3. Gresham's law in integrative instincts (bad instincts driving good instincts out)	Rules-oriented	Canada remains rules-oriented
4. Safeguarding against external shocks?	A big issue given dependence on United States	Canada continues to seek diversification (e.g., China initiatives)
5. Exploring new avenues of collaboration	Yes, discussion of NAMU	Yes, citizenship/border coordination
6. Compatible leadership?	Some disagreements with Liberals, but relatively minor (mostly foreign policy)	Harper government is expected to be more United States-friendly

Source: James E. Dougherty and Robert L. Pfaltzgraff, Jr., eds., "Theories of International Integration, Regionalism, and Alliance Cohesion," in *Contending Theories of International Relations: A Comprehensive Survey* (New York: Harper and Row, 1990), 431–59.

approach to the common security challenges faced by Canadians and U.S. citizens/residents will be difficult, but it must be done soon.

The vision of an emerging trilateral North American community is not dead, but its realization remains many years distant. In the meantime, asymmetrically bilateral relations with Washington seem destined to be the fate of governments in both Ottawa and Mexico City. Both Mexico and Canada would benefit from greater joint activities and joint analysis of the common problems they face in dealing with American vulnerabilities and the ever present threat of loss of access or even just

Table 3.8 Security Community Tenets Pre– and Post–9/11

Dimension	Pre–9/11	Post–9/11
1. Value compatibility	Yes	Yes, expected to increase with Harper government
2. Behavioral predictability	Yes	Yes
3. Mutual responsiveness	Yes	Yes, though Canada still finds key remaining issues—softwood lumber, U.S. foreign policy
4. Value complementarity	Yes	Yes
5. Distinctiveness of lifestyles	Yes, e.g., crime and public health care	Yes, increasingly
6. Reward expectations before burden sharing	Yes	Increasing friction—ABM, Iraq
7. Increasing political and administrative functions	Yes	Yes, albeit in an ad hoc manner
8. Economic growth distinguishing core areas from peripheral areas	Yes, differentiation along regional and sectoral lines	Yes
9. Geographical and social communication linkages	Yes	Yes
10. Multiplication of communications and transactions	Yes	Yes
11. Decreasing barriers to mobility across political boundaries	Yes	No, increasing barriers
12. Increasing political elites	Yes	Yes, though polarization of attitudes toward United States continues

Source: James E. Dougherty and Robert L. Pfaltzgraff, Jr., eds., "Theories of International Integration, Regionalism, and Alliance Cohesion," in *Contending Theories of International Relations: A Comprehensive Survey* (New York, NY: Harper and Row, 1990), 431–59.

reduced access to the U.S. economy. Perhaps under SPP auspices such activities can be stepped up in a timely and productive fashion.

THEORETICAL APPLICATIONS

We can now evaluate the primary theoretical questions of this study, focusing on Canada–U.S. relations:

Table 3.7 summarizes that not much has really changed in Canada as a result of 9/11 in terms of general orientation. The main changes have been in institutional arrangements and attention paid to border security.

Table 3.9 Neofunctionalist Tenets Pre– and Post–9/11

Dimension	Pre–9/11	Post–9/11
1. Economic symmetry among units?	No, United States dominates	No
2. Elite complementarity?	Yes and no, divided	Yes and no, Canadian elite divided in attitudes toward United States
3. Pluralism?	Yes	Yes
4. Capacity to adapt?	High	High
5. Spillover?	High	High
6. Growing transactions?	Yes	Yes
7. Growth in intergovernmental relations?	Yes	Yes
8. Transnational growth?	Yes	Yes
9. Elite socialization?	Yes	Yes
10. Growth in ideological identity?	Polarized	Polarized
11. Increasing interaction with external actors?	Limited and constrained	Limited and constrained
12. Benefit distribution higher and more equitable?	Yes, NAFTA increases benefits to Canadian economy as a whole, but unevenly	Yes, commodities prices, but unevenly shared (e.g., Alberta)
13. Converging perception of external problem?	No	No, still no movement toward Iraq
14. Integration as cost-free?	No	No

Source: James E. Dougherty and Robert L. Pfaltzgraff, Jr., eds., "Theories of International Integration, Regionalism, and Alliance Cohesion," in *Contending Theories of International Relations: A Comprehensive Survey* (New York: Harper and Row, 1990), 431–59.

Table 3.10 Interdependence Tenets Pre– and Post–9/11

Dimension	Pre–9/11	Post–9/11
1. Channels of communications?	Multiple, economic most important	Multiple, economic and security
2. Hierarchy of issues?	Yes, economic issues at top	Yes, economic issues a priority, but security issues increasing
3. Subordination of military?	Yes	No
4. Nature of institutional membership?	Voluntary, emphasizing a wide range	Voluntary
5. Catalyst?	Competitive markets and investment and trade dependence (reducing transactions costs)	Reducing potential transactions costs increases from U.S. concerns about security
6. Placement of regionalism along levels of policy-making analysis?	Bi- and multilateral issues are both important; bilateral more important	Bilateral relations are increasingly the priority; multilateral issues secondary

Sources: Robert O. Keohane and Joseph S. Nye, *Power and Interdependence: World Politics in Transition* (Boston, MA: Little, Brown and Company, 1977), 3–37; and Henry Nau, "From Integration to Interdependence: Gains, Losses, and Continuing Gaps," *International Organization* 33, no. 1 (Winter 1979): 119–47.

Table 3.8 demonstrates that the Harper government represents a step toward the security tenets of the United States. However, the distinctions at the domestic level are decreasing in a few areas, e.g., business regulation and taxes, but the sacred cows of the social welfare system will remain as differences. The Harper government has not clearly revealed how far this shift will be.

Table 3.9 points to a basic continuity in terms of the economic dimension of U.S.–Canada relations. Polarization of attitudes among Canadian elites continues,

Table 3.11 Neorealist Tenets Pre– and Post–9/11

Dimension	Pre–9/11	Post–9/11
1. State as dominant actor?	Yes, provincial consultation begins	Yes, and more proactive engagement with NGOs
2. Policy reflecting internal considerations or international competitiveness?	Policy reflects international competitiveness	Policy reflects international competitiveness
3. Is international competitiveness orderly or anarchic?	Orderly, market competitiveness	Orderly, but fear of change from U.S. security policy

Source: Kenneth N. Waltz, *The Theory of International Politics* (Menlo Park, CA: Addison-Wesley, 1979), chap. 5.

and differentiation in perceived benefits by region and sector also continues. Canadian academics tend to be more nationalistic.

Table 3.10 reinforces our conclusion that security concerns have become an important concern insofar as they threaten Canadian economic interests. Canadian policy-makers are concerned about increasing transactions costs and keen to preempt any American action that reduces market access on security grounds.

Our last table 3.11, points to the fact that Canadian policy-makers have been making proactive attempts to engage with Canadian civil society, partly in response to antiglobalization protests, which registered quite importantly in Canadian media during meetings in Vancouver (APEC), Kananaskis (G-7); and Quebec (SOA) in recent years. Canadian NGOs are also becoming more active and organized, working with international partners. The divisions in Canadian society dating from the 1970s and piqued by NAFTA continue to be worked out peacefully.

4

Mexico and Homeland Security: Revolving Doors and Transient Interests

BACKGROUND[1]

Mexico's 9/11, one might argue, was 9/4: President Vicente Fox Quesada's no-border immigration proposal to George W. Bush during his U.S. visit that week, was summarily crucified by Congress.[2] As what Robert A. Pastor and Rafael Fernandez de Castro call *the controversial pivot* of Mexico–U.S. relations,[3] Congress was expected to oppose the proposal, but Fox was still jolted: His lacklustre communications with Bush after 9/11 reversed the tone of the very special relationship between his country and the United States. In what until then was a honeymoon year, Mexico's *cinco de mayo* was celebrated for the first time in the White House;[4] the first country visited by an incoming U.S. president was no longer Canada but Mexico; and even Tony Blair's Great Britain took a back seat, leaving Fox the pedestal. Distance, indifference, and an outright lack of deference suddenly and chillingly characterized the new bilateral tone.

Mexico's responses to new U.S. security imperatives echoed those of the Cold War, but it is in preserving the post–Cold War embrace that both countries find new challenges. Even as instincts collided, "images seem[ed] so convincing," as *New York Times*' Ginger Thompson observed at the March 2002 UN summit between developed and less developed countries in Monterrey, Mexico. The bilateral relationship, she continued, "seems high on concept, low on content," with Bush still saying "no nation is more important to the United States than this one," and Fox still dreaming "of opening the border to a freer flow of immigrants."[5] One thorn from the past (immigration) exacerbated the 9/11 security temperament, while the NAFTA romance, whose newness was wearing off by 9/11, slipped into obscurity after 9/11.

With the border involving not just illegal immigrants, but also unprecedented drug trafficking and over $650 million of legitimate trade every day,[6] the obvious question of how the adoption of U.S. homeland security affects any or all of these raises an even more slippery consideration: Since these represent bilateralized issues within the trilateral North American framework,[7] is 9/11 bilateralizing a trilateral framework even further with a security imperative? If regionalism is in retreat,

U.S. bilateral network? Ultimately, what do these mean for Mexico, its relations with the United States, and the approach and attitudes toward North American regionalism?

Addressing all three questions, this chapter (a) assesses the impacts of cross-border externalities—emigration, drug trafficking, and security-mindedness—on Mexican foreign policy-making; (b) elaborates 9/11 security impositions and elicitations, in particular institutional responses, procedural constraints, and transactional impacts; and (c) inquires which theoretical prism (security community, neofunctionalism, interdependence, and the realist family of thought), better explains post–9/11 Mexico–U.S. relations at different levels of analysis (Mexico, Mexico–U.S. bilateralism, and North American regionalism). Chapter 6 picks up on leftover issues.

MEXICO'S NEW FOREIGN POLICY THINKING

At least three policy positions of the fledgling Fox administration exposed a different foreign policy orientation: treating the thorny migration topic pragmatically, with a business-like approach; diluting such negative connotations of narcotrafficking as corruption, again driven by business considerations; and establishing a security policy framework, well ahead of 9/11, based upon domestic or bilateral concerns over illegal emigration, drugs trade, money laundering, and indigenous resistance against liberalization/globalization. In the best possible world expected, the third served as Mexico's reward to the United States for reciprocating its stand on the first, while the second sought the public relations goal of image-enhancing.

Although all three receive elaborate treatment in the subsections below, the common themes they portrayed—pragmatism, business-friendliness, and problem-solving policy-making attitudes—ultimately rest upon one fatal assumption: a rosy relationship with the United States. Without the rosiness, those attitudes lose anchor. When Fox's term ended in December 2006, its defining characteristic was rudderlessness: glaring North American unaccomplishment, precisely because mutuality in Mexico–U.S. relations had waned.

New Wine in Old Immigration Cup

Fox's July 2000 election victory depended as much on opening new doors to Mexico's upwardly mobile classes as it did to closing old nepotistic and bureaucratized corporatist practices. Prioritizing entrepreneurship as the instrument of deepening U.S. economic integration, his administration interpreted the prickly immigration issue much like the Europeans had done, at least until 9/11: as another factor of production, like merchandise and services, and thus subject to routine market demands and supplies within the country and across sovereign boundaries. For as long as low-wage jobs remained unfulfilled in the United States, and Mexico had workers willing to accept low-wages, the trade-off was seen as mutually beneficial if left unhindered. It was an ingenious approach to (a) developing Mexico's impoverished south;

(b) diluting tensions and restlessness in the same region; (c) boosting a binational constituency from the 30-odd million expatriates in the United States, a group more cosmopolitan and supportive of regional integration than the traditionally sedentary groups wary of anything foreign; and (d) accelerating Mexico's North American identity and credentials over its Latin counterpart—a tension as old as the country itself.[8]

Toward those ends, Fox was more open than any of his predecessors to giving Mexican expatriates the right to vote in Mexican elections no matter where they lived, thereby seriously reconfiguring electoral constituency weights and threatening vested interests built under 70-odd unbroken years of PRI control.[9] "We are all agreed that this right should be set down in black and white," he asserted. "Its time," he continued, to let up to seven million expatriates vote for the president, and ultimately "to elect their own representatives."[10] He was prepared to open a sixth electoral district, catering exclusively to expatriates. That this reduced representatives in the five existing districts, generated considerable legislative opposition, but prioritized Fox's external orientation. To be sure, the Mexican Congress approved of a legislation to this effect in 1996, under Ernesto Zedillo Ponce de León, but it never (a) clarified who could vote; (b) established the necessary mechanism whereby this could happen; and (c) expected PRI to benefit from the largely anti-PRI expatriate body.[11] Fox capitalized on this opportunity. Institutionalizing his goals, he opened the Office for Mexicans Living Abroad under Candido Morales and Juan Hernandez. Although short-lived, it clearly conveyed his desire to reshape the Mexican–U.S. architecture and reiterate his government being "serious about slowing migration and creating more jobs in the communities."[12]

Unfortunately for him, U.S. decision-making is not quite as centralized and presidentialized as the Mexican was throughout the twentieth century. Immigration policies formulated in Washington, DC, had to reckon with societal pressures locally in a way those made in Mexico City do not have to. In spite of the growth of U.S. presidential powers, as Richard E. Neustadt and others observed,[13] Congress still imposes occasional authority, as the 1973 War Powers Act, the fast-track authority of the 1990s, and controlling the 2001 PATRIOT Act revealed. This was not true of Mexico's legislature when the PRI controlled both branches for 70 years. Beginning with Fox's administration, however, his very victory converted interbranch rivalry into a can of worms for the first time in modern Mexico,[14] over issues as trivial as controlling the president's travel budget,[15] to more underlying commitments as supporting Cuba against the United States,[16] and formulating the country's budget under a democratic mandate.[17] Rather than societal groups in Mexico's border states resisting immigration policy proposed in Mexico City, the failure of Fox's immigration policy proposal encouraged opposition parties from supporting his other proposals, thus generating a policy-making deadlock unknown in the seven decades of what Mario Vargas Llosa dubbed the perfect dictatorship.

The biggest obstacle to normalizing immigration-based feuds surprisingly evolved from routine U.S. policies: Legalizing illegal immigration periodically not only encouraged would-be emigrants, but also conveyed the U.S. inability to control its own borders, even after 9/11 when illegal immigrants spiraled. Since illegal immigrants are hard to count, the U.S. Department of Justice's 1996 figures offer a sobering assessment of the size of the problem: Of five million illegal immigrants, 2.7 million were Mexicans;[18] of the total 1.6 million apprehended that year, 1.5 million were Mexican; and over $1.2 billion worth of narcotics was confiscated from 120,000 of these Mexicans in the entire process.[19] Many scholars contend today's figures to be doubled these.

Table 4.1 lists the policies contributing to these outcomes.[20] The 1965 U.S. Border Industrialization Program sought to curb Mexican emigration by complementing Mexico's effort to promote low-wage *maquila* production along the border, creating twin-city production networks. Yet, Cold War logic aborted the plan: Better to let a job-seeking illegal Mexican into the United States than to expose him to communist appeals from nearby Cuba. When matters got worse, various Simpson-Mazzoli bills from 1982 in both U.S. chambers proposed employer sanctions, which were only implemented from 1986 through the IRCA (Immigration Reform and Control Act). Although the bracero program, begun in September 1942 under World War II exigencies, was terminated in 1964,[21] its philosophy prevailed in IRCA and all policies since, manifested in the annual guest-worker programs. In addition to RAWs (replenished agricultural workers), SAWs (specialized agricultural workers), and LAWs (legalized agricultural workers), IRCA also offered amnesty to existing illegal migrants, letting a loose snowball gather much momentum.[22] The message this emitted to family members of illegal and would-be migrants was that the gates of nirvana was opening, in spite of the appearance of border restrictions.

IRCA proposed introducing the military along the border. Now the Cold War was finally over, and with the Berlin Wall tumbling down in 1989, new walls emerged along the Mexico–U.S. border, the most conspicuous, under Operation Gatekeeper from 1994, being along the Tijuana–San Diego border. Through a December 2005 U.S. legislation, 1,130 kilometer of the 3,200 kilometer border with Mexico is to be walled; and as half of that goal has already been accomplished at the time of this writing in early 2008, the Berlin Wall already looks pale by comparison. With ex-president Fox calling it "shameful," and current president, Felipe Calderón Hinojosa, pleading for "co-responsibility" on a February 2008 U.S. visit which completely ignored the White House,[23] a perennial U.S. need for low-wage Mexican workers will most likely prevent a total Mexico shut-out. Though NAFTA was expected to lift the image of Mexicans being merely low-wage workers, 9/11 indirectly reinforced that image, and quashed, in the process, the pragmatist conversion Fox had in mind.

Would-be migrants were not discouraged. The failed 1990s guest-worker trickles, in turn, flooded the U.S. Hispanic segment, as marriage or sponsorship opened doors to legal migration. Restrictive border patrols, the minutemen campaign being waged by border citizens against Mexicans in Arizona and Texas,[24] and the wall construction prompted would-be illegals to dig tunnels, facilitated no less by narcotrafficking routes dotting the desert. The new illegal immigrant became more resilient than before, hardening social attitudes along the borders. By inviting intangibles, 9/11 opened new windows of vulnerability, unnecessarily pushing illegal immigrants

Table 4.1 U.S. Immigration Policies Toward Mexico

Actual policy (and year)	Components, consequences
Border Industrialization Program, 1965	Introduced *maquiladoras* Did not stop illegal emigration
Simpson-Mazzoli Bill, 1981	Introduced employer sanctions
Immigration Reform and Control Act, 1986	Implemented employer sanctions, guest worker programs (LAWs, RAWs, SAWs), offered amnesty, introduced the military
Operation Gatekeeper, 1994	Built wall around Tijuana–San Diego border; deployed the military and hi-tech equipment

and narcotraffickers to flirt with die-hard Middle East *jihadists* should they come probing.

A hitherto indifferent Mexico government suddenly is as strapped by incoming Central American migration/narcotrafficking flows as the U.S. government was/is with Mexican immigrants. On the one hand, *coyotes* exploit would-be emigrants to the bone, or literally to death, creating a booming business. On the other, Central American gangsters established in Los Angeles and deported to Central America under California's three-strikes-and-you-are-out legislation, began returning to the United States through Mexico, bringing greater danger with them.[25] Combining illegal emigration and drug trafficking, two hitherto uncontrollable forces, they unleashed a powerful punch, with trademark signs for all to see: extort money, rape women migrants, threaten Central American government officials,[26] expand the illegal immigrant pool to Central America, and in short, convert the search for nirvana into a deadly gambit. [27] Rather than serve as a dividing line, 9/11 allowed an expanding illegal phenomenon to simply be incorporated.

If all of the above pre–9/11 policies could not halt the illegal traffic, indeed only encourage it, then post–9/11 policies do not convey any meaningful lessons learned from the experience. As soon after 9/11 as March 2002, Bush urged lawmakers to approve illegal immigration amnesty under Bill 245(I),[28] just as Hispanics displaced Afro-Americans as the largest U.S. minority; Samuel P. Huntington's civilization clash polemics of the 1990s now narrowed to the cultural Hispanic challenge;[29] and a binational population explosion contemptuously exposed governmental vulnerabilities across the border.

One of the doyens of Mexico–U.S. studies, Wayne A. Cornelius, made three penetrating observations: (a) After about 10 years of regional integration between a developed and developing country, the migration flow from the latter to the former is likely to return to the same level; after 15 years, actual migration from the latter to the former is expected to be prevented; and after 20 years, the latter is projected to actually receive migrants from the former. (b) While Mexico–U.S. migratory patterns remained generally "consistent with the prediction of the modified liberalization/migration model," short-term variations occurred owing to the huge wage differentials within Mexico and between the United States and Mexico. (c) Mexico's porous southern borders, combined with increasing U.S. sentiments/safeguards against Mexican immigrants, constrain Mexico from reaping full NAFTA benefits, in turn reducing U.S. benefits.[30]

Ultimately, the Mexico–U.S. illegal immigration fissure is becoming a more dangerous beast than routinely profiled in policy-making and theory-building exercises, evident in how it is fanning out from (a) both these two countries to also Central America and (b) transborder human flows to narcotrafficking. If it continues trumping post–9/11 controls, the Mexico–U.S. border may become nothing but a literal minefield, as in Afghanistan and Iraq.

Unwittingly supporting Fox's no-border immigration proposal, Tito Alegria observes the Mexico–U.S. "binational" or "transborder" area is very unlike the European counterparts because wage differentials exert greater influence on traditional Mexican emigrants than labor supply-demand factors.[31] His study of transmigration through Tijuana and Ciudad Juárez exposes a dual rather than single labor market, legitimizing Mexican emigration in the same way as Central American gangster connections illegitimize it. Only time will tell which side of the equation will triumph, but Mexican governments, facing other crises (crackdown on drug-traffickers, winning popular legitimacy after a bitterly divided 2006 election), may be finding Mexican emigration as their Achilles Heel. Even U.S. attempts to legitimize immigrants by utilizing noncontroversial visas usually given to facilitate business, faces increasingly stubborn domestic opposition.[32] In the final analysis, politics, whether in Mexico or the United States, deepen more than resolve the bilateral immigration problem.

Narcotrafficking Nexus

Demonstrating greater transborder agency cooperation than immigration, Mexico–U.S. drug-control efforts still face an equally formidable but considerably more reactive beast. Even though the Fox administration decisively broke the back of Mexico's cartels and carteleering,[33] splintering the trade is proving more cancerous. The inherited vested interests intertwining policemen, politicians, and military leaders may actually be thriving under the policy-making deadlock alluded to earlier, and the incremental growth of local and regional power blocs may be attributed precisely to this federal-level deadlock, prompting the United States government to issue tourist alerts against visiting certain Mexican towns, much to the chagrin of Mexicans.

On the eve of NAFTA implementation, drug trafficking was already a $100 billion industry, with one of the fastest industrial growth rates in Latin America.[34] By then, according to Peter H. Smith, Mexico was already supplying 80 percent or more of the U.S. heroin market,[35] not to mention serving as the traditional marijuana source and the forthcoming springboard of cocaine. In spite of a series of corrective policy measures, listed in table 4.2, any trafficking interlinking the two countries burgeoned beyond control, exacerbating recriminations.[36] Even though the key drug problem for Mexico was "alcohol and inhalants (glue, ether, paint thinner)," as Gabriela D. Lemus observes, Mexico "increased its antinarcotics activities in response to U.S. pressure."[37] Thus, while Carlos Salinas de Gortari tripled expenditures to $63 million by 1990, the problem also spiraled, helped in no insignificant measure by collusion

Table 4.2 Pre–9/11 U.S. Drug Policies Toward Mexico

Name, sponsor, date	Consequences
Operation Intercept, Nixon administration, September 1969	Harassment of border-crosser increases, no reduction in trafficking, bred antagonism; border closed for 20 days, seen by Mexico as "economic blackmail"
Operation Cooperation, Nixon administration, October 1969	Included Mexico's cooperation, better results
El Paso Intelligence Center (EPIC) established by INS and DEA (Drug Enforcement Agency), 1974	Round-the-clock monitoring to gather intelligence
Campaña Permanente, Mexico, 1975, with Operation Condor as highlight	Eradication programs, interdiction, and flow-disruption efforts adopted; reduced Mexico's share as source country of marijuana (from 75 percent in 1976 to 4 percent in 1981), heroin (from 67 percent in 1976 to 25 percent in 1980); Mexico received military assistance but cartelization also bred
Phase I U.S. drug policy, Reagan administration, 1980s	Emphasizes supply side, not demand side; zero-tolerance adopted; $1.1 billion spent on this
Operation Alliance, United States, 1986	Utilizes (a) customs agents, (b) Border Patrol, and (c) military; creates National Drug Enforcement Policy Board in 1986; shifts attention from domestic "Just say no" campaign to border; meant to be bilateral, became unilateral; does not alter situation: U.S. crackdown in Florida and Caribbean shifts Colombian cartels to Mexico
Omnibus Act, United States, 1986	Requires president to "certify" countries participating in war on drugs: Mexico almost decertified when agent Enrique Camarena assassinated in 1985
1988: Mexico declares drugs a "national security" threat	Policy adopted by President Miguel de la Madrid
Phase II, George H.W. Bush, 1989	$2 billion antidrug campaign, but also supply-side orientation boosted expenditures to $10.6 billion
Mexico–U.S. Agreement on Cooperation in Fighting Drug Trafficking and Drug Dependency, February 22, 1989	Reaffirms joint nature of problem and solution
Operation Border Ranger, California policy, 1989	Introduces unarmed guards at commercial shipments locations and armed guards deployed; Mexico antagonized; aerostatal radar units introduced under this campaign from 1991
National Antidrug Program, Carlos Salinas de Gortari, 1990	A half-hearted initiative coinciding with a surge in drug consumption and addiction

Mutual Legal Assurance Treaty implemented from 1991	Indicates Mexican accommodation of U.S. interests, start of a huge shift
National Program for Drug Control, Evaluation, and Implementation, Carlos Salinas de Gortari, 1992	Highlights interagency, multiple-level cooperation, and establishes Planning Center for Drug Control (CENDRO) under both attorney generals
U.S.–Mexican Extradition Treaty of 1980 implemented from 1994	Another case of joint cooperation
1994–2000: Ernesto Zedillo Ponce de León's three-prong security approach	The approach includes (a) defending Mexico's sovereignty and territory; (b) protecting health of Mexicans; and (c) promoting multilateral cooperation on basis of equality
Operation Casablanca, USA; 1995	Covert operation angers Zedillo by arresting 22 banking officials and retrieving $110 million; creates Mexican dilemma: cooperation with United States on drugs, but also fend off United States from encroachments
Plenary Group on Law Enforcement, February 1995	Adopted by two attorney generals against drugs
High Level Contact Group for Drug Control, 1996	Bilateral initiative
Bilateral Border Task Force created, 1996	Another case of bilateral cooperation
Bilateralism comes full circle by 1998	Mexico deploys 20,000 troops (out of 170,000) for crop eradication, gets planes and helicopters, but misunderstanding increases as equipment fail to operate

Source: Jorge Dominguez and Rafael Fernandez de Castro, *The United States and Mexico: Between Partnership and Conflict* (New York, NY: Routledge, 2001), 37–51.

between cartels and his own administrative officials.[38] Marketing cocaine to Mexico benefited from NAFTA by tapping into the upwardly mobile population segments, especially in schools.

Resolving narcotrafficking involves a Mexico–U.S. clash of cultures in spite of the 1990s cooperation upsurge: Mexico sees it as a demand-side problem, explaining in part its policy-response inertia, and the United States as a supply-side problem, to the point of justifying intervention. Without dissolving some of the attitudes and beliefs behind those embattled positions, a common antiterrorism front appears surreal; and remaining aloof of border U.S. antiterrorism campaigns weakens cooperative threads against narcotrafficking. The *lose-lose* outcome of this vicious cycle is not wanted by either, but too much is at stake to alter the status quo: Too many U.S. drug consumers keep demand levels perpetually high; and too many Mexicans eager to cash in as suppliers risk their lives. Even a military deterrent, elaborated next, may not be sufficient for at least three reasons: (a) the breakdown of Mexican drug cartels under the Fox administration produced multiple local lords, thus making control-efforts next to impossible; (b) the growth of Central American illegal migrants, not with just for Mexico, but through Mexico to the United States, oftentimes in association narcotraffickers knowledgeable with the routes from shipping cocaine to U.S. markets; and (c) the potential defection of soldiers to drug cartels, as exemplified by the elite *Zetas,* trained in the late 1990s by the United States to fight narcotraffickers, from the Mexican military to the Gulf Cartel, and currently engaging Calderón's military in several northern provinces.

Security Cooperation

Just as IRCA introduced the military to check illegal Mexican immigration in 1986, Operation Alliance against drugs also relied eventually on the military, also from 1986. Not for the first time, both countries cooperated over such high-politics threats as indigenous resistance to liberalization and globalization in the mid-1990s. Jorge Dominguez and Rafael Fernandez de Castro detect three patterns in Mexico–U.S. "security" relations over the last century: (a) one of mutual balance until World War I; (b) Mexico's abnegation for the remainder of the century; and (c) Mexico's bandwagoning from the 1990s.[39] Balancing was evident in the war with the United States in the 1840s and the 1907 Washington Conference comediation of restless Central American *porfiriatos.* The United States safeguarded Mexico from European threats in between. Abnegation was also demonstrated in two formats: through the creation of the Mexico–U.S. Defence Commission in February 1942, suggesting a brief PSC,[40] and Mexico's rejection of the Cold War U.S. Military Assistance Advisory Group. Bandwagoning, triggered by illegal immigration and drug trafficking, revived a fairly robust form of military cooperation by the end of the 1980s, and coincided with the emergence of counterinsurgency, dramatized by the 1994 *Zapatista* uprisings in Chiapas. Noting how Mexico's defence forces were caught "remarkably unprepared" against this threat, Dominguez and Fernandez de Castro pointedly asked "whether the United States and Mexico would be allies in a counter insurgency war."[41] Mexico also sought military cooperation with Guatemála against insurgents, thus opening a southern security flank—and getting deeper into U.S. security networks elsewhere—all before 9/11. After 9/11, the picture got mixed: new threats along the southern frontier became illegal migrants, not just from Central or Latin America, but also from right across the world; and drug traffickers, increasingly through gangs, *maras,* originating in the United States.

Historically, Mexico's bandwagoning still occasions frequent outbursts of frustration, finger-pointing, and fury. President Zedillo's three-pronged reformulation of the country's security policy approach in the mid-1990s, amidst the most cooperative phase in the bilateral relationship, admitted the need for U.S. cooperation against drugs but also cautioned the United States against unilateralism, intervention, and excesses, as with the DEA's covert 1995 Operation Casablanca inside Mexico. Of note, a similarly oriented United States, following Enrique Camarena's assassination

10 years earlier, subtly converted Mexican anger into long-term U.S. cooperation. Salinas de Gortari deepened this new approach between 1989 and 1994. Table 4.2 portrays the bilateral antidrug trafficking arrangements concluded during this honeymoon phase. As Guadalupe González González and Stephan Haggard note, "Mexico has never attempted...an anti-American alignment," even in its moments of frustration, finger-pointing, and fury; and that the security community between the two countries "is not the traditional realist one of overcoming a security dilemma...." Rather, it depends on (a) "the willingness and capacity of the smaller power [Mexico] to protect the property rights and economic interests of the larger [United States];" (b) "negative but unintended consequences that arise from geographic proximity," such as illegal immigration and drug trafficking as described here and labeled as "cross-border externalities" by the authors; and (c) "perceptions by the more powerful actor of the underlying political stability, and thus reliability of the smaller one."[42]

The first and third González-Haggard criteria beg more attention. Especially under the expanded transactions under NAFTA, the former conveys an increasing Mexican obligation to protect the economic status quo of virtually unlimited U.S. corporation autonomy. To jeopardize it would boomerang against Mexico's economic interest. Similarly, the third criterion raises the enormous though subtle disincentive for Mexico to reduce its U.S. reliability, for example, by becoming excessively nonchalant toward terrorism. After 9/11, and particularly amidst Mexico's distancing of relations with the United States, both criteria amplify Mexico's own security-based helplessness: It has full freedom to engage in any activity or alliances so long as these do not threaten the United States. From this angle, then, Mexico's helplessness becomes secondary to the geographical context of being situated right next to a 9/11-affected United States. Also from this angle, Mexico's post–9/11 security predicament is no different from its pre–9/11 security predicament: Coercive U.S. policy approaches may immediately trigger Mexican resentment and reactions, but when the dust settles, Mexico is more likely than not to willingly stand beside the United States. Mexico's institutional responses to 9/11 reaffirm this observation. But as previous subsections indicated, neither Mexico nor the United States can control various exogenous catalyzers, such as Central American gangs over illegal immigration and narcotrafficking, in traditional policy disagreement areas. Cooperative efforts could be easily undermined, while disagreement in responses would only worsen the predicament. The present situation is precariously poised somewhere in between: cooperation on paper, with Mexican foot-dragging and U.S. unilateralism producing neither full-fledged cooperation in the trenches nor breakdown—precisely the uncertainty adversarial forces (illegal immigration, narcotrafficking, and gangsterism), have hitherto capitalized on.

MEXICO AFTER 9/11

By experiencing both swings of the security pendulum, Fox's tenure possibly provided the future model. He both proposed the no-boundary immigration proposal and created his own national security agency as a counterpart to the central U.S. Cold War institution amidst the upswing; but as both faded, security became more precarious. Whether Felipe Calderón's pragmatism, business-friendliness, and a problem-alleviating policy-making attitude prevail, remains to be seen, but he faces more figurative and literal walls in those relations than any post–Cold War Mexican president, not to mention those increasingly secular factors, such as terrorism, neither he nor his U.S. counterpart can fully control. Most of all, he faces a lame-duck whose increasingly unpopular war in Iraq seems to have dangled a Damoclean sword upon Republicans in the 2008 presidential elections—so much so, no candidate courts him, Calderón simply avoided him during his 2008 visit, and security priorities suddenly face a worsening economy.

Distinguishing institutional from procedural responses helps understand ballooning predicaments like immigration. By *institutions* is meant either the creation of or the rallying around a formal organization prescribing the procedures through laws, regulations, principles, or interests; and procedural responses may be local, ad hoc, not necessarily dependent on an institution, and inclusive of random and independent citizen or corporation actions.[43] Since immigrants operate with their own logic and resources, often beyond routine expectations, law enforcement officials may have to go outside the loop, that is, the institutional setting, to apprehend them. Individualizing policy responses not only subverts institutionalized expectations, but also localizes rules, laws, and regulations, and decentralizes institutions, sometimes correcting, at other times compounding the relevant problem.

In addition to this distinction, the Dominguez-Castro troika of PSC tendencies—balancing, abnegation, and bandwagoning—also facilitates our comprehension. As becomes evident, periodizing these tendencies as Dominguez-Castro do is unhelpful: After 9/11, all three tendencies operate simultaneously in different policy arenas; that they did so before 9/11 is debatable, but that is for other studies to confirm.

Three sections both identify and illustrate constraints between (a) institutional and procedural policy responses after 9/11; (b) the pre–9/11 regularities inherited by these; and (c) routine trade transactions thereafter. Owing to penetration by narcotraffickers and endemic, enduring corruption, Mexico's institutions carry a dubious reputation. Eliciting governmental response in Mexico, necessitates mobilizing both federal government officials and independent local players, since procedures within normal routine institutions need not follow the rules of the game (as prescribed by the constitution, for example). They may not only override institutional prerogatives, but also feed into the country's civil law traditions: Although civil law is an institution in itself, few people pay much attention to the formal organizations safeguarding laws; and though expected to uphold these institutionally driven laws, too many law enforcement officials resort to ad hoc responses, shifting statutory procedures to a life of their own and driven by inducements for personal gains, such as bribes, misappropriations, misallocations, and the like. Thus, just as procedures often collide with or even displace institutions behind the Mexican policy-making steering wheel, in Canada and the United States, for example, we will often find institutional imperatives behind the steering wheel and rarely discretionary law enforcement official actions over-riding institutions, though corruption is not entirely absent in either.

Institutional Responses

Whether the relationship is causal or coincidental, Fox's about-turn paralleled the fluctuating preferences of Jorge Castañeda, his first foreign secretary. Once an unabashed U.S.-denigrating leftist intellectual more at home with Cuba-Castro-Ché (and more recently accused by Mexico City's *El Universal* newspaper of spying for Cuba), Castañeda became the central protagonist in deepening regional economic integration with the United States using no-border immigration as the lightning rod. In this pursuit, he was to abandon Cuba, and ingloriously at that:[44] To facilitate Bush's visit to the March 2002 UN Monterrey summit, he brusquely asked his prior hero, Fidel Castro, to not come.[45] Then, after 9/11 struck both his immigration proposal and U.S. embrace, he led the campaign to deny the U.S. support for UN Resolution 1441 in the Security Council, which sought the green signal to attack Iraq.[46] Amidst this transition, Castañeda resigned his post, and eventually formed another party to challenge Fox's PAN. Luis Ernesto Derbez, the new Foreign Secretary, was more accommodating with the United States. Fox was thus left empty-handed, much like Mexico in its U.S. relations: In spite of occasional and unsustainable assertiveness, his central tendency favored acquiescence. Derbez himself faced this dragon, albeit in reverse order: Acquiescence in general bilateral relations until the 2005 U.S. border wall-construction legislation hit his guts.

The war against drugs inside Mexico, as previously noted, engendered a fair degree of collaboration with the United States over both intelligence and military security. While helpful as precedence after 9/11, Mexico's responses were nonetheless chaotic, with too many cooks spoiling the proverbial broth. Considerable abnegation toward the United States was matched by interagency rather than interstate differences, and with the least bandwagoning desired or attempted. In the words of a recent analyst, Mexico's intelligence apparatus complexity, "coupled with its institutional baggage from the past[,] has hampered early reform attempts by the Fox administration."[47] Even more pointedly, Christopher Leroy asserts, "a critical challenge for the Mexican government has been the constant threat of penetration by drug cartels and organized crime."[48]

Table 4.3 profiles this intelligence apparatus. Although created in 1989, CISEN faces (a) parallel intelligence agencies, making coordination and central command impossible; (b) increasing demands for congressional oversight, thus failing to act as an instrument of the executive branch; (c) increasing porosity, especially for drug cartels and other crime organizations; (d) virtually no direct or formal linkages with U.S. counterparts, thus remaining isolated in 9/11 countermeasures; and (e) a dubious climate of poor reputation, inadequate funding, even then controlled by the legislature, and leaderlessness.

One consequence of such a weak institution is the increasing desire of counterpart U.S. agencies to pursue their own Mexican goals independently, thus constantly threatening to infringe Mexican sovereignty. When after 9/11, the United States required foreign airplanes to first be thoroughly scrutinized in the port of

Table 4.3 Mexico's Intelligence/Counterinsurgency Institutions

Agency	Responsible to	Duties
Dirección Federal de Seguridad (DFS)	Became too independent	Dissolved in 1985 following high-profile murders (Manuel Buendia and Enrique Camarena)
Centro de Inteligencia y Seguridad Nacional (CISEN): Modeled on CIA and Mossad	Interinstitutional Council (IC), comprised, under the Secretary of Interior, of the Attorney General, and secretaries from Defence, Navy, Public Security, Finance, and Public Administration	Prepares National Security Threat Assessment for IC approval Does not control narcotrafficking measures Conducts HUMINT, SIGINT, COMINT, and IMINT Blamed for not anticipating 1994 *Zapatista* uprisings Serves as affiliate of Interior Secretariat Congress controls budget
National Security Cabinet	Created by President Carlos Salinas de Gortari to supervise CISEN	Created parallel jurisdiction
National Security Advisor	Created by President Vicente Fox Quesada	Lasted only from December 2000 to January 2002 under Adolfo Aguilar Zinser
Other parallel bodies: SSP (Public Security) SEDENA (Defence), SEMAR (Navy), PGR, and PFP (Police)	PFP controls GAT (the antiterrorist group)	GAT in charge of border security and drug trafficking

embarkation before landing in any U.S. airports, procedural changes in Mexican airports by the airlines themselves, augmented by customs officials, uniformed and plain clothed officers, and normal security personnel, were also monitored by the United States. Similar procedures also exist at each overland port of U.S. entry. In the final analysis, although we would expect procedural peculiarities to stray far from institutional imperatives, when they do not, and institutional goals instead get flouted, diminishing institutional legitimacy pushes the public (and other countries) to avoid the institutions. Though not so evident in airports, border outposts constantly battle the bending and breaking of rules, often by forces "superior" to the state—narcotraffickers, for instance. How deeply these forces penetrate the institutions of any given president, and particularly how many back-to-back administrations have they directly or indirectly influenced, ultimately sheds light on how perverted the procedural-institutional relationship has become.

Another consequence encourages what John Bailey calls "the invitation to bureaucratic struggle," as agency-cooperation, both within each country and within them, "will prove even more difficult to achieve as functions are shifted to state and local levels. . . ."[49] This may be the ghost haunting President Calderón, as the 30,000 troops he has deployed against narcotraffickers must now establish a *modus operandi* with local officials, many of whom may be resistant, some of whom may remain on cartel pay-rolls.

Procedural Constraints

U.S. government officials continuously discussed the border after 9/11 with Mexican officials, but progress remains sporadic with Mexico when compared with counterpart efforts in Canada. The December 2001 Canada–U.S. border agreement, seeking what Homeland Security director, Tom Ridge, called a "modern, efficient border of the 21st Century," includes biometric scanning, "smart" cards whereby frequent border crosser receive preclearance, and FAST lanes. About extending these agreements to Mexico, Ridge observed, "it just isn't as mature as it is with Canada. That's a fact." Both illegal drugs and immigration got in the way, he added.[50] Nonetheless, with the 2004 figures of 276 million people, 91 million vehicles, 4.5 million trucks, and 647,000 containers crossing the Mexico–U.S. borders,[51] steps had to be taken. The March 2002 Mexico–U.S. Border Partnership Declaration, signed in the Monterrey UN Summit by U.S. Secretary of State Colin Powell and Mexico's Interior Secretary Santiago Creel, and hailed as a "partnership for prosperity" by their presidents,[52] outlined the "border partnership" measures and adopted a 22-point "Action Plan."

The Border Partnership initiative consists of three chapters on securing (a) the infrastructure; (b) flows of people; and (c) flows of goods. Targeting such sectors as energy, transportation, telecommunications, water and dams, public health, as well as food and agriculture, the infrastructure chapter, emphasizing institutions, established a Binational Steering Committee for the Mexico–U.S. Critical Infrastructure Protection Framework for Cooperation, which had already met five times by September 2004.

The second chapter outlined the adoption of several exemplifying measures (or procedures capable of becoming institutionalized over a period of time if not perverted): (a) border crossing card-holders were given extended visa-time in order to reduce visit frequencies; (b) the Secure Electronic Network for Travelers Rapid Inspection, or SENTRI, program increased lanes from 6 to 13;[53] (c) implementation of the U.S. Visitor and Immigrant Status Indicator System, or U.S.-VISIT program, and the creation of a U.S.-VISIT Binational Working Group, which met at least seven times until October 2003 and subdivided functions into technology, infrastructure, border procedures, and outreach sectors in a Border Management System; (d) to save lives from heat, dehydration, and *coyote* attacks, U.S.-VISIT also established the Border Safety Initiative, or BSI, and the Border Patrol's Search and Rescue Teams, or BORSTAR, which was supplemented by the Mexican government establishing *Grupos Betas* in the Arizona-Sonora region and strengthening those in El Sasabe; (e) the February 2004 U.S.–Mexico Action Plan for Cooperation and Border Safety and a Memorandum of Understanding addressed the issue of immigrant repatriation; and (f) additional resources were diverted, especially by Mexico, to arrest human smuggling and trafficking in persons, or TIPs.

In fact, antismuggling operations remain an evergreen industry. Operation Carlos Loyola in 2001 was followed by Broken Promise (2002), Operation Rescue (April–May 2003), Operation Victoria (2003–04), Operation Samaniego-Valenzuela (2003), Operation Limpieza (2003), Operation Ice Storm (2003–04), and Operation Supersonic (2004).

Addressing flows of goods, the third chapter authorizes seven FAST lanes to be opened,[54] covering 15 percent of bilateral trade, while express lanes going south were also opened. To double the volume of bilateral trade covered, eight more FAST lanes were opened in 2005.[55]

Complementing these measures is the 22-point Action Plan, seven for the infrastructure chapter, eight for flows of people, and seven for flows of goods. Those for the infrastructure chapter address long-term planning, relieving bottlenecks, infrastructure protection, harmonizing port of entry operations, demonstration projects, cross-border cooperation, and financing projects at the border. For the human flow chapter, the eight address precleared travelers, advanced passenger information, NAFTA travel, safe borders and deterrence of alien smuggling, visa policy consultations, joint training, compatible data bases, and screening of third-country nationalities.[56] For the goods-flow chapter, the seven address public-private sector cooperation, electronic exchanges of information, secure in-transit shipments, technology sharing, secure railways, combat fraud, and contraband interdiction.[57]

Routine Transactions: Message in a Bottle?

With NAFTA in its eighth year when 9/11 struck, the critical question becomes how regional economic integration was impacted by the imposition of military security imperatives. More generally, the issue becomes whether North America shifted from an economic integration paradigm toward a PSC. Among the key findings: (a) 9/11 constrained trade; (b) recovery from this negative impact was still underway two years later; (c) whereas Mexican exports to the United States remained virtually unchanged proportionately, imports from the United States declined relatively sharply, opening trade diversification windows should Mexico be interested; (d) since Mexico's trade with the United States continued to fetch handsome surpluses while trade with countries where diversification occurred entailed huge deficits, the United States continued to remain too critical a player for Mexico's economic vitality to be ignored; and (e) since the tenets of both regional economic integration and PSC were fully satisfied even before 9/11, the irrelevance of a paradigm shift questions each paradigm's value within the context of size asymmetry, trade concentration, and a developed-developing country mix.

Statistics rarely convey a complete story or picture, but rightly or wrongly they cast an indelible impression. Table 4.4 presents such an impression from trade figures. Even with the 9/11 impact being the subject of attention, it is possible to capture a broader view, from the moment NAFTA was launched on January 1, 1994, or even its precursor, the CUFTA, was from January 1, 1989, all the way to 2004, the last year for which trade statistics were available at the end of the 2005.

Each country's bilateral trade with the other North American partners is tabulated as a proportion of that country's overall trade. The "pre" scenarios are captured under 1989 and 1993 for CUFTA and NAFTA, respectively. The year 1998 serves as the fifth year benchmark for NAFTA, while each of the years from 2000 constitute the analytically critical years for measuring 9/11 impacts comparatively.

The most dramatic 9/11 impact is clearly the sharp decline in Mexico's imports from the United States as a proportion of its overall import value (second arrow of the top row depicting "Mexico's proportions"): from 73 percent in 2000 to 61 percent the next year, where it stuck up to 2003. The sharpest trade reduction in the broader 2000–2003 period was precisely this one: 2003 Mexican imports from the United States were only 82 percent of the 2000 figure. Table 4.4 also shows the flip side of this (first arrow in second row, under "United States proportion"):

Table 4.4 North American Bilateral Trade (as a proportion of overall trade in percent)

Bilateral Trade	1989	1993	1994	1998	2000	2001	2002	2003
Mexico's proportions of overall trade								
M→U		75.0	80.0	88.0	88.0	88.0	89.0	87.0
U→M		67.0	70.0	74.0	73.0	61.0	63.0	61.0
M→C		5.3	5.8	1.3	2.0	1.9	1.7	1.8
C→M		0.8	0.9	1.8	2.3	2.5	2.6	2.4
United States proportions of overall trade								
U→M	5.8	9.8	9.8	11.6	13.9	13.8	14.0	13.3
M→U	4.8	5.6	7.5	10.0	10.9	11.0	11.3	10.6
U→C	23.0	17.3	21.0	22.6	22.5	22.2	23.1	23.3
C→U	17.0	17.0	19.0	19.0	18.0	18.6	17.7	17.3
Canada's proportions of overall trade								
C→U	71.0	79.0	83.0	85.0	87.0	88.0	88.0	86.0
U→C	63.0	61.0	66.0	67.0	64.0	64.0	63.0	60.0
C→M	0.3	0.4	0.4	0.4	0.5	0.6	0.6	0.5
M→C	1.1	1.9	2.2	2.5	3.2	3.5	3.6	3.6

Source: International Monetary Fund, *Direction of Trade Statistics* (Washington, DC: IMF, various years), different pages.

The next sharpest trade decline was U.S. exports to Mexico as a proportion of its own overall exports, with the 2003 figure being only 89 percent of the 2000 counterpart. What amplifies these figures is that (a) in 2003 Mexico imported less from the United States as a proportion of its overall imports than when it first joined NAFTA in 1994, and even in the last year before NAFTA, 1993—suggesting the evaporating regional integration gains; (b) between 1994 and 2000, as Table 4.5 shows, the proportion of Mexico's U.S. imports to overall Mexican imports climbed rapidly, with 13.4 percent increase from 1997 to 1998, 12.8 percent in the next year, and a whopping 21.1 percent the following year—figures matched by U.S. exports to Mexico as a proportion of overall U.S. exports climbing by 10 percent from 1997 to 1998, 9.3 percent from 1998 to 1999, and another astounding figure of 25 percent increase from 1999 to 2000; (c) expanding Mexican imports from the United States was also matched by Mexico's exports to the United States as a ratio of its overall exports reaching a high upper threshold of 88 percent in 2001, and barely hanging on at 87 percent in 2003—a huge increase from the 75 percent proportion in 1993 and 80 percent in 1994, climbing at the rate of 9.2 percent from 1997 to 1998, 16.5 percent from 1998 to 1999, and 22.6 percent from 1999 to 2000—while the proportion of Mexican exports to the United States to the overall U.S. imports

Table 4.5 Annual Changes in North American Trade Values (in percent)

Bilateral trade	From 1997 to 1998	From 1998 to 1999	From 1999 to 2000	From 2000 to 2001	From 2001 to 2002	From 2002 to 2003	From 2000 to 2003
Mexico's proportions of overall trade							
M→U	+9.2	+16.5	+22.6	−0.94	+1.9	+0.9	−0.97
U→M	+13.4	+12.8	+21.1	−0.89	−0.94	−0.98	−0.82
M→C	−0.7	+57.0	+40.0	−0.91	−0.91	+7.6	−0.9
C→M	+16.0	+28.0	+36.0	+5.4	+5.7	−0.91	+2.5
United States proportions of overall trade							
U→M	+10.0	+9.3	+25.0	−0.93	−0.96	−0.99	−0.89
M→U	+10.0	+13.9	+23.3	−0.98	+2.5	+2.6	+3.4
U→C	+2.6	+5.7	+7.1	−0.93	−0.98	+5.3	−0.97
C→U	+4.0	+11.0	+15.0	−0.96	−0.97	+6.4	−0.99
Canada's proportions of overall trade							
C→U	+1.4	+13.8	+15.6	−0.5	−0.35		
U→C	+2.6	+5.9	+7.1	−0.8	−0.15		
C→M	−0.6	+19.4	+35.6	+11.3	−2.5		
M→C	+1.1	+24.6	+23.7	+0.2	+3.7		

almost doubled from 5.6 percent in 1993 to 11 percent in 2001, spiraling upwardly at the rate of 10 percent (from 1997 to 1998), 13.9 percent (1998 to 1999), and 23.3 percent (1999 to 2000); and (d) just as trade-expansion justified NAFTA for both Mexico and the United States, 9/11 threw a curveball filled with lessons.

Behind the statistics lies the grim reality of a briefly felt severe post–9/11 U.S. economic downturn. Although Mexican exports survived, and indeed might even have profited given the preference for low-wage products over their high-cost counterparts, imports from the United States could have been hit worse and more negatively impacted, pushing Mexico to aggressively seek other partners and shift from NAFTA-induced trade concentration, toward the kind of diversification Mexico explicitly rejected when embracing the Washington Consensus. If there is a message in the U.S. economic slowdown sharply reducing illegal immigration—over 120,000 fewer apprehensions between October 2001 and May 2002—then it surely must be, when push comes to shove, it is not a string of 9/11 security measures but the state of the U.S. economy that halts illegal Mexican immigration.[58] Pushing this farther, since the illegal immigration profile is changing significantly, as previously argued, even a depressed economy might not offer future or long-term safeguards.

Among other lessons: (a) since security imperatives can dampen trade, it might be worthwhile to save for a rainy day; (b) since Mexico's exports were expected to face more stringent barriers entering the United States than U.S. exports entering Mexico, 9/11 may not be the only reason why the proportion of U.S. imports entering Mexico ebbed while the proportion of Mexican exports to the United States more or less held their ground—pointing to either low-wage Mexican exports bucking the line and high-valued U.S. exports paying the price, or to global competition rocking the NAFTA boat, particularly seducing Mexico finally; (c) the global competition thesis is strengthened by Mexico's imports from China increasing 350 percent between 1997 and 2001 and 700 percent between 1997 and 2003, from India increasing 30+ percent between 1997 and 2001 and 160 percent between 1997 and 2003, and from Japan almost doubling between 1997 and 2001 while still registering upwards of 75 percent increases between 1997 and 2003;[59] (d) with Mexico persistently amassing huge deficits in its trade with China, India, and Japan while posting even more surpluses in U.S. trade, regional economic integration under NAFTA was seriously shaken, but not by security imperatives or constraints—rather by interregional trading dynamics, again underscoring the huge impact of globalization; and (e) given all of the above, security imperatives shaking Mexico's trade relations themselves get rattled by an even more powerful trade dynamic.

When all is said and done about 9/11's Mexico–U.S. trade impacts, business interests prevailed, providing light at the end of Mexico's one-tracked trade tunnel should the country wish to exploit the opportunity. It also exposed the vulnerabilities trade faces against terrorism.

Looking beyond the Mexican–U.S. bilateral trade relationship, one is struck how Canada's fate was almost diametrically opposite Mexico's. Imports from the United States as a proportion of overall Canadian imports expanded robustly initially, from

63 percent in 1989 to 66 percent in 1994, before falling to 60 percent in 2003—a fall nowhere as steep as Mexico's, and actually compensated by more significant gains in Canadian exports to the United States as a proportion of overall Canadian exports, from 71 percent in 1989 to 83 percent in 1994 and 86 percent in 2003. With the United States initially imposing more restrictions along Canadian borders than Mexican, trade flows, amounting to more than a billion dollars every day in the largest bilateral trading relationship existing were barely scratched. On the contrary, although Canadian exports to Mexico as a proportion of its overall exports doubled from 0.3 percent in 1989 to 0.6 percent in 2003, while Mexico's exports to Canada as a proportion of Canadian overall imports simultaneously tripled from 1.1 percent in 1989 to 3.6 percent in 2003, traded volumes still remain too negligible to have any significant impacts. That these are growing is healthy for Canada–Mexico bilateral relations, but they do not even come close to offsetting or compensating Canada's relations with the United States. Even more dramatically, whereas 9/11 opened opportunities for Mexico to shed its huge U.S. trade concentration, it actually deepened Canada's U.S. concentration, certainly in terms of the country's exports to the United States, but hardly less in the reverse direction with its imports. Above all, whereas Canada's 1997 imports from Mexico were more or less comparable to those from China in terms of value, by 2003, China was exporting almost 75 percent more to Canada than Mexico was, although Mexico's exports to Canada were almost nine times larger in 1997 and still seven times larger in 2003.[60] Evidences of Mexico's globalization making more noise than its North American regionalization contrast with Canada's regionalization making more sound than its globalization.

Completing the circle, although George W. Bush's presidency began by elevating Mexico over Canada, reverting this ranking in his second-term better fits developments on the ground: Canada not only remains the top U.S. trading partner but also with greater equanimity in its high—and increasing—U.S. trade concentration than Mexico, which not only slipped from the second largest U.S. trading partner, a position it climbed to almost as soon as it joined NAFTA, to the third largest, with the China locomotive overtaking Mexico shortly after 9/11. Bush carries gripes galore: he had them with Jean Chrétien, created them with Vicente Fox Quesada, and faced them increasingly with Paul Martin. With Steve Harper, however, Bush found the stripes he was more comfortable with in North America—restoring Canada to the most special of special U.S. friends, much like Mexico was to him in 2000. This unexpected 9/11 fall-out may be compensated for Mexico by sustaining growth in trade with Canadian and Asian countries. Two caveats remain: how Calderón overcomes the immigration bug, which threatens more in U.S. election years than at other times; and whether Mexico will be seduced by bilateral U.S. charms again, like the Washington Consensus proved to be. Current Mexico–U.S. trade trends will probably run their routine course, and not be significantly altered; and, while both Mexico and the United States remain forever entwined, not all the Canadas, Chinas, and Indias of the world can undo a bilateral bondage come high tide, heavy waters, or tsunamis—for better or for worse.

Canada will not match Mexico over remittance receipts. By virtue of exporting such huge numbers of low-wage workers, Mexico is now one of the top two remittance recipients (India being the other). Adding up the small amounts sent by many of these workers to over 1.25 million households, Mexico was receiving over $9 billion on the heels of 9/11, though in 2003, that shot up to over $13 billion, displacing FDI from the second slot, and after crossing the $20 billion mark in 2006,[61] Mexico's remittances overtook even petroleum income as the largest source of foreign exchange as it approached $25 billion by 2008 even though border walls and controls threaten continued growth.

This comparison probably gets to the heart of the North American network: With frequent expected and unexpected changes under the twin-impacts of regional integration and globalization, glances may be exchanged, nights may be spent together, but a long-term commitment—marriage, for the lack of a better term—may become a spent force even before it glows. To wit, the guns-butter exchange remains a valid force, though exerting less intensity today than before given the multiplication of economic interexchanges; changes within the domestic context, for example, election results, also remain as powerful a potential determinant of international policy outcomes as foreign policy interests may themselves be; and emerging nonstate actors—citizens or corporations—constrain states even under security-driven state-strengthening measures.[62]

POST–9/11 BALANCE SHEET: SECURITY COMMUNITY OR REGIONAL ECONOMIC INTEGRATION?

What do all these institutions, procedures, and transactions add up to in the wake of 9/11 imperatives? The emerging picture of security imperatives constraining the fruits of regional economic integration—the classic security-economic trade-off—highlights institutional-level performances while concealing grassroots actions which together may completely undermine macro-level expectations. Comparing and contrasting the tenets of both paradigms before and after 9/11, as tables 4.6, 4.7, and 4.8 do, the case is made of both paradigms remaining functional, though the freer-flowing integrative efforts and results of the 1990s face an increasing security constraint today.

Table 4.6 overviews how the catalyzers of political/security integration performed before and after 9/11. Was there a purposeful orientation shift, as the first dimension asks? The *yes* answer for both comparative periods belies the different nuances. Before 9/11, Mexico often demonstrated unwillingness and eagerness to cooperate with the United States to stamp out narcotrafficking, as all the various policies in table 4.2 indicated, and in spite of having the rug being pulled from beneath by narcotraffickers penetrating the policy-making system. After 9/11, Mexico's heart, mind, and soul just do not seem to be behind any security integration, but to lay the golden eggs of economic growth, the goose of security cooperation must be accepted, and particularly as rigid regulations for border flows or air travel must be complied with. Mexico's is a classic damned-if-I-do, damned-if-I-don't predicament!

Table 4.6 Catalyzers of Political/Security Integration Compared

Dimension	Pre–9/11	Post–9/11
1. Occurrence of purposeful orientation shift?	Yes, Mexican societal constraints offset by over-enthusiastic state responses	Yes, Only because of U.S. surveillance and monitoring
2. Institutionalization of orientation shift?	Yes, But with extra efforts	Yes, But Mexican niggardliness makes task uphill
3. Gresham's law in integrative instincts (bad instincts driving good instincts out)	Possible, but subordinated to reverse Gresham instincts	High and probably getting higher: Mexico's indifference toward emigrant controls; U.S. subordinating every issue to military security
4. Safeguarding against external shocks?	Not an issue since external shocks were no longer so shocking after Cold War	Huge issue, but interpretations through different nationalistic lenses produces second-best policy outcomes
5. Exploring new avenues of collaboration	Yes, increasingly	No, a steady-state mentality persists
6. Compatible leadership?	Yes, publicly and privately	Yes, but for photo opportunities; attitudinal differences breed less-than-perfect policy outcomes

Source: Karl W. Deutsch, et al., *Political Community and the North Atlantic Area: International Organization in the Light of Historical Experience* (Princeton, NJ: Princeton University Press, 1957), chap. 2.

Given the constrained construction of a Mexico–U.S. security community, the results reflect a laggard Mexico, one-track-security-minded United States, and obvious second-best outcomes. As the second dimension shows, even by institutionalizing the security community orientation shift purposefully before and after 9/11, the going was not smoothened in either period, and became more uphill after 9/11. Similarly, the third dimension highlights how ill-conducive integrative instincts, such as Mexico's indifference or the U.S. security veto, increased after 9/11, while before illegal immigration and narcotrafficking soured blossoming economic integration efforts.

Safeguarding against external shocks—the fourth dimension—was not a pre–9/11 factor of concern, but a huge post–9/11 consideration, exacerbated by both countries viewing those shocks differently, given their nationalistic priorities. In turn, exploring new avenues of collaboration was smoother and fruitful before 9/11, though after 9/11 the tendency has been to conserve the status quo more than to open new areas unless these feed into the defence mentality. Finally, leadership compatibility also changed. The pre–9/11 camaraderie, evident in both private relations and public demonstrations, cooled appreciably after 9/11, without rocking the bilateral cooperation boat, as the leaders continue to cordially engage at regular summits, but the previously conspicuous spark and fire in personal relations remain conspicuous by their very absence today.

If the security community catalyzers cannot throw the bilateral relationship in unfettered light, the corresponding tenets themselves cannot muster the needed gloss. Table 4.7 lists a dozen tenets, the first three from the PSC paradigm, the remainder from the ASC counterpart. Recalling how PSC refers to integrating countries and ASC to domestic integration, we see 9/11 effects dampen, rather than reverse, expectations on both fronts. All three PSC tenets continue to suggest post–9/11 integration, just as they did before 9/11, but with increasing speed-bumps: more values were compatible than not both before and after 9/11, but

Table 4.7 Security Community Tenets Pre– and Post–9/11

Dimension	Pre–9/11	Post–9/11
1. Value compatibility	Yes	Yes over many values, increasingly less in others
2. Behavioral predictability	Yes, mostly converging	Yes, admixture of converging and diverging
3. Mutual responsiveness	Yes	Yes, but with ifs and buts
4. Value complementarity	Yes	Yes, but value distinctiveness also emerging
5. Distinctiveness of lifestyles	Yes, with growing commonalities	Yes, increasingly
6. Reward expectations before burden sharing	Yes	Burden-sharing before reward expectations
7. Increasing political and administrative functions	Yes	Yes
8. Economic growth distinguishing core areas from peripheral areas	Yes, within country and across region	Yes, within country and across region
9. Geographical and social communication linkages	Yes	Yes
10. Multiplication of communications and transactions	Yes	Yes
11. Decreasing barriers to mobility across political boundaries	Yes	No, increasing barriers
12. Increasing political elites:	Yes, with expansion of common ground	Yes, but not always on common ground

Source: Karl W. Deutsch, et al., *Political Community and the North Atlantic Area: International Organization in the Light of Historical Experience* (Princeton, NJ: Princeton University Press, 1957), chap. 2.

after 9/11 noncompatible values also demand attention; behavior predictability both before and after 9/11 emphasize convergences more than divergences, though after 9/11 divergences continue to ascend; and mutual responsiveness also rules at the end of the day, both before 9/11 and after, yet revealing more ifs and buts since 9/11.

Paradoxically, Mexico relates better to the United States through ASC than PSC, although increasing post–9/11 constraints remain a common feature. Revisiting and reconstructing the theoretical tenets may be an urgent 9/11 message, but returning to the empirical front, value complementarity, distinctiveness in lifestyles, and reward expectations before burden-sharing—the fourth, fifth, and sixth dimensions—show the 9/11 speed-bumps with burden-sharing actually preceding reward expectations after 9/11. The next four dimensions, highlighting mostly sociopolitical and socio-economic forces in the two countries, remain viable pre– and post–9/11 forces, while the last two dimensions highlight the differences. Before 9/11, barriers to mobility across political boundaries were decreasing not only to legitimate flows, such as permit-holding border-crossers, trade, and investment, but also illegitimate flows like undocumented migrants and narcotrafficking; yet after 9/11, even as these barriers increase, both illegal flows continue unabated while legal flows took at least a temporary hit. Similarly, political elites have been expanding under integration, but before 9/11, they shared a larger common ground than after, as different orientations and attitudes toward military security and policy priorities continue to whittle the collective platform.

Addressing the economic consequences of political/security integration by plucking out the various neofunctionalist tenets or characteristics, table 4.8 makes two broad conclusions: First, transactions may have dropped, as the sixth dimension acknowledges, but that they remain at extraordinarily high levels (compared to pre-NAFTA or with other countries) suggests (a) the economic consequences have not been as damaging as expected and (b) security safeguards have been institutionalized fairly rapidly and effectively, though without providing a foolproof blanket. In turn, the second conclusion, of a distinctive security-economic trade-off benefiting security revives Cold War patterns, marking a Mexico–U.S. bilateral relationship déja vû. Since neofunctionalism has always been a dispensable dimension of regional integration, as evident in 55 years of West European experiences, it is more exposed to and cohabits with speed-bumps and constraints, ultimately surviving all of them in one form or another. People do need to consume, have a job, travel, and so forth. Events like 9/11 could temporarily slow or stop them, or under-supply the demands, but not shutter them for the long-haul. Unsurprisingly, post–9/11 by and large mirrors pre–9/11 patterns.

If anything, 9/11 marked the dividing line between regional integration and complex interdependence in the Mexico–U.S. bilateral relationship, evident in comparing six interdependency tenets before and after 9/11. The clear message: Interdependency proved weaker than regional economic integration before, but stronger after. There were multiple channels of communications in both periods, as the first

Table 4.8 Neofunctionalist Tenets Pre– And Post–9/11

Dimension	Pre–9/11	Post–9/11
1. Economic symmetry among units?	No, but not a divisive issue any more	No
2. Elite complementarity?	Yes, increasingly	Yes, increasingly; but also increasing divergences
3. Pluralism?	Yes, increasingly	Yes, increasingly
4. Capacity to adapt?	High	High
5. Spillover?	High	High
6. Growing transactions?	Yes	Stalled, momentarily; but thresholds remain high
7. Growth in intergovernmental relations?	Yes	Yes
8. Transnational growth?	Yes	Yes
9. Elite socialization?	Yes	Yes
10. Growth in ideological identity?	Yes, selectively	Yes, selectively; but distinctiveness not abandoned
11. Increasing interaction with external actors?	Limited and constrained	Limited and constrained, but increasing for both countries
12. Benefit distribution higher and more equitable?	Yes, but not necessarily through state initiatives (emigration)	Yes, but not necessarily through state initiatives (emigration, security)
13. Converging perception of external problem?	Yes, and defined economically	Yes and No, External problems not always interpreted similarly (economically and militarily)
14. Integration as cost-free?	Yes	Becoming costly

Source: Joseph S. Nye, "Comparing Common Markets: A Revised Neofunctionalist Model," in *Regional Integration: Theory and Research,* ed., Leon N. Lindberg and Stuart A. Scheingold (Cambridge, MA: Harvard University Press, 1971), 199–218.

dimension of table 4.9 shows, but economic channels overshadowed security counterparts before 9/11, only to be completely reversed after 9/11. Accordingly, the second dimension acknowledges economic integration at the top of a hierarchy of issues before 9/11, but military security alone at the top after 9/11. The third dimension only reiterates this pattern: the military was subordinated before, but economic integration is subordinated now.

On the basis of these relations and orientations, the institutional membership became more involuntary after 9/11 than before in order to accommodate U.S. security networks, while the catalyst of interaction between the two countries was no longer the creation of competitive North American markets, but the search for new knowledge pertaining to terrorism for the United States and new markets for

Table 4.9 Interdependence Tenets Pre– And Post–9/11

Dimension	Pre–9/11	Post–9/11
1. Channels of communications?	Multiple, economic most important	Multiple, security most important
2. Hierarchy of issues?	Yes, economic issues at top	Yes, military issues at top
3. Subordination of military?	Yes	No
4. Nature or institutional membership?	Voluntary, emphasizing a wide range	Voluntary and involuntary, emphasizing both a wide range but also hierarchy
5. Catalyst?	Competitive markets	New knowledge (security tips), competitive markets for Mexico, but outside North America
6. Placement of regionalism along levels of policy-making analysis?	More important than nationalism and globalism	Less important than nationalism and state interests; less important to globalism too

Sources: Robert O. Keohane and Joseph S. Nye, *Power and Interdependence: World Politics in Transition* (Boston, MA: Little, Brown and Company, 1977), 3–37; and Henry Nau, "From Integration to Interdependence: Gains, Losses, and Continuing Gaps," *International Organization* 33, no. 1 (Winter 1979): 119–47.

Mexico, this time outside North America. The final dimension encapsulates bilateral dynamics: They suddenly become less important than state interests and globalization after 9/11, whereas before they were more important than both state interests and globalization.

How does neorealism fare in explaining Mexico–U.S. relations before and after 9/11? Table 4.10 suggests the clear answer to be increasing post–9/11 relevance. Behind the observation lies the rigidification of state interests. The state was dominant both before 9/11 and after, but whereas before 9/11 it was more receptive to a wide variety of nonstate actors, especially corporations, after 9/11, even with a growth of NGOs (nongovernmental organizations), the state is more suspicious. Toward illegal immigrants, a form of nonstate actor, the United States was hostile both before and after, whereas Mexico proved to be more indifferent on both occasions.

Neorealism is weak connecting internal dynamics and international competition. Both were salient for the United States in the two periods, more internal after 9/11 than before, but without abandoning the international context of competitiveness. Whereas the competitiveness was largely over market access before 9/11, it is increasingly over international security threats by terrorists. For Mexico, internal considerations continue to remain dominant, and although North American interests were on the ascendancy before 9/11, afterward Mexico, without abandoning North American interests, is more open to global possibilities.

Table 4.10 Neorealist Tenets Pre– And Post–9/11

Dimension	Pre–9/11	Post–9/11
1. State as dominant actor?	Yes, but with a kinder, gentler approach to nonstate actors (except illegal immigrants)	Yes, and more robustly so: Nonstate actors viewed with suspicion
2. Policy reflecting internal considerations or international competitiveness?	For Mexico, international first, North America next; For United States, both	For Mexico, internal and North America; but more receptive to global
3. Is international competitiveness orderly or anarchic?	Orderly, market competitiveness largely	Anarchic, terrorism breeds ghost-like perception

Source: Kenneth N. Waltz, *The Theory of International Politics* (Menlo Park, CA: Addison-Wesley, 1979), chap. 5.

As the third dimension indicates, market competitiveness was orderly and the war against terrorism more anarchic, again depicting a pre– and post–9/11 difference, as well as the drift toward a neorealist orientation. Nevertheless, an orderly market has not provided a foolproof formula against downturns and depressions, and the anarchy on the Mexico–U.S. border, though increasing, pales in comparison to those along various borders across Africa or Asia.

Finally, both bilateral relationships and those with other countries were driven by states, and continue to be so increasingly, for both countries.

Turning to the three arguments interlinking security community and neofunctionalism paradigms, what evidence do we find?

The first posits any coexistence of security imperatives and regional economic integration will be to the benefit of the former and the detriment of the latter. This was found to be partially true: Trade took a 9/11 hit, but remittances mushroomed; swarming border outposts with all kinds of security procedures certainly imposed trade bottlenecks, from which Mexico continues to recover, but that they are not the *be-all* and *end-all* of a terrorism-free United States was glaringly evident in the continued growth of illegal Mexican and Central American migrants. In turn, both subset expectations of the first argument find vitality: Free-trade arrangements do find security imperatives constraining them, and security imperatives stratifying rather than equalizing communities was also suggested in the expanded post–9/11 role of the Mexican military.

According to the second argument, given the above developments, interdependence characteristics will prevail over all others. This was also found to be true, but only partially: issues belong to a hierarchy in which the military is on the ascendancy, but multiple channels and multiple issues still characterize the Mexico–U.S. relationship. Both subset considerations also find vitality: Mexico's trade diversification is finally underway, but it remains unclear how far or fast this will go; whether it wants to or not, Mexico continues to free-ride U.S. security, in fact, this is a U.S. imposition rather than Mexican desire given the high 9/11 stakes.

Finally, the third argument of interdependence breeding state-society fissures, in turn accentuating more disagreements/conflicts between the countries and between groups, was also found to be true. Nonetheless, integration is also reality, more so now than at any previous time.

CONCLUSIONS

Critical for Mexico–U.S. relations is not that 9/11 may not be the only reason for the poor PSC and REI performances, and why interdependence and realism show post–9/11 growth: Illegal immigration and drug flows, proximity of developing-developed countries, and Mexico increasingly serving as a platform for not just Central American illegal immigration and narcotrafficking, but also East Asian *maquiladoras* production were set to pose security problems independently, thus corroding economic integrative efforts from the very start. If anything, 9/11 accelerated rather than initiated these constraints, suggesting significantly, short of closing the U.S. border, post–9/11 measures and policies are unlikely to halt these flows or arrest inherent problems. Should the border be closed, it would also mark the end of PSC and REI as we have known them to be. If interdependence and realism better describe the bilateral relations as they are already doing, we face a curious plight: Both actually introduce a security dilemma where none really existed before. Transforming Mexico's trade diversification tendencies into external security arrangements would entail an enormously important structural change.

Turning to the volume's hypothesis, given the nature of dynamics at the Mexico–U.S. border, and particularly their nonreplicability along the Canada–U.S. border, the symptoms of bilateralizing Mexico–U.S. relations, as opposed to a trilateralization through NAFTA, better convey early twenty-first-century reality. Not only that, given the Mexico–U.S. border idiosyncrasies, the immediate 9/11 effects suggest those bilateralist features reflecting a staying power other initiatives or developments may not easily displace or duplicate. Trilateralization was a historically brief experimentation or infatuation without the steam-rolling power to continue much longer, but it took 9/11 to reassert the historically prominent and prolonged role bilateral relations have played. This does not mean a breakdown in larger integrative efforts, but in a street car named desire, the back-seat matters. And that may be where PSC and REI may long remain—not outside, but inside—no matter how spellbinding technology demands larger markets.

It is tempting to identify NAFTA as a victim of 9/11, but the Mexico–U.S. relation carried enough warts even through the golden years of NAFTA and faces even to this day more unilateral, grassroots, or transnational activities than bilateral or trilateral state policies. Blaming only 9/11 for North American bilateralism exaggerates the situation. Ironically, the one country to oppose North American economic integration from being extended to Mexico–Canada—may end up better-off in the region, and particularly in its relations with the United States after 9/11, and because of 9/11, than Mexico, the country which profited the most from NAFTA (in terms of trade surpluses, recovery from the 1995 peso crisis, remittances received, and the size of the binational population with the United States). Two implications follow. First, if anything, 9/11 exposed the key victim: Canada when REI is in full bloom, Mexico when PSC reigns; and both Canada and Mexico when either interdependence or realism are on the ascendancy. Second, the true culprit of a deflated bilateral relationship seems to be a tyranny of independent circumstances, rather than Mexico, the United States, or both.

5

Canadian–U.S. Relations Since 9/11: Putting Humpty-Dumpty Back Together?

INTRODUCTION

Although the United States and Canada share about 3,150 miles of common border, their foreign policy interests and interpretations differ markedly. Since 9/11, these views have often clashed over Iraq, Afghanistan, the international criminal court, and the role of the United Nations in world affairs. In addition, steps have been undertaken to avoid a major disruption in the long-standing economic relationship, so much more vital to Canada than to the United States.

Assessing the impact of the new post–9/11 security emphasis on the Canadian–U.S. bilateral relationship, this chapter adopts the following four analytical dimensions: (a) institution building, (b) trade and economic integration, (c) foreign and military policy interests, and (d) military intelligence. A theoretical discourse thereafter reflects selectively on neofunctionalist, interdependent, integrative, and realist tenets in Canadian–U.S. relations. Beforehand, we overview the post–9/11 bilateral changes.

POST–9/11 CONTEXTUAL CHANGES: SHUTTLING BETWEEN STRENGTHS AND WEAKNESSES

Following the United States pressures Canada. This is evident in beefing up Canadian domestic and international security capabilities against potential terrorism, ranging from ballooning budgets to creating PSEPC, a counterpart to the United States DHS. Cross-border dependencies simultaneously impose pressures and offer opportunities. The Bush administration openly cited Canadian energy resources as an important asset in "weaning" the United States off of Middle East supplies. U.S. investment in the auto, mining, energy, and services industries in Canada is extensive. Canada remains the largest trading partner, with China now displacing Mexico for the second spot. Indeed, the northern border was always an afterthought with the Mexican border, where 90 percent of the 12,000 U.S. border agents were posted until 2006, after which the deployment of 36,000 Border Patrol agents to thwart illegal immigrants from Mexico reaffirmed the secondary importance of the Canada–U.S. border.[1]

The first salvo of U.S. anxiety across the border came in response to the so-called "millenium bomber," Ahmed Ressam, who was caught entering the United States (Port Angeles, WA) from Canada with bomb material in his trunk in December 1999.[2] Ressam had entered Canada in 1994, claiming refugee status. He had developed a criminal record over the next five years and lived off thievery and Canadian welfare assistance, but was never deported. In an interview on the PBS show, *Frontline,* a former CSIS director expressed alarm over Canada's lax policies of not requiring valid identification from refugees and stated, "we need a gigantic cultural shift in this country," to reckon with the dangers of a new age of global terrorism.[3] As subsequently revealed, Ressam entered Afghanistan via Pakistan for terrorist training in 1998, before returning to Canada.

The Ressam affair reverberated strongly after 9/11 as U.S. officials suggested that the hijackers had entered via Canada. Though this theory was later disproved, the story had a lasting effect on U.S. perceptions of Canada (and on U.S. perceptions of many Canadians). A series of political speeches and popular press stories lambasted the vulnerable border to the North, and portrayed Canada as a haven for false refugees planning nefarious acts against the United States. "It's a big, porous border," Senator Byron Dorgan, Democrat of North Dakota, observed, "and it's very difficult to secure." Dorgan made headlines in 2001 when he held up an orange traffic cone in the Senate as an example of the kinds of barriers often used to block roads on the *Canadian* border.[4] The United States immediately upgraded border security presence by tripling the number of border agents, setting up five new army and marine bases near the border, and initiating customs checks through the Great Lakes.[5] In October 2006, the U.S. DHS awarded Boeing a $2 billion contract to build a "virtual security fence" over some 6,000 miles of the Canadian and Mexican borders. The system will include large radar towers, the use of unmanned small surveillance planes, and infrared and regular cameras.[6]

Canadians, offended by the "weak link" U.S. argument, see tolerance and acceptance of refugees as core to their central values. They argue that refugees can not be expected to have valid passports if they are leaving the country for fear of torture; their fears have been reinforced when the Canadian government reached a settlement for almost $Cdn10 million and acknowledged that it had been complicit in the deportation of Maher Arar to Syria by U.S. officials. He was jailed and tortured in Syria for a year, while no hard evidence of terrorist connections was found. Moreover, Canadians point out how the United States demonstrated plenty of its own vulnerabilities, as in the case of the actual 9/11 terrorists, and imply that the border with Mexico is the real weak link.

To be sure, Harper's Conservative Government represents a sea change in official Canadian attitudes toward the United States from the Liberals, as discussed in chapter 3. The government has moved swiftly to become a proactive partner in the war on terror, from increasing budgets and cooperation as described later to expanding domestic policing and intelligence. The latter gained steam since the June 2006 arrest of 17 alleged terrorists in Toronto, allegedly with large amounts of ammonium nitrate—the fertilizer-based substance used in the Oklahoma City bombings—reinforcing the government's determination, if not capturing the public's attention. Yet, even Harper, leading the most Conservative and pro-U.S. government since Brian Mulroney in the late 1980s, has limitations on how far he can go to reassure his southern neighbor without offending Canada's independent anti-U.S. constituency. Canada's limited options in its asymmetric relationship were revealed in early 2007 when the WHTI went into place, requiring Canadians to have a passport to enter the United States, as discussed later. This went through despite repeated attempts by the Harper government to at least delay the timetable in order to give more breathing room to implement the changes.

The problems of security and trade led to the SPP initiative by Canada, the United States, and Mexico in 2005 which directly linked security with trade in North America. This effort, so far limited to working groups and analytical papers while awaiting significant budget reallocations, also created impetus for a North American security perimeter, whereby the three countries would share a common entry and exit policy for persons and goods entering the region. Not surprisingly both nationalist and official Canadians have resisted the idea. Nationalists see the relationship with Washington in imperialistic terms, and hope to resist Canada becoming a simple resource repository for U.S. appetites of Canadian water, energy, and other natural resources. They loathe the idea of losing independence in foreign policy, and destroying Canada's avowed welcoming attitude toward refugees, immigrants, support for the human security and peacekeeping agenda, and multiculturalism in general.[7] To be sure, these attitudes are reflected in good part by the much more blaise attitude of the majority of Canadians toward terrorist threats to Canada and the need for military spending, as reported by surveys, and in sharp juxtaposition to widely held U.S. fears.[8] The latter in good part because the people see Canada's relationship with the United States as distinct, and want to avoid the mexicanization of the northern border inviting additional restrictions and less maneuver for them.[9]

From the U.S. point of view, Canada has been a free-rider on U.S. security expenditures from at least 1942. Canada's low defence expenditures can be directly tied to the security the United States provides in a variety of areas, ranging from the NORAD (North American Aerospace Defence) Command to missile defence. The United States is the credible threat that secures Canada, in short. So U.S. requests for increased contribution and vigilance at a time of heightened danger is simply asking for cooperation with mutual benefits.[10]

HIGH-STAKE PERFORMANCES IN THE LOW-POLITICS DOMAIN: BUSINESS-AS-USUAL ON THE ECONOMIC FRONT

Addressing institution-building, trade and economic integration, and foreign and military policy, this section finds routine interactions not only resuming after a brief post–9/11 slump, but also generally performing even better since the Harper government took over. Whether this means Canada does better with the United States when it is the top U.S. priority, or the cooperation brings more free-riding opportunities, Canada still comes off better than under NAFTA-based integration even by refusing to stoop too deep in the war on terrorism.

Institution Building

Since 9/11, Canadian and U.S. government departments and agencies also increasingly worked jointly to improve security along the border. Several new provisions were put into place. The "smart border" agreement, signed in December 2001, contains provisions to secure the flow of people, goods and services, infrastructure, and information sharing across the border,[11] highlighting better binational border coordination. The Canada–U.S. Transportation Border Working Group was created around the core membership of federal and provincial entities. Meeting for the first time in Windsor, Ontario in 2002, to collaborate on an action plan to identify key priorities, including data collection, technology programs, and information exchange, the dialogue involved many government agencies. On the U.S. side were the Federal Highway Works Administration, state departments of transportation along the border, CBP, U.S. DOS (Department of State), and the General Services Administration. On the Canadian were TC, Provincial and territorial governments, Foreign Affairs Canada, Canada Border Services Agency, and the Canadian Food Inspection Agency.[12]

A single alternative inspection system was established through the NEXUS system, designed to facilitate and simplify border crossings for preapproved, low-risk travelers. NEXUS members use designated lanes to reduce traffic delays at various crossings, and may not be subject to regular customs and immigration questioning. As of October 2004, NEXUS had 74,000 participants.[13] Similar NEXUS programs have been launched for air and marine travel, while the CBSA and the U.S. Customs and Border Protection have been acting together since 2005.[14]

In another post–9/11 cooperative activity, Canada and the United States have developed specific recommendations for maritime security and ferry terminals. In 2004, both governments began reinforcing IPFSC (International Port Facility Security Code). Under the agreement, both countries provide reciprocal recognition and acceptance to each other's approved vessel security plans, meaning, in practice U.S.-flagged vessels can meet the Canadian security specification, while U.S. Coast Guard can monitor the Canadian verification of foreign flagged vessels at the Port of Montréal as they enter the Great Lakes Saint Lawrence Seaway system.[15]

Both governments have also established a joint-program, commonly known as FAST. The program, designed for prescreened carriers and drivers to expedite the movement of low-risk shipment across the border, has been operating at the 12 most high-volume border crossings along the Canada–U.S. border. By 2005, about 25,000 drivers were enrolled in the FAST program, with an additional 11,000 pending the interview portion of the "risk assessment" analysis. Facilitating cargo reporting, FAST provides advance information on shipments before they reach border customs officials, so that informed decisions can be made whether or not to examine them. As an extension of FAST, several pilot projects are underway to implement prior full clearance at specific border crossings. Known as VACIS, this procedure has already been installed at seven U.S. rail crossings, and two Canadian border crossings as of 2005.[16]

Canada–U.S. cooperation has also increased in the area of combating fraudulent travel documents, inspection of travel containers, and more vigorous law enforcement cooperation. Both countries have committed themselves to protecting the critical borderland infrastructure and promoting collaboration of security science. Furthermore, both Canada and the United States have decided to review their mutual obligations to international treaties and law, among other mutually beneficial international treaties.[17]

Greater securitization along the Canada–U.S. border means more technological upgrading, cross-border inspection, manpower upliftment, and associated agreements involving governmental, nongovernmental, and private sector entities. But these have varied across major crossings along the long border. The Central Canada-Western Ontario-Michigan-Great Lakes Corridor has been more focused on the volume of trade, which is its central driving point. Indeed, agencies on both sides of the border have taken the primacy of that point into account and have worked to reduce the delay incurred in cargo and human crossings. Along this corridor, in other words, the security impetus has been incorporated into the existing "trade" primacy.[18]

Canada has also had to cope with the United States-led SEVIS and U.S.-VISIT programs.[19] The former intends to track foreign students enrolled at U.S. universities periodically and the latter tracks the movement of most Mexican and Canadian visitors in the United States.

Stemming from the Intelligence Reform and Terrorism Prevention Act of 2004, a WHTI requires all travelers from Canada and Mexico to present a passport or another form of secure documentation to enter the United States from January 1, 2007, a controversial measure whose implementation was delayed by at least one year. The Canadian government tried without success to stave off the program, while concerns prevail about how the new requirements might negatively affect cross-border travel, particularly U.S. tourists who will need a passport now upon reentry. Areas of frequent traffic such as Detroit-Windsor, and particularly tourist destinations, such as Vancouver, BC, and Niagara Falls, NY, remain most concerned.

It is important to note that many of the antecedents for greater control along the border have been in place since 1996, when the United States identified 10 high priority corridors for U.S.–Canada on-land trade and other traffic. Five of these links were through Ontario border crossings; most of the rest were in the western states, linking British Columbia with western United States and Alaska. In other words, by 2001, a hierarchy of border crossings already existed in terms of size and complexity of economic transaction. At the top were the main border crossings along the east, upper-midwest, and Pacific north-west corridors. Below them were a number of less important crossing points. Cross-border transactions along the more marginalized rural checkpoints, important for the border economies nonetheless, were localized. With undermanned Canadian posts, especially in rural areas, the United States continues to raise the pressure ante. In some cases, the posts are manned by just one person during a given shift. In addition, the United States has placed pressure on the

Canadian government to beef up the border enforcement capability of its officers. This effort dovetailed in 2006 with a series of incidents along Canadian borders, where suspected armed criminals attempted to cross the Canadian border. Since border security guards do not carry arms, they must summon the RCMP to try to catch up with the fleeing violator. As a result, in late 2006, the Harper government announced that it was going to move toward arming border security guards and increase personnel at border stations.

Ten priority corridors integrate economic structures between the United States and Canada. Even before 9/11, demands of the international economy had inspired both governments to invest over $US650 million on the Border Infrastructure Fund and the Strategic Highway Infrastructure Program.[20] The priority corridors had already installed high technology equipments to better coordinate speedy cross-border movements of cargo and people. In particular, several of these modernizing efforts focused on the provinces of Ontario, and the Pacific north-west corridor linking Blaine, WC and Douglas, BC.[21]

After NAFTA commenced in 1994, several institutional partnership organizations were created and put in place, not as a substitute to the integrative efforts of NAFTA, but rather to augment them through other bilateral arrangements between Canada and the United States. In particular, the SBP (Shared Border Process) was initiated in 1995, Canada–U.S. Partnership in 1999, and INS-CIC Border Vision and the Cross-Border Crime Forum were in place shortly before September 2001.[22]

In many ways, the new transportation, customs, and immigration requirements have facilitated what observers characterize the "securitization" of North America. But the implementation of the new measures across the areas of bilateral contact has indeed produced very interesting results.

Trade and Economic Integration

Canada and the United States are each other's main trading partners. Total U.S. trade with Canada grew from $US243 billion in 1994 to $US410 billion in 2000, registering an average annual growth rate of 8.9 percent.[23] In addition, Canada is also the largest trading partner for 38 of the 50 U.S. states, thus making it an important economic associate for many.[24] Several trends in the following tables address what the economic impact of post–9/11 security restrictions may be.

Table 5.1 shows that the total value of all U.S. imports from Canada in 2002 declined by 3.2 percent over 2001 and 9.5 percent over 2000. But by 2004, the total U.S. imports had eclipsed the 2000 figures by 10.8 percent. By 2005, the total import volume had increased by 25.5 percent over 2000 with a value of $US290 billion. Consequently, the total volume of 2002 U.S. exports to Canada in 2002 declined by 1.2 percent from 2001 and 10 percent from 2000. However, by 2004, the total value of all U.S. exports to Canada had eclipsed the peak of 2000 by 18.4 percent. By 2005, all U.S. exports to Canada have reached $US212.[25] Not only has the post-2001 decline been made up, but the pace of total trade also picked up, with Canada running consistent surpluses with its southern neighbor.

Table 5.1 Annual U.S. Imports From and Exports to Canada, 1995–2005 ($US billion, figures rounded up)

	1995	1996	1997	1998	1999	2000	2001	2002	2003	2004	2005
U.S. imports	144	156	167	173	199	231	216	209	222	256	290
U.S. exports	127	134	152	156	167	179	163	161	170	190	212

Source: U.S. Census Bureau, Foreign Trade Division, Data Dissemination Branch, Washington DC.

The investment figures mirror trade patterns. After a precipitous decline in FDI flows in 2002 and 2003, table 5.2 illustrates the volume recovery in both directions. In 2005, the Canadian FDI flow into the United States amounted to $US18.5 billion while the U.S. FDI flow into Canada amounted to $US22 billion.

Similar trends characterize FDI stocks, as table 5.3 indicates. Total FDI stocks recovered in both directions after the initial post–9/11 slowdown. By 2005, the total Canadian FDI stocks in the United States amounted to $US144 billion while the U.S. FDI stocks in Canada amounted to $US235 billion.

Movements of people and vehicles between countries make the border important, while the national economies depend on those flows. Table 5.4 reveals the total human traffic entering the United States as pedestrians and in buses, trains, and personal vehicles across the ten border states declined by 16.5 percent in 2005 over 2001. The decline was particularly high along the Vermont (–27.9 percent), Michigan (–24.5 percent), Idaho (–23.9 percent), and Washington (–19.4 percent) border crossings. The total number of about 67 million humans coming into the United States in 2005 is still far below the 95 million mark registered in 2000.

Table 5.5 shows a decline of 9.6 percent in the number of personal vehicles, buses and trucks coming into the United States from Canada. The largest decline was in Michigan (–13.3 percent), with the smallest decline in Alaska (–2.2 percent). The only modest increase was noted along the Maine crossings at 1.7 percent.

Table 5.2 Foreign Direct Investment Flows, 1999–2005 ($US billion)

FDI flow	1999	2000	2001	2002	2003	2004	2005
Canada-to-United States	26.4	27.3	9.2	2.9	3.2	29.8	18.5
United States-to-Canada	22.8	16.9	16.8	13.9	21.4	24.9	22.0

Source: Bureau of Economic Analysis (BEA), 2006.

Table 5.3 Foreign Direct Investment Stocks, 1999–2005 ($US billion)

FDI flow	1999	2000	2001	2002	2003	2004	2005
Canada-in-United States	91	114	92	93	96	126	144
United States-in-Canada	120	132	153	167	188	213	235

Source: Bureau of Economic Analysis (BEA), 2006.

Table 5.4 Number of Incoming Persons: Pedestrians, Passengers in Buses, Trains, and Personal Vehicles (by U.S. state) in U.S.–Canada border (in 000s)

State	1995	2000	2001	2002	2003	2004	2005	2001–05 percent change
AL	376	449	425	428	434	456	459	+8.0
ID	609	533	505	428	381	369	384	−23.9
ME	10,080	8,157	7,002	6,209	6,230	6,885	6,979	−0.3
MI	33,249	33,682	23,294	19,588	17,738	17,411	17,585	−24.5
MN	3,222	3,187	2,875	2,680	2,792	2,989	2,882	+0.2
MT	1,784	1,509	1,352	2,366	744	1,399	1,512	+11.8
ND	2,123	1,800	1,622	1,682	1,621	1,655	1,653	+1.9
NY	26,651	28,158	26,961	28,569	23,625	25,102	22,806	−15.4
VT	3,608	3,340	3,147	3,088	2,865	2,791	2,267	−27.9
WA	19,558	14,960	13,249	10,520	10,024	10,731	10,670	−19.4
Total	101,260	95,775	80,432	77,558	66,454	69,788	67,197	−16.5

Source: Bureau of Transportation Statistics, 1995–2005.

Altogether over 37 million vehicles crossed into the United States in 2005, the number was still far below the 44.5 million mark set in 1995. A 2007 study of personal vehicle traffic patterns in the ports of entry along the U.S.–Canada border by the Border Policy Research Institute suggests a diversity of border experiences along the length

Table 5.5 Number of Incoming Vehicles: Personal Vehicles, Buses, and Trucks (by U.S. status) on U.S.–Canadian Border Crossings (in 000s)

State	1995	2000	2001	2002	2003	2004	2005	2001–05 percent change
AL	144	138	137	134	136	138	134	−2.2
ID	295	269	255	244	219	213	219	−14.1
ME	4,801	4,448	4,001	3,585	3,622	4,087	4,068	+1.7
MI	13,359	14,700	13,464	12,702	11,839	11,752	11,670	−13.3
MN	1,245	1,238	1,180	1,074	1,130	1,159	1,097	−7.0
MT	695	697	678	643	580	631	626	−7.7
ND	1,016	979	957	954	914	950	940	−1.8
NY	12,266	12,900	12,554	12,941	11,658	11,376	11,102	−11.6
VT	1,887	1,931	1,819	1,836	1,745	1,771	1,762	−3.1
WA	8,738	6,853	6,210	5,499	5,262	5,644	5,673	−8.6
Total	44,446	44,153	41,255	39,612	37,105	37,721	37,291	−9.6

Source: Bureau of Transportation Statistics, 1995–2005.

of the border.[26] In other words, there is no single pattern observed at the ports of entry in the post–2003 period, by which time most of the new security features had been put in place.[27] The study points to two separate patterns. First, there has been significant post–9/11 effects (as well as post–2003 securitization) at the four mega ports of entry—Buffalo, Detroit, Blaine, and Port Huron—in terms of the traffic into the United States, which continues to decline, whereas in most of the medium and smaller ports of entry, the pattern has been one of increasing incoming traffic since 2003.[28]

The airline industry attracted considerable attention of the homeland security measures. Since many of the restrictions affected airline passengers, table 5.6 illuminates specific trends in that mode. The number of overnight travel by Canadian residents to the United States registered an increase of about 10 percent in 2005 over 2001. Those who traveled by air also registered a 10 percent increase, while Canadians traveling to United States for just a day registered a 7.7 percent decline. A much stronger decline of over 27 percent was registered for those Canadians traveling by air.

On the other hand, travel data for U.S. citizens going to Canada registered some interesting trends. Those traveling to Canada overnight by land registered a decline of over 7 percent, while those traveling overnight by air showed an increase of 3.5 percent in 2005 over 2001. But the largest decline was registered for those

Table 5.6 U.S.–Canadian Passenger Data, 1990–2005 (in 000s)

Canada–U.S. data	1990	1995	2000	2001	2002	2003	2004	2005
Canadian residents overnight travel to United States	17,263	14,663	14,667	13,527	13,024	12,666	13,857	14,862
By air	4,040	3,802	5,372	4,655	4,181	4,173	4,583	5,120
Canadian residents same day travel to United States	53,170	37,491	27,999	24,842	21,535	21,485	22,191	22,932
By air	136	138	103	95	57	53	57	69
U.S. residents overnight travel to Canada	12,252	13,005	15,189	15,570	16,167	14,232	15,088	14,391
By air	2,372	2,769	3,835	3,782	3,790	3,505	3,932	3,915
U.S. residents same day travel to Canada	22,482	24,325	28,805	27,301	24,711	21,277	19,539	17,264
By air	165	260	533	446	434	411	397	364

Source: North American Transportation Statistics data base, 1990–2005.

traveling by land to Canada for the day (36.7 percent), while those traveling for the day by air showed a decline of 18.3 percent in 2005 over 2001. Altogether, over 37 million Canadians traveled to the United States in 2005 for the same day or overnight, but about 32 million Americans returned the favor in 2005. Extended security checks at the border crossings and at airports probably explain some of the declines.

Some of the declines may have been correlated with declining number of inspections. As table 5.7 illustrates, only 78.5 million inspections were registered at the Canadian border crossings in 2004, while the corresponding number was 100 million in 2001, a decline of 21.5 percent. Inspections at all ports of entry also declined.

These absolute figures have their limitations, however. For example, border crossing figures do not register delays at checkpoints or in transit, which push up costs. Even five years after 9/11, as some have noted, the average time for a truck crossing the border has been slower than before. A 2004 survey by Supply Chain and Logistics Canada and Industry Canada found that 82 percent of the companies reported greater delay at border crossings compared to 9/11, and that these have impacted negatively on their earnings.[29] Of those surveyed, only 35 percent reported having obtained the certification clearance under FAST or similar program across the border.

Studies on the amount of delays produce other interesting findings. For example, economic models show the post–9/11 security measures have contributed to less than expected increase in overall trade. In the absence of these security measures, the overall trade would have been higher by 19 percent in 2002, 26 percent in 2003, and 18 percent in 2004.[30] Of course, these declines cannot be attributed to the new measures alone, but there is no doubt that they played a critical role in the process. Overall, more needs to be done to augment the institutional capacity building and implementation that has been in place since 9/11.[31] More recent empirical studies verify the rising transactions costs of doing business across the border. In an extensive survey of U.S. and Canadian exporters around the Buffalo, NY, area in 2004, Alan D. MacPherson, et al., found evidence of a decline in crossings, and that firms involved in Canada–U.S. trade face higher costs.[32] Canadian exporters have been harder hit than their U.S. counterparts. The amount of paperwork and

Table 5.7 Inspections at U.S. Ports of Entry, 1999–2004 (in million)

	1999	2000	2001	2002	2003	2004
All ports of entry	525.2	534.2	510.6	444.7	427.7	428.9
Land ports of entry	435.3	437.9	414.4	358.4	338.6	333.3
Canadian border	115.9	113.9	100.0	84.0	79.2	78.5
Land inspection as percent of all inspections	82.9	82.0	81.2	80.6	79.2	77.7

Source: DHS, Office of Immigration Statistics, *Performance Analysis System* (PAS) G-22.1.

preparatory effort have led to the mushrooming of new trade services and consulting firms designed to deal with these aspects for a fee.

It is difficult to separate bilateral cooperation efforts and data from the perceptual domain where considerable differences remain. The perceptions have varied about the amount of danger lying ahead. According to official U.S. thinking, the protection of the border on the south side is the U.S. government's responsibility, and that of the north is that of Canada's; in reality, though, much collaboration is needed to make the border regulations less taxing for the movement of goods, services, and people.[33] Both countries, despite the pre–9/11 efforts to expedite economic goods across the main transit points, have had difficulty in fighting the difference in perception of defining what constitutes a threat for operational purposes.

Foreign and Military Policy

Canadian entities have been quite interested in retaining easy access and mobility across the border even under heightened border security, while American negotiators have been much more interested in protecting the border from external threat. A closed United States would disastrously impact Canada. It would be difficult for Canadians to compete within the global economy after 9/11 without cooperation across the border with the United States. In a cultural imagery of "us against them" in the post–9/11 era, Canadians feel increasingly uncomfortable, and some have evoked national sovereignty in their response to U.S. aggressiveness in insisting greater border security.

But the U.S. view of the border has been supported by many from within Canada as well.[34] The image in the United States that Canadian government is weak so it must change its policies and behavior has also gained currency among elements in Canadian society. Changes in Canadian official policy have reflected this in the sense that the crisis in the United States is also in a way Canada's. These considerations have prompted many innovative responses and changes in governmental behavior.

In military matters, Canada has been a part of NORAD since 1958. NORAD's original mission of guarding against the threat of Soviet bombers during the Cold War has been redirected to combat the new security threats.[35] In addition, Canada has been a member of the NATO and has been historically active in many UN peacekeeping operations around the world.[36] It has also been participating in the military operations in Afghanistan under NATO command, supervising, as it does, a risky southern province where its casualties approach the three-figure mark in 2008. It has also been active in the reconstruction of Iraq by providing monetary and technical support.[37]

Despite the Canadian official preference for diplomatic solutions, the country has been a member of the Defence Ministerial of the Americas, the Inter-IANC, the Conference of the Armies of the Americas, and the hemisphere-wide reporting on Confidence and Security Building Measures. In Fall 2002, Canada joined the Inter-American Defence Board, which promotes cooperative security interests in the Western Hemisphere under authority of the OAS (Organization of American States).[38] U.S. NORTHCOM, organized in 2002, has the Canadian airspace under its supervision but has generated sensitive political debate about Canadian sovereignty.[39]

The Canadian dilemma of whether to support U.S. military policy in Iraq has been sustained by several hard facts. First, Canada has had a long standing commitment to using multilateral forums to resolve international disputes. Second, historically it has enjoyed a long, relatively open border with the United States, sustaining a vibrant economic partnership. Canada's preference for the use of multilateral institutions to resolve international conflicts has been well recorded.[40] But successive Canadian governments have periodically cooperated with the United States in armed campaigns abroad, although they have done so only grudgingly. In that respect, the recent Canadian cooperation in the campaign against the *Taliban* and *al Qaeda* in Afghanistan and the recent collaborative efforts in the Iraqi reconstruction efforts are noteworthy. As noted in chapter 3, the new Harper government's aggressive policies and budget shifts represent a significant proactive shift in Canadian foreign policy against terrorism—a movement away from the Canada-as-peacekeeper-and-multilateralist symbol.

Many scholars of U.S. security policy attribute this divergence to stark hard-power differences.[41] According to the World Bank, the Canadian economy is about 2.2 percent of the world economy. With 31 million people, the ratio of the size of the economy to the population is 0.071 (2.2/31). Compared to this, the U.S. economy is about one-third of the world economy (32.6 percent), while it caters to a population slightly over 300 million. The corresponding ratio for the United States amounts to 0.108 (32.6/300), a much more favorable ratio indicating a more solid hard-power base. While the United States possesses about ten times the population of Canada, its economy is 14.8 times larger than the Canadian economy.[42] Of course, this asymmetry in hard power becomes much too large to ignore if the preponderance of the U.S. military power is taken into account. For the record, Canada's military expenditures account for only 2.6 percent of what the United States spends on defence.[43]

After Gulf War I, U.S. military spending declined somewhat until 2000, but in the aftermath of 9/11, it has increased significantly. Based on 2003 estimates, the U.S. military spending is now about 40–45 percent of the world military spending.[44] This asymmetry in economic and military power does not end with Canada. The United States enjoys a disproportionate amount of advantage *vis-à-vis* every other country or a combination of major powers, though concerns about the growing Chinese strength loom large.

Despite the ideological differences in the use of military might in world affairs Canada's economic dependence on the U.S. market dwarfs most other considerations. The United States is the destination for more than 80 percent of all Canadian exports, leaving it vulnerable to possible reprisal from Washington. Pronouncements by prominent Canadian politicians ominously portray these economic stakes.[45]

OF THE BUTCHER, BAKER, AND POLICY-MAKER: INTELLIGENCE COMMUNITIES CONVERGING?[46]

Three subsections compare the two countries in terms of orientations, institutions, and IC dynamics. All three show compatibilities and convergences, but also distinct identities: Whether push comes to shove or not, for both countries cooperation is more likely than not owing to inherent compatibilities and some lasting Anglo-Saxon values; yet how they go about their tasks and both the policy-making environments and resource constraints they face are quite dissimilar.[47]

Thomas Hughes's role orientations offer interesting and useful perspectives. Does intelligence in the two countries play the role of the butcher (keeping intelligence a permanently top-priority concern), baker (formulating consistently high levels of intelligence expenditures), or policy-maker (whose multiple tasks run across the entire spectrum, from the drawing board to the trenches)?[48] Our findings include the following: (a) Canada as the butcher and the United States playing the policy-maker role and (b) both roles being a function of local military cultures and positionings in the international system.

Orientations and Intelligence

Similar security portraits can still produce different outcomes. Winn L. Taplin's definition as consisting "of the collection, analysis, evaluation, and dissemination of information for 'positive' intelligence and counterintelligence and the conduct of Special Activities (covert action)" highlights the pivotal role of its norms.[49] Of course, with the Bush Doctrine raising preemption to a state of the art and terrorism imposing an invisible enemy, positive intelligence no longer suffices; deriving intelligence by hook or by crook as and when needed, and selling it as a real or manufactured product, opens space for what might be called a negative counterpart. Where to draw the line might be the emerging tantalizing question. Nevertheless, Taplin's six general principles in table 5.8 offer a sufficient premise to initiate Canadian–U.S. comparisons.

Nuances, rather than contrasts, riddle the picture. Intelligence derives from international conflict or rivalry for both countries, as the first dimension acknowledges. Canada's intelligence industry began formally after World War I, under a domestic police agency, the RCMP. On the other hand, U.S. agencies, led by the FBI, also began with a domestic agenda only to shift attention abroad during World War II, first under the OSS (Office of Strategic Services) from 1942, and ultimately under the CIA from 1947. Describing both Canada and the United States as security states,[50] Steve Hewitt traces their "perceived domestic threats," not to "hunts for alleged spies," but to "worker and immigrant groups," with "a campaign, inspired by ethnic and class prejudice."[51] Among RCMP's first targets were Russians and other Germans escaping the Soviet revolution and the World War, not directly to Canada, but through the United States. Interestingly, President Franklin D. Roosevelt also instructed FBI Director, J. Edgar Hoover, as early as in 1936 to shift

Table 5.8 Intelligence Principles and Canada–U.S. Comparisons

Principles	Canada	United States
1. Intelligence derives from international conflict or rivalry	Both domestic and international	Domestic origin, international shift, two-flank post–9/11 orientation
2. Conduct or use of intelligence involves secrecy	True	True
3. Clandestine collection of information is the fundamental activity of intelligence	True	True
4. Truth must be the basis of good intelligence	Not always true	Not always true
5. Intelligence in a vacuum is of no value, tardy intelligence is of little value	True	True
6. Special activities must involve native knowledge of the national groups toward which they are directed	Domestically true, not so abroad	True, but by trials and errors internationally

Adapted from Winn L. Taplin, "Six general principles of intelligence," *International Journal of Intelligence and Counterintelligence* 3, no. 4 (1989): 475–91.

attention to "particularly Fascism and Communism" two largely international issues, albeit with domestic implications.[52] While Canada's domestic orientation served British war strategies through World War II, internationalizing the U.S. orientation by subsequently creating the CIA, also extended the FBI's domestic tools and treatments abroad.[53] Even though the DHS centralizes management of both fronts today, the CIA and FBI continue with their overlapping and conflictual mandates independently.

Both Canadian and U.S. orientations bred secrecy and clandestine operations, Taplin's second and third principles. While the RCMP centralized these efforts from the start, which was unusual for a country so decentralized in many other ways, U.S. decentralization was dictated by both size and the constitutional separation of powers. Both the FBI and CIA emerged from amateurish predecessors, the former through the Department of Justice's Bureau of Investigation from 1908, and the latter from the OSS in 1942. Their relationship "was hindered by cultural differences, rivalries, security concerns, legal separation, and jurisdictional 'twilight zones'" from the very start:[54] Whereas the FBI was entrusted to enforce law by catching criminals and showing force, the CIA's more open-ended role was to promote "strategic understanding," meaning finding policy-relevant information while lying low. "For co-operation to succeed," Frederick P. Hitz and Brian J. Weiss argue, both "must become more open and more flexible," not centralized nor necessarily reorganized, since their critical resource, information, becomes meaningless without analysis.

Clandestine operations became increasingly difficult for both, given legislative oversights. Nevertheless, as Stuart Farson notes, both Canada's inheritance of secrecy from Great Britain and the U.S. preference for deference sheltered the former from legislative orders-in-councils, which literally prevents debate, and the latter from benign neglect,[55] until scandals shook both. With Canada's parliamentary culture imposing further impediments and 9/11 restoring U.S. deference, oversight exercises in both countries fall considerably short. When the issue is security, parliamentary question periods become "highly melodramatic and theatrical" and parliamentary debates "usually superficial," in Roy Rempel's views.[56] In the United States, cause-effect relations often get obscured or swamped by attitudes or agency sclerosis. As Melvyn A. Goodman observed, after Pearl Harbor, President Franklin D. Roosevelt appointed a military and civilian commission to examine how and why the attacks could not be anticipated, but after 9/11, "President George W. Bush, CIA Director George Tenet and the chairmen of the Senate and House intelligence committees were adamantly opposed to any investigation or postmortem."[57] Even when an investigation began in June 2002, the automatic participation of CIA Inspector General, Brito Snider, was denied; but placing the review under the FBI challenged separation of power principles and practices.

Both the fourth and fifth principles, emphasizing the penchant for truth as well as the worthlessness of intelligence in a vacuum or late intelligence, respectively, were meant to be broken: no cloak-and-dagger exercise prioritizes honesty, and fabricating much-needed information, under pressure, is not uncommon. Both the CIA and FBI in the United States and Canada's RCMP raised deviations to new levels. Canadian Prime Minister Lester Pearson was forced to appoint the MRC (Mackenzie Royal Commission) in 1966 to investigate RCMP university surveillance techniques, and Pierre Trudeau's 1981 MC (McDonald Commission) investigated the more serious charges of the RCMP's Security Service Division "planting bombs, burning barns, stealing documents, intimidating sources," and so forth.[58] In the United States, the WMD rationale launching the March 2003 Iraqi invasion was clearly based, not on erroneous, but deliberately false, information.[59]

Taplin's last principle also bears the nuanced stamp of the first—availability of native knowledge. Unique among western powers, Canada does not have any foreign intelligence service,[60] thus "native knowledge" abroad receives less attention. During the Cold War and after, however, three high-profile cases revealed RCMP ineptness and backfiring ingenuity: Igor Guezenko's 1946 revelation of Soviet espionage in Canada, under the very noses of the RCMP; creating what Reg Whitaker calls "abstract files" during the Cold War of supposed "spies who might have been," leading the distinguished historian and diplomat, E. Herbert Norman, to commit suicide in April 1957 against false charges;[61] and the supply of false information, either by the CSIS, created in 1984 as recommended by the MC, or RCMP, on Maher Arar, a Canadian citizen of Syrian origin, to U.S. intelligence, leading to his U.S. arrest, deportation to Syria, and arrest and torture in Syria, before being freed and compensated by the Canadian government in 2007.

U.S. flaws have been no less dramatic and frequent. They constantly pop up in Afghanistan and Iraq currently, where native knowledge is based on grand or false assumptions, such as Ahmad Chalabi vouching U.S. troops would be feted by Iraqis for removing Saddam Hussein, rather than prior knowledge through training. Even before intelligence studies became fashionable, Roger Hilsman, Jr.'s "picture-puzzle analogy," distinguishing "a lifetime of dealing with realities" from "a lifetime habit of dealing with libraries," seems to have gone out of style.[62] Producing specialized experts, rather than training special forces, goes farther in filling such gaps, but relying on trials-and-errors reduces policy outcomes and CIA reputation. Even the CIA's country-study reports, often written by off-shore experts addressing off-shore publics, ignore local perspectives, breed misperceptions, and produce bad policies.

Principles aside, ideas and norms also shape orientations. Donald Snow's recent specifications of the various forces behind strategic culture, illustrates the argument.[63] We extend his treatment of the United States to Canada to not only level the comparative playing field, but also shed light why the two countries, even with so many similarities, differ critically. Table 5.9 compares Snow's two categories of *forces:* background (or conditioning) influences, and direct strategic culture impacts, and paves the way for a comparison of norms in table 5.10.

Both Canada and the United States share plenty over the three background influences: a sense of history, geographical endowment, and cultural heritage. Yet, Britain's Canadian engagement and U.S. absence makes a difference. Institutionalizing intelligence is of recent origin in both countries. Still Edward F. Sayle convincingly

Table 5.9 Elements of Strategic Culture and Mexico–U.S. Comparisons

Categories	Canada	United States
Background Influences:		
1. Sense of History:	1. Goes relatively deeper given Britain's role	1. Relatively shallow
2. Geographical Endowment	2. Neighbor of superpower, but British links	2. Absence of a European-type hostile neighbor context
3. Cultural Heritage	3. Anglo-Saxon	3. Anglo-Saxon
Factors Directly Affecting Strategic Culture:		
1. Democratic Institutions	1. Yes, from the start	1. Yes, from the start
2. Role of Media	2. Constant influence	2. Constant influence
3. Suspicion of Government/Military	3. Yes: stems from colonial and national divisions	3. Yes, but for constitutional reasons
4. Mobilization-Demobilization Pattern	4. Prevails	4. Prevails
5. Notion of Invincibility	5. Not really	5. Yes, from the start
6. Preference for Total Wars	6. No preference for any wars	6. Yes, after World War II and in nuclear age
7. Tradition of Citizen-Soldier	7. Not at all	7. Not really a factor nor a tradition

Source: Donald Snow, *National Security: Defence Policy for a New International Era* (New York, NY: St. Martin's Press, 1995), 42–65.

Table 5.10 Intelligence and Institutional Norms: Canada–U.S. Comparisons

Institutional norms	Canada	United States
1. Institutional survival	Prevails	Prevails
2. Secrecy	Prevails	Prevails
3. Intelligence exceptionalism	To an extent, yes	Increasingly yes
4. Ambiguous mandate	Yes	Yes
5. Confederal structure	More centralizad	Yes
6. Flexible accountability	Increasing pressures to	Yes
7. Separation of intelligence from law enforcement (police)	Mixed	Yes
8. Competitive intelligence	Yes	Yes
9. Separation of intelligence from policy	Increasingly so	Increasingly no
10. Policy support	Largely	Yes
11. Can-do attitude	Not really	Yes
12. Primacy of intelligence analysis	Not really	Yes, increasingly
13. Emphasis on current intelligence	Yes	Yes
14. Provision for accurate, timely, and relevant intelligence	Yes	Yes

Source: Michael A. Turner, "A Distinctive U.S. Intelligence Identity," *International Journal of Intelligence and Counterintelligence* 17, no. 1 (2004): 49; but see 42–61.

and energetically traces U.S. intelligence back to the founding fathers, explicitly identifying the first president, George Washington, as "the manager of intelligence" in 1790.[64] Canadian eyes and ears were also opened from the very moment the British North American Confederation was established in 1867. The U.S. Fenian Brotherhood, relishing the defeat of the British-supported U.S. South in the civil war, threatened to take Canada from Britain to liberate Ireland.[65] Not much came of these initial intelligence-necessitating occasions, since state-building became the priority in both countries. Building democratic states, however,[66] impinged upon intelligence.

Geography and culture contradicted each other: the former kept the New World far from Old World entanglements; while Anglo-Saxon ties brought the two together. Without the hostile West European neighborhood, U.S. intelligence evolved without urgency, but Canada, sharing the same disposition, had to absorb Britain's European preoccupations. Secrecy, drama, and celluloid portrayals, as Mark Phythian points out,[67] became part of the intelligence folklore; and as British–U.S. cooperation increased in the early twentieth century,[68] these traits acquired an Anglo-Saxon tone. Canada depicted them more directly than the United States.

The seven factors directly influencing strategic culture depicted more similarities than differences. With democratization producing institutions more or less simultaneously in the two countries, the media became an early and constant watchdog. Citizens kept abreast of developments, the attention given was a function of how dramatic they were, but they kept a distance from the government and the military. This was more a consequence of constitutional politics in the United States, going back to the founding fathers, while in Canada field politics proved more influential. Neither the Indians nor French were warm about the Anglo-Saxon government, while the steady stream of immigrants over time reduced identity with the government even more. On the other hand, western Canadians were too far from, and never too comfortable with, the federal government, reflecting, as they frequently complain, a bunch of extraneous, sometimes unCanadian eastern interests.

Since democracy and the military do not always move in sync, as previously discussed, after participation in any war, pressure builds to demobilize the military quickly. Increasing reliance on a voluntary force may be the future wave in democracies, as in Canada and United States now. On the other hand, the fifth dimension invincibility is relevant only for the United States. Even in the 1830s, Alexis de Tocqueville predicted the United States would become a world power, sowing the seeds of the invicibility that became twentieth-century-reality; but since Canada never really sought global leadership under Britain's influence or on its own, it was perfectly happy to remain secluded, eventually to play a secondary role to the United States. Thus, Canada never developed the sixth characteristic of preparing for a total war, unlike the United States after World War II, when the communist and terrorist threats successively necessitated what George F. Kennan proposed against the Soviet Union, a "long-term, patient but firm and vigilant" approach.[69] Interestingly, both countries lack a citizen-soldier tradition, the seventh feature, in spite of an expanding U.S. military-industrial complex, which Canada does not claim on such a grand scale.

In a recent study of U.S. intelligence, Michael A. Turner identified a number of norms, which table 5.10 lists and applies to Canada as well. They reinforce the mixed comparative findings of table 5.9. Among the similarities, both Canada and the United States believe in secrecy (second norm), give intelligence an exceptional status in governmental affairs (third), grapple with the ambiguities of the intelligence mandate (fourth), face increasingly flexible accountability (sixth), facilitate a competitive intelligence industry, given the multiple agencies involved (eighth), and utilize intelligence to support policies (tenth).

Differences stem less from the process of intelligence-making than from geographical and demographical constraints. Given its sparse population over a huge chunk of territory, much of it uninhabitable, Canada cannot but survive in a confederal system, and although the United States is almost as large, a more hospitable climate permits integrative infrastructures, its far larger population provides military depth, and its greater engagements in foreign wars built not just one capable and substantial military institution, but several. Thus, as the fifth dimension notes, centralizing U.S. tendencies contrast Canada's decentralized patterns. Similarly in the seventh dimension, which recognizes Canada's intelligence springing from a law enforcement background (Royal North West Mounted Police [RNWMP] and DP), it acquired and finessed the infrastructure of conducting espionage; while in the United States, the CIA–FBI tussle at the very outset confirmed a long-term separation of police and intelligence functions.

Whereas politicians increasingly keep a distance from intelligence agencies in Canada (ninth), for political or other reasons, with homeland security, the United States is reducing that distance between intelligence activities and policy-making. Intelligence is also being accepted by the U.S. public as a necessary evil, whereas in Canada, it is largely seen just as an evil. As George W. Bush informed Congress on September 20, 2001, he would "lead, oversee, and coordinate a comprehensive strategy" under the OHS,[70] his message found receptive U.S. ears, but one a Canadian leader would probably not emit to Canadians. Given the background influences and sources/nature of threat, intelligence agencies in the United States increasingly show a can-do attitude (eleventh), what outsiders dub a gung-ho approach. They vie for policy-making primacy post–9/11 (twelfth), emphasize concurrent intelligence (thirteenth), and prioritize the timely availability of accurate and relevant information (fourteenth). Canada has neither the intention nor the infrastructures to evince a can-do attitude, while intelligence remains a subordinate activity. Satisfying both the thirteenth and fourteenth norms reveals another fundamental feature of Canadian intelligence: It cooperates silently and ungrudgingly with its U.S. counterparts, as evident in neutralizing the possible terrorist plot near Toronto during June 2006 through coordinated arrests of several suspects.

Institutionalization and the Intelligence Community

Turner's application of IR (international relations) theories to intelligence offers a meaningful start to this institutional Canada–U.S. comparison. Recognizing how the realist and constructivist schools of IR thought may respectively be reduced to interest and power relations, on the one hand, and norms and identities, on the other, Turner's argument of "strategic culture" evolving only through a historical process applies to both Canada and the United States:[71] Both had roughly parallel growth, but nuances may be found even through theoretical lenses. Although he identifies the United States fulfilling the realist criteria and fitting into that framework better,[72] we argue that, over time, it has shifted in the constructivist direction, since continuity and cumulative growth create the longer historical process for the norms and identities of an IC, as well as bedfellows through trials and errors. Canada fits the constructivist IR paradigm even better owing to a longer cumulation, but we also argue that Canada's IC shows signs of consociationalist mediating patterns:[73] elites capable of accomodating diverging preferences, implying both secrecy and a competitive field,[74] as well as transcending cleavages to preserve larger interests against fears and costs of political fragmentation. Given Canada's parliamentary system, with its fusion of powers, as opposed to the U.S. separation, even though Canada is littered with competitive intelligence agencies,[75] political leaders have been able to prevent guerrilla warfare among them to preserve Canadian unity, perhaps through side-payments or other clandestine concessions.

To understand the IC, though, we first turn to Thomas F. Troy. Defining it as "the collection of those entities loosely knitted together by a number of committees," he identifies the U.S. DCI, a position broader and higher than Director of CIA, as the head of this collection from as far back as July 1947.[76] Since then, the U.S. IC was neglected, with even the DCI hardly more powerful in 1976 than in 1947.[77] Growth at the base has not deepened authority at the top, again probably the result of agency rivalries. Canada is not only comparable, but also offers an arguably tighter IC owing to the centralizing efforts of political leaders. There is no Canadian counterpart to the DCI, thus softening theoretical linkages, but intelligence, lacking a parliamentary constituency, has rarely reached the commanding heights of Canada's consociationalist policy agenda. Whereas DHS centralization enhances presidential control and seemingly reassures the public, Canada's CSIS is constantly debated in the public, thus preventing not only politicians from claiming ownership, but also reforms from being effectively undertaken.

Of course, 1947 was not the start of the U.S. IC.[78] Seeds of the current "Big Three" were sown by the original "Big Three" from the 1880s: the ONI (Office of Naval Intelligence) was created in 1882 by the Bureau of Navigation, only to be incorporated by the Chief of Naval Operations by World War I; the U.S. army matched this by creating the Division of Military Information in 1885 under the Miscellaneous Branch of the Adjutant's General Office, eventually becoming the Military Intelligence Division, or G2, by the end of World War I; and the Department of Justice founded the Bureau of Investigation in 1908, later to become the FBI. Perhaps the most powerful FBI director, J. Edgar Hoover, coordinated all three agencies, ONI, G2, and FBI. Yet, by World War II, when Troy counted more than 50 agencies collecting intelligence, the DOS rose to prominence after creating its own OSS, which also controlled the Office of War Information and Board of Economic Warfare.[79] Troy notes how all these agencies (a) were both independent and insulated, (b) belonged to a larger uncoordinated whole, and (c) had a specific chain of command.[80]

Even before President Harry S Truman's 1947 National Security Act created its own Big Three,[81] he experimented with the NIA (National Intelligence Authority), DCI, and CIG (Central Intelligence Group) from January 22, 1946. Major General William J. "Wild Bill" Donovan, head of OSS, campaigned against the three 1946 institutions, blaming the CIG for lacking "civilian control and independence," and the NIA for being no more than "a debating society."[82] With the National Security Act, NIA became the NSC, DCI was made a civilian post, and the CIG became the CIA. According to Troy, the CIA's IC included all of the following: the CIA itself, departments of State, Energy, and Treasury, the FBI, DIA (Defence Intelligence Agency), National Security Agency, army intelligence, navy intelligence, air force intelligence, Marine Corp intelligence, and various offices in the defence department. Over 80 percent of these, he contends, belonged to the DOD. As one can see, quite a network evolved, but with it came compartmentalization, and thereby an IC not fully serving as a community. In Hughes's terms, one might argue the U.S. intelligence system was filled with butchers, bakers, and policy-makers even before 9/11; after 9/11 the fear is not the absence of relevant actors nor the constraints of congressmen, but the coordination of the many.

Canada's institutional experiences were similar, but the threat was not (a) from abroad; (b) significant enough; or (c) capable of over-riding preponderant U.S. influences. Although scarred by scandals from at least 1946, the RCMP continues to remain as obstreperous after 9/11 as it was heavy-handed after World War I with East Europeans and trade unionists. From 1984 it faced new competition from the CSIS. The division of labor between the two is as unclear as between the FBI and CIA; but unlike their U.S. counterparts, both RCMP and CSIS escape legislative oversight, inspite of repeated claims of both transparency and accountability. Their political subordination is as complete as the independence and influence of the FBI, CIA, and now DHS.

The CSIS Act also created the SIRC, an independent external review body, with three to five members, all sworn Privy Councilors, and appointed by the prime minister on the basis of consultation with all political parties—yet another consociationalist pattern. Its budget allocations, however, rarely allow more than three SIRC members and a staff of only 16,[83] thus handicapping any meaningful oversight. Clearly, Canadian intelligence is too financially constrained to play the baker's role, thus leaving just the butcher (RCMP) to hold the fort.

In addition, the CSIS must report to the SG through the IG (Inspector General), while Parliament has its own OAG (Office of the Auditor General) also reviewing CSIS. Accountability and oversight are not review functions,[84] as Farson points out, while parliamentary procedures prove counterproductive. For example, fears of antagonizing the prime minister encourage play-safe approaches in the question-period, while security and intelligence generally receive a lower agenda placement. Canada lacks even the theoretical foundations of the U.S. Congress in bringing intelligence agencies to task.

After 9/11, a new, more centralized legislation, Bill C-36, upgraded intelligence: By making terrorism a crime, it enhanced RCMP power, while the CSE was authorized to intercept communications. When Chrétien resigned in 2003, Paul Martin elevated the security and intelligence portfolio, directly placing it as a deputy prime minister portfolio under the PCO.[85] It also spawned public debates over the extent of interrogative intrusiveness, rights curtailment, and so forth. Yet the underlying question still remains if the skeletons will come out of the Canadian closets.

The U.S. 9/11 responses also entailed breathtaking changes; but even though DHS exerts more influence over the IC, it still does not control all intelligence agencies, the CIA and FBI being notable exceptions. In between 1947 and 2001, Troy found at least four clusters, or subcommittees: (a) the DCI managing the Secretariat, counterintelligence, planning and policy, programming and budgeting, and eight committees; (b) the National Foreign Intelligence Board, though under the DCI, managing the same eight committees in addition to five others; (c) the National Intelligence Council filled with analytical groups; and (d) the Intelligence Producers Council. While the DCI managed this CI, in 1953, Congress created the Deputy DCI to run the agency itself, creating two institutionalized streams.[86]

IC development is also affected by policy-makers bringing different idiosyncrasies. Taking the NSC as an example, Cecil V. Crabb and Kevin V. Mulcahy show how four different roles can emerge by mixing policy-making responsibility (PMR, that is, drawing-board functions) and implementation duties (ID, or trench activities) along high and low saliences. Henry Kissinger exemplifies high PMR and high ID; Walt Whitman Rostow the mixture of high PMR but low ID; Robert McFarlane the converse picture of high ID but low PMR; and Colin Powell and Brent Scowcroft of low PMR and low ID.[87]

Whether the National Security Advisor's role is administrator, counselor, coordinator, or agent, we return where we began, to roles. Within the IC, Hastedt finds at least five types of loyalties: to the president, profession and organization, a political cause, the law, and to the congress and public. During the Cold War, he found Allen Dulles (1953–61) and Richard Helms (1966–73) reflecting loyalty to the CIA; William Casey (1981–87) to a political cause, in this case, the Reagan revolution; and John McCone (1961–65) to a mixture of law (legislation) as well as congress and public.[88] After 9/11, we argue, the third (political cause) may get greater emphasis than the fourth and fifth (the law, Congress and the public), in the United States, in spite of increasing accountability and personnel changes. Applying these to Canada dramatizes the different professional and political cultures: the butcher, baker, and policy-maker can converge in the United States but not in Canada; and the political difference between the fusion of power, which should promote that convergence, and a separation of power, which should encourage divergence, could be a big reason why.

THEORETICAL PRECEPTS AND EVALUATIONS

Canada's balancing game between its foreign and military policy goals and the economic imperatives profoundly impact the extent to which the various neofunctional attributes can be assessed. Although huge economic asymmetry remains, governmental change alters the political will. Under Steve Harper's Conservative Party alliance government, much more conciliatory gestures have been made in the security arena. Several cooperative provisions under the "smart border" agreement have indeed created a regional institutional base whose dynamics cannot remain purely national. Yet, if integration is evolving, how do we describe it?

Integrative tenets (both neofunctionalism and security community) should find more relevance. Increasing interaction through new fora, organizations, and task forces can only enhance greater elite complementarity between the two countries and bode economically well, as a neofunctionalist explanation would posit, and as table 5.11 summarizes. Spillover is expanding, as too transactions, intergovernmentalism, and transnational growth. Converging perceptions of specific foreign policy issues as well, in particular North Korea and Iran, remain opportunities for the Harper government. Though it is ideologically similar to Bush's government, conservatism is not exactly alike in the two countries, where nationalism also evokes quite discordant sentiments against each other (over tariffs, for example). Increases

Table 5.11 Neofunctional Attributes Five Years After 9/11: Canada–U.S. Relations

Dimension	Canada–United States
1. Economic symmetry	Much asymmetry still remains; the ratio of the U.S.–Canadian economies in terms of the size is 7:1
2. Elite complementarity	Greater complementarity under Prime Minister Harper than under Chrétien
3. Pluralism	Broader disagreement over foreign policy goals still remain but practical concerns have led to instrumental agreements and implementation of several institutional features
4. Capacity to adapt	In the immediate aftermath of 9/11, reaction was limited; but since then, the pace has picked up; a greater convergence of practical concerns over terrorism has closed the bilateral expectation gaps
5. Spillover	Robust spillover; the internal bifurcation of sentiments over the U.S. posture after 9/11 has largely subsided
6. Growing transaction	The extent of total economic transaction has actually exceeded the pre–9/11 peaks in 2004–05 and growing
7. Growth in inter-governmentalism	Expansion under NAFTA; continues alter 9/11 through intelligence agencies
8. Transnational growth	Has grown with a short decline after 9/11, as a response to the U.S. policies but also as a response to growing globalization
9. Elite socialization	Greater historical socialization between United States and Canadian elites continues
10. Growth in ideological identity	Is much more sector specific in developing a generally common ideological identity with the United States
11. Increasing interaction with external actors	Greater interaction with Mexico in areas of technology, security information and patents, and NATO participation in Afghanistan
12. Benefit distribution higher an more equitable	Since 9/11 the cost of border transaction increased in the immediate aftermath but is progressively declining (though still higher than pre–9/11 days)
13. Converging perceptions of external problems	Issue-specific convergence higher on North Korea, Iran, and the general treatment of terrorism, but grudging acceptance of the inconvenience of economic dependency with the United States
14. Integration as cost free	Although economic transaction levels have now exceeded the pre–9/11 levels, much greater social and infrastructural cost is incurred

in defence spending seek to repair Canadian military capabilities which had deteriorated over the last decade under the Liberal governments.

Table 5.12 echoes similar patterns and directions for basic security community tenets.[89] With values as their bedrock, 9/11 helped the two countries deepen and more and extend ties, even making values the linchpin of the bilateral relation.

Canada inevitably embraced U.S. pursuits, and the United States inevitably switched special friendship from Mexico back to Canada. Two events mark that transition markedly: George W. Bush violated the traditional inaugural foreign visit of U.S. presidents to Ottawa to reaffirm the bilateral relationship in 2001 by going to

Table 5.12 Security Community, Canada–U.S. Relations, and 9/11 Impacts

Dimension	Descriptions
1. Value compatibility	Never in doubt: differences are political, not over values, such as democracy, economic liberalism, and even between intelligence agencies, though perhaps not over military culture
2. Enhanced predictability	A diminishing factor, not because of mutual relations, but by how external developments increasingly impinge those relations
3. Mutual responsiveness	Increasing function under Harper and Bush; but never low enough to create concerns, not even between Chrétien and Bush
4. Value complementarity	Increasingly so after an initial post–9/11 dip; most evident through new institutions created after 9/11
5. Distinctiveness in lifestyles	Governmental (fusion versus separation of power) and security culture (leader versus follower) very different in the two countries, but easily compensated by value complementarity (in #4), and many sociocultural economic, and philosophical similarities
6. Reward expectations before integration	Not at all attempted with security, nor evident before, over security: *with or against us* as a rallying call serves as a stick, not a carrot
7. Increasing political and administrative functions	Yes, very much so; increasing function over 9/11, and not necessarily because of 9/11
8. Economic growth distinguishing core from periphery	Yes, some areas (two coasts) benefit more from economic integration than others; but also Canada increasingly becoming less core than periphery of United States, given its increasing economic and security dependence
9. Expansion of geographical and social communications	Very true before 9/11, and continues to be prominent after 9/11 in spite of restrictions
10. Multiplication of communications	Very true before 9/11, and continues to be prominent after 9/11 in spite of restrictions
11. Decreasing barriers to mobility	Not at the official level (U.S. restrictions not popular in Canada); but otherwise fewer restrictions between the two than any two other countries
12. Increasing political elites:	Yes, an unfortunate spillover of integration (which promotes business sectors over, for example, agricultural), Canadian consociationalism (networking among group leaders), and U.S. Republican leadership

Mexico City; but in 2005, he returned to Ottawa, signalling a big Mexico snub this time.

Even 9/11 could not stop transborder flows across the most open boundary in the world. Except for a minor post–9/11 dip, trade, investment, and human flows returned to the very high pre–9/11 years, sometimes exceeding those levels. It was only a matter of time before Canada joined the war on terrorism in substantive terms. The NATO role in Afghanistan pointed to a need out there that could only be solved through U.S. participation and Canadian collaboration. Whether this leads to deeper engagement remains uncertain, but increasing Canadian deaths has not impacted Canada's commitment, although public concern may also be growing.

Table 5.13 shows the Canada–U.S. relationship to be more integrated than interdependent. More communications channels bind the two countries, with economic issues at the top, though security, a growing interest, is not far behind; the military remains subordinate, which is why we subordinate interdependency to integration, while both countries can boast of membership in multiple viable institutions, both economic and security; similarly, catalysts of change can be found in both economic exchanges with regionalism (of two countries) vying for as much attention and interests as the national.

Table 5.13 Interdependence Versus Integration: Canada–U.S. Relations

Dimension	Canada–U.S. relations
1. Channels of communication	Both interdependent (bureaucratic-level cooperation) and integrative forces (trade and investment) seem to be operating; societal and transnational too
2. Hierarchy of issues	Economic issues are still at the top of Canada's agenda due to the stake in dealing with the United States; security and terrorism are quickly catching up with greater institutional coordination and integration
3. Subordination of the military	Military still subordinated to the civilian authorities but security related issues have given them greater leverage in Canada.
4. Nature of institutional membership	Institutional engagement over security and military matters have returned but economic integration still the top item on the agenda (Canadian commitments to UN, human rights, development); may face more challenges abroad and constraints within for Canada For the United States, institutions remain instruments of state interests, thereby raising an interdependent tenet over others
5. Catalysts of change	Global economic forces and Canadian economic dependence on the U.S. market continue as trilateral or bilateral catalysts of integration.
6. Placement of regionalism along levels of policy-making analysis	Regionalism, in the form of a North American security perimeter, seems to be as vital to Canada as its own national interest, and probable de-emphasizing past multilateral preferences; U.S. prioritizes both national and global interests (latter through leadership lenses)

Table 5.14 The Realist Concerns: Canada–U.S. Relations

Dimension	Canada–U.S. relations
1. State as dominant actor	Although military and security concerns are still the matters of the state on economic and regional matters provincialism (thus state at the provincial level) has returned, but the extent of NGOs and private sector involvement is also high at several interaction points, and thus explain variation across the major border crossing points with the United States
2. Policy reflecting internal or external competitiveness?	Competition in both domains impacting policies: divided governments in both Canada and the United States; and global terrorist threats exemplified by forces engaged in Afghanistán for both
3. Is international competitiveness orderly or chaotic	Canada sees some light at end of túnel, based on its Afghanistan experiences; disorderly U.S. international view generates more dim conclusions, given the Iraqi fiasco

Finally, table 5.14 addresses realist tenets. Although the Canadian federal government still dominates foreign policy-making, provincial, private, and social interests independently seek transborder coalitions. Thus the federal government cannot alone stand for Canada abroad, weakening its authority in times of crisis—a fate the United States also shares, in a slightly different way, after the 2006 elections reduced Bush's policy-making authority in the Congress. Internal competition is evident in both countries with the alliance government in Canada and a divided U.S. government (Democratic Congress and Republican President). International competition generates less Canadian concerns if the domain is the military, but increasing interest if it is economic—a pattern likely to hold unless something dramatic happens to Canadian participation in Afghanistan, either intensifying it further or leading it to withdraw. For the United States, both are vitally important, security more than economic. On balance, Canada's global orientation shows more optimism at the start of 2007 than the United States.

CONCLUSIONS

We draw five conclusions. First, the Canada–U.S. bilateral relationship is far richer theoretically than on empirical grounds: Theoretically, with the exception of neorealist expectations, it not only satisfies all the tenets of integration (neofunctionalism and security community) and interdependence, but also shows overall post–9/11 relevance, demonstrating how they have withstood pressures of unfavorable and formidable circumstances; empirically, nuances abound everywhere (driven by ideological or personality adjustments, military and governmental cultures, external circumstances), sometimes obstructing the bilateral relationship (Chrétien-Bush sparring), at other times adapting (Harper and a Democrat-controlled U.S. Congress to each other). To a large extent, there is little the two countries can do to control them, since societal and transnational linkages, as well as commonly felt external threats, bypass the governments, either binding the people or distancing them.

Second, opportunity-cost considerations underlie the relationship. Both countries were exposed to the costs of relational disruption, if only briefly, after 9/11, but neither wishes an encore; dependency sentiments never seem to be too far from the surface in Canada, but somehow actual benefits, free-ridership opportunities, or simply the helplessness in changing the status quo, overrides them; and Canadian support, no matter how flimsy or rhetorical, serves more than its weight in gold to U.S. public relations at home and abroad.

Third, Anglo-Saxon values survived the relational collapse before 9/11 (when Bush refused to make the traditional first foreign visit to Ottawa), in part due to intelligence agencies still collaborating, and immediately after 9/11 (when Chrétien's support for the war on terrorism was more rhetorical than substantive), dramatized by the June 2006 collaboration between the intelligence agencies of both countries to defuse a terrorist act in Ottawa through last-minute arrests. That possible threat brought home the war on terrorism to Canadians, who could only feel more empathy for their southern neighbors; and the entire war on terrorism, carrying with it an Islamic-versus-Christianity flavor, carries the underlying message of tightening Christian bonds, including other Anglo-Saxon countries. The message also elevates Anglo-Saxon contributions to Western civilization, such as some of the products of the English Enlightenment (democracy, economic liberalism, harnessing intelligence, technological development, and cutting-edge weaponry), all of which help, in one way or another, streamline approaches, instruments, and bonds in an unpredictable war.

Fourth, while not abandoned nor neglected, trilateralism, regionalism involving more than three countries, and multilateralism have implicitly or explicitly been subordinated to this bilateral relationship by Canada and the United States. NAFTA, the FTAA, the WTO (another Canadian proposition), and the United Nations are examples of compacts not very high on the policy-making agenda of either country after 9/11, and clearly not above the bilateral relationship. True they did not fade away because of 9/11 or became matters of diminishing interest within Canada and the United States: Some face other big problems, like the WTO over trading concessions to developing countries. Regardless, their benign or malign neglect only reaffirms the value of the Canadian–U.S. bilateral relationship. No matter how it is belittled or undermined, at the end of the day, it is this bilateral relationship which stands more robustly than many others. If anything, 9/11 exposed that dramatically by dragging it through a lot of accumulating dirt.

Finally, a much broader interpretation of "security" is in order. As threat perception recedes, U.S. homeland security efforts are likely to be embedded in efforts to foster a broader notion of "societal security" or "total defence," rather than strictly military security. In particular, the notion of "North American Security Perimeter" has gained much coinage in recent years, not only by scholars studying the dynamics of U.S.–Canada relations but also by leading think-tanks in the United States, such as the CFR (Council on Foreign Relations).[90] Whether Canada can maintain its claim of distinct values while cooperating with U.S. directives for security cooperation in order to ensure economic flow remains to be seen, but if the past is any guide, this proposal may be very welcome in Ottawa. After all, it was as participant of a PSC during the NATO years that Canada was baptized into the international arena, and as an independent foreign policy-maker; and Canadians do not need to be reminded how NATO was proposed, and in fact imposed upon a reluctant United States, by Canada.

6

Post–9/11 Mexico–U.S. Relations: Green Pastures, Rough Patches, Muddled Outcomes

INTRODUCTION

Given the post–9/11 U.S. imperatives of tightening loose security ends and filling missing security gaps, and Mexico's economic priorities, how have integrative efforts along both fronts evolved? Do they show unilateralism, bilateralism, or trilateralism?

Distinguishing between state and societal dynamics directs policy-making and institutional discussions to the state, and independent individual and group behavior analysis to society. With illegal migrants and drug flows, for example, individual or group behaviors affecting the Mexico–U.S. borders triggered state policing actions, generating a different kind of state-society interaction. Some of these actions and behaviors were previously acknowledged, to some extent even explained. Our task here is to examine the interaction along security and trade dimensions along two additional strands. The first examines 9/11-driven integrative possibilities over intelligence services, given the two different military cultures; the next turns to trade as well as a host of externalities. Externalities for us simply refer to two-thirds of what Guadalupe González González and Stephan Haggard utilized in their treatment of this same bilateral relationship almost a decade ago: drugs and migration.[1]

INTELLIGENCE WITHOUT POLICY, OR POLICY WITHOUT INTELLIGENCE?[2]

Overviewing Mexico–U.S. Security/Intelligence Comparisons

If the war against terrorism is to succeed, and certainly if the United States remains behind the steering wheel, a *modus operandi* must evolve with Mexico, given the long, porous common border. Yet, intelligence occupies a very different position on the policy-making agenda of both countries. The security culture within both further discounts any significant streamlining. For homeland security to deliver, what are the key areas of differences and how might commonalities induce cooperation?

Examining U.S.–Latin American security threats, Paul Todd and Jonathan Bloch raise the question if the approaches reflect "intelligence without policy," or "policy without intelligence." We do not have an answer for the entire region, but the Mexico–U.S. relationship since 9/11 betrays a little bit of both, for not just Mexico, but also the United States. "Intelligence without policy" simply means awareness not backed up by, or translated into, action, while "policy without intelligence," rather than the exact opposite, essentially means an action without doing the relevant homework. Selective policy treatments avoid these pitfalls, but overall assessments seem to be riddled with such gaps in both countries. Blaming politicians or administrative officials does not help: Externalities could drive issues or policies out of even their control. A study of Mexico–U.S. relations becomes a study of both promises and pitfalls.

Given the past history of both countries, this section addresses intelligence from three angles: orientations, institutions, and prospects of an IC. Owing to the length of the chapter, frequent summaries highlight the key issues leaving the key findings for the concluding section.

Orientations and Intelligence

Building upon Winn L. Taplin's definition of intelligence, as applied to Canada and the United States in the previous chapter,[3] this chapter examines his six principles for Mexico and the United States, then turns to David Snow's security culture determinants and Michael A. Turner's norms. Table 6.1 sets the stage.

Unlike in the Canada–U.S. case, we find the first principle, of intelligence deriving from international conflict or rivalry, producing quite different answers for Mexico and the United States, setting the tone for the overall picture. While it holds for

Table 6.1 Intelligence Principles and Mexico–U.S. Comparisons

Principles	Mexico	United States
1. Intelligence derives from international conflict or rivalry	Not really	Mostly true
2. Conduct or use of intelligence involves secrecy	True	True
3. Clandestine collection of information is the fundamental activity of intelligence	True	True
4. Truth must be the basis of good intelligence	Not always true	Not always true
5. Intelligence in a vacuum is of no value, tardy intelligence is of little value	True	True
6. Special activities must involve native knowledge of the national groups toward which they are directed	Domestically true, not so abroad	True, but by trials and errors

Adapted from Winn L. Taplin, "Six General Principles of Intelligence," *International Journal of Intelligence and Counterintelligence* 3, no. 4 (1989): 475–91.

the United States, its irrelevance for Mexico produces at least two contrasting, rather than overlapping, orientations, and security cultures, masking a variety of procedural similarities. Secrecy and clandestine operations—the second and third principles—remain the same, as too the fourth and fifth principles, respectively emphasizing the penchant for truth, as well as the worthlessness of intelligence in a vacuum or if late. Neither the fourth nor the fifth principle has been prioritized in either country: Mexico's military intelligence prediction of a *Zapatista* uprising before it actually happened on January 1, 1994, was ignored by politicians and civilian officers,[4] just as the WMD U.S. argument to justify the March 2003 Iraqi invasion was patently false.[5] As postulated before, questionable principles push positive intelligence and counterintelligence in *negative* directions. Both Mexico and the United States illustrate this. Mexico's military knew of local tensions in Chiápas because deployment provided native knowledge, which policy-makers, far removed in Mexico City, did not have. While Mexico's native knowledge is mostly domestic, the United States must rely upon native knowledge abroad. As repeatedly evident in Afghanistan and Iraq, native knowledge is being acquired through trials and errors, and a lot of money, not necessarily through prior training. Similar erroneous approaches characterized the Vietnam War 40 years earlier, but apparently not enough lessons were learned: Created to fight guerrillas, the Green Berets proved too feeble for the occasion,[6] and the special forces deployed in Afghanistan and Iraq also seemed to have been moving in circles.

As in chapter 5, we augment our treatment of principles through a comparison of Donald Snow's two categories of security culture forces. These are background influences (what he calls conditioning forces), and direct strategic culture impacts, presented in table 6.2. We then compare Michael Turner's norms in table 6.3.

Both Mexico and the United States differ sharply over the three background influences: a sense of history, geographical endowment, and cultural heritage. Both Mexico and the United States began institutionalizing intelligence in the 1880s, but the prior history of each made a difference: Mexico's was one of perpetual conflict, the United States's of state-building. While Alexis de Tocqueville's detection of democratic ingredients in the United States was noted in the previous chapter,[7] if he had gone south, he might have agreed with Peruvian poet Mario Vargas Llosa of Mexico being a *perfect dictatorship.* Suspicion and a democratic distemper highlighted the civil-military tussle until at least World War II, delaying democracy until the twenty-first century.[8] Like in the United States, Mexican intelligence institutions would be compartmentalized from the very outset, but whereas U.S. intelligence was legitimized by foreign wars, Mexico's counterpart sprang from domestic conflicts. The playground of intelligence and politics were kept far apart in Mexico.

Geography and culture played their parts too. Even before U.S. intelligence was institutionalized from the 1880s, Mexico's frequent competition with Guatemala and the United Province of Central America necessitated intelligence, but domestic divisions diverted energy from that task. When the United States began institutionalizing intelligence, it curiously drifted toward its several cultural roots, to Anglo-Saxon criteria,[9] such as secrecy, drama, and celluloid reaffirmation; Mexico could

Table 6.2 Elements of Strategic Culture and Mexico–U.S. Comparisons

Categories	Mexico	United States
Background Influences:		
1. Sense of History	1. Goes relatively deep	1. Relatively shallow
2. Geographical Endowment	2. Location next to a superpower in recent history	2. Absence of a European-type hostile neighbor context
3. Cultural Heritage	3. Hispanic	3. Anglo-Saxon
Factors Directly Affecting Strategic Culture:		
1. Democratic Institutions	1. Not until very recently	1. Yes, from the start
2. Role of Media	2. Too recent to configure	2. Constant influence
3. Suspicion of Government/ Military	3. Yes: stems from social conflicts, corporatism	3. Yes, but for constitutional reasons
4. Mobilization-Demobilization Pattern	4. Prevails	4. Prevails
5. Notion of Invincibility	5. Not really	5. Yes, from the start
6. Preference for Total Wars	6. No: preference for lesser wars	6. Yes, after World War II and in nuclear age
7. Tradition of Citizen-Soldier	7. Evaporating, and almost gone	7. Not really a factor nor a tradition

Source: Donald Snow, *National Security: Defence Policy for a New International Era* (New York, NY: St. Martin's Press, 1995), 42–65.

not turn to its own colonial master, Spain, not only because Spain was not a hallmark name in intelligence, but also because, unlike Britain, Spain was in decline and eventual introversion after losing its colonies in the Western Hemisphere. This may have mattered since intelligence resonates with the rise and decline of great powers, and invokes balancing imperatives,[10] none of which Spain could offer at the end of the nineteenth century.

All seven of Snow's strategic culture determinants would be shaped differently by these background forces. U.S. democratization (first) produced institutions faster than in Mexico,[11] thus making the media (second) an earlier and more constant watchdog than in Mexico, and whereas the distance from government and the military (third) in the United States stemmed from a constitutional background, dictated by the separation of powers, in Mexico the sources were corruption, social inequities, and ideological rivalries. Only in the twenty-first century, for example, have Mexican military archives been opened for public and media scrutiny, and the president can be elected freely, rather than be designated. Demobilizing the military (fourth), however, is a common pattern, facilitated by Mexico's shift from military rule to civilian after World War II, while democratic U.S. impulses automatically demobilize the military after any war engagement. Invincibility (fifth), as a determinant, highlights the differences. Given its size, resources, and military victories, the United States was dress-rehearsing for this from its very birth, and one of the first thresholds, the

1848 Treaty of Guadalupe-Hidalgo, ironically nipped any invincibility claims in Mexico. Likewise, even though the United States has recent and ongoing experiences with total, long-term wars (sixth), as a nuclear power, it has no choice but to prepare for perpetual total wars—unfathomable factors in Mexico. Both lack a citizen-soldier tradition (seventh), in spite of an expanding post–World War II U.S. military-industrial complex, but whereas Mexico's citizen-soldier tradition ended only recently, the United States never developed one.

Institutions and Intelligence

Table 6.3 profiles similarities and differences in terms of Turner's norms. Among the similarities, both Mexico and the United States believe in secrecy for intelligence-building (second norm); accept ambiguity of the intelligence mandate (fourth), as discussed previously; retain a confederal nature of the intelligence structure, given the multiple independent agencies involved (fifth); display an increasingly flexible accountability (sixth), especially for Mexico; how intelligence activities remain largely separate from law enforcement, or policy functions (seventh); why the intelligence industry is competitively inclined given the multiple agencies involved (eigth); and how intelligence supports policies (tenth).

Table 6.3 Intelligence and Institutional Norms: Mexico–U.S. Comparisons

Institutional norms	Mexico	United States
1. Institutional survival	Scope not available	Prevails
2. Secrecy	Prevails	Prevails
3. Intelligence exceptionalism	Increasingly no	Increasingly yes
4. Ambiguous mandate	Yes	Yes
5. Confederal structure	Yes	Yes
6. Flexible accountability	Increasingly so	Yes
7. Separation of intelligence from law enforcement (police)	Yes	Yes
8. Competitive intelligence	Yes	Yes
9. Separation of intelligence from policy	Increasingly so	Increasingly no
10. Policy support	Yes	Yes
11. Can-do attitude	Not really	Yes
12. Primacy of intelligence analysis	Not really	Increasingly yes
13. Emphasis on current intelligence	Yes	Yes
14. Provision for accurate, timely, and relevant intelligence	Yes	Yes

Source: Michael A. Turner, "A Distinctive U.S. Intelligence Identity," *International Journal of Intelligence and Counterintelligence* 17, no. 1 (2004): 49; but see 42–61.

Where they differ is largely in terms of institutional survivability (first). In the United States, the same institutions survive presidential changes, in Mexico they do not. Whereas several independent intelligence orbits prevail in Mexico, owing to conflictual history, civilian governments have kept them at a distance (ninth), in the United States, the DHS made a valiant effort to centralize inherently competitive intelligence agencies. Bush's desire to "lead, oversee, and coordinate a comprehensive strategy,"[12] was matched by Mexico's Vicente Fox Quesada's establishing a NSC, before 9/11 in fact. Mexico's NSC has played a low-keyed policy-making role ever since, struggling as it is to even survive in 2007, while the DHS does not supervise the FBI and CIA. Nevertheless, with a can-do attitude (eleventh), U.S. intelligence agencies vie for post–9/11 policy-making primacy (twelfth), emphasize concurrent intelligence (thirteenth), and prioritize the timely availability of accurate and relevant information (fourteenth). For Mexico the attitude is relaxed, while intelligence remains a subordinate activity, even after the Central American threats of the 1980s, indigenous revolts in the 1990s, and drug-trafficking throughout.

Institutionalization and the Intelligence Community

Since Turner's "strategic culture" evolves through a protracted historical process, Mexico's stunted outcome contrasts with the snowballing U.S. counterpart.[13] Administrative overhaul every six years in Mexico thwarts institutional growth and military/intelligence coherence, but the U.S. infrastructure is both resilient and growing. Prevailing political circumstances would lead one to believe Mexico's intelligence should be deepening, given the wide arrays of potential problems, but it seems, after spending an entire century civilianizing the military inheritance, the system remains exhausted.[14]

A number of IC-related observations may be articulated. First, the U.S. intelligence system is graduating from the roles of the butcher and baker to the intelligence *policy-maker,* while Mexico's still remains at the butcher stage, since it has neither the baker to supplement its efforts nor the possibility to convert into a policy-maker. Second, as Mexico's intelligence and policy-making move in diverging directions, U.S. convergences do not betray if there is a consistent leader-follower pattern. Third, although Turner identifies the United States fulfilling the realist criteria and fitting into that framework better,[15] we argue, continuity and cumulative growth shifted it in the constructivist direction. On the same debate, finally, Mexico's intelligence cannot display either the constructivist claims, given the truncated and competitive atmosphere, or the realist counterpart because of its corporatist subordination to civilian leadership.

The U.S. DCI and the Mexican president head the IC in each country,[16] though intelligence has rarely, if ever, been at the commanding heights of any Mexican presidential policy agenda and only from 1947 in the United States. We make two observations. First, with Mexican intelligence and policy moving in opposite directions, as just noted, even converging U.S. patterns do not convey a consistent leader-follower pattern: Which agency is leading is not always clear; and whether they follow policymakers, or vice versa, is also mixed. Second, although Troy finds the U.S. experience consistent with the realist paradigm, we argue that it is reflecting constructivist colors, given its continuity and cumulative institutional growth, while Mexico's is drifting from its constructivist origins, when a political party would set the norms and create identity networks, in an unknown direction. Competitiveness within U.S. IC is consistent with realist thinking, and Mexico's own brand of realism comes across in President Felipe Calderón Hinojosa deploying a growing number of troops—presently 30,000—to combat drug cartels and defecting *Zeta* elite troops from the military.

Like in the United States, Mexico's institutional growth evolved in compartmentalized form, with the catalysts emanating, not from abroad, as in the United States, but from within and amidst a more hostile IC environment. Fox's 2001 NSC, which sought to salvage intelligence from this plight, assumed strong bilateral U.S. relations. Disagreement over an immigration proposal one week before 9/11 essentially pulled the rug from underneath Mexico's most robust institutional transformation in recent history, one capable of unleashing the strongest of forces, since they were bilateral, against drug-trafficking.[17]

Just as Mexico's post–World War II civilianizing process as well as electoral disjunctures every six years prevented both centralizing and cumulating intelligence experiences, as the civilian-military tussle subsided, a string of other security problems, increasingly dubbed as *externalities* emerged: the environment, drugs, and migration, to which James F. Rochlin adds indigenous protests and democratization.[18] If Mexico's NSC was created to tackle these, its evaporation from the headlines summarizes Mexico's case: Using Troy's terms, it has neither a butcher nor a baker strong enough to shape policies, even to stand robustly on their own.

THEORETICAL INTERPRETATIONS

What do our Mexico-specific and United States-specific discussions predict for security integration of the two countries? Comparing apples with apples, on the one hand, and apples with oranges, on the other, become two entirely different exercises, but necessary in the case of Mexico and the United States. In terms of apples against oranges, the United States has been, and continues to want to be, a world leader, both economically and militarily, and its orientations, institutions, and idiosyncrasies, tinged directly by 9/11 attacks, reflect this extroversion. By contrast, Mexico has historically been insulated, and desires to remain so for as long as feasible under liberalizing and globalizing pressures, thus possessing orientations, institutions, and idiosyncrasies considerably more modest and in scope, weight, and purposes. At the same time, 9/11-related priorities demand they must converge, in other words, both must transform into the same genus, apples against apples, for example, over certain functions, such as waging the war against terrorism, through parallel, if not the same, orientations, institutions, and idiosyncrasies.

Mexico–U.S. Peculiarities

Ground-level dynamics get more exposure and elevation here than their drawing-board counterparts, in other words, how foot-soldiers execute the general's commands becomes more critical. We repeatedly distinguished institutions from procedures to capture this dynamic: In the case of Mexico, the distinction mattered, since many procedures, rather than taking an institutional, thereby predictable, turn, deviated. Illegal emigration exemplified one consequence of, for example, border personnel turning a blind eye and eliciting a more pervasive Mexican nonchalance; or even more blatantly, narcotics flowing across boundaries with hands-on engagement of not just state officials, but state officials at the very top, such as a former president's brother and military generals. Thus far, at least illegal emigrants have not been terrorists, and narcotraffickers have not catered to terrorism. Yet, the future remains a hostage to these possibilities. It is in this sense that institutional principles, norms, rules, and decision-making procedures may be bended, sometimes broken, but invariably stray from expectations. Encapsulating some, though by no means all, of such gray-area possibilities, table 6.4 directs attention to six peculiarities, out of possibly many more, dictated by our country-specific investigations: central intelligence command, state-society relations, financial resource-base, steering wheel versus back-seat positioning and perceptions, extent of public mobilization, and human rights impacts.

Peculiarities such as these usually slip through the policy-making cracks, indicating either deliberate neglect or low-agenda importance. If security is the overriding concern, as 9/11 demanded it be for the United States, we would expect intelligence command to be centralized. The huge step taken in this regard by establishing DHS still fell short by leaving the CIA, in particular, out of its ambit, in the process producing unnecessary sniping and, even worse, reversing the policy-making process by making desired goals justify the chosen policy instrument. Faulty intelligence leading to the March 2003 Iraqi invasion was inexcusable, but that the decision to invade should have manipulated the rationale leaves little sympathy for the outcome sought or legitimacy to rally the public.

If intelligence could not be centralized in the United States, expecting Mexico to do so would be unrealistic. Fox's well-intentioned effort to upgrade it against the narcotrafficking upsurge, may not be enough to reverse the momentum of history. It was not just not in the Mexican interest, as much as it was for the United States, to centralize intelligence agencies, but Mexico's narrow security scope also contrasted with the global U.S. outreach, imposing very different hierarchies of interests, and thereby needs for centralized responses. Yet, the centralization issue speaks of an orientation determinant, or reflection, not often brought to the forefront.

As the second dimension points out, security inverts broader state-society relations within both countries and between them. A large literature posits the United States as a pluralist society,[19] shifting toward possible post-pluralism,[20] that is, from influencing legislators over policy-making, interest groups anchored themselves in the various bureaucracies as the New Deal brought more governmental intervention. If we

Table 6.4 Peculiarities Affecting Mexico–U.S. Security Integration

Dimension	Description
Central intelligence command	Absent in both: DHS does not control CIA, CISEN does not fully embrace military, thus promoting territoriality, competition, suspicion, and arrested policies in key existing security agencies
State-society relations	An inverted pattern persisting: state imposes security interests upon society in pluralist/post-pluralist United States, but societal pressures (illegally and/or indirectly) permeate state security interests in corporatist Mexico
Financial resource-base	Diametrically opposite possibilities: Capacity of being fully or predominantly diverted toward military needs in the United States, but huge population at the margin prevents large military allocations in Mexico
Steering-wheel versus back-seat positions/perceptions	Behind the steering-wheel, the United States carries an open-ended threat perception, inviting concerns or reports from anyone about almost anything; in the back-seat, Mexico can only afford to look after top-priority concerns or reports, free-riding largely, United States picking up the tab
Extent of public mobilization	Security imperatives more likely to be made the typical citizen's top priority in the United States than in Mexico: more divided Mexican state (not necessarily society) dilutes public attention-span; corruption also delegitimizes state actions
Human rights impacts	Guantánamo, representing the most noninstitutionalized U.S. response over security threats (no principles, norms, rules, or decision-making procedures; at least not at all in conformity with those existing in open society), parallels the same human rights violations Mexico is known for (torture, maiming), whether perpetrated by criminals or officials, past or present

examine U.S. security interests, on the other hand, and especially under DHS, we find a dominant policy-making thrust originating, not from interest groups, but from within the government, from the executive branch, typically from the president—a pattern not far removed from corporatism,[21] but not depicting pluralism.[22] Mexico, which epitomized corporatism for as long as the United States embraced the New Deal,[23] is more used to the president or his party determining policy interests—until Fox's electoral victory. From the year 2000, societal interests seem to be creeping into broader Mexican policy-making processes,[24] including security. Intelligence archives have been opened up for public scrutiny for the first time, inviting scholarly evaluations, while even illegal emigration and drug trafficking bring society into the policy-making process as determinants. Security anchors, then, reflect quite different perceptual bases in both countries, and contrary to the models we apply to the two: top-down executive preferences in the United States, and increasingly lateral, societal influences in Mexico.

Addressing a parallel phenomenon, the third dimension identifies how converting security into an overriding citizen concern is easier in the United States than in Mexico. This may be the advantage of the executive branch playing the predominant security role over the Congress, as was just discussed; and if handled adroitly, the executive branch is capable of diverting commensurate state resources to prosecute security interests. Mexico has not been able to make security an over-riding citizen concern in modern history, and even if it could, resources cannot so easily be diverted to the military when so many other pressing demands remain. Thus, the United States possesses the elements of a military/security culture in a way Mexico is losing it. Gerard S. Vano's definition of military culture as "that complex interdependency of strategy, politics, economics, technology, socioideology," suffices here:[25] When a military-industrial complex develops in the United States,[26] Vano adds, it automatically becomes the "epitome of Western military culture," since military purchases by the rest of the world props up so many other countries. Not so in Mexico, where it lacks appropriate roots, especially since World War II, even though Mexico is one of those military purchasers. Roderic Ai Camp, foremost in the study of Mexican civilian-military relations, points out how the proportion of Mexican military office-holders in the government declined from Porfirio Díaz's 55 percent during 1885–88, after hitting a peak of 64 percent under Venustiano Carranzo's 1914–15 administration, to 32 percent after the PRI assumed office in 1929, 19 percent during World War II, 10 percent during the first half of the 1970s, and 5 percent when neoliberalism was adopted between 1982 and 88.[27] General Avila Camacho, the last military president, left office in 1946.

In turn, these perceptions also get impacted by where the policy-making anchors are positioned, for example, behind the steering wheel, that is, managing hands-on policy implementation or formulation, or in the back-seat, in other words, facing the consequences of another country's policies, either reluctantly or as a free-rider. The fourth dimension highlights this peculiarity, with the United States behind the steering-wheel, and Mexico in the back-seat. Whereas the U.S. position reflects greater sensitivity toward security threats, much like driving on a pot-hole filled stretch of road, it both invites those threats by being on the road, and interprets almost anything as constituting a security threat; Mexico, on the other hand, can rally behind the United States when circumstances get sticky and shelter underneath the U.S. security umbrella, even elicit U.S. support by crying "wolf" should the need arise, although thus far Mexico has simply kept a dignified distance from 9/11-related security obsessions by attending other more serious preoccupations at home.

Given both the third and fourth dimensions, the public can be more quickly mobilized on security threats, real or perceived, in the United States than in Mexico. By the same token, the public can also bring the government to its feet more briskly in the United States than in Mexico. Education and mass media are not necessarily the reasons why. With more people living at the margin in Mexico, the gravity of security concerns cannot be sold as convincingly to people whose top priorities remain food, clothing, shelter, and so forth. Not only does the evaporation of privilege threaten developed country citizens more than their less developed counterpart, but also the acquired hubris from successfully defending that privilege also seems to be the rewards only citizens of great powers can boast.[28] Mexico faces additional constraints to mobilizing the public: Its governmental agencies and officials carry a reputation of being corrupt,[29] thus alienating citizens unnecessarily. Although Mexicans can summon deep and universal nationalism, somehow these same sentiments dilute themselves when extended to security issues. Again, this could be a function of Mexico's introverted security culture.

Table 6.4 touches on an issue climbing rapidly on the list of public concerns worldwide, itself a function of widespread democratization, globalization, and liberalization, among other factors. Human rights abuses typically characterize societies where democracy is under-supplied, gender, or ethnic inequalities remain the norm, or protecting narcotrafficking or other illegal operations produce torture, violent competition, and other extreme forms of behavior. Mexico faced, and still faces, these, though campaigns to arrest them also serve as a common pattern. What is striking about the war on terrorism is how the United States unleashed some of the most horrific human rights abuses or denials for any democratic country at any time. Utilizing Camp Guantánamo unilaterally, indiscriminately, clandestinely, and barbarically since 9/11 undermines many of the legitimately positive claims or credits of the United States.[30] Official Guantánamo actions remain "off-limits" from public scrutiny, thereby escaping the institutional network (they do not generically represent principles, norms, rules, and decision-making procedures as regime theorists would expect), but more recently, there is also a drive to start institutionalizing these deviant behaviors. New Defence Secretary Robert Gates' submission of the Military Commissions Manual legitimized "hearsay" and "coerced statements" as instruments against Guantánamo detainees in trials.[31] It gives judges "wide latitude to decide what evidence may be presented" against 80 of the 400 detainees currently held.[32] In the final analysis, human rights face an Achilles Heel even in democracies as a consequence of security imperatives.

Institutions and Orientations

Shifting from peculiarities to actual institutions and orientations, post–9/11 security imperatives revitalize neorealist and interdependence arguments at the expense of neofunctionalism, security community, or any other integrative theses. Several institutions built upon these weaker theories still anchor nonmilitary dynamics, but explanations become complicated. A hodgepodge of just about every tenet under the sun claims top-priority when not a single one is strong enough to win the day. Even neorealist and interdependent theories, with their characteristics more or fully satisfied than ever before, cannot return to their robust Cold War forms during the 1970s. Something seems to be missing even with the prevalence of every feature, player, and paradigm.

Table 6.5 examines the 9/11 difference for the 12 features of security community for Mexico and the United States. The overall message is one of retreat: either tenets adjust to the new reality with difficulty, or explanations fail completely.

Table 6.5 Security Community, Mexico–U.S. Relations, and 9/11 Impacts

Dimension	Descriptions
1. Value compatibility	To an extent, yes; but difficult to find across the board (of issues)
2. Enhanced predictability	Evaporating feature under security: Mexico's behavior more predictable than United States under new circumstances
3. Mutual responsiveness	Yes, but vastly different in degree: U.S. agility contrasts with Mexican indifference
4. Value complementarity	Not in the broad sense, though over specific issues (border controls, drugs), efforts underway to make them complementary
5. Distinctiveness in lifestyles	Very exposed: Mexicans less security-minded than U.S. citizens; and security culture very different in the two countries
6. Reward expectations before integration	Not at all attempted with security, nor evident before, over security: *with or against us* as a rallying call serves as a stick, not a carrot
7. Increasing political and administrative functions	Yes, very much so; increasing function over 9/11, and not necessarily because of 9/11
8. Economic growth distinguishing core from periphery	Yes, and very much like before: relevance for security imperatives unclear, perhaps not at all important
9. Expansion of geographical and social communications	Very true before 9/11, and continues to be prominent after 9/11 in spite of restrictions
10. Multiplication of communications	Very true before 9/11, and continues to be prominent after 9/11 in spite of restrictions
11. Decreasing barriers to mobility	Not at the official level (U.S. immigration check-points discouraging Mexican visitors); yes at the unofficial level (booming illegal Mexican migrants)
12. Increasing political elites	Not increasing, but not evaporating either: the glow conspicuous by its post–9/11 absence; elites face other priorities in Mexico

Different military cultures shape different value systems (first). Fewer security-based values tie Mexico and the United States after 9/11, and those that do, may just be symbolic or rhetoric. For example, Mexico supports the war against terrorism, but only with words, not with troops or any hands-on engagements. It directly opposed the war against Iraq in 2003,[33] indicating how compatibility is diminishing.

So too is behavior predictability (second), more so for Mexico of U.S. behavior than United States of Mexico's. This may not be an indictment against the United States, since the war on terrorism is itself a nebulous engagement against, at times, invisible enemies. However, it threatens integration between the two countries.

As it threatens integration, mutual responsiveness also diminishes (third). Mexico's disillusionment with its immigration proposal rejection the week before 9/11 set the stage for this turnaround, although without an ample military culture, it is questionable if, or when, with an immigration agreement, Mexico could fulfill security needs after 9/11. Shifting from economic integration to security integration is a giant leap for a country neither interested in Cold War alliances, nor a member of NATO. The United States also treated Mexico like all other countries, rather than the special friend it became in 2000—a mere subject of the "with us or against us" dictum. Even then, the U.S. responsiveness made no attempt to strike the symmetrical posture it did during the 1990s with free-trade.

As with value compatibility, value complementarity did not fully blossom (fourth). Where they did, it was negative, and over long-established bilateral issues of controversy: drugs, illegal immigration, and so forth.

As these differences grew sharper, both countries demonstrated greater distinctiveness in lifestyles (fifth), especially since security meant different priorities for both. Ironically, this is a necessary trait for a security community; but in this case, lifestyle distinctiveness exposes disintegrative connotations more than integrative, calling into question its utility and relevance as a tenet.

Exigency, and not reward expectations (sixth), drove Mexico and the United States to each other. Whereas the United States adopted a unilateral posture with an ultimatum, Mexico did not seem interested in any security-based rewards, even more in paying any security costs.

Expanded post–9/11 collaborative political and administrative functions (seventh) satisfied United States rather than bilateral security demands. As frequently alluded to, these addressed long-established controversies rather than any new 9/11-related development; and although those controversies have security concerns written all over them, the positions of the two sides on them were as different after 9/11 as before.

The security community tenet of distinguishing core from peripheral areas of economic growth (eighth), did not seem relevant to 9/11 or to security integration at all; while both the dimensions of geography and social communications, as well as multiplication of communications (ninth), expanded, independent of 9/11. Their expansion had a lot to do with integration, globalization, and liberalization; but this expansion across national boundaries faced more barriers after 9/11 than before, as the ninth dimension notes. Just after 9/11, for example, all U.S. borders were briefly closed; since then, all flows go through more restrictions than ever before. These did not reduce communications growth (tenth). In turn, barriers to mobility across national boundaries (eleventh) did not decrease, even though communications may have expanded (since not all communications go across formal border check points: telephones do not, neither the internet—two burgeoning industries in the border areas and between the two countries given the huge binational population).

Finally, the increase of elites (twelfth) did not emerge as a noteworthy factor. To be sure, elites did increase, but neither was their emergence or increase necessarily related to security, nor were they acting jointly over either bilateral relations or terrorism: elites under economic transactions promoted bilateral interests much more conspicuously than they did after 9/11, and they acted together more often before 9/11 than after.

If the security community paradigm did not resonate with security developments on the ground after 9/11, the neofunctionalist paradigm also suffered. Table 6.6 guides this discussion. Owing in part to its total neglect of military and security considerations, neofunctionalism lost its relevance after 9/11 even though many of its tenets remain viable. As a discussion of those tenets reveals, tenets alone do not explain any given full picture: idiosyncrasies and peculiarities impinging paradigms constantly can shake any explanatory framework.

Economic symmetry (first) never prevailed across North America, but it may be to the credit of NAFTA, and how NAFTA encouraged neofunctionalist thinking, that the seven years of regional integration preceding 9/11 permitted the most concerted and sincere efforts at leveling the North American playing field: NAFTA's dispute settlement arrangements, for example, illustrate those painstaking efforts. Nevertheless, 9/11 irrevocably changed the order, not by abandoning NAFTA's arrangements, but by shifting priority to security issues. In this new playing field, size matters; and North American asymmetry was not only reinforced, but sharply so.

Elite complementarity (second), a necessary vehicle of integration, was also not abandoned. It remained confined largely to the economic domain, entering the security domain only under two circumstances: on U.S. terms; or full conviction, and thereby U.S. embrace, of the 9/11-generated security imperatives. Neither spoke for Mexico, until at least 2007; and only the latter gained belated ascendancy in Canada under Steven Harper.

The neofunctionalist emphasis on pluralism (third), also becomes sensible under economic integration; but when security integration faces terrorism and an invisible enemy,[34] pluralism may not be helpful. By some coincidence, though, Mexico's shift to full-fledged pluralism coincided with the 9/11 season: Fox's election followed the abandonment of *dedazo* by Ernesto Zedillo Ponce de León, and his victory ending seven decades of one-party rule also breathed sighs of North American democratic relief. In the United States, however, 9/11 curbed some human rights and democratic behaviors, while introducing clandestine methods, such as telephone or internet eavesdropping (until relaxed by the Democrat-controlled Congress in 2007).

Adaptation (fourth) is the hallmark of integration, vital for economic survival, but expectedly restrictive for military/security. True both Mexico and the United States had to adapt to new circumstances after 9/11, but how this was done also matters: It was a matter of urgency for the United States, but foot-dragging for Mexico. Spiraling illegal Mexican emigration only exposed the hollow adaptation to security needs across the U.S. borders; while harsh U.S. responses, for example, building walls, only alienated Mexican policy-makers to the point of creating a vicious cycle and lose-lose outcomes for both.

Spillover takes on new meanings under security integration and when illegal flows (fifth), such as humans or drugs, accompany routine trade flows. Neofunctionalism only focused on trade, investment, and legal human flows, not any of the rest.

Table 6.6 Neofunctionalism, Mexico–U.S. Relations, and 9/11 Impacts

Dimension	Descriptions
1. Economic symmetry	Not relevant for security integration; did not exist for regional economic integration either
2. Elite complementarity	Not really salient (or relevant) over security integration
3. Pluralism	Not a factor: Both countries more pluralistically oriented after 9/11 then before, since Fox's election was without *dedazo* (for the first time), and U.S. evangelism boosted voting turnout
4. Capacity to adapt	Difficult to adapt: Mexico to U.S. security needs, United States to Mexico's ostensible illegal emigration role and to an indifferent war-on-terrorism role/approach
5. Spillover	Forced spillover did take place; illegal spillover (migrants) also took place, but natural spillover over security not conspicuous after 9/11
6. Increasing transactions	Not threatened over the long-haul across borders, but security did not create any new transaction increases; Mexico slipped to becoming the third largest U.S. trading partner after 9/11, and imports less from the United States than before 9/11, but neither of these were security-driven outcomes
7. Growth in intergovernmentalism	More so after 9/11 than before, but the warmth also seems to be diminishing
8. Transnational growth	Not enhanced by 9/11, and certainly not over security issues, for example, Mexico did not support UN Resolution 1441, sponsored by the United States
9. Elite socialization	Not out of security issues, and because of the lackluster performance on this front, other dimensions also took a hit
10. Growth in ideological identity	Not under security issues, in fact, there has been a distinct diminution under the same two land-owing, probusiness presidents (Bush and Fox)
11. Increasing interactions with external actors	For the United States, this was true; for Mexico, to a lesser degree and not driven by security motives
12. Benefit distribution higher and more equal	Neither contention proved true: There were no mutual benefits over security issues, hence distribution did not arise; and equality in both benefits and distribution also not relevant
13. Converging patterns of external problems	This has just not happened; diverging patterns may be closer to reality than converging
14. Integration as being cost-free	Not really: it has been costly, and would be so under security arrangements even if both partners were on the best of terms; but integration over security is not being pushed precisely because it may have high (social) costs in Mexico

The result has not just been a policy-making quagmire along the Mexico–U.S. frontiers, but also exacerbated by Mexico's southern borders suddenly becoming more porous and increasingly vulnerable to cartels, gangs, and possible terrorists using Central America as a platform. These considerations are not chimerical:[35] Deported Central American gangsters from Los Angeles, for example, make the return journey through Mexico to escape not just the grinding poverty, but also the alienation in an unknown society, transacting drugs to pay the way in the process. It remains only a question of *when*, not *if*, a rendezvous with terrorist entrepreneurs occurs. Post–9/11 security measures have barely touched these concerns.

As with spillover, transactions across the Mexico–U.S. borders have expanded (sixth), sometimes feeding North American integration, at other times global integration, as more and more Asian companies use Mexico or Central America as production platforms for low-wage U.S. sales.

Both increasing transactions (sixth) and intergovernmentalism (seventh) demonstrate growth, but along economic and social lines, not nearly as much along security lines. Security concerns prompted a growth of intergovernmental interactions no doubt, but translating governmental agreements on the ground has not been as fluent as desirable, leaving pockets of vulnerability almost everywhere along the borders.

Transnational growth (eighth) elite socialization (ninth), and growth in ideological identity (tenth) also show increasing gaps. Socializing among policy-making elites over security issues has not produced the warmth, amity, and vision characterized by NAFTA. Indeed, the sharply asymmetrical playing field even undermines elite socialization. One consequence is not just a perceptual gap between the leaders, but one feeding into the security culture gap referred to earlier. A common ideology does not bind the two countries, or their leaders, in the war against terrorism.

Increasing interactions with external actors (eleventh), that is, players outside North America, also reflect asymmetry: more so for the United States than for Mexico; and not necessarily in conjunction with each other. Mexico's unspoken concern about the United States is that the war against terror necessitates interaction with too many other countries and organizations, thus reducing the attention-span for Mexico even under good times.

Under economic integration, benefit distribution being higher and more equal (twelfth), converging patterns of external problems (thirteenth), and integration as being cost-free (fourteenth) were valid, robust, and catalytic features; but under security integration, all three show exactly opposite results. Benefits have been too few, if any, for the bilateral relations, and not at all reflecting equal distribution; external problems are not breeding identical perceptions on either side of the Río Grande (and increasingly even within the United States); while security integration increasingly imposes costs, not only from protection against illegal flows, but also the growing proportion of the national pie being diverted to the military.

Neofunctionalism originally emerged to help the excessive exuberance of economic integration, and the possibilities this entailed, to political realities: David

Mitrany's functional thesis even bypassed the state; Ernst B. Haas and others brought the state back in but, as seems evident, more as a lame-duck or rebounding board than as an active participant. Neither fitted security considerations, even though both postulated their thesis amidst the most grim security circumstances of the twentieth century—the World War II and the Cold War, respectively. Yet, even the cursory admission of the state appears grossly inadequate to meet the explanatory needs of the war on terrorism today.

As table 6.7 suggests, interdependence arguments fill many of the missing blanks of integration theories like neofunctionalism. Like under integration, interdependence is able to explain, and necessitates, multiple channels of communications between partners (first). Mexico and the United States satisfied this criterion, but struggle with other table 6.7 dimensions. Integration demands the evaporation of any issue hierarchy (second), while interdependence facilitates it when economic integration is the subject. Under security integration, interdependence restores the hierarchy, and as the third dimension specifies, the military returns to the top (third). Economic integration or interdependence requires institutional affiliation (fourth), the former at the expense of the state, the latter at state's command. With security integration, the state is fully in command, like the U.S. chief executive. Like other countries, Mexico was told it could be either with or against the United States, a difficult choice for a country accessing nearly half of all U.S. land borders, but uninterested in antiterrorism war engagements. Whereas integration sees technology as catalysts of change (fifth), interdependence relies on new knowledge, which includes technology. Under security considerations, technology also is not enough: HUMINT rises to the fore, thus interdependence comes closer to explaining it than integration. Finally, whereas integration pays more attention to the regional level than the state or even global integration (sixth), interdependence pays equal attention to all three. North American security integration after 9/11 again gravitates toward interdependence: Nationalistic preferences remain foremost, but regional and global integration become vital instruments of state policy preferences. In an age of terrorism, decision-makers in Washington must know what their counterparts have in mind in other critical capitals.

If interdependence does better than integration to explain the post–9/11 Mexico–U.S. relationship, does it facilitate going to the explanatory extreme—to neorealism?

Table 6.8 gives us the mixed answer: for the United States it does, not at all for Mexico—again reaffirming the different military cultures in both. Their only agreement is to be found in the first dimension: state as the dominant actor. Both Mexico and the United States believe in this. Even in the wildest moments of regional integration, Mexico never subordinated state presence and interests to any supranational, transnational, or international body; while the proposition never took hold of policymakers or academicians in the United States even when it was proposing the League of Nations and the United Nations, or its corporations were scattering production activities in multiple countries.

Table 6.7 Interdependence Versus Integration in Mexico–U.S. Post–9/11 Relations

Dimension	Descriptions
1. Channels of communications	Still multiple after 9/11 security integration
2. Hierarchy of issues in those channels	Clearly restored: security for United States, economic matters for Mexico; and neither country can talk meaningfully to the other about their top priority issues
3. Placement of military in that hierarchy	Prioritization for the United States; still subordinate for Mexico
4. Membership in institutions	Deficiency noticeable for both: Security cooperation attempted more through parallel state institutions, not bilateral, nor regional, nor even multilateral—at least in Mexico–U.S. relations
5. Catalysts of change	Security dynamics on the ground, but outside of North America, not technological innovation (though deployed only along borders)
6. Relationship between nationalism-regionalism-globalization levels of analysis	Very much a return to nationalistic preferences

The second and third dimensions find Mexico and the United States poles apart, given the underlying differences and weights over a security culture. Mexican policies reflect primarily upon internal dynamics, such as party competition; for the United States, policies reflect not only internal competition between parties, but also and sometime primarily, international competition—for example, against the Soviet Union during the Cold War, or against terrorism after 9/11.

Finally, the respective views of competition also differ. For Mexico, since it is almost exclusively domestic, there is an element of order: parties win or lose elections, then try the next time, and so forth. True, the 2006 elections was chaotic; but that was an exception. Although charges of electoral fraud have historically been more common in Mexico, there has not been a political breakdown, at least

Table 6.8 Neorealism, Mexico–U.S. Relations, and 9/11

Dimension	Descriptions
1. State as dominant actor	Yes, very much restored
2. Policy reflecting internal or international competition	For United States, it is international threat possibilities, not competitiveness; for Mexico internal developments
3. International competition orderly or disorderly?	Both: For United States, if seen through conventional warfare, it is orderly but growing; if seen through terrorism lenses, it is selectively anarchic. For Mexico: Question is not so pertinent, but economically, competition seems to be natural and orderly; through security, it is more anarchical than before

not until 2006. In the United States, there is also the orderliness of political competition within, in spite of recent procedural malfunctions, but the overriding influence has been the anarchical view of the world outside, and how failure in competing with challenges abroad would permit this anarchy to prevail within.

Summary

Walking through the tenets of the various schools, Mexico–U.S. relations still reflect a mixed-bag today. In and of itself, the observation is not any reason for panic. Seen within the context of developments in the last fifteen years, however, the bag looks more weighty, less manageable, and even less a source of future pathways or confidence. This is a source of concern. Adjusting to changes is not a new state preoccupation, but when the parts do not add up to the whole, a blueprint is absent at any crossroads, or disconnections outweigh connections, then optimism plays second fiddle to pessimism. And that is but the start of a vicious cycle.

STILL ROLLING: MEXICO–U.S. TRADE BOOM AND BURSTING CROSS-BORDER EXTERNALITIES

Turning to trade and externalities, the mixed-bag theme constantly resurfaces here too. This section assesses the impact of border securitization on the overall U.S.–Mexico trade, immigration, drug-trafficking, and the overall border dynamics against that setting; and it does so under five consecutive rubrics: trade, drugs and illegal immigration, institutional capacity building, trilateralism, and a theoretical discussion of all of the above. Largely due to historical, economic, cultural, and political reasons, Mexico consistently follows anti-interventionist foreign policy prescriptions, and pays respect to domestic national sovereignty, and self-determination.

The closer the economic ties between Mexico and the United States, the more the asymmetries become visible, sometimes as a diminishing function, at other times increasingly. Consider income and population growth: Whereas Mexico's 1990 GDP (gross domestic product) of $US238 billion was only 4 percent of the U.S. GDP and its 86 million people 34 percent of the U.S. population, by 2004, this GDP expanded to $US676 billion, or 5.7 percent of the U.S. GDP, while its 104 million population constituted about 35 percent of the U.S. population.[36] Together with Canada, they helped make the NAFTA the world's largest regional market at the time, with Mexico's U.S. trade expanding tremendously after 1994. On the eve of 2001, the United States accounted for over 85 percent of Mexican exports whereas in 1993, this share was 82.8 percent,[37] creating interdependence of sorts to go with the symmetrical-asymmetrical pushes and pulls.

Mexico–U.S. relations, on the other hand, have been neither antagonistic nor carefree. The sheer number of the people and vehicles crossing the Mexico–U.S. border dwarfs the Canada–U.S. border counterparts, but these have had to confront post–9/11 security regulations. Home to 12 million people, the Mexico–U.S. border, like the Canada–U.S. borderland, has its own dynamic, spread across

48 counties in four states: Arizona, California, New Mexico, and Texas.[38] Although the United States and Mexico share over 1,900 miles of common border, many policies have been openly divergent.

Bilateral Trade and Movement of People

At first sight, trade shows a promising picture. One NAFTA benefit was Mexico's significant and repeated trade surpluses with the United States. Table 6.9 shows U.S. imports from Mexico have consistently outpaced U.S. exports to that country since 1995. In the immediate aftermath of 9/11, the total U.S. imports from Mexico in 2002 actually registered a 3 percent increase over 2001 but less than 1 percent decline over 2000. By 2003, the total dollar value of U.S. imports from Mexico had exceeded the 2000 peak of $US136 billion by 2 billion dollars. By 2005, the U.S. imports represented an increase of 25 percent over the 2000 total amount, and although a lot of U.S. imports were oil and intraindustry exchanges, border restrictions did not get in the way of these flows. Whereas the oil flows invite even more stringent U.S. vigil, the intraindustry, or *maquila,* networks, show the underlying interdependent and asymmetrical relationship between the two economies: cheaper U.S. products would be impossible without low-wage Mexican labor.

U.S. exports to Mexico in 2002, declining 2.9 percent from 2001 and 11.7 percent from 2000, took longer to recover than imports. By 2004, exports had recovered to the dollar level of total exports registered in 2000. But by 2005, total U.S. exports to Mexico of $US120 billion marked an 8 percent increase over 2000. The total trade value with Mexico has now exceeded its pre–9/11 peaks, although China pushed Mexico from being the second largest U.S. trade partner to the third slot. Overall, this represents a significant strengthening of the Mexico–U.S. relations, despite the reported delays and increased militarization of the common border.[39]

Since many of the border security measures restrict unwanted personnel entry, it is important to examine travel data along the Mexico–U.S. border. Table 6.10 examines the incoming personal travel data by states along the Mexico–U.S. border. Between 2001 and 2005, the total number of persons entering the United States from Mexico as pedestrians and in buses, trains, and vehicles, declined by 10.9 percent. Except for the 38 percent increase in New Mexico border crossings, in Arizona, California, and Texas, the flows declined, suggesting a critical pattern, of illegal and legal flows shadowing each other, though for entirely different reasons: Illegal flows

Table 6.9 U.S.–Mexico Trade Data, 1995–2005 ($US billion)

	1995	1996	1997	1998	1999	2000	2001	2002	2003	2004	2005
U.S. imports	62	74	86	95	110	136	131	135	138	156	170
U.S. exports	46	57	71	79	87	111	101	98	97	111	120

Source: U.S. Census Bureau, *Foreign Trade Division, Data Dissemination Branch* (Washington DC, 2006).

shifted to the Arizona desert after security-checks and walls sprang up around well-established entry-points in California and Texas; and any kind of flows, legal or illegal, spur informal economies at transit points. Nevertheless, in absolute numbers, about 235 million persons crossed the border legally in 2005, far below the peak number of 290 million reached in 2000.

Table 6.11 shows the number of personal vehicles, buses, and trucks did not significantly change, with the total number of vehicles crossing into the United States increasing by only 1 percent in 2005 compared to 2001. The absolute number exceeded 107 million if all border crossings in the four states are added. However, except for the state of California border crossings, the number of incoming vehicles slightly declined along the rest of the border. But because the increase in the volume along the California crossings was to the order of 16 percent, it more than compensated for the decline elsewhere.

According to table 6.12, the air travel data present interesting trends. The total number of overnight travel by Mexican residents to the United States during 2001–2005 registered an increase of 9.6 percent, comparable to the 9.1 percent increase in total number of U.S. residents' overnight travel to Mexico. Between 2001 and 2005, the percentage increase in travel by air increased by 26.7 percent from Mexico to the United States and by 29.2 percent from the United States to Mexico. The total number of air travels in both directions eclipsed the respective peaks reached earlier during 2000–2001. The total number of same-day travel by Mexican residents to the United States registered a modest increase of 2.7 percent during 2001–2005, still below the peak number of 116.2 million reached in 2000. But the total number of same day travel by U.S. residents to Mexico registered a decline of 3.4 percent during 2001–2005, far below the peak number of 81.5 million reached in 2000.

These data remain consistent with the data on U.S. domestic airline passengers for the same time period. According to Bureau of Transportation statistics, in July 2004, the total number of monthly airline passengers surpassed the peak number of 65.4 million registered in the month of July of 2001. By July of 2005, the monthly total of airline passengers had reached 74 million.[40]

The cross-border air travel data in particular remain consistent with the upbeat data on passenger traffic on the U.S. domestic airlines since 2004, which likely indicates a greater level of confidence.[41]

The Bureau of Transportation statistics indicate about 80 percent of passenger vehicle trips across the border with Mexico involve same-day travel to participate in daily activities, such as commuting to work, shopping, visiting family and friends, and accessing schools or healthcare.[42] The passenger data both on land and on air reveal that that part of the border dynamics has been negatively affected since 2001. The delays and the restrictions put in place have either caused fewer people to travel or have made travel more expensive if the alternative is to take to the skies.

The events of September 11, 2001 brought in great vigilance along the Mexico–U.S. border although Mexico was not home to a single terrorist involved in the 9/11 events. Nonetheless, the country in general and the border in particular faced the consequences of an increased securitization across the border. The fact that

Table 6.10 Number of Incoming Persons and Vehicles (in 000s): Pedestrians, Passengers, and Personal Vehicles by state

State	1995	2000	2001	2002	2003	2004	2005	2001–05 percent change
Arizona	29,205	35,419	32,899	36,758	33,790	34,511	32,757	–0.04
California	46,183	94,842	90,520	88,626	90,530	85,909	84,285	–6.9
New Mexico	611	1,776	1,544	1,961	1,897	1,880	2,136	+38.3
Texas	127,574	158,331	139,030	125,895	119,902	120,123	115,787	–8.0
Total	203,573	290,368	263,993	253,240	246,119	142,423	234,965	–10.9

Source: Bureau of Transportation Statistics, 1995–2005.

Table 6.11 Number of Incoming Vehicles Along Mexico–U.S. Border (in 000s) : Personal Vehicles, Buses, and Trucks by state

State	1995	2000	2001	2002	2003	2004	2005	2001–05 percent change
Arizona	8,637	10,663	10,451	10,753	10,240	10,532	10,340	−1.06
California	12,912	32,331	31,351	33,179	33,880	35,818	36,417	+16.1
New Mexico	349	504	12,554	12,941	11,658	11,376	11,102	−11.5
Texas	42,856	53,586	51,709	49,854	47,821	48,943	49,284	–4.6
Total	64,754	97,084	106,065	106,727	103,599	106,669	107,143	+1.0

Source: Bureau of Transportation Statistics, 1995–2005.

Table 6.12 Mexico–U.S. Passenger Data, 1990–2005 (in million)

Mexico–U.S. data	1990	1995	2000	2001	2002	2003	2004	2005	2001–05 percent change
Mexican residents overnight travel to United States	7.0	8.2	10.6	11.6	11.4	10.5	11.9	12.7	9.6
By air	0.9	0.8	1.4	1.5	1.5	1.6	1.8	1.9	26.7
Mexican residents same day travel to United States	91.5	94.7	116.2	112.0	112.7	111.9	116.4	115.1	2.7
By air	n.a.	n.a.	n.a.	n.a.	n.a.	n.a.	n.a.	n.a.	–
U.S. residents overnight travel to Mexico	16.4	19.2	19.3	18.6	18.5	17.6	19.4	20.3	9.1
By air	3.6	4.7	6.7	6.5	6.2	6.7	7.7	8.4	29.2
U.S. residents same day travel to Mexico	64.0	63.5	81.5	77.1	75.3	68.7	72.1	74.5	–3.4
By air	n.a.	n.a.	n.a.	n.a.	n.a.	n.a.	n.a.	n.a.	–

Source: North American Transportation Statistics Database, 1990–2005.

Table 6.13 Inspections at U.S. Ports of Entry, 1999–2004 (in million)

	1999	2000	2001	2002	2003	2004
All ports of entry	525.2	534.2	510.6	444.7	427.7	428.9
Land ports of entry	435.3	437.9	414.4	358.4	338.6	333.3
Mexican border	319.5	324.0	314.3	274.4	259.4	254.7
Land inspection as percent of all inspections	82.9	82.0	81.2	80.6	79.2	77.7

Source: DHS, Office of Immigration Statistics, Performance Analysis System (PAS) G-22.1.

greater vigilance is present along the Mexico–U.S. border is illustrated in table 6.13. The total number of inspections in all ports of entry declined consistently since 2000. Land ports in particular registered a sustained decline in total number of inspections. For example, the total number of inspections registered at 358 million in 2001, while by 2004 the number had declined to 333 million. Decomposing data at the Mexican border entry points, it can be seen that the total number of inspections have steadily declined since 2001. An explanation could be people seeking other forms of entry not requiring inspection, in particular illegal modes of entry. However, it is possible that absolute numbers alone do not convey the full picture, since inspections can be quite intense even though these have been fewer. Nonetheless, it is possible to use these data to indirectly reflect the impact of the post–9/11 securitization of the Mexico–U.S. border.

Commensurate with this declining trend in total inspection has been a sustained increase in the total number of border patrol agents along the border. For example, table 6.14 shows there were 8,700 agents along the border, in 2000; by fiscal year 2004 that number had increased to 10,500. Although not available from the same date source as yet, after 2006, over 36,000 U.S. border patrol agents were deployed along the Mexico–U.S. border to protect both the walls being constituted (370 miles complete in early 2008—roughly half the projected target) and the desert-land in between.[43]

Establishing a causal logic to the spiraling undocumented worker apprehensions along the Mexico–U.S. border is difficult. As can be seen from table 6.15, the number of apprehensions quickly declined to 960,000 from 1.2 million in 2001, but increased to 1.2 million in 2004. The total number of apprehensions of undocumented immigrants probably represents a switching of their points of entry. As the number of border patrol agents posted along certain corridors increased, mainly along the Arizona and Southern California borders, would-be migrants moved to unprotected areas along the New Mexico and Texas borders, a move that was not entirely unanticipated, but confirming the need for a comprehensive U.S.–Mexican immigration strategy.

The relations with Mexico are complex, largely due to the vastness of jurisdictions on both sides of the border. As stated earlier, the border area on the U.S. side encompasses 48 counties in four southwestern states. In addition to that, Texas and New Mexico have about 1,300 unauthorized *colonias,* unincorporated semirural communities

Table 6.14 Number of Border Patrol Agents On-board, 1994–2004 (in 000s)

1994	1995	1996	1997	1998	1999	2000	2001	2002	2003	2004
4.1	4.5	6.0	6.5	8.0	8.2	8.7	10.0	10.2	10.4	10.5

Source: U.S. Department of Homeland Security, U.S. Customs and Border Protection, *Performance and Annual Report.* Various issues, available at www.cbp.gov/linkhandler/cgov/toolbox/publications/admin/cbp.

90 percent of all border patrol agents are stationed along the U.S.–Mexican border; the rest along the U.S.–Canadian border.

without sufficient basic facilities of water, electricity, and waste disposal systems. About 30 percent of all foreign born population in the United States today is from Mexico, with an additional 6.2 million undocumented immigrants.[44]

In the 2003 budget, the U.S. president allocated nearly $US11 billion for increased border security, including $US380 million for the ICE to construct a state of the art entry-exit system.[45] This additional funding is expected to modernize the border transit system in order to facilitate a seamless air, land, and sea border between the two countries, the ultimate goal of which is to ensure U.S. security while permitting a fast movement of legitimate goods, services, and people across the border crossing-points. Of course, any coercive measure across the southern border that infringes upon the lifestyle of the border communities is bound to invoke strong political and cultural undercurrents.

Despite the militarization of the southern border, the number of trucks passing through the Mexico–U.S. border crossings increased by 63 percent during 1994–2004.[46] The volume of the land inspections, as stated earlier, has declined between 2000 and 2004. As observed, so far 370 miles of fences dot the Mexico–U.S. border, mostly in California and Texas.[47] A 2006 legislation approved by both houses of the U.S. Congress authorized the construction of an additional 700 miles of border fence.[48]

War on Drugs and Illegal Immigration

Mexico has been included in the annual certification by the U.S. State Department as a major drug transit or drug-producing country. This is an important characterization since the drug policy has now been fully integrated into a broader notion of national security. The 2006 fiscal year certification list by the Secretary of

Table 6.15 Apprehension of Undocumented Immigrants Along Mexico–U.S. Border (in 000s)

1994	1995	1996	1997	1998	1999	2000	2001	2002	2003	2004
1,000	1,250	1,450	1,350	1,460	1,480	1,650	1,210	960	950	1,200

Source: U.S. Department of Homeland Security, U.S. Customs and Border Protection, *Performance and Annual Report,* Various issues, available at www.cbp.gov/linkhandler/cgov/toolbox/publications/admin/cbp.

State designated Mexico, along with Afghanistan, the Bahamas, Bolivia, Brazil, Colombia, Dominican Republic, Ecuador, Guatemala, Haiti, India, Jamaica, Laos, Myanmar, Nigeria, Pakistan, Panama, Paraguay, Peru and Venezuela.[49] Although certification does not necessarily imply a lack of cooperation with the United States over drug-control, it does indicate a tense area of bilateral contact with Mexico.

Illegal drug problems are rather complex, encompassing not just Mexico and drug-trafficking, but also U.S. society and official policy. The U.S. drug policy on illegal drugs has included elements of extradition, eradication, and interdiction. Each component of the drug problem is thus associated with the consumption of drugs in the United States and the production and trafficking of drugs in Mexico and the larger Latin America. Studies have reported a direct correlation between drugs and criminal violence.[50]

Mexico has become the transit point for drugs aimed at the U.S. market. Observers have noted that as much as 70–90 percent of all illegal drugs entering the United States use Mexico as the transit route.[51] Along the Mexico–U.S. border, kidnappings have flourished along with drug trade. Much of the illegal arms found in Mexico have been traced back to the United States, so the pressure on Mexico to do more has only limited impact. The U.S. hard-line policy on illegal immigration and the proposal to expand the border fence is only likely to complicate cooperation in this important area of mutual security.

Although the previous Fox administration in Mexico had collaborated with the United States in security matters, in the area of illegal drugs there were considerable problems. Over the six years of the Fox administration, drug-related violence plagued many Mexican states, claiming as many as 2,000 lives in 2006 alone, over 9,000 in the six years of the Fox administration.[52] Of these, feuding drug gangs accounted for 500 murders in 2006, mostly in key northern states along the U.S.–Mexico border as well as Michoacán.[53]

The administration of President Felipe Calderón commenced with a similar crusade against narcotrafficking, hoping to increase cooperation with the United States. Immediately after his inauguration, in December 2006, 7,000 federal troops were dispatched to the state of Michoacán to combat drug operations. About 600 acres of marijuana crops were destroyed in this operation.[54] In January 2007, the Mexican government dispatched 3,000 federal troops to the Northern city of Tijuana to combat drug-related organized crime,[55] while thousands more were sent to Acapúlco in the first week of February following the murder of government officials by ostensibly drug traffickers.[56] The troops were backed by 28 boats, 21 airplanes, and 9 helicopters.[57] A similar campaign against *Zeta* defectors from the military in Tamaulipas is underway in 2008. Given the high correlation between illegal drugs, gang-related violence, and potential terrorism implications, the new Calderón administration proposed that the share of the internal ministry's budget on national security and intelligence be increased to 40 percent from the current level of about 20 percent.[58]

Yet, Calderón's vigorous campaigns belong to an emerging pattern: presidents begin their terms in similar dramatic fashion, before tapering off as the tenure approached its end. Fox's much publicized initial efforts broke the Tijuana Arellano cartel, capturing or killing three of the notorious brothers, in addition to putting behind bars several other kingpins. Midway through his tenure, though, splinter factions replacing the cartels essentially ruled many border towns. Even the U.S. State Department frequently warned tourists against visiting those towns.

Though less important than cocaine, illegally cultivated marijuana reportedly declined by 75 percent since 2004 due to increased Mexican government involvement, especially in Sinaloa and Michoacán.[59] Increased cooperation led to 63 individuals with cross-border drug trafficking, and extraditing them to the United States on December 1, 2006 by the Calderón administration.[60] Efforts to institute a national drug czar in Mexico, along the lines of the United States hope to better coordinate the antidrug operations.[61] The U.S. DEA has solicited permission to open offices in three of the most drug-related violence ridden cities of Mexico: Nuevo Laredo, Matamoros, and Nogales.[62] These offices, once installed, are expected to oversee the protection of U.S. property and interests, including the consular offices in the area.

Marijuana, however, is a far more harmless contraband than the cocaine industry, which rakes in more money and is far more deadly. Here there has been less success, especially with the sources falling outside of Mexico, or along Mexico's coasts; and increasingly these rely upon Central American gangs, many of whose members were returning to the United States, from where they were expelled for illegal activities.

Over time, the matters of illegal drugs and the interdiction of other banned substances have been collapsed into military operations in and around Mexico and the general Central American neighborhood. The U.S. Southern Command's jurisdiction has been extended over Central and South America, and the Gulf of Mexico. The U.S. NORTHCOM has also extended its jurisdiction over Mexico and Central America to a minimum of 500 miles.[63] In that regard, since 2000, the U.S. DOD has created four new FOLs (forward operating locations): Manta (Ecuador), Queen Beatrix (Aruba), Hato (Curacao), and Comalapa (El Salvador).[64]

The increased coordination in establishing security operation across the Caribbean has been strongly correlated with a growing consensus between the United States and Mexico on the issue of illegal drugs as a growing threat to the hemisphere. The greater use of the military to fight the production of illegal drugs and supply centers across Latin America has been viewed with increased apprehension. But the militarization of the illegal drugs issue in the Andean countries and the strong involvement of the United States in the process have had little effect in stemming the flow of illegal narcotics into the United States.[65]

The reaction of groups within Mexico in the production and transportation of illegal drugs is very much a reaction to the successful domestic controls exercised by the United States. For example, although increased interinstitutional cooperation has been observed in the security matters, the flow of Mexican methamphetamine into the U.S. multiplied. This has been largely due to the federal crackdown on domestic U.S. production of such material.[66] Recently, the *Los Angeles Times* reported that as the number of super labs producing methamphetamine declined from 125 in 2003 to 12 in California in 2006, those of Mexican origin seized along the U.S.–Mexican border increased by 50 percent, from 4,030 pounds in 2003 to 6,063 pounds in 2005.[67] If such trends continue, coordination to combat potential terrorists could be adversely affected.

Illegal Immigration

The issues of illegal drug and national security are complicated by the thorny problem of illegal immigration along the Mexico–U.S. border. With the increasing bundling of terrorism and crime globally, the issue of illegal immigration, unless handled judiciously, could make matters worse. Immigration can be a powerful tool of American "soft power" if those who come and live in the United States build up positive experiences in and about American society. On the other hand, it could (a) harden attitudes in U.S. societies, such as reflected by supporters of the Minutemen project, for example; (b) spill over into Mexico, and deepen anti-*gringo* sentiments; and (c) ultimately disrupt positive bilateral developments. Just as a positive image can be a catalyst for greater integration of the Mexican economy and society with the United States and Canada,[68] a negative image can produce exact opposite effects.

Both legal and illegal Mexican migration to the United States, though spiraling since 1994, has had a long historical precedent (as noted in chapter 4). During World War II, Mexican contract labor provided needed manpower in agriculture, as the U.S. domestic labor largely shifted to industry. The *Bracero* Program was instituted in 1942 to help alleviate the labor crunch in agriculture. At the peak of this program in 1956, about 450,000 Mexican workers were permitted in the United States.[69] The program, however, was terminated in 1964, but replaced by guest worker programs from 1986 under the IRCA. The demand of labor in the U.S. economy has contributed to a severe surge in both illegal and legal migration of labor over the years. For example, from 1946 to 1954, the apprehension of illegal immigrants on the southern border increased from under 100,000 to over 1 million.[70] U.S. policy responses were stumped by such structural forces as the unfolding U.S. economic transformation.[71] When, in the aftermath of the 1965 immigration reform legislation, a surge in non-European immigration to the United States became a political issue, the 1976 amendments to the Immigration and Nationality Act imposed a limit of 20,000 per country limit on labor visas. This significantly affected Mexico, which had previously been subject to a hemispheric limit of 120,000.[72] The uncontrollable nature of illegal immigration continued and in 1986 IRCA proposed the introduction of military safeguards, yet encouraged illegal immigrants by providing large-scale amnesty.[73] Subsequently, the Immigration Act Amendment of 1994 failed to alleviate the problems of Mexican immigration since it provided only 55,000 new visas to be distributed among the countries that had sent fewer than 55,000 legal immigrants in the previous five years.[74]

During the 1990s, border control with Mexico was transformed from a low-priority issue to a high-profile event attracting much media coverage. As mentioned earlier, the number of border patrol agents more than doubled between 1993 and 2000, just as cross-border trade increased and the coercive control measures were put in place. These measures included fencing in parts of the border, new equipment and surveillance technologies along with new personnel.[75] Two trends went in opposite directions because the two issues were being treated separately.

Many of the new security regulations put in place after 9/11 merely extended what was already in process to enforce border control. Consistent with our first hypothesis of securitization, the new measures through the USA PATRIOT Act (2001) and the Enhanced Border Security and Visa Entry Reform Act (2002) were restrictive in nature, as some of the data on passenger and vehicular travel discussed earlier bore out.

The warning by a U.S. *Task Force on Immigration* on the triple threat of drug smuggling, illegal immigration, and rising violence along the Mexico–U.S. border can derail the limited institutional cooperation gained so far in other areas, such as trade and security of the infrastructure. The DHS reported that of the 1.2 million illegal aliens apprehended in 2005, 165,000 were other than Mexican. Of these 165,000, 650 were from special interest countries.[76] It is important to note that Central American migrants increasingly use Mexico as a transit point on their way to the United States.[77] Many notorious Central American gangs, including the *Mara Salvatrucha* and *La-18,* have been noted to have used Mexico to travel to and from the United States.[78] The suspected networking between Central American gangs and *al Qaeda* members in Central America has made the issue of illegal immigration of Central Americans to the United States through Mexico quite important.[79]

Drug smuggling, human trafficking, and gang operations have also been reported to be correlated, all indicating heightened security threats to both countries.[80] It is interesting to note that such increase in threat has coincided with increased cooperation between the United States and Mexican authorities on law enforcement. How long that continues remains a critical question.

Institutional Capacity Building

Creating the DHS elevated security in bilateral relations. Although the status of the DHS did not settle the historical roles played by the CIA, the FBI, and the DOD intelligence analysis units, it nonetheless set the ball rolling in changing institutional capacity building south of the border. Despite tension over the new wall and an increased presence of border patrol agents and an additional 6,000 members of the various National Guard Units along the border, many capacity-building institutional initiatives were taken after 9/11.[81] A smart border agreement with Mexico was signed in March 2002, as an extension of the one between Canada and the United States in December 2001. Under the 22-point agreement, both President Bush and Mexican President Vicente Fox Quesada announced the then-SENTRI program would be expanded to include specific commuter lanes at high volume ports of entry along the Mexico–U.S. border.[82] The program was designed to set up advance passenger information exchanges for flights between Mexico and the United States, and develop systems for sharing other information and intelligence. Given the availability of the necessary technologies, these multilateral information sharing programs to make the borders were, frankly, futuristic.[83] The upbeat cross-border air travel data discussed earlier can be explained in light of such institutional cooperation.

More crucial is the political will to implement these technological empowerment programs, given the tensions between the United States and Mexico over immigration and drugs, among other issues.[84] Effective law enforcement across international borders is more of a possibility if major technical and financial assistance is given to lesser developed countries, such as Mexico. How the Canada–U.S. border outpaces the Mexico–U.S. border with new technology reveals another North American asymmetry.

Whether the Mexican government can assure the United States and Canadian partners of the reliability of Mexican data systems to share sensitive information through the electronic media remains a big question. The Canada–United States border system already shares a fair amount of sensitive information, but the Mexico–United States system is still a testing ground for such sharing of sensitive financial and technical information.[85] Despite these limitations, in addition to the cooperation described earlier, a series of institutional capacity-building efforts have taken place since 9/11 along the U.S.–Mexican border or between the United States and Mexican authorities.

The USDA (U.S. Department of Agriculture), the FDA, and the Mexican agencies SAGARPA (*La Secretaria de Agricultura, Ganaderia, Desarrollo Rural, Pesca y Alimentacion*) and *La Secretaria de Salud* signed a cooperative agreement in September of 2001 to enhance food safety measures which would include sharing of critical information. The USDA's Food Safety and Inspection Service and SAGARPA are expected to jointly undertake steps to ensure the safety of meat, poultry, and egg products in both countries.[86] Such emphasis on food security can be directly related to the broadening of the security definition on the part of Washington. Public health issues figured prominently in the NSS document circulated in 2006.[87]

A Mexico–U.S. Consultative Committee formed between USDA and Mexico's Ministries of Agriculture and Economic Development studies the critical issues of trade, market access, sanitary measures, and information exchange in areas such as biotechnology, and animal and plant health. Through a Rapid Response Team, it helps the two countries over emerging trade issues, with the main goal being to avoid considerable disruption in the booming trade sector.[88] One of the limitations of NAFTA is that it has not created many institutions to address the issues of unforeseen disruption in the economies due to external political forces or terrorist attacks. In that context, one of the consequences of 9/11 could be the creation of many more institutional arrangements across sectors to quickly analyze and recover from future disruptions of such nature.[89]

The U.S. Department of Energy also created a binational sustainability laboratory, the primary goal of which is to foster long-term, sustainable economic development along the Mexican–U.S. border. The laboratory is expected to help new small- and medium-sized enterprises and strengthen existing ones in providing technical, business, marketing, and financial expertise necessary to help industries on both sides of the border. This is a long-term project but nonetheless aims to improve the quality of life along the border by enhancing the average household income.[90]

The Department of Justice's Border Coordination Initiative coordinates the management of the border between several agencies (Immigration, Customs Service, Coast Guard, and the Department of Agriculture) to facilitate a more efficient strategy to interdict drugs, undocumented humans, and other contraband, such as chemicals or arms. Along with the larger Border Coordination initiative, several smaller initiatives, such as the Border Safety Initiative and Southwest Border Initiative, were put in place after 9/11. The former intends to minimize injuries and death along the Mexico–U.S. border, the latter, in coordination with intelligence gathering Mexican agencies, to counter illegal drug activity by disrupting the established drug transportation routes.[91] We clearly see the hypothesized interactions here between states and at state-society levels.

On the one hand, the 2004 U.S.–Mexico Partnership Treaty for Prosperity outlines a series of steps for both countries to pursue in order to increase economic and labor opportunities in lesser developed areas of Mexico;[92] and on the other, the 2003 Mexican government unilaterally launched *Centinela,* an operation designed to strengthen the detention operations of certain unauthorized immigrants and improve measures to target organized crime and human trafficking along the border.[93] Again, cooperation becomes fundamental, institutionalized, and ongoing, even though it is unlikely to hit everyday headlines.

In 2004, Mexican and U.S. governments signed a Memorandum of Understanding to assist each other in managing migratory flows and in protecting the human rights of immigrants.[94] Embedding OASSIS (Operation Against Smugglers and Traffickers in the Safety and Security Initiative) from 2005, both countries expanded existing agreements and formalized a permanent program against human smuggling. Preventive measures, providing assistance to victims, and promoting information exchanges were part and parcel of these programs connecting states and societal groups, even individuals.[95]

Both Mexico and the United States, along with Canada, are part of the trilateral SPP, launched in 2005, which committed itself to enhancing broader security while at the same time facilitating cross-border movement of people, trade, and overall economic cooperation. A trilateral agreement is thus made to expedite border crossings by expanding the existing traveler and trader programs, and improving the infrastructural facilities at entry ports. Institutionally, the agreement calls for a single, integrated traveler program by 2008,[96] with similar agreements being negotiated on other important security issues, like food safety. The members of the Trilateral SPP have been working on harmonizing the regulations across the three countries on standards of food and other product safety issues, including the elimination of duplicate testing and certification processes.[97]

The NACC was also formed in 2005 among the three countries to develop competitive industries in North America. Cooperation would lead to clean energy technologies, energy conservation, and market facilitation, thereby build greater energy security and promote sustainable development.[98]

The U.S. Department of Transportation has created the National Corridor Planning and Development Program of which Coordinated Border Infrastructure Program is an important part. The program, among others, provides financial support for transportation and safety infrastructure improvement and serves the border regions near Mexico and Canada.[99]

The Border Anti-Smuggling Coalition, the Container Security Initiative, and the C-TPAT are also in place since 9/11 to help the customs agencies of both countries to share passenger information via the Advance Passenger Information System. Presently in the implementation stage, once completely functional in Mexico, it is expected the reciprocal exchange of data will allow the law enforcement in both countries to apprehend individuals with ties to criminal organization expeditiously. These arrangements indicate a move beyond the narrow definition of border and national security.

A national security law was passed in January of 2000 in the Mexican Congress to establish a NSC to improve military, intelligence, immigration, and civilian law enforcement cooperation on security issues, including terrorism.[100] As we previously noted (this chapter and chapter 4), the NSC has struggled to find firm footing; but the idea behind it has not been abandoned nor compromised.

As evident from the section above, multiple institutional structures have been created or upgraded since the events of 9/11 despite the divergence in overall foreign policy goals of both countries. Of course, the extent to which these institutional creations and/or agreements have produced expected outcomes is another issue.

TOWARD TRILATERALISM?

In general, six years after 9/11, without another recorded attack on the U.S. soil, a much broader interpretation of "national security" may be in order. We have already indicated that along the Canadian–U.S. border, the role that private sector groups on both sides have played is particularly important in fostering a stronger cross-border dynamic, despite the continuing delays in completing transactions between the two countries.[101] But as the perception of immediate terrorist threat recedes, U.S. homeland security efforts are likely to be embedded with greater frequency on broader efforts at "societal security," or "total defence" of North America as a whole.

Scholars have advocated the notion that to combat security threats in a powerful way, the efforts must be actor-focused and not state-focused, as happened during the Cold War.[102] The initial toughening up of the U.S. northern and southern borders in the aftermath of 9/11 represented a continuation of such state-based threats. However, the instruments of the military and other law enforcement may project an outwardly aggressive image; in real terms they actually create more hardships for the innocent populations and commercial entities caught in the cross fire.[103] But analyses of the causes of terrorism and the multiple dimensions of security have become grossly inadequate.

Several others in the United States have also advocated changing the very definition of the border.[104] Currently, the border is used in the narrowest possible physical sense of the word, but the more relevant definition of the border should be much broader, originating in places from which people migrate and end in places where migrants eventually settle.[105] Such an approach would humanize the border without compromising on the security issues that may focus along the narrow national borders on terrorism, illegal drugs, and crime.[106]

Important think-tanks also weigh in on the issue of security and national borders in North America. For example, the CFR has recommended that a North American "security perimeter" be in place by the year 2010. A significant part of the reasoning behind such a broader trilateral approach to the issue of security lies in the fact that since the beginning of NAFTA in 1994, the economic, cultural, and social ties between the Canada, Mexico, and the United States have deepened to such an extent that it would be impractical to apply a segmented approach to the various issues that inhabit the borders. In order to better approach the bundling of the interconnected issues of security, trade, and economic integration, it would be prudent to establish a North American Economic and Security Community. The community would include the three countries of Canada, Mexico, and the United States. Its boundaries would be defined by a common external tariff and an outer security perimeter, which would stretch from the Mexico–Guatemala border in the south to the Canadian Arctic in the north.[107]

Other think-tanks, such as the Brookings Institution, have also argued in favor of a broader approach to the issue of national security. Although the DHS creation was a good start, its already manifested weakness in dealing with disasters caused by natural forces, such as Hurricane Katrina in 2005, exposed the fact that the national security efforts cannot be solely focused on a narrow interpretation of the threat. Instead, a broader collaborative approach should be pursued with other countries in combating not only the sources of terrorism but also the causes of other natural and human-made disasters.[108] Incentives have been proposed to involve the private sector in ensuring the broader security of North America.[109] These intellectual arguments indicate a significant change in approaching the issues of national security. The fear of a strong trade-off between economic integration, on the one hand, and achieving a false sense of physical security, on the other, has largely been countered.[110] In that respect at least, these support the direction of trilateralism in North America, if not globally.

THEORETICAL PRECEPTS AND EVALUATIONS

Three theoretical formulations shed most light in Mexico–U.S. relations: neofunctionalism, interdependence, and realism.

Testing the tenets of the neofunctional propositions in the case of U.S.–Mexican relations, several observations can be made. Economic asymmetry between the two countries is likely to still incapacitate institutionalized attempts at security cooperation. This is more likely to affect both partners negatively. In contrast to the immediate aftermath of 9/11, in the five-odd years since, relations have relatively warmed up with the new Mexican administration, signifying high elite complementarity.[111] However, the border fence and immigration issues will continue to dampen cooperation. Table 6.16 outlines the U.S.–Mexico relations five years after 9/11.

While the third trait, pluralism, did not prove relevant after 9/11 or in pre–9/11 and post–9/11 comparisons, the fourth, adaptation, clearly shows diminishing post–9/11 salience: the United States has priorities elsewhere, and Mexico is not too keen about those priorities. Trade still flows in large volumes across the boundaries, but as the fifth feature points out, spillover is everywhere except over military security: It is not that both countries confront each other, but Mexico's indifference to military security often increases U.S. intervention, especially over drug-trafficking pushing the relationship in a negative intervention, especially over drug-trafficking, adding a negative tone to the relationship.

In terms of transactions, growth is evident in volumes, but Mexico slipped from the second U.S. trading partner to third, and Mexico is also importing proportionately less from the United States, as chapter 4 observed. Intergovernmental relational growth, the seventh characteristic, has been at the expense of pre–9/11 supranational tendencies; while transnational growth also remains high, indicating how wedlocked both countries remain. Although elite socialization was high before 9/11 under economic integration, 9/11 introduced an unusual but short-lived breach, indicating how the two countries cannot ignore each other, especially at the decision-making levels.

The eleventh feature of increasing interaction with external actors speaks more for the United States than the largely introverted Mexico, especially owing to its indifference toward the war as terrorism (a contrast with Canada). Neofunctionalist benefits still accrue for both countries, but increasing costs over the Mexico–U.S. border contrasts the Canada–U.S. border. Because of the different external orientations noted with the eleventh trait, the thirteenth characteristic also finds United States seeking this, Mexico not so interested. Finally, hitherto cost-free neofunctionalist integration faces more constraints, thereby pushing up costs, after 9/11.

Applying the tenets of interdependence versus integration theories to the bilateral relations, table 6.17 captures two observations. First, NAFTA has contributed to a greater integration of the two economies as tariffs fell in record pace, as channels of communications expanded, issue-hierarchy disappeared, and military considerations fell before 9/11. However, 9/11 did not expand institutional engagements, whether within NAFTA or with other regimes. In spite of trade remaining a significant catalyzer, and investment a diminishing one, both Mexico and the United States shielded behind national preferences over regional or multilateral after 9/11. Although 9/11 introduced disruptions, the overall forces of integration continue advancing. But these forces are likely to be affected by the link between economic growth and externalities (such as immigration). Second, although the military continues to be subordinated to the civilian command in both countries, the use of the military in combating illegal drugs operations and violence has increased. This may give the Mexican military a much more powerful say in bilateral security negotiations, possibly expediting greater interdependence, although the United States would like this

Table 6.16 Neofunctionalist Attributes, 2006

Dimension	Mexico–United States
1. Economic asymmetry	Asymmetry persists *vis-à-vis* Mexico; the ratio of the U.S.–Mexican economies in terms of the size is 20:1
2. Elite complementarity	Low complementarity with the Fox administration immediately after 9/11 was a recent aberration (but recovered somewhat in the third and fourth years); under Calderón's administration, relations have so far been warmer
3. Pluralism	Not terribly relevant after 9/11, perhaps reflecting the diminishing role of neofunctionalism after 9/11
4. Capacity to adapt	The degree of pre–9/11 adaptation by both countries to each other clearly seems to be missing post–9/11
5. Spillover	Spillover is evident in many economic issue-areas, but not catching on over military security; the extent of popular bifurcation of sentiments as a reaction to U.S. policies is still greater five years after 9/11
6. Growing transactions	The extent of total economic transaction has actually grown faster by the second and third years after 9/11 and has eclipsed the pre–9/11 peaks, and is growing much faster
7. Growth in intergovernmentalism	Despite inherent tensions, limited intergovernmentalism has been created; more so on military economic, and security matters than on social matters and reflecting bilateral more than trilateral concerns
8. Transnational growth	Has grown after a short decline post–9/11; grown faster than with Canada since the third year after 9/11
9. Elite socialization	Fox took this to a peak before 9/11 before plunging to a recent low; Calderón reestablishing this element
10. Growth in ideological identity	Export-oriented regions in the North have identified more with the United States than the politically sensitive central and south Mexico; but externalities constrain proper growth
11. Increasing interaction with external actors	Much greater interaction with United States and Canada in areas of technology, security info and patents; Mexico conspicuous by placing almost all eggs in North American basket
12. Benefit distribution higher and more equitable	Since 9/11, costs have been greater over Mexico–U.S. border than Canada–U.S. border; still considerably higher than the pre–9/11 days, due to increased militarization of the border
13. Converging perceptions of external problems	Mexico's introversion contrasting with U.S. extroversion feeds into quite dissimilar interpretations across the board
14. Integration as cost free	Although economic transaction levels have now exceeded the pre–9/11 levels, Mexico faces greater social, emotional, and human cost (at the border) than Canada

to be extended to multilateral security arrangements. The issues of Central American gang-related violence and illegal transit through Mexico may also form a catalyst and help push for greater integration on security issues, but again, these pale into insignificance against U.S. security considerations. Ultimately, state-society tension is expected in the United States because of this ordering.

On the other hand, table 6.18 depicts neorealist concerns continuing to bypass Mexico. Though the central government continues to play the role of the main arbiter in Mexico versus the provincial governments, legislative differences weaken the state, and thereby Mexico's limited external role diminishes even further. It has not traditionally been a country involved in global or regional power balances, at least since World War II, but since its vital interest is the bilateral relationship with the United States, how the United States responds to global competitiveness becomes

Table 6.17 Interdependence Versus Integration in Mexican–U.S. Relations

Dimension	Mexico–United States
1. Channels of communication	Interdependence has been a constant in Mexico–U.S. relations, maturing into trade integration under NAFTA, but resurging again after 9/11; integrative efforts over security after 9/11 have not been absent, but need as much vigor and enthusiasm as for economic integration; thus communications remains high, but the tone varies
2. Hierarchy of issues	Immigration, an externality, remains at the top, sometimes with security issues; broader developmental and environmental concerns remain low in the hierarchy
3. Subordination of the military	Military is subordinated to civilian authorities but increasing use of the military to quell domestic unrest and to protect southern Mexican border with Guatemala; concerns about possible repercussions on Mexican authority structure increasing; not willing to go full-speed with the United States against terrorism
4. Nature of institutional membership	Limited integration on military and security institutionalization since 9/11, and even NAFTA has not expanded nor deepened since 9/11
5. Catalyst	Increasing interdependence and integration with the United States in the northern Mexican provincial economies, but southern and central Mexico countervail these tendencies as sources of disruption (illegal emigrants, narcotrafficking, and so forth), suggesting trade and investment to be catalyzers, but externalities as constraints
6. Placement of regionalism along levels of policy-making analysis	Since North American security perimeter is still narrowly conceived, state interests will dominate over regionalization and globalization processes; increasing function after 9/11 for both countries

Table 6.18 The Neorealist Concerns in Mexican–U.S. Relations

Dimension	Mexico–United States
1. State as dominant actor	Mexican central government is still the dominant actor but specific political will and actors within still determine how the state is used. The new president in Mexico has shown much more activism in dealing with security and illegal drugs so far, but neorealists pay more attention to external than internal threats
2. Policy reflecting internal or external competitiveness?	Internal divisions may constrain state policy-making, a development realists do not worry about too much; but external competitiveness continues to be neglected by Mexico given its heavy U.S. accent
3. Is international competitiveness orderly or chaotic	The international context for Mexico remains essentially the United States, with economic engagements much more important than military; but after 9/11, U.S. relations show both order and chaos, given its global commitments and priorities against terrorism

an indirect Mexican concern. So far after 9/11, Mexico has distanced itself from U.S. global pursuits.

CONCLUSIONS

Six conclusions may be drawn from our comparative studies of Mexico and the United States in terms of security and economic integration. First, in spite of many odds, both historical and contemporary, the Mexico–U.S. relationship remains a critical component of the security and economic welfare of both. Endogenous problems, like Mexico's indifference to 9/11 in the initial days and the overpowering economic asymmetry in the region, did not prevent the proliferation of common institutions. Exogenous problems, particularly the externalities, strain cooperation: If not checked, these could impose more irreversible bilateral damage than terrorism. Common to both types of problems is the salience of bilateralism over trilateralism or regionalism; even unilateralism inevitably seeks a bilateral exit. Determining which way the wind will blow, we posit, is not a helpful exercise, since too many unlike vectors are at play to forge a common picture. Through the strengths and weaknesses, though, our salient finding is simply: Damaging this bilateral relationship would make victory in the war against terrorism impossible.

Second, although we find institutions exerting a stabilizing role, as they should, our study also underscores the need to come to terms with the peculiarities (*procedures* in our parlance) in the bilateral relations. Oftentimes reflective of cultural traits, these peculiarities will not automatically go away; but streamlining them and living with them offers the best hope of redressing many attendant problems, or externalities. Our study reaffirms both Mexico and the United States having two very different military cultures and two very different economic orientations; yet common institutions were still developed on both fronts to satisfy the common needs of both countries, suggesting how the drug-trafficking and illegal immigration externalities can also be contained if handled symmetrically by both countries, and particularly if peculiarities within Mexico (corruption, above all) can be arrested.

Third, behind states, as well as their policies and institutions, this chapter finds societal groups performing essential tasks both enhancing and challenging the bilateral relationship independently. Whether as individuals or in groups, these actors were not only most evident with migration and drug-trafficking, but also silently present in the trade, investor, business executive, and think-tank sectors. When official relations become sour, we found nongovernmental interactions silently performing compensatory roles, suggesting how the positive side of the externalities equation can be brought to bear on the negative side. One implication of this is the need to not look only at the state to resolve bilateral problems. As engaged actors, individuals and groups can also chip in.

Fourth, integrative and interdependent relations under both security and economic fronts consistently satisfy our expectation of binational policy structures (that is, without claims of single-state sovereignty), such as many forms of trade, while others remain very nationalistic, such as immigration. In turn, we found theory-specific applications producing weaker explanations than multiple-theory applications.

Fifth, although we did not find security considerations or imperatives providing the prerequisites of economic interaction, since NAFTA was progressing independently, we expect the future to show more security-based determinants: Both drug-trafficking and illegal Mexican emigration have spiraled after 9/11, but most importantly, external forces, that is, forces from outside Mexico and the United States, and therefore outside the control of Mexico and the United States, increasingly participate in these illegal flows. This is a concern now, and a possible source of future threat.

Sixth, impressed by the admixture of rational choices (welfare-enhancing behavior, such as trade), constraints (externalities), cultures (environmentally driven behavior), and history, we see a future reflecting that mixture: combining integration and interdependence, security and economic, national and transnational. In that sense, retreating from the grand visions of the 1990s (*north americanization,* for example) may produce some pessimism; but by grappling with concurrent problems, a more realistic future of conflict and cooperation can be bequeathed to the generations to come.

7

Canada, Mexico, and Homeland Security: Oddballs

INTRODUCTION

After putting their hearts, minds, and souls into NAFTA, Canada and Mexico went their separate ways over post–9/11 security integration. Why did their orientations differ? How theoretically and empirically relevant is the Canada–Mexico partnership in a region driven by weighty bilateral relations?

Both questions derive from the project's three arguments and underlying hypothesis. The first argument posits that security considerations prevail in any trade-off with economic integration, converting FTAs into strategic trade compacts if needed. Integrative behavior, in turn, is overtaken by interdependence, with trade diversification and security free ridership as spin-offs. Third, state-society tensions increase—internally, intergovernmentally, and transnationally. Hypothetically, U.S. homeland security shifts North America's trilateralist trajectory toward bilateralism, invoking three contexts/levels of analysis: domestic, regional, and external (beyond North America). Policy-making is at the domestic level, comparing policy responses brings in the region, and 9/11 responses impose the external.

Institutionalized 9/11 responses operationalize all three contexts. As the United States moved toward homeland security, Canada responded through Bill C-36, Mexico through the CISEN Act and Border Action Plan. Comparing both historically exposes two intelligence cultures,[1] raising the regional question how NAFTA was impacted, and the external query of whether U.S. neighbors stand united in the war against terrorism.

This chapter is organized accordingly. Three sections address each of the three levels/contexts, and then a fourth draws conclusions and projects implications.

BROAD DOMESTIC CONTEXT

Given the lack of depth and sufficiency in the Canada–Mexico bilateral relationship, this chapter departs from the others by examining the impacts of a variety of traditional elements (leaders, their guiding philosophy or ideology, party politics, policy priorities, the resource base, including the state of the economy, and public opinion). It then assesses the intelligence institutions. Trade and investment, since they are paltry, both absolutely and relatively across North America, are omitted, but without significantly undermining the comparisons between Canada and Mexico, pre– and post–9/11 climates, and initial versus subsequent post–9/11 phases. Table 7.1 guides the first set of discussions.

Personalities

The chemistry between leaders matters: Harmony or disharmony between them shapes policy preferences, but need not necessarily predict outcomes. Canada's Jean Chrétien (1992–2003) never really got along with George W. Bush before 9/11, and afterwards only half-heartedly.[2] This disagreeable chemistry contrasts with the very warm relation he had with William H. Clinton. Until 9/11, both Vicente Fox Quesada and George W. Bush were each other's best friends, and together pushed Canada to the background: Bush broke diplomatic tradition by making his first

Table 7.1 Domestic Contexts in Comparative Light

Elements	Pre–9/11		Post–9/11	
	Canada	Mexico	Canada	Mexico
1. Personalities	Jean Chrétien	Vicente Fox Quesada	Jean Chrétien, Paul Martin, Stephen Harper	Vicente Fox Quesada, Felipe Calderón
2. Guiding philosophy/ ideology	Liberalism	Conservatism, Washington consensus	Liberalism-Conservatism	Conservatism
3. Political party in charge	Liberals dominate in 1990s	PAN displaces PRI on eve of 9/11	Liberal, Conservative	PAN
4. Policy Priorities	Harmony with United States until Bush's 2000 elections; divergences thereafter until Harper's 2006 victory	Immigration agreement as fulcrum to deeper integration	Active: yes to war on terrorism, no to Iraq war; from limited to greater partnership	Passive: sympathy to war on terrorism, no to war in Iraq; from camaraderie to aloofness
5. Resources/ State of the Economy	Available/Good	Available/Good	Available/Good	Available/Good
6. Public Opinion	Wary of United States	Hopeful toward United States	Steady shift from wariness to identity	Shift from hope toward suspicion

foreign visit to Mexico, instead of Canada, in 2001, only to reverse gears in 2005. Unfortunately for the Mexico–U.S. relationship, the immigration deadlock haunted five of Fox's six-year tenure, and President-elect Felipe Calderón assumed office in December 2006, three months after the U.S. Congress voted to build up to 700 additional miles of walls on the Mexico–U.S. border.[3] Steve Harper's 2006 victory strengthened U.S. relations, a shift his predecessor, Paul Martin, initiated in fits and starts from 2003.[4] In Canada's 2006 election campaign, however, Martin's belittling of Bush brought back memories of Chrétien.[5] Unpredictable personal chemistry complicates politics-as-usual.

Philosophy/Ideology

Martin's fluctuating U.S. relations also suggest ideological identity cannot be taken for granted. Personality can trump philosophical and ideological preferences, but identical philosophical orientations or ideological preferences do not always enhance bilateral relations. Fox and Bush were both from the same side of the ideological spectrum, but their relationship showed more constraints than opportunities. Fox reluctantly accepted the U.S.-driven CAFTA (Central American Free Trade Agreement), and kept the FTAA, another U.S. initiative, at arm's length. On the other hand, Harper's conservative background and a rosy Bush relationship cooled rather than warmed against the relentless one-track minded U.S. war-on-terrorism approach. As recently as September 2006, for example, Harper personally told Bush the September 2002 deportation of a Canadian citizen, Maher Arar, to Syria, was "inappropriate conduct," and how the United States should "back off."[6] Just as similar philosophical orientations and/or ideological preferences do not automatically spruce bilateral relations, preventing ideological adjustments leaves leaders in limbo, as with Fox, and unnecessarily magnifies suspicion, as in the Mexico–U.S. relationship.

Party Politics

There is no question 9/11 events were condemned by all North American parties across the entire political spectrum. Yet as the dust settles, we find calls for more strident policy responses from the right side of the political spectrum than from the center and certainly from the left,[7] suggesting how party politics, philosophical orientations, and/or ideological preferences eventually intervene. Again, exceptions exist: Fox's conservative PAN tepidly supported the war on terrorism, and actually opposed launching the Iraq war, while Martin's Liberal Party offered the United States more support in the war against terrorism than Chrétien's Liberal Party. U.S. identity, which became more of a Canadian ballot-box issue than Mexican, goes beyond economic philosophy into values over the role of family, position on abortion, and so forth. It also plays less of a Mexican ballot-box issue than Canadian owing to a lower election frequency (once in every six years in Mexico, two in the last six years for Canada). When Mexico's leaders identified more with the United States than Canada over economic philosophy over the last two decades, Mexican election campaigns were more ignited than Canada's. Canada's noneconomic identities have helped soften prickly U.S. ties, a claim Mexico cannot make as robustly.[8]

Policy Priorities

If personality can be salient, so too can policy priorities: 9/11 did not alter any significant Canadian policy priorities in the way it accelerated Mexico's policy shift. To be sure, 9/11 killed Mexico's hope of an immigration deal, even though Fox's proposal was rejected by the U.S. Congress one week before 9/11; not just that, U.S. security imperatives since 9/11 virtually guarantee an immigration agreement will not be concluded in the foreseeable future. Without this deal, Fox's domestic policy agenda crumbled, and his administration accomplished little, if anything, of substance. Since no simple Canadian policy proposal or measure was placed in a sine qua non trajectory as Mexico's immigration deal was, Canada's lower expectations buffered a similar collapse. Though both Canadian and Mexican trade, investment, and tourism policies remain utterly dependent on the United States, Canada may reap more future U.S. rewards than Mexico: When the United States was counting, as if for the last time, the number of special and ordinary friends, and enemies after 9/11, Canada had one foot in, Mexico neither.

Flexibility opens options, rigidity closes them, but Washington's approval matters most. The high predictability of a rigid policy approach not changing suggests Mexico will not modify its immigration stance, but Canadian flexibility absorbed policy reversals and prime ministerial changes better. Among the consequences, Mexico's virtuous cycle of NAFTA-based growth could become vicious under a security policy priority, in turn embittering public opinion, but Canada's middle-range policy responses prevent public opinion extremities. Whether Washington officials approve or not also become an incentive or disincentive to change. Canada is currently riding the incentive wave, and Mexico the disincentive, reversing Mexico's warm and Canada's cool embrace of the original NAFTA proposal being accepted by the United States.

Foreign policy implications may last longer: The United States foreign policy pursuits may be more gung-ho with Canada's backing than with Mexican. With Harper's Canada restored to its primary place on the U.S. special friend list, and post-Fox Mexico at another foreign policy-making crossroads, the obvious casualty is likely to be NAFTA. Canada and Mexico will most likely continue as top U.S. trading partners, but more out of bilateral exigencies than trilateral euphoria. Previous Mexican crossroads, prompted by economic bail-outs in 1982, 1988, and 1995, pushed foreign policy considerations over domestic politics, but with the 2006 elections reasserting domestic politics over foreign policy considerations, Mexico's experiences signal a broader phenomenon: domestic needs demanding greater attention and resources than foreign policy pursuits, a predicament never far from the surface in Canada or the United States.

Resources/State of the Economy

Apparently, though 9/11 inflicted several, short-term economic shocks, especially in the United States, both its largest trading partners at the time were in North America and emerged unscathed. In spite of their deep U.S. dependence, both benefited enormously from post–9/11 oil-price hikes. Still, Mexico was displaced from the second-largest U.S. trading partner spot by China. Since neoliberalism places the private sector instead of the state behind the direction of trade, Mexico's privileged U.S. position was eroding regardless of 9/11: More *maquiladora* migration to China from Mexico threatened jobs; yet, since NAFTA imposes limits on how much and what kind of trade can be pursued outside the NAFTA framework, the stealthy return of state interventionism amidst ferocious capitalism might convert NAFTA arrangements from regional economic integration to strategic trade. Since this would accent the uneven playing field, Mexico could easily become an increasingly reluctant partner. Having fought with the United States in the Korean, Persian Gulf, and Kosovo wars before the war on terrorism, Canada is more experienced with strategic trade arrangements than Mexico.[9]

Public Opinion

"Nous sommes les Americaines" was a conspicuously short-shrifted North American attitude after 9/11, more so six years later. Canadians and Mexicans were outraged against launching the 2003 Iraqi war.[10] Subsequent leadership changes shifted public opinion in Canada, at least to some small degree, but the policy shift from aloofness to engagement, has been more dramatic than public appreciation shifts. The presence of both an anti-U.S. reservoir of public sentiments and post–9/11 U.S. unilateralism, particularly at the expense of fundamental human rights, suggest public opinion may not necessarily be a Canadian policy-making motor. Mexicans have a historically deeper reservoir of United States-based resentments, and the immigration deadlock is seen not just for its inevitability by Mexicans, but also for vindicating all the arguments against NAFTA over the past 15 years, particularly by Mexicans.

Since 9/11, Mexico's leaders have retreated behind public opinion, rather than shape it, evident in its shifting responses to UN Resolution 1441. Between October 2002 and March 2003, Mexico fluctuated from playing politics to extracting U.S. concessions to fully opposing U.S. positions, from promoting expediency to resigning behind public preferences.[11] Fox's blank administrative record could easily be construed by sympathetic future historian as evidence of statesmanship: following public opinion rather than free-riding on it, as elected officials must do in a democracy.

Table 7.2 ranks the various comparative elements, and profiles the Canadian–Mexican similarities and differences just discussed.

Of the six elements, table 7.2 lists personality as the most influential, followed by guiding philosophy and/or ideological preference and party politics, with the least influential being resources/state of the economy. Policy priorities and public opinion lie in between. As the similarity/difference column indicates, both these in-between elements had quite different impacts in the two countries: Migration casts a

Table 7.2 Domestic Context: Relative Weight, Similarities, and Differences

Elements	Relative weight	Similarities/Differences
1. Personalities	Most influential for both countries	Similarity in both: robustly present
2. Guiding philosophy/ ideological preference	Somewhat influential for both countries	Similarity in both
3. Party priorities	Somewhat influential for both countries	Similarity impacting both: but 9/11 created greater partnership in Canada than in Mexico.
4. Policy priorities	Very influential for Mexico in short-term and influential for Canada over medium term	Different in both degree of impact and across the time-span
5. Public opinion	Secondary influence in both countries	Different in both: U.S. support increases over time in Canada but decreases over time in Mexico
6. Resources/state of the economy	Not a current factor in either country	Similarity in both by having negligible impact over the short-term; over the long-term, may benefit Canada more than Mexico

long-term gloom across Mexico, in turn worsening public opinion; Canada was spared of both. Party politics generally hugged this pattern, fluctuating between the positive and negative in Canada, but generally deteriorating in Mexico, with the United States as a central, though not the only, causal factor in both countries.

Do specific and direct 9/11 institutionalized responses alter the above picture? Scrutinizing the post–9/11 intelligence institutions, the next section reinforces Canada's better post–9/11 positioning without improving Mexico's plight.

Institutionalizing Intelligence

For a century until September 11, 2001, Canadian and Mexican efforts to institutionalize intelligence were sporadic, shifted from ultrasecrecy toward transparency only under pressure, swayed between domestic and foreign imperatives, displayed a rare bipartisanship, and demonstrated an uncanny *americanization* without even registering as more than a blip on the U.S. intelligence radar. It was a chekered history of scandals, unnecessary red herrings, and disregard for accountability. Political and perceptual differences with the United States further constrained the maturation of institutionalized intelligence, while *quid pro quo* approaches toward the United States have been more uneven than smooth. The net North American result of inadequate and insufficient coordination further magnifies the inherent regional asymmetry.

Finding Canadian–Mexican parallels behind the lack of regional coordination and symmetry is difficult, with the intelligence culture of both countries too far apart to expect U.S. association to narrow differences. A comparative scrutiny of the evolution of institutionalized intelligence, causal factors (triggers), and consequences in tables 7.3, 7.4, and 7.5 leads to these conclusions.

Disaggregating the past century into four arbitrary phases recognizes the catalytic role of wars. These phases comprise the period upto and including World War II, the Cold War era until the mid-1980s, the post–Cold War phase until 9/11, and the post–9/11 era.

Table 7.3 shows how intelligence was domesticated, irrespective of external triggers, in both countries. Canadian intelligence was directed most forcefully against undesirable immigrants during World War I, in spite of earlier threats from Fenians in the 1860s,[12] and Indian nationalists in the early part of the twentieth

Table 7.3 Triggering Intelligence: Canadian–Mexican Comparisons

Phases	Canada	Mexico
World War II and before	Fenians as threats (1860s–1870s) Indian nationalists as threats German and Irish migrants from United States during World War I as threats Labor antiwar protests (1917–20) World War II shifts threats abroad	Domestic sources: revolutionaries against Porfirio Díaz's authoritarianism Unclear apex in chain of command, civilian or military leadership
Cold War: 1945–85	1969 MRC Security report finds intelligence institutions networking too closed and secretive, like in Britain; proposes civilianization and accountability, hands-on government engagement, and elimination of RCMP from intelligence services MC reports, 1979–81: also proposes civilianization 1981 Charter enhances public consciousness, produces aborted Bill C-157 in 1983 Patriation Act 1980–81 divisive Pitfield committee reviews C-157 CSIS adopted: last trudeauvian legislation, June 1984	Domestic sources: civilian control endures at apex of chain of command Foreign sources: World War II alliances with United States at first, then sporadic antidrug campaigns became more regular and substantial as the Cold War ended
Post–Cold War upto 9/11	Air India terrorist act, 1985: treated with Cold War paradigm	CISEN created with greater theoretical emphasis on development; but practical problems with drug trafficking, then insurgency
9/11 and after	Bill C-36 of October 2001	March 2002 Border Plan: 22 points

century; and in Mexico dovetailed the suspicion, secrecy, and sabotage of Porfirio Díaz's authoritarian rule (1884–1910), breeding a peculiar CMR (civilian-military relationship).[13]

World War I demanded more specialized intelligence in Canada than in Mexico. British engagement dragged Canada in, but the 1917 Bolshevik revolution brought the threat back home: Suspicion of Germans fleeing to the United States, and thence Canada, was displaced by a Canadian Red scare, articulated most vociferously by the Conservative Montreal lawyer and maverick C.H. Cahan. Noting "considerable mental unrest among the peoples of Slavic origins," he singled out the Russians and Ukranians, for "the dissemination in Canada of the Socialist doctrines."[14] His influence later created a reds-under-the-bed mentality reminscent of the United States better-dead-than-red McCarthy scare at the outset of the Cold War.[15] Mexico grabbed attention when Léon Trotsky settled in the country subsequently. However, both Canadians and Mexicans were more concerned with other domestic developments: Canada's labor unrest and Mexico's all-consuming nationalist revolution. When Canadian workers refused to enlist in the war, Robert Borden's Union government invoked the War Measures Act, and secretly developed PHF (Personal History Files), through the RNWMP west of Port Arthur and Fort Williams, and the DP (Dominion Police) in the east. Canada's Criminal Investigation Branch secretly monitored labor activities.

World War II externalized intelligence concerns, more so in Canada than Mexico. Intercepting German intelligence, *Abwehr,* produced the SIGINT industry from 1940, while collaboration with Britain and the United States in holding foreign spies and soldiers in Camp X, near Toronto, anticipated future intelligence-based cooperation.[16] Mexico's U.S. alliance during World War II institutionalized intelligence to a far lesser degree.

Whereas Canada's intelligence institutions absorbed the essence of the Cold War, Mexico's were less influenced, if at all. Both, however, faced similar societal pressures increasingly during the Cold War: the growth of democratization, grassroots consciousness, accountability, and resource management. Even though Canada's intelligence was spawned and groomed by Great Britain before the Cold War, as the Cold War subsided, Canada's intelligence, based on greater transparency, became a model for the mother country.[17] This is not to say it epitomized accountability and responsibility,[18] but huge procedural changes suggested it was silently, independently, and unconsciously, becoming more americanized than British. For example, the intelligence agencies were now more exposed to legislative oversight, as in the United States, rather than the parliament reform driven by the executive branch, as in Britain.[19] Stuart Farson makes the most of this distinction, leaving us to conclude Canada may be getting the worst of both British and U.S. intelligence systems: Oversight hearings in parliament relay government policies more than invite review or probe potential problems,[20] and without a constituency, intelligence barely attracts the parliamentarian's interest.

Mexico's *americanization* was influenced by joint U.S. operations against drug trafficking and domestic transparency demands. The 2002 Federal Law for

Information Access opened Defence Secretrariat (SEDENA) documents, in turn galvanizing a news magazine, *Proceso,* under Kate Doyle's editorship from March 2, 2003. Canada's Access to Information Act did this from 1982. However, neither has cleansed the parlors of intelligence from turf-fighting, secrecy, and accountability.

Institutionalized Canada–U.S. collaboration of the 1940s lost a lot of its bite and weight for Canada as the Cold War dragged on. Though the NORAD Command and the NATO continued, Canada's increasing displeasure at U.S. unilateralism, particularly under Pierre Trudeau, contrasted with the expanding bilateral Mexican–U.S. engagements toward the last part of the Cold War over equally prickly issues, like drug trafficking, illegal migration, and money laundering. Nevertheless, the values behind Canada's U.S. cooperation penetrate deeper than those behind Mexico's U.S. relations.[21]

Owing to those values, the Cold War ending impacted Canada's intelligence network minimally, but raising the ante with Mexico did not expand shared values commensurately. Given its CMR framework, any Mexican intelligence or military identification with the United States requires political identification with the United States first. Beyond rhetoric and photo opportunity summits, this has not happened on the Mexico–U.S. front after 9/11, but on the Canadian–U.S. counterpart, both political and military identification have increased, though in compartmentalized form and only at bureaucratic levels. Using Allan D. English's disaggregation of Canada's military culture into the cultures of the army, navy, and air force, even after the three services were merged in the 1960s,[22] they continue to "build bridges between Canadian and American servicemen and servicewomen who work in the same environments."[23] More so, he might have added, than with politicians in their own country. While civilian control of the military is also a holy idea in Canada and the United States, neither has ever had any history of military governments like Mexico. While CMR breeds one type of values, its absence breeds yet another; and the twain are not the same. The United States has no choice but to constantly reinvent the adjustment wheel to both types on both borders.

The events of September 11, 2001 exposed how recovery from value gaps differs. Canada and the United States recovered from the Chrétien-Bush personality clash better and faster than Mexico and the United States could from the Fox-Bush immigration deadlock. Canada's adjustment to U.S. DHS's new standards profited from a history of joint experiences in NORAD, NATO, and over intelligence, but without much depth of collective experiences, Mexico could not similarly benefit. Different responses were vividly exposed by the implementation of the DHS-supervised border agreements: The Canada–U.S. border faced fewer implementation problems or other hindrances than the Mexico–U.S. border, which attracted even more illegal migrants than before. By merging domestic and external contexts, 9/11 catalyzed the need for intelligence coordination without motivating Mexico as much as it did Canada.

Slow institutionalization in both countries reflected environmental uncertainty. Bureaucratic insulation, independence, and an arrogance incompatible with democracy promoted self-help over cooperation, but reforms have been farther in between and fewer in Mexico than in Canada. Mexico's one-term presidency prevents institutions from developing roots, but Canada's CSIS also lacks political ownership and treats reforms superficially. Kenneth G. Robertson argues that "the integration of CSIS into the central intelligence process has not yet taken place" because CSIS (a) is an ad hoc creation; (b) has different accountability standards from other agencies; (c) lacks a given mandate or departmental obligation other than serving as a watchdog; and (d) continues as an expression of the RCMP police culture rather than developing an intelligence culture.[24]

We see a much more cluttered Canadian scorecard in table 7.4 than Mexican. As a result of British empire membership, reflecting an Anglo-Saxon identity and NATO affiliation,[25] Ottawa officials entered the London-Washington security and intelligence loop, but by minimizing the U.S. cooperative agenda, Mexico only fed authoritarianism through its more introverted outlook. From the DP and RNWMP during World War I to the 1984 CSIS, Canada's dominant institution evolved incrementally rather than fundamentally through external pressures—either war or revolution abroad or domestic public opinion about them; while Mexico's even more glacial shift from the *Secretaria de Gobernación* in 1918 to CISEN in 1985 was largely externally driven, by drug traffickers and illegal migrants.[26] Greater intelligence network independence reflected the military subordination from the very beginning in Canada, when the Department of External Affairs took sole charge under Borden's Union government; but Mexico's military governments until World War II deformed subsequent institutional growth by thwarting civilian control.[27]

Table 7.4 shows sputtering growth of the country's intelligence institutions, in part due to how security was defined. Canada's military interpretation obscured an equally and increasingly persistent emphasis on human welfare;[28] Mexico's was just as ambivalent: open-ended development. CISEN's interpretation of national security not only widened over time, but also shifted from such mundane bureaucratic tasks of obtaining, processing, and interpreting information toward substantive case-by-case evaluations. Even as state security interests change every six years, behaviors remain corporatist. By definition, corporatism requires inclusiveness,[29] but faces Mexican turf-mindedness, while Canadian turf-mindedness also defies consociationalist policy-making patterns.[30] Further, Mexico's more hands-on president within a one-party political network weakens turf-mindedness in a way Canada's prime minister could not in a multiparty parliament. Whether transparency changes Mexico's patterns still remains an open question.

General Porfirio Díaz paradoxically began the civilianizing process in Mexico, which continued with the revolutionaries after him.[31] Although the seeds were sown between 1934 and 1940 during General Lázaro Cárdenas's presidency, Camp traces "the revolutionary process from military to civilian control in a symbolic and concrete fashion" to Miguel Alemán's 1946–52 presidency.[32] To professionalize politics, Cárdenas built four corporate divisions under party control by 1938: labor, popular, agrarian, and military sectors. This was under the PRM (Party of the Mexican Revolution), hitherto called the PRN (National Revolutionary Party), and a precursor of PRI. His centralized control over property, the presidency, and industries, on the

Table 7.4 Institutionalizing Intelligence: Canada–Mexico Comparisons

Canada	Mexico
1914: Military Service Act, DP to oversee security	1918: SG (*Secretaria de Gobernación*): Ander President Venustiano Carranza: included the secretariats of government, interior, and state
1917: Cahan challenge and proposal: PSB (Public Safety Branch) under Department of Justice, with Bureau of Investigation Labor unrest against war enlistment	1929: DC (*Departamento Confidencial*): disaggregated political information acquisition and imparting distributive justice
1918: Cahan proposal to establish two orders-in-council in October (to prohibit policy unionism, and to ban strikes	1938: OIP (*Oficina de Información Publica*): DC shifted political situation toward supplying confidential information
1919: Collapse of Cahan phenomenon, PSB abolished, and, under War Measures Act, RNWMP empowered west of Port Arthur and For William, DP east of these; growth of secret PHF and CIB (Criminal Investigation Branch)	1942: DIPS (*Departamento de Investigación Política y Social*): added to OPA duties by investigating foreigners during World War II
1940: SIGINT under Examination Unit of DEA; Ogdensburg Agreement in August (stepping stone to NORAD)	1947: DGS (*Dirección General de Seguridad*): established under the president to examine national security issues
1942: CJIC (Canadian Joint Intelligence Committee): Proposed first post-war document, Foreign Intelligence in Peacetime, and JCB (Joint Coordination Bureau)	1967: DGIPS (*Dirección General de Investigaciónes Políticas y Sociales*): took over such DIPS functions as investigating sociopolitical problems, gambling, and executive SG functions, and supplying briefs to any federal ministry
1945: General Foulkes proposes strategic intelligence (with components of military, political, scientific, economic, demographic, and geography), SIGINT, and counterintelligence	1977: DGIPS given such new tasks as establishing a documentation center and conducting security-based polls
1946: JCB and Foulkes proposals rejected, and foreign espionage (HUMINT) disbanded JIB (Joint Intelligence Board) created, with DEA in charge over military CBNRC (Communications Branch of the National Research Council) absorbs Examination and Discrimination units CJIC goes out of business	1985: DGISN (*Dirección General de Investigación y Seguridad Nacional*) merged DGIPS and DFS to coordinate stages of intelligence production, avoiding duplication, and enhancing respect

1969: McKenzie Royal Commission: proposes civilianization process; and elimination of RCMP	1989: CISEN created
1979–81: MC proposes civilization process	CISEN Act
1984: CSIS adopted: last Trudeauvian legislation, shows Canadian innovation, and marks further drift from British model toward United States	2002: 22-point Border Plan
Bill C-36, October 15, 2001: elaborated below	

Source: "CISEN: Antecedents," http://www.cisen.gob.mx.

one hand, and acceptance of the "no reelection" principle, on the other,[33] edified Mexico's state corporatism and political culture, bringing CMR fully under civilian leadership.

José López Portillo (1976–82) defined state security in terms of development, while Miguel de la Madrid (1982–88), by elevating personal freedoms, justice, and social peace as key security criteria, invited transparency. Both Carlos Salinas de Gortari (1988–94) and Ernesto Zedillo Ponce de León (1994–2000) boosted transparency through their antidrug U.S. collaboration.[34] Coming from a different party, Fox enhanced accountability and visibility in Mexico, but his post–9/11 intelligence securitization appears aimless without political ownership. Canada's 1966–69 MRC ushered in more transparency,[35] while the 1979–81 MC reaffirmed the need for political ownership.[36]

In the aftermath of 9/11, both the PRI and PRD sought congressional control of intelligence. Article 73, Paragraph 28 was amended to facilitate this in 2003, although Article 89, Paragraph 6 also authorizes the president to manage security. By sloughing off its tainted reputation and assuming more responsible postures, CISEN could fit into and facilitate 9/11 needs, but distinguishing the extent of executive power from the open-endedness of legislative oversight bedevils the new Mexico. One notices how incomplete *americanization* and destabilized corporatism breed more uncertainty.[37] Could domestic political differences undermine North American responses to terrorism more than inadequate or insufficient intelligence-driven convergences? Different methods and motivational levels hinder all three countries from producing a coherent singular strategy.

Canadian intelligence-police competition defies the key consociationalist trait of elite cooperation.[38] Since RNWMP policed west Canada at a time of increasing East European influxes,[39] it not only "became increasingly concerned about the apparent rise in radical activity," but associated radicalism with these migrants.[40] RCMP was first asked to manage internal espionage, sabotage, and subversion, only to win additional powers after Igor Gouzenko's 1945 defection exposed an espionage network in Canada and the United States.[41] War-time collaboration, however, elevated the JIB, modeled after the British war-time agency of the same name, to supervise similar functions from June 1946. "From 1946 to the 1960s," Reg Whitaker argues,

"Canadian intelligence policy was bound by a set of particular institutional arrangements and one overarching assumption. Everything was premised on the Cold War . . . Detailed public and parliamentary scrutiny was, by and large, counterproductive and perhaps even dangerous."[42] Exclusive networking and blind-folded red-baiting trampled democratic processes, leading Prime Minister Lestor Pearson to appoint the MRC in 1966 "when questions were being raised in Parliament about security clearance procedures and surveillance techniques used at various universities." His successor, Pierre Trudeau, appointed the MC in 1979 when it was clear the RCMP was "transgressing the law. . . planting bombs, burning barns, stealing documents, intimidating sources, and the like."[43] Both the 1969 MRC and 1981 MC reports proposed separating police and security tasks. RCMP resisted both, but succeeded only with the first.[44] Clearly consociationalist lines were not connecting.

RMA and RIA during the 1980s could be one reason why. RMA introduced sophisticated intelligence gathering techniques affecting COMINT, and more diverse means of extracting HUMINT; on the other hand, RIA invoked, in Martin Rudner's words, a "quantum leap in information technology and information processing. . . [whose] operational backbone. . . is an advanced technological architecture for Command, Control, Communications, Computers, Intelligence, Surveillance, and Reconnaissance (C4ISR)."[45] Both this widening gap and the evaporation of the domestic-external divide led Elinor Sloan to argue, very much in the Bush Doctrine spirit, "the best defence is a good offense." She continued, "The United States and Canada should give roughly equal weight to homeland security and defence measures and measures to defend the homeland abroad."[46] RCMP took upon itself to coordinate both fronts.

Wartime arrangements produced post-war collaboration at first. For example, the Examination Unit and Discrimination Unit, jointly operated by Britain and the United States, became Canada's CBNRC; NATO emerged from wartime collaboration under a Canadian initiative;[47] and the August 1940 Ogdensburg Agreement between Prime Minister MacKenzie King and President Franklin D. Roosevelt laid the foundation of the NORAD agreement from May 12, 1958.[48]

Pierre Trudeau's CSIS Act of June 21, 1984, was his last legislation, which his successor, the Conservative, Brian Mulroney, barely changed, not because it was picture perfect, which it was not, but because he had other priorities. CSIS was filled with innovations, such as the creation of the Office of an IG and the SIRC. Although these would never see the full light of day, they sorely filled huge existing blanks.[49]

Over a sclerotic 40-year interim, the RCMP neither anticipated nor correctly appraised the October 1970 FLQ (*Front de Liberación du Québec*) separatist terrorist act. This, in spite of the 1967 "Key Sectors" program reform in the D Branch, the counter-subversion unit. RCMP was founded on the belief "that communist subversion constituted the main threat to the Canadian state," which, Steve Hewitt informs us, "restricted its ability to understand the new forces and threats associated with the 1960s. . ."[50] "RCMP follies," in turn, raised accountability as an issue, challenging the ultrasecretive British intelligence system and enhancing the oversight-based U.S. counterpart. Whitaker's distinction between public and agency mandate accountability nothwithstanding,[51] CSIS created five accountability strands of its own:[52] (a) a statutory mandating purposes and limits; (b) specifying responsibility with the Deputy Minister and the SG; (c) establishing two institutions of external review, the IG, answerable to the SG and the SIRC, answerable to the parliament; (d) legitimizing the previously illegal judicial warrants as a form of control; and (e) a five-year parliamentary review by the Commons or with both the Commons and Senate.

The CSIS-RCMP joint relationship contrasts with the mutual independence the CIA and FBI show toward each other. Disaggregating Canadian intelligence into security, foreign, military, and criminal, the 1984 legislation placed CSIS in charge of the first with authority to bring RCMP in; the CSE took charge of the second, and eventually became the largest intelligence institution; National Defence supervised the third; and both CSIS and RCMP the fourth. Since 9/11, both CSIS and RCMP received fresh powers to (a) adopt new terrorism-related laws; (b) employ electronic surveillance against target groups; (c) enhance investigative hearings of the police; (d) penalize those aiding or abetting terror groups and individuals; (e) censor selectively; and (f) arrest in anticipation.[53]

CSIS's TAU kept in contact with community leaders of expected problems, combining functions with ICC to feed the EII, and streamlining government agencies at various policy-making levels involve counterintelligence more than counterterrorism. Police and intelligence functions do not always blend.[54] With terrorism falling under Canada's Criminal Code penal jurisdiction, whose responsibility is local, not federal, the CSIS-RCMP tussle is further jostled;[55] and with SIRC and EDIG reviewing CSIS activities, 9/11 produced a Canadian alternative hugging U.S. expectations.

Although Roy Rempel sees the SIRC as "the only truly independent external review body in Canada's security and intelligence community," he also suggests the bipartisan selection of its three to five Privy Council members constrains effective decision-making, while meagre resources undermine human rights monitoring. While Paul Martin's 2003 Action Plan allocated more resources and encouraged oversight, other problems remain. Rempel generally faults a lack of "a commitment to less partisanship on security and intelligence matters," and calls parliamentary deliberations *theatrical* since only "a few top politicians and bureaucrats" dominate.[56] Farson argues, "[t]he twin cultures of deference and secrecy remained unchallenged until the 1970s," in both Canada and the United States, but even after a five-year CSIS review in 1995, the OAG found "serious deficiencies" with foreign intelligence and the CSE, and SIRC serving as a parliament "surrogate."[57] Intelligence hearings, for example, became meaningless.

The SIRC operated under constraints. First, Trudeau's MC initiative fell by the wayside and Mulroney's greater FTA interest with the United States unwittingly widened the gap between the IC and the government; second, RCMP prevented CSIS access to the Canadian Police Information Centre, and independently created National Security Investigation Division; third, when Canada faced terrorism first-hand with the 1985 Air India flight explosion, it could only respond with an outdated Cold War paradigm, not one against terrorism;[58] and fourth, after the Cold War, the national security "temperature" dipped considerably.

Although Jean Chrétien reportedly never put a foot inside the National Defence Department,[59] Martin's mending of U.S. fences proved only half-hearted, leaving Steve Harper on track to restoring not just the traditional Canadian cordiality with the U.S. military, but also the traditionally hawkish Conservative party positions on security.

Though "designed to enhance the federal government's capacity to protect Canada," and "contribute more effectively to international efforts aimed at combating global terrorism,"[60] Justice Minister Anne McClellan's Bill C-36 compensates for CSIS inabilities. It defines terrorism for the first time, authorizes terrorist cell penetration, channels intelligence across various levels, and coordinates local-provincial problems.[61] It also specifies various offenses and penalties, permits the police to judicially supervise investigations and sanctions, elevates electronic surveillance, provides power to withhold critical information, and authorizes arrest based on suspicion, thus dispensing with the innocent-until-found-guilty tradition.[62] Finally, Bill C-36 promotes cooperation by ratifying the International Convention for the Suppression of the Financing of Terrorism, and the International Convention for the Suppression of Terrorist Bombings. Restricting Canadian liberties however, makes it unpopular.

Summary

Shaped by personalities, philosophy/ideology, party politics, policy priorities, and public opinion, in that order, the domestic context exerted its own share of influences without bringing the two countries together. Balancing behavior, predicting alignment among weaker neighbors of a powerful country, did not emerge after 9/11. Yet, neither did the two blindly bandwagon the United States. Mexico's immigration *quid pro quo* attempt failed. Canada hopped aboard only under Harper, but since the U.S. identity it seeks is one of mutuality, against Mexico's identity search for complementarity, it stands to reap large rewards. If so, the post–Cold War North American orientation is likely to shift again, with the United States rethinking its southern interests.

REGIONAL CONTEXT: ONE FOOT IN, ONE FOOT OUT

The regional context reiterates this theme. It examines, in particular, three clusters of issues: (a) the institutional responses of the two neighbors to 9/11 events and the subsequent adoption of a homeland security mentality in the United States, (b) the commercial consequences for the two neighbors, and (c) a theoretical discussion of the above dynamics/findings. Table 7.5 profiles the discussions.

Institutional Responses

Although both Bill C-36 and CISEN have been previously compared, four additional features posit Canada as an arguably more reliable U.S. antiterror partner than Mexico: (a) timing; (b) focus; (c) constraints; and (d) public responses.

Table 7.5 Regional Context: Comparative Empirical Observations

Empirical Elements	Canada	Mexico
1. Institutional Responses	Bill C-36 (October 15, 2001)	CISEN (1989), CISEN Act, 22-point Border Plan, (March 2002)
2. Commercial Consequences	Increasing trade dependence on USA	Distinctive diversification of imports from United States

Turning to timing first, Bill C-36 was a direct and immediate response to 9/11, CISEN existed from 1989 but no immediate responses emerged. Chrétien kept a personal distance from Bush, but his administration largely aligned with the Bush administration over the need to combat terrorism; and after 9/11, Fox's personal relationship with Bush was strained, as too his administration's with Bush's. The results: greater U.S. intrusion in Mexico, and unilateralism aggravating Canada.

The antiterror foci differed vastly. CISEN targeted narcotrafficking through U.S. coordination, Bill C-36 was driven by antiterrorism. Given the overlap between narcotrafficking illegal immigration, the United States emphasized the Mexican border more than the Canadian. This is not to say Canada escaped scot-free: The largest open border in the world faced more restrictions than ever before, which galvanized the Smart Border agreement or counterpart agreements with Mexico faster than expected. Canada's own antiterror drive, culminating in numerous 2006 Toronto arrests, assuaged the United States; Mexico did not have any counterpart experiences or receive any compliments.

Yet CISEN automatically faced more constraints than Bill C-36. Its agenda is more diversified, and ubiquitious corruption across the entire administrative structure leads to greater U.S. intervention.[63] Canadian institutions, on the other hand, synchronize automatically with their U.S. counterparts, in spite of Chrétien's distaste of Bush. Harper's personality and ideological preference revived Canadian–U.S. warmth, but institutional streamlining compensates for too frequent changes of the chief executive. Nevertheless, public opinion remains the Achilles' Heel of Canada's intelligence institutions.

Finally, public responses to Bill C-36 and CISEN as antiterror institutions also contrasted in Canada and Mexico. There were no Mexican counterparts to the Canadian debates linking Bill C-36 to the Charter of Freedoms, or to any other issue. In addition to different public moods about 9/11, Mexicans view CISEN with suspicion, and Canadians Bill C-36 as controversial. Canadians worry about constrained constitutional rights, Mexicans about just getting CISEN to work routinely.

Commercial Consequences

Good economic times currently in Canada and Mexico mask potentially significant structural changes. After 9/11, Canada's trade dependence on the United States deepened further while Mexico's U.S. imports declined conspicuously.

Just as Canada was not interested in diversifying U.S. trade, Mexico saw it as a temporary boon.

Caveats abound. First, under the Washington Consensus fundamentals of privatization and liberalization, trade cannot be regulated by the state, meaning Mexican diversification was a market-driven phenomenon. Second, emerging North American economic patterns may be very unrelated to 9/11 or state policy-making: Since China's North American forays were independent of but coincided with 9/11, Mexico's diversification did not convey retaliation for a failed immigration policy proposal.

Nevertheless, the two post–9/11 commercial consequences open windows of opportunities and vulnerabilities for both U.S. neighbors. For Canada, by coinciding with the revival of Canadian–U.S. relations, they helped solidify an antiterror partnership, but elevated Canada as a terrorist target. The June 2006 Toronto arrest of alleged terrorists raised Canadian stakes, widened the theater of threat, and posed a difficult question: If directly related to Canada's Afghanistan engagement precisely when Richard Haass of the U.S. CFR talks of the "iraqification of Afghanistan,"[64] then a bold policy shift is obviously backfiring; and if not related to Afghanistan, the problems go deeper, as across West Europe, into social maladjustments for Muslim immigrants. For Mexico, diversifying trade fulfills a historical aspiration and holds the promise of making the country more independent of, and thereby more robust in, its dealings with the United States; yet, by exposing the country to greater market fluctuations and possible economic disruptions, U.S. bailouts may no longer be as automatic as before.

Theoretical Disconnections

From a U.S. homeland security view, Canada–Mexico bilateral relations simply do not belong to any of the theoretical frameworks under assessment in this project. Regional integration theories offer the least helpful explanations, interdependence fares slightly better, and neorealism, like the glass half full, also remains half empty.

Table 7.6 confirms why the tenets of security-based integrative paradigms do not enlighten us on the Canadian–Mexican regional plank. Beginning with the absence of explicitly shared values, in the first dimension, the intelligence networks in the two countries carry too different histories to easily blend and permit the value complementarity sought by the fourth dimension. Mexico's CMR trajectory and Canada's greater harmony with the U.S. intelligence system do not bode well for this particular bilateral relation, meaning the second dimension feature of network predictability becomes less relevant, though not impossible, and mutual responsiveness in the third dimension becomes meaningless in the absence of interaction.

The one security community trait fitting very well is the fifth: the Canadian and Mexican intelligence lifestyles keep them apart, with no evidence of modifications. With 9/11 and terrorism as external impositions, the sixth dimension characteristic of reward expectations before absorbing the burdens of regional integration also fails to connect with realities. The seventh dimension requirement of increasing political

Table 7.6 Conditions of Pluralistic and Amalgamated Security Communities: The 9/11 Difference

Dimension	The 9/11 difference in Canadian–Mexican security community
1. Value compatibility	No evidence of institutionalizing shared values; in fact, Mexico's civilian-military relations constrain prospects of shared values, while Canada's military services more historically compatible with United States
2. Behavioral predictability	Increasing transparency demands compel intelligence agencies in both countries to be more predictable, but little in common
3. Mutual responsiveness	Evident among political and economic leaders; not enough joint military action to measure this
4. Value complementarity	Hypothetically yes, but no real-life cases
5. Distinctiveness in lifestyles	Intelligence culture very much so
6. Reward expectations before burden sharing	Reverse is more reality: burden sharing of homeland defence as means toward rewards of stability and economic prosperity
7. Increasing political and administrative functions	Clearly these have expanded, but for different reasons: For Canada directly from terrorist threats; for Mexico because of expanding flows of illegal transactions predating 9/11
8. Economic growth distinguishing core areas from peripheral	Quite likely prevalent in both countries, but relationship with a security threat not at all clear; and no evidence of higher growth areas in both countries integrating faster than areas of lower growth
9. Geographical and social communications linkages	Clearly linkages of all sorts have expanded between both countries, but not caused by nor impacting security factors
10. Multiplication of communications and transactions	These have also clearly expanded, but independent of any security threats: economic transactions began expansion from before 9/11
11. Decreasing barriers to mobility across political boundaries	In general not a factor, but 9/11 increased restrictions to cross-border flows, thereby demanding more time, in turn reducing potential interest in crossing borders
12. Increasing political elites	Yes, in both countries, but relationship with a security paradigm is difficult to establish

and administrative functions is satisfied, but differently: Canada reacted directly and substantively to 9/11, Mexico adapted an existing institution for the purpose, displayed less enthusiasm, and let the United States build the 2002 Border Plan. The remaining five dimensions explicitly expose (a) growth, but not due to 9/11, security causes, or broader terrorism, and (b) how security-based integration is not a bilateral pursuit for Canada and Mexico and, indeed, is another ballgame entirely different from economic integration, which satisfies every one of the 12 features very well. Paradigm relevance is questioned.

If the security community could not explain 9/11 security outcomes for the Canada–Mexico dyad, does regional integration theory do any better? Table 7.7 plots the 14 characteristics of neofunctionalism, representing the prerequisites, processes, and perceptions. In a nutshell, it mirrors the pitfalls of table 7.6. Economic symmetry never existed (first), but its relevance is questionable, especially when asymmetrically positioned United States and Canada have long enjoyed a healthy security community and economic integration, but similarly positioned Mexico and Canada have not. While this bilateral relationship has witnessed the growth of elite complementarity (second), pluralism (third), and adaptability (fourth), and benefited from economic integration, circumstances imposed by 9/11 and the U.S. DHS simply do not connect with these traits. It is not their irrelevance, since they explain the Canada–U.S. dyad, but somehow the Bush dictum of with or against us seems to be creating an even larger category of *ho-hum* countries, such as Mexico, in between. The mechanism of how they connect with countries in the with camp, such as Canada, is absent, but so too the will on the part of Mexico.

Spillover is traceable in Canada, but not in Mexico (fifth), where 9/11 responses are not spilling over into other policy areas, but institutions and interests of other policy areas, such as illegal immigration, spill over to fill terrorism security gaps. While Bill C-36 spills over into the domain of Charter freedoms, CISEN illustrates Mexico's reverse case. Reward expectations before burden sharing (sixth), increasing political and administrative functions (seventh), economic growth distinguishing core areas from peripheral (eighth), and geographical/social communications linkages (ninth) show again developments unfolding comprehensively under economic integration, but not quite connecting with security impulses. Ideological identity (tenth), as well as increasing interaction with external actors (eleventh), becomes irrelevant when only one country, Canada, participates in the post–9/11 paradigm, but without Mexico as a partner. Ultimately, the last three dimensions portray the inherent dilemma: they remain very true for economic integration and for other bilateral relations in North America, but simply do not touch a Canada–Mexico security relationship.

If integration/community theses do not help, can the bilateral relationship be of a lesser kind, a half-baked form of integration or community, such as interdependence? Table 7.8 tells us a familiar story: It takes two to tango. Canada is inside the post–9/11 ballpark and adjusts to any paradigm applied to the war on terrorism, but Mexico is not interested in entering, thus weakening half of any given equation. Responses to 9/11 and U.S. DHS did not open any significantly new Canadian–Mexican channel of communications (first), leaving existing channels to define the relationship. Those channels, in turn, seem to be inversely related, with Mexico still keeping economic integration at the top and Canada raising military security to the top (second), if not immediately after 9/11, then certainly after the Toronto arrests of July 7, 2006. Both countries subordinate the military (third), but they do so under different circumstances. It is axiomatic under CMR to keep civilian control of the

Table 7.7 Neofunctionalist Prerequisites, Processes, and Perceptions: Any 9/11 Difference?

Dimension	Any 9/11 difference?
1. Economic symmetry among units	Not really, though there is a minimum threshold both satisfy; above all, not really pertinent against a security threat
2. Elite complementarity	This has been demonstrated in nonsecurity areas, but no evidence over security
3. Pluralism	More now than in the past; but relevance to security threat not evident
4. Capacity to adapt	Yes, to different degrees: Mexico's slower response to 9/11 and war on terrorism differs from Canada's late but full-fledged engagement
5. Spillover	Thus far, security issues have not spilled over too significantly to other policy areas; in the case of Mexico, the reverse is more true: resources pertaining to and interests reflecting narcotrafficking control spilling over into terrorism monitoring
6. Growing transactions	Yes, but this was as true before 9/11 as after, raising questions if security or 9/11 is the reason why
7. Growth in intergovernmentalism	This should increase, but within the Canada–Mexico dyad, still within the nonsecurity domain
8. Transnational growth	Yes, but not because of security considerations or causes
9. Elite socialization	Yes, but more out of nonsecurity interests
10. Growth in ideological identity	Hypothetically possible, but nothing special emerging from the security context of 9/11
11. Increasing interaction with external actors	More true for Canada than Mexico, especially through engagement in ISAF/NATO in Afghanistan; Mexico's reluctance very evident
12. Benefit distribution higher and more equitable	Not really relevant to the security, 9/11, or terrorism dimensions of concern
13. Converging perceptions of external problems	This is true, evident in the get-togethers the three chief executives have every once in a while, and sometimes in addressing security issues
14. Integration as cost free	Not under the extant security climate

military, as in Mexico, but in Canada, where the military has never run the government before, political control has also varied, becoming tight during wars or loose as at present. Canada's greater interest in institutional membership (fourth), contrasts with Mexico's lesser. Canada would like to see such membership catalyze change (fifth), but for a catalyst to be relevant to Mexico necessitates acceptance of its immigration proposal. Finally, the nationalism-regionalism-globalism levels of analysis also show both countries presently placing national interests at the top

Table 7.8 Interdependence Versus Integration: Insights

Dimension	9/11 Difference on Canada–Mexico Relation
1. Channels of communications?	Security issues did not really open any new channel, and unclear if integration is even being sought through security issues
2. Hierarchy in these channels?	Yes: security clearly below other, especially economic, channels for Mexico; as a variable for Canada, driven by circumstances
3. Subordination of the military?	Yes: but for different reasons and to different degrees: For both, civilian control of military is fundamental, but stems from a history of no military control in Canada and a civil-military history of fluctuating fortunes in Mexico; and though the military is under direct political control in Mexico, in Canada political leaders have often not claimed ownership of military/intelligence institutions
4. Membership in institutions?	Membership in the war on terrorism is important; more important is military engagement against terrorists: On both counts, Canada is far ahead of Mexico; Mexico not interested in military engagement
5. Catalysts of change	U.S. acceptance of migration-based *quid pro quo* is Mexico's critical catalyst of change; Canada's comes from battlefield results, since it has committed itself fully to the war on terrorism
6. Relation between nationalism-regionalism-globalism levels	For different reasons, national interests suddenly drive both Canada and Mexico: For the former to prevent a global threat, for the latter to compensate for missed regional opportunities

(sixth), yet Canada directs these toward global outcomes more than regional, Mexico to regional over any global.

If interdependence fares so poorly,[65] one other paradigm remains for the suitability test: neorealism. Table 7.9 lists the three characteristics of neorealism. The first one emphasizes state as the dominant actor. Both countries satisfy this tenet. Does the policy reflect domestic or international competitiveness? This second feature elicits another mixed bag, with Canada more interested in halting the growth of global terrorism, thus placing international competitiveness ahead of domestic interests, while Mexico, uninterested in the global setting, finds regional interests slipping away too, thus concentrating more of its interests in the national setting. Not many countries can do so these days. Both countries also face internal political divisions, with Harper leading a coalition government, and the legitimacy of Calderón's government challenged even before he assumed office. Finally, the third feature asks if the international setting is anarchical or orderly. From the Canadian view, it must be anarchical in order to justify the deployment of troops to its public and to win the war against terrorism, but for Mexico, like constructivists, anarchy is what states make of it, and the international setting shows more order than anarchy.

Table 7.9 Neorealism: An Achilles Heel?

Dimension	The 9/11 Difference in Canadian–Mexican relations
1. State as a dominant actor?	Yes, very much so, and security strengthens the state's position
2. Policy reflecting internal or international competitiveness?	Canada is more concerned with the global configuration in the war on terrorism, Mexico increasingly in its internal development
3. Is international competitiveness orderly or anarchic?	International competitiveness is both: orderly if seen through the prism of conventional warfare, but anarchic through terrorism lenses

Summary

However we interpret the regional context, the bottom line involves the hub-and-spoke image of the United States being too central to its neighbor's economy for them to drift too far, engage each other to balance U.S. interests, or adopt another paradigm. Whether Canada and Mexico have interest in the antiterrorism campaign or not, they will still face all the consequences if the United States is targeted again, though differently: Canada on the terror battlefield, Mexico on the economic. No Canadian or Mexican leader or policy can neglect the cold logic of size influencing outcomes, more concretely of U.S. policy-making impacting Canada and Mexico one way or another, directly or indirectly, in the trenches or policy drawing boards, whether policy responses emerge independently or not. Whether this means bandwagoning is the only option left for Canada/Mexico or not is addressed in the next section.

EXTERNAL CONTEXT

Three dimensions of the external context include actual war, war alignments, and converting free trade into strategic trade. If trade exchanges make the external context significant, terrorist campaigns amplify its urgency. Both theaters of war, Afghanistan and Iraq, pose the greatest threats to North America, the United States for obvious reasons, Canada for becoming an increasingly assertive partner in that war, and Mexico for unwittingly possessing multiple entry points into the United States.

George Bush's with or against dichotomy sets up another external framework, very much like the Cold War options of the Soviet Union and socialism, or the United States and capitalism. It did not work then, since the nonaligned countries wanted neither, and faces complications even today: Canada or Mexico may not be comfortable with countries the United States places in the with group, such as Pakistan, and they may have good relations with countries the United States categorizes in the against group, such as Iran. Supporting the war against terrorism becomes a slippery slope leading Canada or Mexico to participate in antiterrorism operations, preserving peace in defeated countries, as Canada in Afghanistan, or promoting democratization in liberated countries, also in Afghanistan. Participation, in turn, invites terrorism home.

Similarly, a third dimension extends the antiterrorism crusade to trade, displacing free trade arrangements with *quid pro quo* security safeguards. U.S. FTAs in Southeast Asia against China is an example, with connections, under the policy approach of competitive liberalism, to trade arrangements made in the Americas, for example through FTAA, CAFTA, or NAFTA.[66] Thus, while the immediate U.S. military defence against terrorism is North American and fits the contours of NAFTA and supervised by the DHS, the economic counterpart goes beyond North America to the rest of the world, creating misconnections, ambiguities, and possibly contradictions. Canada and Mexico may have no choice but to uncomfortably be absorbed in this tide.

Bill C-36, CISEN, and the External Context: Disconnections Epitomized

Interpreting the external context reveals more differences than congruences between Bill C-36 and CISEN. Various nonexhaustive dimensions in table 7.10 reaffirm the underlying message: In spite of theoretically supporting the United States, CISEN and Bill C-36 show different social pulses and external orientations.

Turning to the first of the ten dimensions, timing exposes two different country responses and types of countries. From the moment CISEN was created, Mexico had a Central American focus, which is still in tact after 9/11, but Mexico's interest does not extend beyond that. Canada's, on the other hand, is in Afghanistan and world-wide, at least through NATO. These orientations go hand-in-hand with the origins and consequences of the triggers. Mexican triggers come from within, Central America, and the United States, with 9/11 as only one of them, perhaps not even the most important one. Canada, contrariwise, sees 9/11 as central to its orientation, given its top billing, permits it to determine other policy changes, and uses it to rationalize external engagements. In turn, security is not only interpreted differently, but also impacts differently: Mexico's development interpretation is nationalistic, was neither tested nor targeted by terrorists, and leaves the United States wondering if Mexico is on board or not; Canada's security is defined by terrorism, and it will go wherever terrorism threatens.

The next four dimensions address domestic dynamics. Turning to public opinion on 9/11 in the fourth dimension, Mexico is mostly a spectator of global developments, concentrating largely on U.S. impacts; in addition to all of the above, Canadians have troops carrying the flag in distant lands to worry about. The fifth dimension asks if any 9/11-related domestic controversy is externally related. For Mexico, it is not, for Canada it is through multiple linkages, especially all the principles in its Charter, and the covert nature of its intelligence institutions within a democracy. The sixth dimension similarly inquires about external consequences of political change. Mexico's biggest political change, the 2000 election results, did not shake the external context, although democratization rippled far and wide,

Table 7.10 Neighborly Watchdogs?

Dimension	CISEN	Bill C-36
1. Timing in a Global Perspective	CISEN was neither product of 9/11, nor extended beyond North and Central America	Direct product of 9/11, eventually breeding external engagements
2. External Origins and Consequences of Triggers	A diverse bunch of external triggers, with 9/11 as only one, and not even the most determining one	9/11 as central, determining, top priority, and rationale for external engagement
3. Security Impacting more than the Region?	Security defined in terms of state development; not directly tested by terrorists: makes United States even more wary, and limits antiterrorism cooperation; and not externally impacting	Yes, after the terrorist plot was broken in Toronto; directly tested by terrorists; cements relations with U.S. counterparts
4. External Components of Public Reactions	U.S. engagements outside interpreted warily	Going beyond N. America perennially popular to offset United States; tolerated after 9/11 to correct Canadian threats
5. External Context as part of any Domestic Controversies?	No: public is indifferent toward CISEN, does not look beyond	Yes: Charter-related debates; on war against terrorism; and intrusive domestic intelligence
6. External Consequences of Political Change?	Not really: Survived the biggest change in 2000 with expanded agenda	From symbol of peacekeepers, Canada shifting to a warrior state
7. Capacity to Broaden Scope/Framework?	Quite unlikely at present	Very likely, and indeed underway
8. Connection between North American Agreements and other External compacts?	Not in Mexico's interests: Mexico prefers to treat policies separately	Yes: All roads should lead to multilateralism
9. Does long-term prosperity involve External Context?	Not really, but if so, only as *quid pro quo*	Willing to go all the way
10. North American Relations within Global Security Climate?	Not a necessary context	Imperative context

but Canada's 9/11-triggered political change led to a shift from defensive force deployments to force engagements, with all its consequences. Likewise for the seventh dimension: Mexico is too inwardly oriented to broaden any frameworks, Canada has no choice but to go wherever terrorism surfaces.

The last three dimensions address the regional context within the external purview. Are North American agreements connected with other agreements beyond the region, as the eighth dimension asks? CISEN is not interested in this, and Mexico prefers to treat each agreement on its own merit. By contrast, Canada's holy grail terminates in multilateralism: It always did, and still does. Therefore, NAFTA or FTAA can only be expected to move toward multilateralism, just as Bill C-36 and U.S. homeland security must extend to the global war on terrorism. The ninth dimension inquires if the external context is related to the country's or region's long-term prosperity. Without *quid pro quo* policy arrangements, Mexico's interest is not triggered, but Canada's long-term prosperity is seen as originating in and remaining related to the external context. Finally, the relation between North American relations and the global security climate is not seen as necessary by Mexico, though Canada treats it as being imperative.

CONCLUSIONS AND IMPLICATIONS

After recapitulating what the study set out to do, this section summarizes the findings first. Then it draws implications along the same contexts/levels of analysis previously utilized.

Conclusions

Two questions were asked: Why did both U.S. neighbors put their hearts, minds, and souls into NAFTA-based economic integration but not security-driven integration? What is the theoretical relevance of the Canada–Mexico relationship?

Turning to the first one, three themes kept recurring in the study: (a) NAFTA was seen as a win-win situation by both Canada and Mexico, but 9/11 elicited three different Canadian responses from three different prime ministers, while rejection of Mexico's immigration deal turned off its U.S. interests just when 9/11 struck, and casting with it the die in Mexico–U.S. relations. (b) The yardsticks were different: NAFTA measurement was largely material, but the 9/11 measurement is the human being, through values, lives lost or saved, and beliefs. (c) NAFTA represents arrangements that could easily function symmetrically in the three countries, however not only were the starting points of post–9/11 arrangements asymmetrical, but they also asymmetrically tilted in favor of the United States, damn the torpedoes!

The second question also raised three themes: (a) The Canadian–Mexico bilateral relation was the least developed in North America, and therefore the most vulnerable to theoretical fitting. (b) Whereas the Canadian–Mexican bilateral relationship had NAFTA-based linkages, it had virtually no security-based linkages, and in fact, security-based discontinuities or gaps may even dilute the existing strength of overall

Canada–Mexico links more than fortify them. (c) Both Canada and Mexico realized balancing the United States was more costly than failing to strengthen their own bilateral relationship, indeed security was an issue they could both agree to disagree upon, especially as it was interpreted in terms of the United States. For both it was a rendezvous of sorts with history: Mexico's history is one of distrust and suspicion toward the United States, Canada's filled more with war-time collaboration and Anglo-Saxon values than friction over size and unilateralism.

Three broader arguments were raised in the larger project. The first is, in any competition between security and economic integration, security would prevail, converting free trade into strategic trade; security priorities, secondly, elevate interdependence over integration, encouraging trade diversification and security free-ridership; and the third, with interdependence displacing economic integration, state-society tensions mount, internally, intergovernmentally, and transnationally.

We clearly noticed how NAFTA was subordinated to security considerations for both Canada and the United States; and though Mexico still prioritized it, without reciprocal gestures from its two partners, Mexico was left stranded with this interest. In fact, trade diversification emerged as an alternative. Added to these secular developments, both Canada and Mexico also adopted stringent border measures against terrorists, in the process also inhibiting free flows of trade, investment, and humans. With North American regional integration already facing speedbumps not imposed by 9/11, returning to the heady early days of regional splurges and orgies may not be easy, and certainly is not foreseeable at present.

The second argument of interdependence displacing integration was also found to be true, but not to the point of making the Canada–Mexico relation a model of interdependence. Both Canada and Mexico free-ride on U.S. security, but for different reasons: Canada because it is an active player in the war on terrorism, and therefore bandwagoning with a heavyweight is only logical; Mexico reluctantly, since it is not interested in the war on terrorism, but must make some face-saving gesture to the United States to fall back on should the terrorist threat suddenly, and unexpectedly, evaporate. Though Canada deepened its trade dependence on the United States after 9/11, Mexico's diversification was not state driven. Even with more symptoms of interdependence prevalent across North America by 2006 than before 9/11, the Canada–Mexico relation over security was not large or important enough to make interdependence the label of choice.

Finally, the third argument was adequately supported by North American dynamics. State-society tensions emerged over Bill C-36's restrictions of inalienable rights of citizens in Canada; and CISEN's reputation and handling of narcotraffickers continued Mexico's blemished tradition of state-society tensions. Transparency became a growth industry in both countries. On the intergovernmental front, though Canada and Mexico remained far apart over security matters, Canada witnessed see-saw relations with the United States, while Mexico never really warmed up to the United States after 9/11. This is international relations as seen by realists. Finally, transnationally, Canada's Afghanistan engagement, representing one strand of transnationalism, with the enemy they fought, terrorists, constituting another, also spiked its own vulnerability to terrorism. Mexico's transnational experiences remain historical and unrelated to 9/11: narcotraffickers and illegal migrants, as well as forces organized to combat these.

The project's hypothesis of the U.S. homeland security shifting North America's trilateralist trajectory toward bilateralism was found to be very true for both Canada and Mexico. Over security affairs, Canada relied on the United States, Mexico went solo, and neither Canada nor Mexico showed more than rhetorical interest in cultivating bilateral relations on this front. Over economic relations, matters were significantly different from war. In the final analysis, however, when push turns to shove, military interests rule over even the most robust economic force.

Implications

Three contexts/levels of analysis previously utilized anchor the implications: domestic, regional, and external.

Just as policies were subordinated to personalities or personal preferences, these in turn, appeared to have been driven more by values than reason. This is the most important finding within the domestic context/level. While values attach to just about every policy, this study found those attaching to security sink deeper and reflect more basic instincts than those attaching to economic behavior: NAFTA brought out self-help, but the security-driven self-help displaced NAFTA from the front-burner. Implications go beyond the weakening of NAFTA: They return attention to leaders, and the capacity of leaders to create circumstances, rather than the other way around, an attritional process in which, unfortunately, might will be right—at least for the only occasion that matters under the circumstances: the present, not the future. Analysts may need to pay more attention to leaders for both what they represent and how they compare with their contemporaries.

The weakening of NAFTA sends several regional shivers. In addition to accenting the war industry, investors are likely to shift resources to portfolio from FDI, to securities and bonds more than to manufacturing plants, in the process fueling boom-bust cycles. North America has the most to suffer, just like it had the most to gain during the NAFTA years: It boasts the largest world economy, three of the top-fifteen economies, the largest bilateral trading partnership, and the most prominent trading arrangement between developed and developing countries—ideal for speculators, and particularly with tumultuous energy prices. Because the United States is the top trading partner of more countries in the world than any other, a cough here could mean a fever there, and influenza somewhere else. War has never been friendly to economic development, integration, and welfare; and it is unlikely to be more compassionate to economies because the threats are more terroristic. Destabilizing North American regional economic integration implies a domino effect whose impact scale remains the only unknown.

The growth of values and the decline of economic foundations are not the only worrisome external forces: Five years of the war on terrorism have produced more terrorists rather than reduced them, an observation based on the sudden growth of

Taliban fighters in Afghanistan, Pakistan's recognition of *Taliban,* Iraq's descent into a splinter state, Iran's acquisition of nuclear capability, and North Korea exploding its own nuclear bomb, among others. Many more Canadas will be needed if the goal is to fight terrorism; contrariwise, many more Mexicos will help external threats to peter out on their own, rather than be allowed to proliferate under foreign presence. Whichever way, the most positive North American implication is of terrorism not revisiting the region since 9/11. That is cold comfort when terrorists proliferate overseas and more coffins come back, and all just to reassert which is the better of subjective values.

8

9/11, Theory, and the *North America* Idea: Trilateralism on Trial?

INTRODUCTION

Given the starkly different, if not contradictory, Canada–U.S. and Mexico–U.S. relations after 9/11, chapters 5, 6, and 7 suggest trilateralism to be an idea whose time has not yet come to North America. Unlike NAFTA's starting point of three bilateral agreements seeking trilateral outcomes, responses to 9/11 across North America laid the seeds not only of finite bilateralism, but also bilateralism based on the frank unilateral interests of the United States. Such observations do not clinically abandon trilateralism, however. Without trilateral institutions, previous chapters noted the resilience of various trilateralist procedures, processes, pressures, and sentiments. Might they endure longer than the war on terrorism? Could they recast security integrative efforts more positively? Europe's experiences offer useful historical lessons on the roles of sequence and holism.

Facing thresholds as perilous as 9/11, the ECSC was able to expand its agenda within the first decade,[1] membership throughout the next three, promoted supranationalism by fits and starts, and permitted fragile supranational institutions to mature—all in spite of the 1965 Empty Chair crisis,[2] the 1969–71 monetary crises,[3] and four decades of the Cold War. Although North American integration is not doing too badly by those standards, it could also take stock of, and place, one-shot episodes into a larger integrative framework, much like the Europeans did by making their institutionalizing efforts stick through newly created bureaucracies. This is not impossible in North America, given the pathfinding measures of the 1990s. What is impossible is to permeate North America's greater power asymmetries. At least our study buttresses that observation. We nonetheless believe a variety of different paths still facilitate North American integration.

NAFTA's past history suggests the staying power of lesser issues, and how these have subtly promoted trilateralism. With obvious and emphatic attention on bilateral trade and investment arrangements, NAFTA silently and successfully pushed various sticky arrangements through the labor and environmental side-agreements.[4] Both established secretariats, in Dallas and Montreal, respectively, dealing with, and adjudicating complaints from the entire region, from Alaska to Central America. In addition to these modest examples of supranationalistic tendencies was the more robust display of intergovernmentalism:[5] the innovative and regular trilateral summits, for example. Of course, these trilateralist initiatives may flounder or fail, but giving up on them because of a changed post–9/11 agenda, would be akin to letting the baby out with the proverbial bath water.

Contradictory post–9/11 bilateral performances should not obscure the big North American picture highlighting the largest world economy and two of the top three most voluminous bilateral trading relations in the world at the start of the twenty-first century. In spite of the fears imposed by 9/11, people have to eat, earn an income, and continue with some basic needs of life; corporations have to find external markets to survive, and thereby provide domestic jobs while competing globally; and policy-makers must ultimately depend on the typical citizen's vote and corporate operations. Transactions and travel remain indispensable to these, and increasingly across boundaries. Looking beyond, post–9/11 bilateralism is consistent with these trends.

Chapters 5, 6, and 7 do not posit bilateralism as a comprehensive North American force, nor of the three bilateral relationships belonging to the same specie. How common are the bilateral-specific claims across North America? What is the strength of the nonbilateral claims, and do they predict trilateralism? Ultimately, what can other integrative experiences learn from post–9/11 North America?

Taking a stab at those questions, for whatever it is worth, we redirect the same theoretical tenets toward a trilateral analysis. We pay more attention to illustrating similarities and differences here rather than argument validation, since many cases, descriptions, and examples already exist. Beginning with the integrative theories (neofunctionalism and security community), we shift to the interdependent family (interdependence, neorealism) of explanations, before assessing the principles and norms of intelligence, to find answers to the above questions.

POST–9/11 TRILATERALISM: INTEGRATIVE THEORIES

Tables 8.1 and 8.2 facilitate discussions, the former through neofunctionalist lenses, and the latter through security community counterparts. Generally, we find economic integration offering more trilateralist hope than security integration, but although trilateralist security integration cannot at all be dismissed, present circumstances and preferences provide them neither a favorable setting nor hope in the immediate future. More importantly, security considerations were not found to be in a zero-sum relationship with economic integration: Economic integration was constrained, but not reversed nor diversified significantly, if at all, by 9/11 or its aftermath.

Neofunctionalism

Of the 14 neofunctionalist tenets, only five pose trilateralist (and bilateralist) problems: the first, tenth, eleventh, and thirteenth. Before elaborating, the others can be dismissed first. As chapters 5, 6, and 7 showed, 14 years of NAFTA either coincided with, or directly fostered, growth in all of the nine remaining tenets.

Table 8.1 Neofunctionalist Tenets, 9/11, and North America

Tenets	Trilateral discussions
1. Economic symmetry	Underlying problem: surfaces every now and then, but always on people's mind
2. Elite complementarity	Success story under NAFTA, equally forceful after 9/11
3. Pluralism	North America more pluralistic after 9/11 than before with Mexico's democratization taking irreversible directions with the 2000 elections
4. Capacity to adapt	Clearly evident in adjusting trade to security screenings, as well as leaders to each other, under changed circumstances
5. Spillover	Continued growth: at state level (new institutions) and societal (people, groups, corporations)
6. Growing transaction	Continued growth: Canada still top U.S. trading partner, Mexico third
7. Growth in intergovernmentalism	Huge growth, with creation of several bilateral border regulations: Bush's 2007 budget reduced domestic spending but sharply increased border allocations
8. Transnational growth	Still very high: NAFTA's side agreements functioning at peak capacity
9. Elite socialization	Unaffected by 9/11: extensive and intensive networks
10. Growth in ideological identity	No new post–9/11 North American ideological identity: support for war against terrorism remains rhetorical trilaterally, but very substantive in the Canada–U.S. bilateral relationship
11. Increasing interaction with external actors	North America acting as a unit with external actors is still a pipe dream, complicated by 9/11
12. Benefit distribution higher an more equitable	All three countries have benefited from NAFTA (but gripes have also mounted); however, distribution is not equal between them or even within each
13. Converging perceptions of external problems	More divergences than convergences after 9/11
14. Integration as cost free	Yes, improvement over Canadian nationalism, Mexican import-substitution, and punitive U.S. trading actions: all reduced transactions costs, and short-term losses from shifting policies largely produced long-term gains

More summits involving all three countries were held during those 14 years than all trilateral summits put together previously (second and ninth), while business leaders also convened in greater numbers than ever before. In turn, not only more people, but also more policies, spilled over from one arena to another across the national boundaries (fifth); transactions expanded and multiplied (sixth), the three governments established more institutions (seventh), while more businesses and societal groups, including even individuals, flowed across those boundaries (eigth). Since these were all welfare-enhancing actions, opening new doors all the time, trilateralist integration proved more beneficial than the Canadian nationalism of the 1970s,[6] Mexico's import substitution until the 1980s,[7] and the punitive U.S. trade measures of the 1970s–80s.[8]

Behind these economic, political, and social flows, North America became more democratized (third). Canada and the United States have long-established claims in this regard, but Mexico was also able to unshackle itself from the last chains of authoritarianism. Mexico's free-trade moves leading up to the February 1990 Davos proposal to create NAFTA was not initially accepted by Canada; but by September that year, realizing the inevitability of NAFTA, Canada joined the negotiations, and wholeheartedly at that. This adaptation mirrors Mexico's approach to the United States: Instead of apprehending the United States as the great colossus (fourth), Mexican migrants, both legal and illegal, showed how the shark could be tamed.[9] None of these forces—transactions, liberalism, adaptations—were decisively diminished by 9/11.

Where there were problems, 9/11 was not necessarily the reason why. The first of these is economic symmetry (first in table 8.1). Arguably prevalent in the first half of the nineteenth century, economic symmetry has not only been absent in a dramatic way, but is unlikely to become a regional trait in the foreseeable future. Integrative efforts managed to not only to get underway regardless of it, but also helped absolute welfare levels improve in each of the three countries. Interpreting it as an impediment is the equivalent of escaping the problem. Within asymmetrical conditions, many opportunities have been found and created, and even more adjustments have been made by Canada and Mexico. In the final analysis, though, it remains the straw that could break the back of North American integration, since the fear is commonplace, often invoked in negotiations, and resorted to in the last-gap argumentation when all else fail. It stalks North America as a ghost, not only enlivened by 9/11, but also aggressively referenced by the United States after 9/11.

The second impediment is the growth of ideological identification (tenth). Unpopular though it was, and unworkable in an asymmetrical setting, the Washington Consensus, did become an ideology all three countries officially embraced at one point or another. Yet it does not cover a number of broader North American dynamics, such as individual travel or societal networking across borders; and remains widely unpopular, though very appealing to selected probusiness groups. Compounding a common ideology are cultural barriers (e.g., Anglo-Saxon versus Hispanic; English versus Spanish), political preferences (the 9/11-driven with-us-or-against-us U.S. ideology), and even economic directions (nationalized versus private enterprises). If anything, 9/11 only sharpened these differences, and ultimately, integration might face its most formidable opponent in them. That, however, is likely to remain a long-term problem, a predicament hardly affecting consumers, corporations, politicians, or voters, driven as they are by short-term instincts and horizons. They have also not curtailed more integrative ideologies (environmentalism, for example, or respect for human rights), thus leaving room for trilateral hopes.

Increasing interaction reflecting a North American entity has been attempted only superficially and in less-important policy areas, such as environmental protection, therefore interacting as a North American unit with external actors is still too new and experimental (eleventh). The only reassurance lies across the Atlantic Ocean: It took the European Community almost 40 years to be able to act together abroad, and be accepted in international/multilateral institutions as a single entity. North America has a long way to go.

Integrative benefits have been welfare enhancing but not distribution-equalizing, due in part to the prevalent asymmetry between countries, to which one might add intracountry asymmetry. Every country can find grievances attributable to NAFTA, with the agricultural sector and farmers being blatantly common residues. In addition are distributional inequalities within countries, with the farm sector and rural residents again being the common victim. These are structural problems, irremediable with any single, specific policy. They existed before 9/11, and will continue to be there. The only hope is to not let the grievance grow.

Finally, external problems, that is, those outside North America but affecting North America, will continue to be interpreted differently by the three countries: Diverging responses to UN Resolution 1441 to invade Iraq illustrated deeper differences and could be the source of future misinterpretations. Before 9/11, the three countries could point to more converging patterns than diverging, a pattern inverting itself after 9/11 (thirteenth). How long the 9/11 shadow lasts may hold an answer to the North American convergent-divergent tussle, but in and of itself, this dimension probably will not upturn all the others: All three countries have been learning to agree to disagree.

In summary, the five dimensions together could pose formidable integrative problems across North America. So far, the other nine dimensions have withstood these pressures. How much longer they can continue doing so is a question without a drawing-board answer: Events and developments in the trenches can alone do that; but since that potentially invokes individual action from more than 435 million people in the region, individual citizens could be the decisive factor. European integration side-stepped the middle and lower classes for over 50 years, and paid the price when citizens in some countries voted against the constitution to ventilate accumulating frustrations. North American integration could be stumped at the national level even before any North American constitution reaches the drawing board, indicating why any trilateralist shift remains precarious and uphill.

Security Community Tenets

How does a security community integration framework fare? We argue each one of the 12 tenets in table 8.2 is double-edged, with values constituting one reason for the subjective underpinning. Measuring flows and transactions is quite different from measuring values. Some values change, others do not even if external

Table 8.2 Security Community, 9/11, and North America

Tenets	Trilateral discussions
1. Value compatibility	Could work both ways, depending on how political entrepreneurs cultivate/disseminate values
2. Enhanced predictability	Over economic performances, yes; over terrorism, no
3. Mutual responsiveness	Valid, but also invites an eye-for-an-eye, tooth-for-a-tooth mentality (Fox's delayed 9/11 sympathy to Bush for not accepting his immigration proposal)
4. Value complementarity	Depends on the value, economic or security, for example, easier over the former than the latter trilaterally; bilaterally, it depends on which two countries are being paired
5. Distinctiveness in lifestyles	North American lifestyle is difficult to create, given the cultural, social, and political differences; but a North American economic personality may be easier on the basis of policy convergences more than institutions
6. Reward expectations before integration	True for economic integration; not a viable proposal in a security-driven atmosphere
7. Increasing political and administrative functions	Yes, too many examples litter previous chapters
8. Economic growth distinguishing core from periphery	True, cities and coastal areas have benefited many more than the hinterland; 9/11 will not alter the pattern, but lower the scale of growth
9. Expansion of geographical and social communications	True both before and after 9/11
10. Multiplication of communications	True both before and after 9/11
11. Decreasing barriers to mobility	True both before and after 9/11 (even for illegal flows from Mexico)
12. Increasing political elites	True both before and after 9/11

circumstances change. They can be the source of considerable flux, but in hard times, also a source of reassurance.

We posit the first six tenets depend more on subjective forces than objective, and the second six more on objective than subjective criteria. At least the second six can be measured by commonly accepted yardsticks, and in fact, have their counterparts in neofunctionalism, either directly or indirectly. Under NAFTA, we have witnessed the trilateral growth of political and administrative functions (seventh), core areas being distinguished within each country from the peripheral (eighth), geographical and social communications expanding (ninth), in fact, overall communications multiplying (tenth), barriers being lowered (eleventh), and political elites increasing everywhere, whether through political parties or not (twelfth).

The subjective six tenets carry elements of objectivity. Subjective individual values become more objective through aggregation (a person's values being more subjective than a group's), but the interpretive criteria will always be debatable. Not only are values slippery (they can be activated or kept on the back burner at one's will), but the typical person also carries multiple values, often too many to be counted, sometimes even at odds with each other. Core values acquired in childhood may subsequently be modified by education, exposure, dialogue, and mistakes. Our point is simple: values may go in multiple directions simultaneously, creating ambiguities; but rejecting them on the analytical front is equally perilous.

Turning to the first six tenets, North America shows both compatible and incompatible values (first: welfare enhancing versus warfare-enhancing policies), enhances both predictable and unpredictable outcomes (second: gross domestic production figures versus terrorist attacks), elicits mutual responsiveness or neglect (third: support for the war against terrorism against the specific March 2003 opposition to war on Iraq), promotes value complementarity and confrontation (fourth: over legal immigration versus illegal immigration), evoking lifestyle distinctiveness through integration and conformity (fifth: accepting English, French, and Spanish as official North American languages versus conforming to just English), and expects both rewards and costs of North American integration (sixth: lower transactions costs from free movements across boundaries versus the lower costs translating into lower incomes, especially for the underprivileged, such as farmers).

Unlike neofunctionalism, which survived the 9/11 militarism and ramifications, a budding security community, even given increasing unpredictabilities based on the greater reliance on subjective determinants, could prove stronger because of its value-based structures. Security imperatives touch life-death issues more directly than economic imperatives, and summon those bedrock values faster than all other values. In North America, this slants an uneven playing field even more so, as Anglo-Saxon values across one border outstrip Hispanic values across another. To the extent security community overlaps neofunctionalist tenets, the security community alternative is safe and steady; where it does not, probabilities of derailment and reversals are much higher simply because those "safer" values shelter with greater ease under nationalistic frameworks than regional (that is, between countries, not a region within a country).

In a nutshell, whereas North American neofunctionalism begins with bilateralism and intergovernmentalism while pushing toward and probing trilateralism and supranationalism, a North American security community begins with bilateralism and intergovernmentalism. The critical paradigm difference may be how values find a better anchor with military considerations than economic integration. This may explain why Canada vaulted over Mexico in U.S. interests after 9/11, and why extending the Canada–U.S. security community, prevalent even during the Cold War, to Mexico may not be possible, at least not in its current form, given both a negative historical mind-set and inflaming contemporary cross-border externalities. Theoretically, we understand better why amalgamated and pluralistic security communities, though pitched as two different paradigms, are more wedlocked than independent. Both need bedrock values, and these types of values do not significantly change for any given person, country, or paradigm.

POST–9/11 TRILATERALISM: INTERDEPENDENT THEORIES

Tables 8.3 and 8.4 motivate new discussions, the former spelling out interdependent, the latter neorealist, tenets. Overall, interdependence offers a stronger explanatory framework for North America than neorealism, although neorealism may still remain the most appropriate lens for evaluating post–Cold War United States, very much like it was during the Cold War itself.[10] Old habits die hard, but security imperatives even prevent them from blending with other habits. Since neorealism does not apply to Mexico's case in the least and captures Canada's experiences only with a lot of imagination, interdependence serves as a more reliable North American option. It has the additional advantage of being a fall-back when integrative theories collapse, or when integration fails. The magic behind why integrative theories persisted for over 50 years, despite all odds, is their ability to keep one foot on familiar ground (intergovernmentalism for neofunctionalism; values for security communities), while the other explores the unknown (supranational variations for neofunctionalism; expansion through communications and transactions as media

Table 8.3 Interdependence, 9/11, and North America

Tenets	Description
1. Channels of communication	Expanding before and after 9/11, but questionable criteria for interdependence since integration lays stronger claims too
2. Hierarchy of issues	Neorealism explicitly places military at top (as in the United States), integration places nonmilitary issues at top (as with Canada and Mexico), and interdependence fluctuates (to some extent Canada and Mexico after 9/11)
3. Subordination of the military	Explicit in Mexico and pre–9/11 Canada, largely in post–9/11 Canada, not at all in United States
4. Nature of institutional membership	Used to be pre–9/11 Canadian preference, after 9/11 Canada prefers NATO command over United States; Mexico's only preference is North American institutionalization, not global or multilateral; institutions serve as U.S. instruments to promote state interests
5. Catalysts of change	New knowledge for Canada and Mexico; new knowledge, power distribution, and terrorist activities for United States
6. Placement of regionalism along levels of policy-making analysis	Canada preferred multilateralism before 9/11, now nationalist preferences prevail, especially if attached to U.S. interests; Mexico preferred regionalism pre–9/11, now both regionalism and nationalism; U.S. always preferred nationalism, all others serving as instruments of state policies

for security communities). Interdependence acts as a conservative form of intergovernmentalism, which is precisely the relationship table 8.3 captures.

Whereas the first tenet is explained by both integrative theories being considered, the second and third tenets shake the integrative boat. With 9/11 pushing security to the top of all issues in the United States and to a higher ranking on Canada's agenda than before, Mexico has no choice but to adjust to the reordering without displacing economic growth from the apex of its own hierarchy. Until Mexico becomes more directly involved in the war on terrorism, this order will not change; and until then, interdependent interpretations are likely to do better than integrative in North America. The fourth, fifth, and sixth dimensions, therefore, probe both options, suggesting greater integration between Canada and the United States over security owing to more familiar and reliable values, but more interdependent Mexico–U.S. relations owing to policy differences, nuances, and cultural incompatibilities (officially adopting Spanish as a second U.S. language, for example).

Whereas institutional membership dilutes pure state identification, we find all three North American countries pursuing institutional membership selectively: Canada's integrating interests were restricted only to the United States until 1990, and then, as it embraced NAFTA, it also mellowed to the OAS, pursued the APEC (Asia-Pacific Economic Cooperation), FTAA, and so forth, while also participating under NATO in Afghanistan; Mexico has never been interested in NATO; and the United States perennially ignores the OAS. Thus, all three fall in between state-based interdependence and institutional ascription.

Catalysts of change can be the power distribution (neoliberalism, interdependence), or new knowledge (integration). In North America, only the United States accepts and can initiate the first, with both other countries impacted directly by it; and though the United States is by far most important source of new knowledge (such as technology), the scope to create it is even more in less developed countries, like Mexico, as they tackle increasingly new issues, for example, moving up the technology ladder from a *maquiladora* low-wage base. However, new U.S. knowledge is likely to disperse more widely outside the United States than new Mexican knowledge, or even Canadian, given its wider and deeper trade links, investment attachments, and cultural influences. With a foot in both camps, the United States is better able to induce Canada and Mexico in both than Canada or Mexico can the United States.

Finally, in the nationalism-regionalism-globalism sequence, interdependence is stronger at the former end while integration begins anywhere on the right of it along the spectrum: the farther to the right, the more the integration. North American patterns have been fluctuating along this spectrum, with Canada's historical preference of being located on the extreme right of the spectrum, though any location on the right-hand side of nationalism is acceptable. Mexico will not go to the extreme right, while a narrowly defined regionalism, meaning only North American, suggests the nationalistic pole as the area of central tendency, certainly historically; and national interests clearly serve a *sine qua non* United States role, though it freely explores both regional and multilateral/international/global options as instruments of national interests.

It is hard to envision the United States changing its posturing: World leaders need to keep one foot out there, probing the rest of the world, while the other stays at home to assert everything leadership stands for (values, institutions, resources, popular mood, and so forth). In turn, Canada and Mexico shifting too far to the right cannot be expected because of the restraining effects of the United States, which also happens to be their own locations of central tendency. What 9/11 did was essentially shift the center of gravity more to the left along the spectrum, though not necessarily to the extreme left. Integrative thrusts retreated from wherever they had been on the right side of the spectrum.

Can a left spatial spectrum shift, as opposed to an ideological spectrum left, be better explained by neorealism? After all, national interest has been the traditional interest of realism,[11] and when influenced by distribution of power considerations, becomes the central concern of neorealism. Table 8.4 clearly asserts these to be dominant U.S. characteristics, less so for Canada, and still less so for Mexico. While all three countries claim sovereign equality, they are not at all equal, in terms of (a) state-society relations and (b) relative state capabilities. By emphasizing the strength of the state, the second dimension posits how state strength becomes a function of how it is able to manage societal interests within the country. Canada has always been weak on this, divided as it is between Anglo-Saxons and French, as well as between the east and west of the country; Mexico has a far stronger state, given its authoritarian past, yet still unable to control the many divisive elements, such as north-south imbalances, the preponderant place of Mexico City in the country, and integrating indigenous groups. The U.S. fluctuates, at times unable to rise above pluralistic differences, especially when different parties control the legislature and executive, and at other times united by external threat, as 9/11. Finally, the third dimension of international competitiveness captures Mexico's refrain from participation in the international milieu, Canada's greater interest in nonmilitary global competition, and the U.S. interest in global military and economic competitiveness, with the military clearly

Table 8.4 Neorealism, 9/11, and North America

Tenets	Description
1. State as dominant actor	Canadian state weak, Mexican strong, U.S. fluctuating: interest groups and ethnic/national divisions get in the way
2. Policy reflecting internal or external competitiveness?	Canada has an alliance government, Mexico is politically fractured, United States has different parties controlling the two key branches: internal competition is high in 2007, weakening state capabilities abroad
3. Is international competitiveness orderly or chaotic	Canada engages in nonmilitary competitiveness, which is more orderly than military; Mexico is not interested in this criterion; and United States believes only in international competitiveness, with military considerations over-riding economic

setting the tone after World War II and 9/11, and raising economic competitiveness to the U.S. policy-making apex only between the end of the Cold War and 9/11.

In short, there is much to be said about the interdependence theories: They can explain almost any rainy North American development; though brighter moments may be better explained by integrative theories, interdependence theories cannot so easily be dislodged.

POST–9/11 TRILATERALISM: INTELLIGENCE INSTINCTS

Tables 8.5, 8.6, and 8.7 examine the intelligence infrastructure to inquire if the three countries can engage in the war on terrorism if push comes to shove (or alternately, they somehow agree on full-fledged security integration). Integration on the basis of intelligence assumes a PSC. The previous section attributed one of the weaknesses of a trilateral PSC to segmented values; this one looks at the mechanics in case of a hypothetical tripartite engagement against terrorism. Since intelligence cannot operate in open space, a subject, object, and procedural connections between them must exist. With terrorism as the subject, the object and procedural connections can be gleaned from principles (table 8.5), strategic cultural elements (table 8.6),

Table 8.5 Intelligence Principles, 9/11, and North America

Principles	Trilateral discussions
1. Intelligence derives from international conflict or rivalry	Very disintegrative: Not an initial Canadian orientation, but increasingly becoming so, reaffirming U.S. collaboration (with CIA); not at all a Mexican principle; and a robust, catalyzing U.S. principle
2. Conduct or use of intelligence involves secrecy	True for all three countries
3. Clandestine collection of information is the fundamental activity of intelligence	True for all three countries
4. Truth must be the basis of good intelligence	True for all three countries by denial: In practice all three countries remain open to questionable means
5. Intelligence in a vacuum is of no value, tardy intelligence is of little value	True for all three countries
6. Special activities must involve native knowledge of the national groups toward which they are directed	True for all three countries within different contexts: For Canada and Mexico native knowledge has been very domestic, though Canada may be dragged by the war on terrorism to external settings; for United States, native knowledge can be both domestic and international, increasingly the latter owing to the prerogatives of a world leader

and institutional norms (table 8.7). In a nutshell, they reaffirm Anglo-Saxon values, Canada–U.S. integration, Mexican indifference, and U.S. leadership—precisely the inherently uneven North American playing field economic integration made a valiant but unsuccessful attempt to level.

Through trilateral eyes, the six table 8.5 dimensions offer two contrasting explanatory clusters: (a) trilateral parallels, with the second, third, fourth, and fifth principles representing secrecy, clandestine information-collection, foundations in truth (which none of the three countries pay any respect to), and the fact that intelligence becomes meaningless in a vacuum or if tardy and (b) trilateral disjunctures with the first and last principles. Internationalizing the premise of intelligence automatically eliminates Mexico (it is not even interested in war-on-terrorism participation), bothers Canada (whose intelligence evolved against perceived domestic threats but prior ties with U.S. counterparts led to free-riding internationally), and speaks only and fully for the United States. As such, utilizing native knowledge, the sixth principle, essentially means the domestic level for Mexico and Canada, but the whole world for the United States, as for example, about Iraq to serve policy interests in Washington—creating North American levels of analysis problems, especially for the turf-minded agencies in the three countries. Forging partnerships may be useful, as between Canada and the Untied States, but integrating the disparate agencies demands more attention and resources than any of the countries can offer, or show interest in.

Table 8.6 Strategic Cultural Elements, 9/11, and North America

Determinants	**Trilateral discussions**
Background influences:	
1. Sense of history	More important for Mexico, least for United States, Canada in between
2. Geographical endowment	No hostile-neighbor syndrome for United States; neighborly gravitational pull for Canada and Mexico
3. Cultural heritage	Two streams without opportunities to adjust to each other adequately well
Factors directly affecting strategic culture:	
1. Democratic institutions	Prevalent in all three countries.
2. Role of media	Prevalent in all three countries.
3. Suspicion of government/ military	Prevalent in all three countries.
4. Mobilization-demobilization pattern	Prevalent in all three countries.
5. Notion of invincibility	Only in United States, not in Canada or Mexico
6. Preference for total wars	Only in United States, not in Canada or Mexico
7. Tradition of citizen-soldier	traces in all three countries, historically dominant in Mexico, but not too important for any of the three countries

Even under the best-case scenario of all three countries providing the needed attention and resources, their endowments might still pull the rug from beneath a North American intelligence regime. Table 8.6 highlights the huge differences in two clusters: background/conditioning forces, as well as the direct elements of strategic culture. The three background/conditioning determinants—sense of history, geography, and culture—dramatize all the ingredients integrative efforts can do without, at least for the purpose they are being used here. They cannot even be assumed away. In our previous discussions, we have made a case of how the physical and cultural endowments produced quite different intelligence orientations, interests, and constraints. These, in turn, constrain rather than enhance integration.

Table 8.6's second set of factors, affecting strategic culture, is less forbidding, but since they are premised upon the first set, they have their inherent constraints. All three countries have democratic institutions (first), face full media scrutiny (second), harbor suspicion against government and/or military (third), and share

Table 8.7 Intelligence Institutional Norms, 9/11, North America

Institutional norms	
1. Institutional survival	Not necessarily in Mexico, elsewhere a long tradition of this
2. Secrecy	Prevalent in all three countries
3. Intelligence exceptionalism	Not in Mexico, elsewhere very true
4. Ambiguous mandate	Prevalent in all three countries
5. Confederal structure	Not in Mexico, elsewhere very true
6. Flexible accountability	Not in Mexico, elsewhere very true
7. Separation of intelligence from law enforcement (police)	Prevalent in all three countries
8. Competitive intelligence	Prevalent in all three countries: many agencies in each country
9. Separation of intelligence from policy	True of Canada and Mexico, not the United States, especially after 9/11
10. Policy support	Not true in Canada and Mexico, but increasingly true in United States
11. Can-do attitude	Only United States demonstrates this
12. Primacy of intelligence analysis	Only United States demonstrates this
13. Emphasis on current intelligence	Prevalent in all three countries, but U.S. networks usually get there before their Canadian or Mexican counterparts
14. Provision for accurate, timely, and relevant intelligence	Prevalent in all three countries, but U.S. networks usually get there before their Canadian or Mexican counterparts

mobilization-demobilization patterns (fourth). With only the United States evincing invincibility (fifth), not only through its resources but also out of its preferences, it is the only country fully geared for total war engagement (sixth). Whereas all three countries have had citizen-soldier historical experiences (seventh), only in Mexico were they institutionalized, but in no country have these left a continuing tradition, or remain important presently. Even if the four similarities facilitate integration, they are unlikely to serve intelligence purposes as much as the Kantian *foedus pacificum* of democratic countries.[12] In the final analysis, democracy becomes the single most salient and silent thorn behind intelligence pursuits.

If indeed such an integrative effort is pursued, the norms that must first be satisfied for it to flourish, provided in table 8.7, may become a less demanding task. Out of the 14 norms listed, we find only one cannot be fully supplied (first), while four others show fragility (third, ninth, eleventh, and twelfth). The only one not fully supplied is institutional survival (first): Facing a change every six years, sometimes significantly, at other times modestly, Mexico's political system and structures still need more roots almost a century after its constitution was adopted. Intelligence agencies, in turn, remain obvious victims. Deliberately subordinated so as not shake the system, Mexican intelligence does not share the exceptional status Canadian and U.S. intelligence agencies do (third); it is as separated from policy-making as it is not in the United States (ninth), lacks any assertive can-do attitudes as the U.S. counterpart displays (eleventh), and does not command primacy in agenda-setting as in the United States (twelfth). Canada identifies with Mexico over the ninth, eleventh, and twelfth norms.

CONCLUSIONS

Assessing the trilateral prospects through intelligence lenses closes the door of trilateralism even more emphatically. Even if the leaders wanted to pursue a North American security community, the necessary conditions (experience, facilitative culture, institutional orientations, and instincts) do not exist, while the sufficient conditions (many of the norms) constitute too brittle a framework to develop something as urgent. Mexico's indifference should not be taken too lightly: nonintervention has long been a Mexican tradition, and it is not as internationalist as Canada or the United States to suddenly put on a global cloak. Without will and interest, no institution can last too long.

The chapter clarifies why North American trilateralism (a) should be encouraged along economic lines where the necessary conditions prevail; (b) feeds on commonalities between various bilateral partnerships, of which there are not many presently; (c) springs ultimately from the will, interest, and institutional orientations within each country, all in short contemporary supply; (d) is an issue-specific pursuit, with some issues facilitative, and other restrictive, thus inhibiting a comprehensive categorizing; and (e) must assume unilateralism of varying degrees, minimal unilateralism producing hypothetically stronger trilateralism, maximal weaker forms, with its source being only the United States. In short, trilateralism is not dead because of

9/11, it remains in abeyance, waiting for the right combination of purposive agency and circumstances to revive it in an evolving and tailored form for North America's idiosyncratic relations.

Minefields are not uncommon in international relations; and navigating between them is also a routine expectation. Therefore, North America, as such, is not closed to trilateralism, but the pathways may be more precarious than usual and demand a more uphill climb than perhaps elsewhere.

9

Conclusions: North American Tango—Only For Two

RECAPITULATING ARGUMENTS

North America awoke to a constrained post–9/11 security-driven future after relishing regional economic integration during the 1990s. With the world's largest economy exerting enormous gravitational effects on Canada and Mexico, the United States had no choice but to prioritize security considerations. How its two relatively pacific neighbors responded remained the only variable. Hypothesizing that North American trilateral pursuits, would shift toward bilateralism, no matter how widely or deeply, we postulated three arguments, each with its own implications.

The first argument simply posited simultaneous security and economic integration elevates the former over the latter, with two implications: (a) strategic trade considerations would displace FTAs and (b) security imperatives would promote hierarchy over community on issues and in relationships. Our second argument stated that retreating from economic integration in the face of increasing security imperatives would promote interdependence over integrative relations, but the process would encourage (a) trade diversification and (b) security free-ridership. We finally argued the net effect of interdependence displacing integrative thrusts would enhance state-society fissures; and in turn generate conflicts between (a) states, (b) social groups themselves, and (c) social groups across state boundaries. What do our country-specific and bilateral North American investigations show?

OVERALL FINDINGS: REGIONALISM AT BAY?

Chapters 2, 3, and 4 clearly convey the country-specific retreat from trilateralism in the United States, Canada, and Mexico, respectively, while the bilateral inquiries in chapters 5, 6, and 7 also show disparate forms of unilateralism: the United States asserting its dominant position, Canada riding an ambiguous wave, and Mexico's abnegation predicting retreat. A trilateral examination in chapter 8 dimmed any immediate return to the go-go North American orientations of the 1990s even further. Both the hypothesis of North American bilateralism and its off-shoot arguments were reaffirmed.

First, security imperatives received higher priority over economic integration in the United States and Canada, but not in Mexico. For the United States, this was a logical response, while Canada's value overlapping with the United States partially mollifies its irreversible U.S. economic dependence. Mexico, on the other hand, continued prioritizing economic integrative interests. Without active U.S. engagement on U.S. terms, economic integrative measures languished behind security imperatives, reviving a North American issue-agenda hierarchy reminiscent of the Cold War.

Second, the findings do not show interdependence and integration to be in a zero-sum relationship: Patterns of interdependence were neither new nor dominant whether the issue was security or nonsecurity, but were not the only reason why integration stalled in all three countries. Among the subset arguments, only Mexico's imports from the United States have diversified; its exports, as well as Canada's overall trade remain highly dependent on the United States. Two coincidental circumstances cloud the direct 9/11-triggered security and economic integration connections: On the one hand, illegal Mexican emigration to the U.S. spiraled during the period under study, thus bringing an old and somewhat more passive issue on to the front-burner of terrorism protection. On the other, China's displacement of Mexico as the second largest U.S. trading partner in 2003 broke the magical NAFTA claim of making the top-two U.S. trading partners North American. In the aftermath of 9/11, Mexico–U.S. relations were unusually and unnecessarily compounded by the illegal immigration cross-border externality, while China's surge highlights the nature and numbers of secular factors intervening in the homeland security nexus, underscoring the need to not belittle economic relations. Both Canada and Mexico became U.S. security free-riders, Mexico unwittingly and Canada willingly.

Third, state-society relations were not disrupted, but were left more dangling than before. There was enough sympathy in Canada and Mexico for 9/11 and 9/11-related events in the United States; but the one-track U.S. responses, in particular through its increasingly institutionalized approach, dimmed enthusiasm quickly. Canada's support shifted from the rhetorical to hands-on engagement, Mexico's emerged grudgingly. Partisanship was not the only reason behind Canada's initial reluctance, and immigration proved to be the dominant explanation for Mexico's distance. State-society relations struggled, reflecting personality clashes, partisan differences, and cultural resonance, with implicit Anglo-Saxon values buoying Canada–U.S. relations, and identifying Hispanics with illegal immigration exacerbating Mexico–U.S. relations. More than 9/11 events, these attitudes divided societies within each country: The 2006 Liberal defeat in Canada was largely over domestic issues (corruption, incompetence), but the Conservative victory elevated pro-U.S. social groups; Mexico's PAN won the 2006 elections but the disruptive PRD defeat struck a chord with a historical anti-U.S. sentiment; and illegal Mexican emigration divided Republicans—those against immigrants versus those favoring a guest worker program at both the Republican-dominated legislative and the Republican presidential levels. Losing the legislature to the Democrats in 2006 left the immigration bill even more unpredictably positioned. In all three countries, society was more divided in 2008 than in 2001.

COUNTRY-SPECIFIC FINDINGS: BIRDS OF DIFFERENT FEATHERS?

Country-specific interpretations further elaborate some of the overall findings. We begin with the country directly impacted by 9/11, then turn to its two neighbors in alphabetical order.

United States

Four findings deserve attention: (a) a mammoth administrative overhaul still at odds relating mechanics and purposes; (b) growing asymmetry in relations with the two U.S. neighbors; (c) subcontracting security to private actors expanding state-society relations in new directions; and (d) a perceptual North American convergence of terrorism as a threat matched by divergence over instruments to be used.

First, the largest bureaucratic reorganization since World War II did not improve coordination over intelligence analysis and cogent security policy formation. Competing agencies and blurred lines between foreign and domestic threats remain the obvious consequences, but predict more subtle mismatches elsewhere over time.

Second, with growing post–9/11 economic asymmetry *vis-à-vis* both Canada and Mexico, interdependence pressures have been strengthened over their integrative counterparts. Economic transactions between the United States and its neighbors seem to have recovered from 9/11-imposed disruptions and security impositions, or at least adjusted to them, costly though the measures have been. Expanded military-security cooperation reaffirms interdependence and bilateralism.

Third, a conspicuous shift seems to be taking place in supplying and safeguarding security, from state prerogatives toward private sector participation. Subcontracting of this type is new, expands state-society relations, and seems to be following the FTAA pattern of subcontracting economic initiatives across the Western Hemisphere. Whether this pattern spreads to Canada and Mexico or not, not only the U.S. government but also U.S. private security firms seem set to dominate this industry across North America (possibly globally, as evident in Afghanistan and Iraq).

Finally, a general convergence of perceptions with Canada and Mexico over the external threats posed to North America by *al Qaeda* coexists with divergence over what specific methods to utilize. At least two forces may be catalyzing this development. One is that, as just alluded to with the third finding, immediate post–9/11 U.S. reactive and coercive security policies are embracing more interactive means, thus either broadening the threat as perceived through state prisms, or diluting the state's rigid threat perception through more societal inputs. The other simply reflects mismatches in policy goals and instruments: Not only have specifications of broad policy perceptions become difficult, but with more agencies and countries involved, how to respond to broadly construed threats is also posing problems. The net effect may be diminishing terrorist threats but increasing institutional preparedness.

Canada

Canada's unavoidable U.S. economic dependence influences all its responses, with at least three implications merging in the study. First, measures to assure a continuing free flow of goods, services, and investment accelerated the interplay of economic and security policy instruments and institutions at all governmental levels—federal, provincial, and local, as well as within Canada and across U.S. boundaries. In turn, Canada's response to exigencies and emergencies, both at home and abroad, may increasingly remain at the mercy of bureaucratic territoriality and in-fighting. As in the United States, the bureaucracy emerges a big winner of 9/11-driven overhauls.

Second, Canada cannot but tip-toe U.S. policy responses—unwittingly accenting bilateralism over trilateralism, both in economic ties (since trade with Mexico is so meager) and over security imperatives. The bilateral approach is also not breaking new ice: Even before NAFTA, Canada shared the longest free-trade boundary in the world and the largest trade partnership; even before 9/11 and Afghanistan, Canada shared security integration partnership with the United States through NATO, an institution first proposed by Canada to a reluctant United States immediately after World War II. What 9/11 did was to elevate Canada from the back-seat of economic integration to the front-seat of security imperatives, reviving many common values and predicting a rosier future economic partnership.

Finally, other distinctive Canadian values and policies, such as multilateralism and strong civil liberties, may be sacrificed to placate the giant to the south. Even its integrative initiatives are unlikely to shift from the backburner. With bilateralism as the order of the day, Canada's ingenuity will be in how to prevent other relations from languishing beyond a point of no return.

Mexico

At least five empirical findings characterize Mexico's 9/11 responses and adjustments: (a) cross-border externalities may be vetoing Mexico's well-intentioned U.S. integration efforts; (b) resistance to being dragged outside North America against its wishes; (c) bilateral U.S. ties becoming the bedrock of North American relations, with flourishing bilateral Canadian relations serving as a sideshow; (d) free-riding U.S. security arrangements opening increasingly irreversible border vulnerabilities; and (e) U.S. economic integration becoming pivotal to Mexican welfare and security. There is no ranking of these, since each depends on different circumstances, which can be as independent as they can overlap.

First, from being a pre–9/11 thorn, cross-border externalities affecting Mexico–U.S. relations may become a post–9/11 cancer. Illegal migration and narcotrafficking have posed problems for a long time, but their explosion after 9/11 (a) feeds into the elevated sense of insecurity among the U.S. citizens; (b) suggests the Mexican government is doing nothing tangible to arrest the problems; (c) catches the Mexican government off-guard since no democratically elected government can seriously clamp down on the movement of people; and (d) invites flows of other illegal actors, such as terrorists, to saddle up on the Mexican horse. Environmental incompatibilities, differentials in labor standards, indigenous uprisings, leftist turnarounds, or even democratic deficits did not appear as dangerous externalities in this study, but their potential to capitalize on tensions and disrupt routine relations should never be underestimated.

Second, Mexico's helplessness stems in part from it being blamed for a number of developments originating outside of Mexico, increasingly over illegal immigration, drug-trafficking, low-wage Asian production for U.S. sales, and terrorist entrepreneurs scoping the porous Mexico–U.S. borders. Alone, it cannot handle these, and certainly not when domestic tensions remain unresolved. Only through U.S. cooperation can these be resolved, but given a difficult historical relationship with the United States, the more symmetrical the terms of cooperation, the more likely Mexico will partner resolutions effectively.

Third, Mexico's conversion of its bilateral U.S. ties into some sort of a holy grail, suggests the country's inability to separate the heart and the mind. Its preferences and actual outcomes increasingly diverge, in part from how rationality is interpreted in both countries: Mexicans view it flexibly, involving a more relaxed approach, behavior, and conversation in which neither side must lose; by contrast, the commonly tight, adversarial U.S. view promotes interest maximization and cost minimization, a process more likely to produce both winners and losers. Mexicans feel a lack of U.S. reciprocation, whereas in the United States, Mexico is seen as not doing enough (with whatever issue at stake). Concretely, Mexico sees emigration as a rational response to the U.S. work-force demands and sociocultural gaps in the United States (e.g., Hispanic migrants wanting to marry a Hispanic spouses and live amidst their extended family in the United States); in the United States, it is seen more as a cultural threat than an economic or social necessity, even as relative poverty generating excess supply. Mexico's flourishing Canadian relationship obscures a reality: if push turns to shove, only the United States can be banker, family, and paramedic at the same time, leaving Canada a bystander.

Fourth, Mexico has been open to, and has collaborated with, the United States in securing airports, ports, and borders; but it is not in the interest, style, tradition, or expectation of Mexico to sit behind the security steering wheel. Mexico not only has other, welfare-based priorities, but civilianizing authoritarian processes seem to still be underway, albeit silently. Permitting the military to encroach upon the political or administrative systems is unacceptable, and interventionist policies abroad have not been a Mexican tradition.

Finally, as one of the pure supporters of the Washington Consensus (one of Latin America's earliest to liberalize and privatize), Mexico is confused why the neoliberal music must be slowed down: It fears more losses than gains, as mounting domestic divisions reveal.

NORTH AMERICA'S BILATERAL RELATIONS: PROMISE-FILLED FINDINGS

We turn to findings from our bilateral chapters (chapters 5, 6, and 7). For obvious reasons, these are treated in the following order: Canada–United States; Mexico–United States; and Mexico–Canada.

Canada–U.S. Relations

We draw five conclusions: (a) this relationship is more insightful theoretically than empirically; (b) it is based as much on opportunity-cost considerations as on values; (c) though neglected in policy-making considerations, Anglo-Saxon values oftentimes rescue both under tight circumstances; (d) the bilateral relationship overrides the frequent placement of trilateralism or multilateralism at the policy-making pedestal; and (e) a broader notion of security gains more currency in this bilateral relationship than others.

First, the Canada–U.S. bilateral relationship is far richer theoretically than on empirical grounds. With the exception of neorealist expectations, it not only satisfies all the tenets of integration (neofunctionalism and security community) and interdependence, but also shows overall post–9/11 relevance, demonstrating how they have withstood pressures of unfavorable and formidable circumstances; but on the ground, it faces all sorts of nuances, as opposed to constraints, driven by ideological or personality adjustments, military and governmental cultures and external circumstances. Contrasting cases of blending with the United States can be cited, for example, Canada fully satisfying integrative tenets, when it also carries so many interdependent features in its U.S. relations. To a large extent, there is little the two countries can do to control these paradoxes, since societal and transnational linkages, as well as commonly felt external threats, bypass the governments, either binding the people or distancing them, not to mention the more slippery value variable.

Second, opportunity-cost considerations not only underlie the relationship, but also coexist with contrasting value imperatives. Both countries were exposed to the costs of relational disruption, if only briefly, after 9/11, but neither wishes an encore; dependence sentiments never seem to be too far from the surface in Canada, but somehow actual benefits, free-ridership opportunities, or simply the helplessness in changing the status quo, over-rides them; and Canadian support, no matter how flimsy or rhetorical, serves more than its weight in gold to U.S. public relations at home and abroad. Apart from these, values tie these two countries more solidly than any (or many) other pair(s) in the world, exemplified by their both sharing the longest unprotected borders and largest bilateral trading relationship in the world.

Third, Anglo-Saxon values unwittingly came to the rescue of both countries when relations collapsed before 9/11 (when Bush refused to make the traditional first foreign visit to Ottawa), and immediately after 9/11 (when Chrétien's support for the war on terrorism was more rhetorical than substantive). That possible threat brought home the war on terrorism to Canadians, who could only feel more empathy for their southern neighbors; and the entire war on terrorism, carrying with it an Islamic-versus-Christianity flavor, silently tightens Christian bonds, including between scattered Anglo-Saxon communities (Australia, Britain, Canada, the United States, and so forth, for example). The message also elevates Anglo-Saxon contributions to Western civilization, such as some of the products of the English Enlightenment (democracy, economic liberalism, harnessing intelligence, technological development, and cutting-edge weaponry), all of which help, in one way or another, streamline approaches, instruments, and bonds in an unpredictable war.

Fourth, this bilateral relationship subordinates even trilateralism (NAFTA), regionalism (FTAA), multilateraliam (WTO, another Canadian proposition). True they did not fade away because of 9/11 or of diminishing interest within Canada and the United States: Some face other big problems, like the WTO's over trading concessions to developing countries. Regardless, their benign or malign neglect only reaffirms the value of the Canadian–U.S. bilateral relationship.

Finally, this bilateral relationship could catalyze a broader interpretation of "security." As threat perceptions recede, the notion of the "North American Security Perimeter" has gained much currency in recent years, not only among scholars studying the dynamics of U.S.–Canada relations but also by leading think-tanks in the United States, such as the CFR.[1] Whether Canada can maintain its claim of distinct values while cooperating with U.S. directives for security cooperation in order to ensure economic flows, remains to be seen, but if the past is any guide, this proposal may be very welcome in Ottawa.

Mexico–U.S. Relations

Many of the findings from the Mexico case study spill over into the bilateral Mexico–U.S. relations. Three receive additional attention.

First, 9/11 had the effect of introducing a security dilemma for the first time along the Mexico–U.S. border, perhaps in Mexico–U.S. relations. It stemmed from a function of increased DHS-driven U.S. military attention along the borders and Mexico's abnegation; magnifying the historically cat-and-mouse treatment of the illegal migration. Illegal immigration in and of itself was not sufficient to generate a security dilemma; but when combined with drug trafficking and potential terrorist infiltration, it constitutes a full-fledged threat. Escalating deterrent forces, as presumed under a security dilemma, reduce the threat, but when these push the adversary to also escalate—the typical "arms race"—in this case between U.S. deterrent forces (more military deployment and walls, for example) and illegal forces (immigrants, drugs, terrorists)—unconventional measures also enter calculations: Would-be illegal migrants shift from regular border-crossings near big towns, for example Tijuana-San Diego, to the Arizona desert, then from desert-crossings to tunnel-crossings; from utilizing males as vehicles of drugs to females, or even children; from carrying contraband materials as portable luggage to ingested "food"; and so forth. A battle of wits eventually becomes deadly.[2]

Second, monocausal explanations of increasingly complex bilateral relations increasingly explain less and become irrelevant. A tyranny of circumstances fuels the worsening of relations: Beginning with Fox's migration proposal being knocked down by the U.S. Congress, climaxing with different 9/11 responses, and connecting with so many externalities, the relationship has become overloaded, demands more patience and cooperation than both leaders and the public can supply, either because they have other priorities or gotten tired of playing the same old game over and over again,[3] and remains at the mercy of illegitimate forces overpowering well-intentioned survival efforts. There is no parallel to this bilateral relationship in North America or the Western Hemisphere.

Finally, the golden moments of Mexico–U.S. relations came during the pre–9/11 NAFTA years, when even Canada took a back seat; yet 9/11, symbolizing bilateralism and policy incongruence, not only reduced the bilateral relationship into a routine affair, but also displaced Mexico from the U.S. front-seat of special friendship for Canada. Clearly good times and bad times trigger different values, thus necessitating different trends–a monumental *realpolitik* lesson for Mexico.

Canada–Mexico Relations

Previous observations also echo under Mexico–Canada relations. Two capture the comprehensive picture.

First, NAFTA was seen as a *win-win* Mexico-Canada undertaking, in spite of Canada's initial reluctance to admit Mexico, but 9/11 proposes a less rosy relationship even in the best of times. It is difficult to sustain the flourishing relations of the 1990s when 9/11 orientations differ so vividly, another indication of how peculiarities can override institution-friendly forces. Whereas Canada could converge with U.S. expectations, Mexico did not want to even try; and for both to sustain booming relations under contradictory posturings clearly pressures the relationship. As noted, meager trade relations deprive those relations of much substance; if and when the whistle blows, diverging policies could collide, if not here and now, then at some point in the future. Consequently, while 9/11 strengthened the U.S. need for both countries, perhaps at the expense of their own bilateral relationship, the missed opportunity of the fruits of economic integration for both exposed its thin underpinnings.

Second, just as a flourishing NAFTA downsized the Canada–Mexico bilateral relationship, security integration belittles the bilateral relationship further. As North America's least developed bilateral relationship, it became the most vulnerable to attrition after 9/11 by lacking security hinges. Canada's traditional prioritizing of human security over military security would have opened pathways into the hearts, minds, and souls of Mexicans, and actually connected with substantive concerns in Mexico. But when Canada went the other way, Mexico was left flat-footed. Mexico's post–9/11 import diversification tendencies opened another opportunity to reduce U.S. vulnerability, but actual diversification did not involve Canada. It seems, unless the two countries can streamline their U.S. orientations, there may not be enough mutualities in the Canada–Mexico relationship. Thus, even on a bilateral basis, few and far-in-between integrative seeds handcuff both countries over both security and economic integration. Interdependence does a better explanatory job than integration, as evident in, and reflected by, intrastate and transnational tensions both constantly face.

THEORETICAL FINDINGS: LOST PARADIGMS?

We raise six issues for consideration: (a) While several theories simultaneously claim at least partial validity, those reaffirming the state offer better explanations than those going beyond it in supranational directions. (b) Increasing state defencelessness and vulnerability prevents full-blown unilateralism, and reduces effective integration to the minimum possible relationship: bilateral. (c) Value considerations increasingly speak for, side with, and sharpen theoretical identities and divisions. (d) The key clash seems to be between welfare-enhancing and warfare-enhancing theories. (e) Doctrines and policy-making appear to be less related to each other, especially in Canada and Mexico. (f) Country-specific peculiarities need more theoretical attention than predictable institutionalized prescriptions.

First, the dominant finding seems to be the multiplicity of post–9/11 theoretical claims, raising the perplexing and subjective task of ranking them for relevance. NAFTA's resounding success in integrating the North American countries could not prevent 9/11 from ditching neofunctionalist or regional economic integrative tenets; yet even before 9/11 and without necessary security catalysts, neofunctionalism and regional economic integration were being overtaken by globalizing forces and larger regional initiatives demanding more attention than smaller counterparts: FTAA, for example, demanded more attention than NAFTA in the years immediately preceding 9/11; while theories describing disruptive forces were gathering more momentum by capturing more of reality than integrative theories. James Rosenau's theory of turbulenceand even the *Zapatista* uprising, explained Mexico's widening income gap better than integration theories could.[4] Arguably 9/11 halted sputtering integrative North American effects; but even then, state-based theories like realism, neorealism, and interdependence, which do much better, still cannot explain the big picture adequately. Interdependence performed better by proposing too little; neorealism also proposes too little, but could not anchor in Canada or Mexico.

Second, interdependence also scored high by exposing issue sensitivity and issue vulnerability, topics of renewed interest in the region after 9/11. All three countries realized the costs of disruption: consumer preferences in all three depend on imports; exports keep consumers happy and bring home the bacon; and the inability of caging Canada's multicultural society or Mexico's burgeoning binational population. This last feature also poses a potential U.S. security threat: multicultural Canada, for providing possible transit ways to possible terrorists, and Mexico's binational population platforming more illegal immigrants. Since the only alternative to bilateral cooperation with the United States is unilateral U.S. action, Canada and Mexico deliberately stopped at the water's edge; while the weight of unilateral actions also prevented the United States from going the full distance. By offering more leeway, bilateralism proved more sensible in Canada, Mexico, and the United States.

Third, bilateralism funnels values and sentiments with greater purity than broader or multilateral settings. If 9/11 did North American countries a favor, it was to flesh out the multiple values, distinguishing the central ones from the peripheral. For example, values behind immigration and military security identified adversaries and friends better; and unfortunately, since these paralleled dominant cultural fissures in the region, Hispanic for the former and Anglo-Saxon in the latter case,[5] 9/11 had the effect of dramatizing North American cultural boundaries. Security community tenets emphasize values more explicitly than the other theories, revealing again the limits of North American security integration. After 9/11, theories seem to acquire relevance only if values receive some formal treatment.

Fourth, 9/11 put in sharper relief the distinction between welfare and warfare goals—and thereby resource allocations, policy commitments, and ultimately those very value judgments just discussed. Canada sought to balance both; Mexico sympathized with the war against terrorism, but opted to promote domestic welfare; and the United States went full-speed into the warfare zone again with a full and one-sided commitment. Constitutional, political, democratic, and popular prerogatives played more important catalyzing roles in Canada and Mexico than in the United States, exposing once again how difficult integration may become in North America.

Fifth, in all of these choices and crossroads, the gap between policy-makers and theories or doctrines only widened. Few, if any, of the theories or doctrines considered, address dilemmas of the three countries today: Diffusive domestic Canadian pressures not only weaken the state, but also prevent the fulfillment of many state-based expectations in the various theories; Mexico's many externalities simply cannot enter the analytical plane of any extant paradigm; and the dominant enemy the U.S. faces, terrorism, cannot even legitimately fit any theoretical framework. Previously there was more order. Canada's and Mexico's shift to neoliberalism elicited so many theory/doctrine applications, like those being tested in this study, we could situate Canada's nationalism of the 1970s into the realist framework, Mexico's import substitution along the lines of Raúl Prébisch and other dependency theorists, and U.S. Cold War participation into neorealist expectations. Not so with 9/11. It came when theories and doctrines were already breaking down; and in its aftermath, too many theories clutter the analytical plane, often ignoring variables critical to explaining the puzzles, to be meaningful. Domestic considerations, externalities, and illegitimate actors need to find a more secure place in theories if only to make them fulfill their explanatory and predictive goals more fittingly.

Sixth, in reaffirming bilateral realities over trilateral relations, 9/11 also promoted country-specific peculiarities over predictable institutional outcomes. For example, 9/11 exposed the Mexico–U.S. border to be very different from the Canada–U.S. border to even think trilaterally over security affairs; and although both borders also differ over trade relations in some critical ways,[6] 9/11 shifted sufficient attention from the economic domain to even make those differences relevant. Depending on how long into the future 9/11 casts its shadow, neofunctionalism and regional economic integration theories, because they are so detailed and Panglossian, may remain on the back burner or be exhausted as explanatory tools. By contrast, variations of parsimonious realism and interdependence may capture those country-specific peculiarities better and thereby offer more fruitful explanatory frameworks for at least the short-term future.

SUMMARY

When all is said and done, North America will plod along, still boasting two of the largest bilateral trading relations, housing almost half a billion of relatively prosperous people, and probably better insulated from terrorism than any other parts of the world. None of these lines are etched forever in the sand, but the flexibility needed to adjust to them may find no better a laboratory than North America: More than any other region of the world, North America is living at the cutting edge of the dynamics constituting international relations: war, peace, development, nationalism, multilateralism, technological growth, to name but a few. How the three countries respond to these, even in their idiosyncratic ways, offer lessons other countries and regions could profitably utilize.

Notes

CHAPTER 1

1. The February 2006 U.S. Defence Department QDR (Quadrennial Defence Review) acknowledged the United States to be "engaged in what will be a long war," mostly against "new and elusive forces," and involving "catastrophic challenges," such as the use of WMD by terrorist groups and/or "rogue states." From Adam Brookes, "US military plans for 'long war,'" *BBC News* (February 4, 2006), http://news.bbc.co.uk/2/hi/americas/4678942.stm. Yet, the mid-term November 2006 elections conveyed a strong public desire to withdraw: Winning a majority in both chambers, Democrats shifted the onus from *if* there should be withdrawal to *when* withdrawal would take place. In December 2006, a bipartisan committee under Ronald Reagan's Secretary of State, James Baker III, and former Democrat congressman, Lee H. Hamilton, also proposed a phased exit in case "the Iraqi government does not make substantial progress toward the achievement of milestones on national reconciliation, security, and governance. . . ." By the end of 2006, the U.S. military engagement in Iraq surpassed its World War II engagement of three years and eight months, and Iraq was unofficially in a civil war, with the death toll of U.S. troops hitting peaks last recorded in Fallujah in 2004. See Robert Burns, "Combat death tolls at a high: worst 4 months for US; shift to urban fight cited," *Philadelphia Inquirer* (February 8, 2007), A1–A2. Also see Baker and Hamilton, *The Iraq Study Group Report: The Way Forward, A New Approach* (New York, NY: Vintage Books, 2006), 61. Although General David H. Petraeus's *surge* calmed Iraq and particularly Baghdad, no one familiar with Iraqi politics has yet claimed this to signal an irreversible development.

2. We treat the three countries alphabetically, except where U.S. security imperatives demand greater priority, as in this sentence. Our conception of *North America* is the same as in the NAFTA (North American Free Trade Agreement), with Canada, Mexico, and the United States entwined through three bilateral pacts, conveying more what Andrew Moravcsik describes as *intergovernmentalism* rather than supranationalism. See Moravcsik, "Negotiating the Single European Act," *The European Community: Decision-Making and Institutional Change,* eds., Robert O. Keohane and Stanley Hoffmann (Boulder, CO: Westview Press, 1991), 41–84.

3. Stephan Haggard and Guadalupe González González, "The United States and Mexico: A Pluralistic Security Community?" in *Security Communities,* ed., Emanuel Adler and Michael Barnett (Cambridge, UK: Cambridge University Press, 1998), 295–332.

4. Its various manifestations articulated by John L. Gaddis, *Strategies of Containment: A Critical Appraisal of Postwar National Security Policy* (Oxford, UK: Oxford University Press, 1982).

5. This is not to say security studies were discarded or neglected. Stephen M. Walt, who distinguishes between method-driven approaches from problem-driven, contends applying formal rational choice theory to "real-world security issues," may have been "most useful for enhancing the precision of the theory," it "lacks rigorous empirical support" and "has not led to powerful new explanations." After 9/11, our study suggests, this "method-driven" approach was displaced by 9/11, a "problem-driven" counterpart. See Walt, "Rigor or Rigor Mortis? Rational Choice and Security Studies," *International Security* 23, no. 4 (Spring 1999): 45–46, but see 5–48.

6. No better an example than David Mitrany's lofty *functionalism.* Proposed to create a long-term working peace and end a catastrophic war, it was replaced by Ernst B. Haas's *neofunctionalism,* which not only restored the state in the analytical framework, rather than eliminate it in the way Mitrany did, but also, and critically, subsumed how Mitrany's outcome could still be attained by keeping the state at an analytically low pecking order of attention. Robert Gilpin's view of security constituting the *necessary* condition and economic pursuits serving as the *sufficient* condition was evident in West Europe, where the U.S. security provision through NATO permitted European economic integration, but also bred security free-riders. Likewise in North America: Canada and Mexico free-riding US security interests, unless they explicitly decide not to (for other reasons). See Mitrany, "The Functional Approach to World Organization," *International Affairs* 24, no. 3 (July 1948): 350–63; and ———, *A Working Peace System* (Chicago, IL: Quadrangle Books, 1966, originally 1943). Also Haas, *The Uniting of Europe: Political, Economical, and Social Forces, 1950–1957* (Stanford, CA: Stanford University Press, 1958); and Gilpin, *U.S. Power and the Multinational Corporation: The Political Economy of Foreign Direct Investment* (New York, NY: Basic Books, 1975), esp. chap. 1.

7. For a summary, see Richard Feinberg, *Summitry in the Americas: A Progress Report* (Washington, DC: International Institute of Economics, 1997), esp. chap. 1.

8. The first for the United States was with Israel, in 1984.

9. Elaborated by Gilbert R. Winham, *Trading With Canada: The Canada–U.S. Free Trade Agreement* (New York, NY: Priority Press Publications for Twentieth Century Fund, 1988); and Frederick C. Mayer, *Interpreting NAFTA: The Art and Science of Political Analysis* (New York, NY: Columbia University Press, 1998), respectively.

10. Explained in Richard Feinberg, "The Political Economy of United States' Free Trade Arrangements," Paper, Berkeley APEC Study Center (BASC), University of California, Berkeley, March 21–22, 2003.

11. George Bush, *The National Security Strategy of the United States of America* (Washington, DC: The White House, September 2002). Critically examined by John Lewis Gaddis, "A Grand Strategy of Transformation," *Foreign Policy,* no. 133 (November–December 2002): 50–57; and Donald C.F. Daniel, Peter Dombrowski, and Rodger A. Payne, "The Bush Doctrine is Dead: Long Live the Bush Doctrine," *Orbis* 49, no. 2 (Spring 2005): 199–212.

12. Includes four elements: (a) transform international politics, since a state's domestic regime determines foreign policy; (b) great threats can be defeated through preventive action; (c) unilateralism is the most effective approach; and (d) peace and stability require U.S. primacy. See Robert Jervis, "Understanding the Bush Doctrine," *Political Science Quarterly* 118, no. 3 (2003): 365, but see 365–88.

13. Mr. X, "The Sources of Soviet Conduct," *Foreign Affairs* 25, no. 4 (July 1947): 566–82. As a State Department official, Kennan could not use his own name, and signed off as Mr. X.

14. Joel Sokolsky's distinction, from "Northern Exposure? America's Homeland Security and Canada," *International Journal* 60, no. 1 (Winter 2004–05): 36–44.

15. Its most forceful proponent was U.S. Trade Representative, Robert B. Zoellick. See Feinberg, "Bilateral Trade Agreements in the Asia–Pacific: Origins, Evolution, and Implications," Berkeley APEC Study Center (BASC), March 21–22, 2003, University of California, Berkeley.

16. From the $US429.6 billion sought in the 2006 budget, the 2007 defence budget sought a 12.1 percent increase to $US481.4 billion, with DHS outlays climbing from $US32 billion to $34.3 billion, a 7.2 percent hike. From Michael Abramowitz and Lori Montogomery, "Holding Firm on Budget: To Boost Military, Avoid Tax Hike, Bush Plan Would Limit Domestic Spending," *Philadelphia Inquirer* (February 6, 2007): A1, A6. Also see Sally B. Donnelly, "When Can the U.S. go?" *Time* (February 27, 2006): 15.

17. Ronald L. Jepperson, Alexander Wendt, and Peter J. Katzenstein distinguish between "formal institutions or security regimes" between countries, like NATO, and sociological forces influencing state identities. The "cultural environments affect not only the incentives for different kinds of state behavior but also the basic character of states [or] 'identity.'" Thus, there are "formal institutions or security regimes" involving countries, as in NATO, as well as state *identities* reflecting *sociological* forces. From "Norms, Identity, and Culture in National Security," in *The Culture of National Security: Norms and Identity in World Politics,* ed., Katzenstein (New York, NY: Columbia University Press, 1996), 33, but see 33–35. Robert O. Keohane on the sociological forces in "International Liberalism Reconsidered," in *The Economic Limits to Modern Politics,* ed., John Dunn (Cambridge, UK: Cambridge University Press, 1990), 183–84; and Frederick Frey, "The Problem of Actor Designation in Political Analysis," *Comparative Politics* 17, no. 2 (January 1985): 127–52. *Coyotes:* Middlemen in migratory flows. They not only extract exorbitant amounts for smuggling humans, but also possess a nefarious reputation of deserting the would-be migrant, raping women migrants, and even remaining receptive to transporting drugs.

18. See "China 'to dwarf G7 states by 2050'," *BBC News* (March 6, 2006) http://news.bbc.co.uk/2/hi/business/4770590.stm.

19. Michael Mastanduno, "Preserving the Unipolar Moment: Realist Theories and US Grand Strategy After the Cold War," in *Unipolar Politics: Realism and State Strategies After the Cold War,* eds., B. Kapstein and Mastanduno (New York, NY: Columbia University Press, 1999), 138–81.

20. Elinor C. Sloan, *Security and Defence in the Terrorist Era: Canada and North America* (Montreal and Kingston: McGill-Kingston University Press, 2005), 44, but see chaps. 4–5.

21. This standard U.S. definition of regimes more or less satisfies what we mean by institutions, although we recognize the merits of counterarguments in the relevant literatures. Since our study is of North America, where this regime definition is widely (though not exclusively) utilized, the debate, though important, is not pertinent for our work. Definition from Stephen D. Krasner, "Structural Causes and Regime Consequences: Regimes as Intervening Variables," *International Organization* 36, no. 2 (Spring 1982): 186, but see 185–206. Critiqued by Volker Rittberger, ed., with the help of Peter Mayer, *Regime Theory and International Relations* (Oxford, UK: Clarendon Press, 1993), and especially articles by Andrew Hurrell, "International Society and the Study of Regimes: A Reflective Approach," ibid., chap. 3; and Harald Müller, "The Internalization of Principles, Norms, and Rules by Governments: The Case of Security Regimes," ibid., chap. 15.

22. See, among others, Reg Whitaker, "Cold War Alchemy: How America, Britain, and Canada Transformed Espionage into Subversion," *Intelligence and National Security* 15, no. 2 (Summer 2000): 177–210.

23. From Samuel P. Huntington's article title, "The Hispanic Challenge," *Foreign Policy,* no. 141 (March/April 2004): 30–45.

24. Max Weber, *The Protestant Ethic and the Spirit of Capitalism,* eds., Talcott Parson and R.H. Tawney (Dover, UK: Dover Publications, 2003).

25. Without being exhaustive, the following, largely collective works, reflect a vast literature: Edward J. Chambers and Peter H. Smith, eds., *NAFTA in the New Millennium,* (La Jolla, CA: Center for U.S. Mexican Studies, University of California, San Diego, and Edmonton, AB: The University of Alberta Press, 2002); Nora Lustig, Barry P. Bosworth, and Robert Z. Lawrence, eds., *North American Free Trade: Assessing the Impact* (Washington, DC: Brookings, 1992); Robert A. Pastor, *Towards a North American Community: Lessons from the Old World for the New* (Washington, DC: The Petersen Institute, 2001); Robert A. Pastor and Rafael Fernandez de Castro, eds., *The U.S. Congress and North America: The Controversial Pivot* (Washington, DC: Brookings, 1998); Ricardo Grinspun and Maxwell A. Cameron, eds., *The Political Economy of North American Free Trade* (New York, NY: St. Martin's Press, 1993); and Carol Wise, ed., *The Post-NAFTA Political Economy: Mexico and the Western Hemisphere* (College Park, PA: The Penn State University Press, 1998).

26. Harold C. Relyea, "Organizing for Homeland Security," *Presidential Studies Quarterly* 33, no. 3 (September 2003): 603, 611; but see 602–24.

27. Title of Charles P. Kindleberger's pivotal work, *The World in Depression, 1929–1939* (Berkeley, CA: University of California Press, 1973).

28. Relyea, "Organizing for Homeland Security," 607.

29. Truman's middle name is not an abbreviation.

30. DHS and HSD used interchangeably in entire manuscript.

31. Bruce Maxwell, *Homeland Security: A Documentary History* (Washington, DC: CQ Press, 2004), 429–30.

32. Maxwell, *Homeland Security,* xxi–xxii.

33. Relyea, "The Law: Homeland Security: The Concept and the Presidential Coordination Office—First Assessment," *Presidential Studies Quarterly* 32, no. 2 (June 2002): 400–01, but see 397–411.

34. Relyea, "Organizing for Homeland Security," 617.

35. From Relyea, "The Law: Homeland Security," 400.

36. Ibid., 401.

37. Bruce Berkowitz, "Intelligence for the Homeland," *SAIS Review* 24, no. 1 (Winter–Spring 2004): 1, but see 1–6.

38. Kate Martin, "Domestic Intelligence and Civil Liberties," *SAIS Review* 24, no. 1 (Winter–Spring 2004): 8–11.

39. PATRIOT is an acronym: Providing Appropriate Tools Required to Intercept and Obstruct Terror. See US Congress, "PATRIOT Act of 2001," HR 3162, 107th Congress, 1st Session, October 24, 2001. Available at http://www.epic.org/privacy/terrorism/hr3162.html.

40. Also called the National Commission on Terrorist Attacks Upon the United States.

41. Note how the usage of transformation here parallels Gaddis's (2002), both referring to more than a significant and evolutionary change.

42. Deborah C. Barger, "It is Time to Transform, not Reform, US Intelligence," *SAIS Review* 24, no. 1 (Winter–Spring 2004): 26–30.

43. On Canada's proposal, see Winham, *Trading With Canada,* esp. chap. 3; on Mexico's see Mayer, *Interpreting NAFTA,* chap. 3; and on North America, see Robert O'Brien, "North

American Integration and International Relations Theory," *Canadian Journal of Political Science* 28, no. 4 (December 1995): 693–724.

44. Stéphane Roussel, "Honey, are you still mad at me? I've changed, you know..." *International Journal* 58, no. 4 (Autumn 2003): 571–90.

45. Andrew Cohen, "Canadian–American Relations: Does Canada Matter in Washington? Does it Matter if Canada Doesn't Matter?" *Canada Among Nations 2002: A Fading Power* (Toronto, ON: Oxford University Press, 2002), 34–48.

46. Haggard and González González, *Security Communities.*

47. Fox gives a more upbeat description of these events in his autobiography, *Revolution of Hope: The Life, Faith and Dreams of a Mexican President,* written with Rob Allyn (New York, NY: Viking Press, 2007).

48. Examples of this new type include, at the multilateral level, the United Nations, and at the regional CSCE (Council for Security and Cooperation in Europe), ASEAN (Asian Southeast Asian Nations), and the OAS (Organization of American States).

49. Jill Sinclair, "Canada's International Security Policy," in *Natural Allies? Canadian and Mexican Perspectives on International Security,* ed., Hal P. Klepak in *Changing American Series,* no. 2 (Ottawa: Carleton University Press and Canadian Foundation for the Americas—FOCAL, 1996), 158–59, but see chap. 8.

50. Roger Gibbins, "Meaning and Significance of the Canadian–American Border," in *Borders and Border Politics in a Globalizing World,* eds., Paul Ganster and David E. Lovey (Lanham, MD: SR Books, 2004), 153, but see chap. 10.

51. Paul Ganster and Alan Sweedler, "The United States–Mexican Border Region: Security and Interdependence," *United States–Mexico Border Statistics Since 1900,* ed., David Lovey (Los Angeles, CA: University of California Los Angeles, Latin American Center Publications, 1990).

52. Gibbins, *Borders and Border Politics,* 161–62.

53. See Peter Chalk and William Rosenau, *Confronting the "Enemy Within": Security Intelligence, the Policy, and Counterterrorism in Four Democracies* (Santa Monica, CA: RAND Corporation, 2004), 26–27.

54. Chalk and Rosenau, *Confronting the "Enemy Within",* 27–28.

55. Ibid., 48–53.

56. See Ronald J. Daniels, "Introduction," in *The Security of Freedom: Essays on Canada's Anti-Terrorism Bill,* eds., Daniels, Patrick Macklem, and Kent Roach (Toronto, ON: University of Toronto Press, 2001), chap. 1; quote from chap. 3, bill, provisions from chap. 4.

57. Reference to the *Charter of Rights and Freedom.*

58. Gary T. Trotter, "The Anti-Terrorism Bill and Preventative Restraints on Liberty," *Security of Freedom,* 239, quote from 246–47.

59. Kent Roach, "The Dangers of a Charter-proof and Crime-based Response to Terrorism," *Security of Freedoms,* 131–50, quote from 131.

60. Ibid., 132.

61. Ibid., 132–33.

62. Ibid., 138–39.

63. Ibid., 142.

64. Sujit Choudhry, "Protecting Equality in the Face of Terror: Ethnic and Racial Profiling and s.15 of the Charter," *Security of Freedom,* 367–82, quote from 367.

65. Audrey Macklin, "Borderline Security," *Security of Freedom,* 383–404, quote from 384.

66. Christopher Leroy, "Mexican Intelligence at a Crossroad," *SAIS Review* 24, no. 1 (Winter–Spring 2004): 111–18.

67. Karl Deutsch, Sidney A. Burrell, and Robert A. Kann, *Political Community and the North American Area: International Organization in the Light of Historical Experience* (Princeton, NJ: Princeton University Press, 1957).

68. Jorge Domínguez and Rafael Fernandez de Castro, *The United States and Mexico: Between Partnership and Conflict* (New York, NY: Routledge, 2001).

69. Haggard and González González, "The United States and Mexico," 295–332; and David Mares, "Strategic Interests in the U.S.–Mexico Relationship," in *Strategy and Security in U.S.–Mexico Relations: Beyond the Cold War,* eds., John Bailey and Sergio Aguayo Quesada (La Jolla, CA: University of California Press for Center for U.S.–Mexico Studies, 1995), chap. 2.

70. This is the extent to which we will treat the overloaded concepts of values and culture —just their impacts on security. Neither are dominant subjects of our analysis, and to go beyond their strict relation to security opens up too many cans for this manuscript alone to address. However, we encourage other studies to pick up the pieces as and where needed.

71. Essentially meaning potatoes and beer, pork and lumber—issues of long and bitter trade disputes.

72. Robert O. Keohane and Joseph S. Nye, *Power and Interdependence: World Politics in Transition* (Boston, MA: Little, Brown 1977): 3–37.

73. Henry Nau, "From Integration to Interdependence: Gains, Losses, and Continuing Gaps," *International Organization* 33, no. 1 (Winter 1979): 119–147.

74. Robert Gilpin, "Integration and Disintegration on the North American Continent," *International Organization* 28, no. 4 (Autumn 1974): 851–74.

75. Charles Pentland, *International Theory and European Integration* (New York, NY: Free Press, 1973).

76. Haas, *Uniting of Europe,* 1958.

77. Harald von Riekhoff, "The Impact of Prime Minister Trudeau on Foreign Policy," *Canadian Foreign Policy: Historical Readings,* ed., J.L. Granatstein (Toronto, ON: Copp Clark Pitman, Ltd., A Longman Co., 1993), 286–99.

78. J.L. Granatstein, "The Mulroney Government's Policy, 1985," ibid., 73–86.

79. Jorge Chabat, "Mexico's Foreign Policy and NAFTA: The Tools of Interdependence," in *Bridging the Border: Transforming Mexico–U.S. Relations,* eds., Rodolfo O. de la Garza and Jesús Velasco (Lanham, MD: Rowman and Littlefield, 1997), chap. 2.

80. See Peter H. Rossi, James D. Wright, and Andy B. Anderson, *Handbook of Survey Research* (New York, NY: Academic Press, 1983), 69–79.

81. George W. Bohrnstedt, "A Quick Method of Determining the Reliability and Validity of Multiple Item Scales," *American Sociological Review* 34 (1969): 542–48.

82. Richard F. Curtis and Elton F. Jackson, "Multiple Indicators of Survey Research," *American Journal of Sociology* 68 (1962): 195–204.

83. Alexander L. George and Andrew Bennett, *Case Studies and Theory Development in the Social Sciences* (Cambridge, MA: MIT Press, 2005).

CHAPTER 2

1. The White House, *The National Security Strategy of the United States of America* (September 2002): 1, as published on CommonDreams.Org.

2. Ibid., 1.

3. For example, see Joseph S. Nye, "Soft Power and American Foreign Policy," *Political Science Quarterly* 119, no. 2 (2004): 255–70, but see 257–8.

4. Ibid., 257.

5. In political science, there is a significant amount of literature that focuses on "weak states," which is appropriate here. Weak states are those that are incapable of protecting their borders or citizenry from terrorist infiltrations. In addition, these states are also limited in their abilities to undertake societal transformation. See, for example, J. Migdal, A. Kohli, and V. Shue, eds., *State Power and Social Forces* (New York, NY: Cambridge University Press, 1994), 7–15.

6. The White House, *The National Security Strategy* (September 20, 2002): 3, as published on www.CommonDreams.Org.

7. Ibid., 2.

8. Eurobarometer, #59 (Spring 2003).

9. Pew Global Attitudes Project, *Views of a Changing World June 2003* (Washington DC: Pew Research Center for the People and the Press, 2003), T-132.

10. Andrew Bacevich, *American Empire: The Realities and Consequences of U.S. Diplomacy* (Cambridge, MA: Harvard University Press, 2002); Max Boot, "The Case for an American Empire," *The Weekly Standard* (October 15, 2001): 4.

11. John Arquila and David Ronfeldt, *The Emergence of Noopolitik: Toward an American Information Strategy* (Santa Monica, CA: RAND, 1999).

12. Robert Kaplan, "Islam vs. the West," *Rolling Stone* (August 7, 2003): 38; William Kristol, "A Classicist's Legacy: Empire Builders," *New York Times*, Week in Review, (May 4, 2003).

13. John Lewis Gaddis, "Bush's Security Strategy," *Foreign Policy*, no. 133 (November/December 2002): 50–57.

14. John D. Kelly, "U.S. Power, After 9/11 and Before it: If Not an Empire, then What?" *Public Culture* 15, no. 2 (2003): 247–69.

15. The White House, *The National Security Strategy of the United States*, 2002.

16. Ibid., 47.

17. "Privatization of War" is the expression used to describe nonstate groups who operate simultaneously in various parts of the world. The expression is taken from Joseph Nye, "Soft Power and American Foreign Policy," *Political Science Quarterly* 119, no. 2 (2004): 259.

18. Daniel Benjamin, Steven Simon, and Richard Falkenrath, "The War of Unintended Consequences," *Foreign Affairs*, 85, no. 2 (March/April 2006): 1–6, taken from www.foreignaffairs.org.

19. State Department, Terrorism Report, "Western Hemisphere Review" (2006): 155–6.

20. Ibid.

21. http://www.dhs.gov/xabout/structure/index.shtm, 1.

22. The information on the Departmental Agencies, components, and advisory panels are obtained from the web site: http://www.dhs.gov/xabout/structure/index.shtm, 1–3.

23. Ibid., 2.

24. Frank Deffer, Assistant Inspector General of Information Technology, U.S. Department of Homeland Security, Testimony before the House Committee on Homeland Security, Subcommittee on Intelligence, Information Sharing and Terrorism Risk Assessment, September 13, 2006.

25. See Joshua Rovner and Austin Long, "The Perils of Shallow Theory: Intelligence Reform and the 9/11 Commission," *International Journal of Intelligence and Counter Intelligence* 18, no. 4 (2005): 609–37, but see 614–15.

26. This is an ongoing task. Furthermore, in 2005, John Negroponte was appointed as the new National Intelligence Chief with the responsibility of coordinating the various security and

defence related intelligence gathering and analysis operations, and streamlining DHS with other agencies in the federal bureaucracy. See Jeffrey T. Richelson, "From Director of Central Intelligence to Director of National Intelligence," *The National Security Archives* (December 17, 2004).

27. Frank Deffer, Assistant Inspector General, Information Technology, DHS, Testimony before the House Subcommittee on Intelligence, Information Sharing and Terrorism Risk Assessment, September 13, 2006, 6–7.

28. Ibid., 7–8.

29. David Zavada, Assistant Inspector General for Audits, DHS, Testimony Before the House Committee on Government Reform, July 27, 2006.

30. The 9/11 Commission Report, *Final Report of the National Commission on Terrorist Attacks upon the United States of America* (New York, NY: W.W. Norton, 2004), 339–40.

31. Ibid., 215–41.

32. Philip Heymann, *Terrorism and America: A Common Sense Strategy for a Democratic Society* (Cambridge, MA: MIT Press, 1998).

33. Cynthia M. Grabo, *Anticipating Surprise: Analysis for Strategic Warning* (Washington, DC: Joint Military Intelligence, 2002).

34. Gregory F. Treverton, "Intelligence Law Enforcement, and Homeland Security," *The Century Foundation Homeland Security Project Report* (Santa Monica, CA: RAND, 2002).

35. Arthur S. Hulnick, "Does the U.S. Intelligence Community Need a DNI?" *International Journal of Intelligence and Counter Intelligence* 17, no. 4 (2004): 710–30.

36. Ibid., 718–19.

37. Thomas Duffy, "New DOD Intelligence Directorate will have Broad Policy, Program Influence," *Inside the Pentagon* (March 27, 2003).

38. Michael A. Turner, *Why Secret Intelligence Fails* (Dulles, VA: Potomac Books, 2004).

39. Arthur S. Hulnick, "Indications and Warning for Homeland Security: Seeking a New Paradigm," *International Journal of Intelligence and Counter Intelligence* 18, no. 4 (2005): 593–608, but see 603.

40. James D. Marchio, "The Evolution and Relevance of Joint Intelligence Centers," http://www.cia.gov/csi/studies/vol49no1/html_files/the_evolution_6.html, 1–2.

41. Calculated from World Development Report, 2005.

42. See Michael Waslin, "The New Meaning of the Border: U.S.–Mexico Migration Since 9/11," Paper presented at the Conference on *Reforming the Administrative Justice in Mexico,* Center for US–Mexican Studies, University of California, San Diego, May 15–17, 2003.

43. Hazelton, PA, township is now embroiled in a lawsuit, in which its ordinance banning employment, residence, and access to medical and educational facilities to those who are in the United States illegally has been challenged.

44. Frederick P. Hitz and Brian J. Weiss, "Helping the CIA and FBI Connect the Dots in the War on Terror," *International Journal of Intelligence and Counter Intelligence* 17, no. 1 (2004): 1–41, but see 33–35.

45. The Center for Constitutional Rights, *Report on The State of Civil Liberties: One Year Later* (2002).

46. Civil Rights Act of 1964, Doc Number: PL 88-352, Titles I and II.

47. "The State of Civil Liberties: One Year Later, Erosion of Civil Liberties in the Post 9/11 Era," Center for Constitutional Rights, http://www.ccr-ny.org/v2/print_page.asp?.

48. Discussion available at http://opendoors.iienetwork.org/?p=89207.

49. Peter Karl Kresl, "NAFTA and Its Discontents," *International Journal* 60, no. 2 (Spring 2005): 417–28.

50. See Peter Andreas, "The Mexicanization of the US–Canada Border," *International Journal* 60, 2 (Spring 2005): 449–51. Also see Ruth Jamieson, Nigel South, and Ian Taylor, "Economic Liberalization and Cross-border Crime: The North American Free Trade Area and Canada's Border with USA," *International Journal of the Sociology of Law* 26 (1998): 256–58.

51. According to Canadian officials, the amount of Canadian marijuana sold in the United States annually is worth between $US4 billion to $US7 billion, Reported in Quentin Hardy, "Inside Dope," *Forbes* (November 10, 2003).

52. "The Debate Over the North American Security Perimeter," *The Century Foundation Homeland Security Project,* Issues in Brief, January 2003, 1–15, but see 1.

53. Peter Andreas, "Redrawing the Line: Borders and Security in the Twenty-first Century," *International Security* 28, no. 2 (2003): 78–111.

54. In 2002 alone, the Department of Justice spent $US34 billion in efforts to stop CTAs (Clandestine Transnational Actors) across from the Mexican border. The Immigration and Naturalization Service, before its merger with DHS, spent $US2.5 billion in border reinforcement. These two expenditures alone indicate that Mexico–US border has become quite militarized. See ibid., 88.

55. Tom Godfrey, "US Nabs 8,000 Sneaking Over Border," *Toronto Sun* (September 17, 2002): 26.

56. Charles Doyle, "The USA Patriot Act: A Sketch," *CRS Report to Congress* (April 18, 2002): 3.

57. To that effect, the DEA has launched in Mexico an extensive training program for both the law enforcement and the prosecutorial staff.

58. Notable among these measures are the US PATRIOT Act, adopted in October 2001, Aviation and Transportation Security Act of November 2001, and Enhanced Border Security and Visa Entry Reform Act (EBSVERA) passed in May 2002. See Cresencio Arcos, "The Role of the Department of Homeland Security Overseas," *Heritage Lecture* No. 849, 7 June 2004 (Washington, DC: Heritage Foundation, 2004).

59. The Canada–U.S. Smart Border Declaration that was signed in Ottawa on December 12, 2001, states that both countries will cooperate in identifying high risk goods while at the same time facilitating the flow of low risk goods. See *Security at Canada's–U.S. Borders: The Smart Border,* http://www.international.gc.ca/anti-terrorism/declaration-en.asp.

60. Miguel Pickard, "Tri-national Elites Map North American Future in "NAFTA Plus," *IRC Americas Report,* 1–12.

61. Ibid., 2–3.

62. For example, an *al Qaeda* associate was reportedly spotted in Honduras allegedly contacting the notorious *Maras* gang during September of 2004. This raises the probabilities for the *jihadists* connecting with the gangsters in the ill-protected southern borders of Mexico. See Ana Arana, "How the street gangs took Central America," *Foreign Affairs* 84, no. 3 (May/June 2005): 104.

63. Joseph Tulchin, "Hemispheric Security: Is the OAS the Answer," Woodrow Wilson Center for International Scholars, Special workshop on Security 2003.

64. Taken from *World Development Report,* 2006 (Washington, DC: Oxford University Press, 2007), 292–93.

65. "Responsible Reform of Immigration Laws Must Protect Working Conditions for All Workers in the U.S.," http://www.aflcio.org/aboutus/thisistheaflcio/ecouncil/ec02272006e.cfm.

66. Stephen Clarkson, "Smart Borders and the Rise of Bilateralism," *International Journal* 61, no. 3 (Summer 2006): 588–609.

67. Douglas Massey interview on NPR, February 2006.

68. Richard N. Haas, "Supporting US Foreign Policy in the Post-9/11 World," *Studies in Intelligence* (2003): 1–8, http://www.cia.gov/csi/studies/vol46no3/article01.html.

69. John McCain, Charles Hagel, and Lindsey Graham, all Republican incumbent Senators, are generally identified with the Libertarian wing of the Republican Party.

CHAPTER 3

1. E-mail correspondence: douglasr@sfu.ca and ahira@sfu.ca. We gratefully acknowledge the financial support of PIERAN (*Programa Interinstitucional De Estudios Sobre La Regíón De América Del Norte*) of Mexico. We would like to thank Imtiaz Hussain, Satya Pattnayak, Emmanuel Brunet-Jailly, Stuart Farson, Alex Leger, Eric Hershberg, Margaret Purdy, and Howard Cody. Field Research was conducted by Andy Hira in Ottawa in September 2006 and by Douglas Ross in November 2007. Off-the-record commentary was received from officials of the PSEPC, the Privy Council, the Department of National Defence, the Ministry of Finance, and the Coast Guard. Special thanks are owed to Alex Leger of PSEPC and Aaron Hywarren of DND for their kind assistance in arranging some of the interviews. Alex Leger, Peter Avis, and Imtiaz Hussain provided valuable editorial comments. Thanks too to Dr. James Fergusson of the University of Manitoba who organized a defence and security policy workshop in Ottawa in 2007. Previous versions of this paper were delivered in Mexico City in April 2006, where they benefited from the commentary of Dr. Edward Mansfield and Mtra. María Pía Taracena Gout. A revised version of the paper was presented at the Anchorage, Alaska, ACSUS meeting in September 2006, and subsequently published in *Canadian American Public Policy.* Patty Hira helped edit the final copy.

2. Alexander Netherton, Allen Seager, and Karl Froschauer, eds., *In/security: Canada in the post–9/11 World* (Burnaby, BC: Centre for Canadian Studies, Simon Fraser University, 2005).

3. Stuart Farson, "From '49th Parallel' to 'security perimeter': Changing Conceptions, Values and Structures Along the U.S.–Canada Border," in *Homeland Security: Protecting America's Targets,* vol. 1, ed., James J.F. Forest (Westport, CT: Praeger Security International, 2006), 55–75.

4. Frank P. Harvey, *The Homeland Security Dilemma: The Imaginations of Failure and the Escalating Costs of Perfecting Security,* Report (Calgary, AB: Canadian Defence and Foreign Affairs Institute, July 2006).

5. Kim Lunman, "Majority Support PM's Stand on War in Iraq, Poll Indicates," *Globe and Mail* (June 16, 2003).

6. Brian Laghi, "Majority Opposed to Afghan Mission," *Globe and Mail* (February 24, 2006).

7. J.L. Granatstein, Gordon S. Smith, and Denis Stairs, *A Threatened Future: Canada's Future Strategic Environment and Its Strategic Implications* (Calgary, AB: Canadian Defence and Foreign Affairs Institute, Fall 2007).

8. Brian Laghi, "Canadians Warm to Tax on Energy Use, Globe–CTV Poll Says," *Globe and Mail* (October 19, 2006).

9. Granatstein, *Whose War Is It? How Canada Can Survive in the Post–9/11 World* (Toronto, ON: Harper Collins, 2007), 150; David G. Haglund, "Quebec's 'America problem': Differential Threat Perception in the North American Security Community," *The American Review of*

Canadian Studies 36, no. 4 (Winter 2006): 552–67; and Brian Bow, "Out of Ideas? Models and Strategies for Canada–U.S. Relations," *International Journal* 62, no. 1 (Winter 2006/2007): 123–42.

10. Granatstein, *Whose War Is It? How Canada Can Survive in the Post–9/11 World* (Toronto, ON: Harper Collins, 2007).

11. Janice Gross Stein and Eugene Lang, *The Unexpected War* (Toronto, ON: Penguin Canada, 2007).

12. Jennifer Welsh, "Damned if we didn't, damned if we did," Review of *The Unexpected War,* by Janice Gross Stein and Eugene Lang, *Globe and Mail* (October 27, 2007).

13. Gross Stein and Lang, *The Unexpected War* (Toronto, ON: Penguin Canada, 2007).

14. David Pugliese, "'High-risk' Military Projects Over Budget, Behind Schedule," *National Post* (October 29, 2007).

15. Nils Orvik, "Canadian Security and 'defence against help'," *Survival* (January–February 1984): 26–31.

16. Paul Koring, "Citing 'liberal' Immigration Laws, U.S. Blasts Canada on Terrorism," *Globe and Mail* (April 29, 2006).

17. Alia McMullen, "Battling the Border Blues," *National Post* (December 15, 2007).

18. John Ibbitson, "Homeland Security: The Next Threat to Canada," *Globe and Mail* (August 16, 2007).

19. Andrew Mayeda, "Double Forces in Afghanistan, Think-tank Says," *National Post* (November 22, 2007).

20. For detailed Canadian views see Canada, Department of Foreign Affairs 2005; and Canada, Department of Foreign Affairs and International Trade (DFAIT) 1999.

21. Keir A. Lieber and Daryl G. Press, "The Rise of U.S. Nuclear Primacy," *Foreign Affairs* 85, no. 2 (March/April 2006): 42–54.

22. See Denis Stairs, *The Diplomacy of Constraint: Canada, the Korean War and the United States* (Toronto, ON: University of Toronto Press, 1974) and Douglas A. Ross, *In the Interests of Peace: Canada, the United States and Vietnam, 1954–1973* (Toronto, ON: University of Toronto Press, 1984).

23. Tom Keating, *Canada and World Order: The Multilateralist Tradition in Canadian Foreign Policy* (Oxford, UK: Oxford University Press, 2006).

24. Edelgard Mahant and Graeme S. Mount, *Invisible and Inaudible in Washington: American Policies Toward Canada* (Vancouver, BC: University of British Columbia Press, 1999).

25. Estanislao Oziewicz, "Poll Finds Support Soft for Iraq War," *Globe and Mail* (March 1, 2006).

26. Jeff Sallot, "War Could Spawn Terrorists, CSIS Chief Says," *Globe and Mail* (October 21, 2005).

27. Mike Blanchfield, "52% of Canadians Support Operation," *National Post* (March 4, 2006); and Michael Den Tandt and Campbell Clark, "Canadian Takes Charge of Coalition in Kandahar," *Globe and Mail* (March 1, 2006).

28. Laghi, "Majority Opposed to Afghan Mission" (February 24, 2006).

29. Mike Blanchfield, "Government, Not Generals, Will Decide Mission: Harper," *National Post* (March 8, 2006).

30. Gloria Galloway and Ingrid Peritz, "Troops Won't Stay Unless All Parties Agree, PM Says," *Globe and Mail* (June 23, 2007).

31. CanWest News Service, "Quebecers Want Canadian Troops Brought Home," *Vancouver Province* (August 24, 2007).

32. Alan Freeman, "Canadian Troops Will Leave in 2009, Dion says," *Globe and Mail* (July 5, 2007).

33. W.D. MacNamara, and Ann Fitzgerald, "A National Security Framework for Canada," in *Geopolitical Security,* ed., H. Segal (Montreal: Institute for Research on Public Policy, 2005), 81–104.

34. For the original statement of the 'Defense Against Help' thesis, see Orvik, "Canadian Security and 'defence against help'," 1984.

35. Jocelyn Maynard Ghent, "Did He Fall or Was He Pushed? The Kennedy Administration and the Collapse of the Deifenbaker Government," *International History Review* 1 (April 1979): 246–70.

36. Ross, "Canada's Functional Isolationism and the Future of Weapons of Mass Destruction," *International Journal* 54, no. 1 (Winter 1998–99): 120–42.

37. Ross, "Foreign Policy Challenges for Paul Martin: Canada's International Security Policy in an Era of American Hyperpower and Continental Vulnerability," *International Journal* 58, no. 4 (Autumn 2003): 533–70.

38. Stephen Clarkson, *Uncle Sam and Us: Globalization, Neoconservatism and the Canadian State* (Toronto, ON: University of Toronto Press, 2003) and Granatstein, *The Importance of Being Less Earnest: Promoting Canada's National Interests Through Tighter Ties with the U.S.* (Toronto, ON: CD Howe Institute, 2003).

39. Michael Ignatieff, "Canada in the Age of Terror—Multilateralism Meets a Moment of Truth," in *Independence in An Age of Empire: Assessing Unilateralism and Multilateralism,* ed., G.F. Walker (Halifax: The Centre for Foreign Policy Studies, 2004).

40. Donald Barry, "Chrétien, Bush and the War in Iraq," *American Review of Canadian Studies* (Summer 2005): 234–5.

41. Major-General Lewis MacKenzie (ret.), "Afghanistan Was Never an Option," *National Post* (April 24, 2003).

42. Peter Boag, "Restore Unity Along the U.S.–Canada Border," *Aviation Week and Space Technology* (January 23, 2006).

43. On the counterproliferation imperative in U.S. policy, see David S. McDonough, "The New Triad, Bunker Busters and 'Counterproliferation Wars': Nuclear Primacy and its Implications for Canadian Security Policy," in *The Dilemmas of American Strategic Primacy: Implications for the Future of Canadian–American Cooperation,* eds., David S. McDonough and Douglas A. Ross (Toronto, ON: Royal Canadian Military Institute, 2005).

44. Barry, "Chrétien, Bush and the War in Iraq," 237, n.15.

45. Farson, "From '49th Parallel' to 'security perimeter'."

46. David Bond, "Expanding NORAD," *Aviation Week and Space Technology* (August 9, 2004).

47. See Ross, "Foreign Policy Challenges for Paul Martin" (2003), p. 535, n. 5; and Ross, "American Missile Defence, Grand Strategy and Global Security," in *The Dilemmas of American Strategic Primacy: Implications for the Future of Canadian–American Cooperation,* eds., David S. McDonough and Douglas A. Ross (Toronto, ON: Royal Canadian Military Institute, 2005), 42.

48. Paul Koring, "Tories Plan New Defence Pact with U.S.," *Globe and Mail* (February 20, 2006).

49. For a review of such indecision see Andrew Richter, "A Question of Defense: How American Allies are Responding to the US Missile Defense Program," *Comparative Strategy* 23 (2004): 143–72; and James Fergusson, "A Strange Decision in a Strange Land: The Irrelevance of Ottawa's Missile Defence 'No'," *The Dilemmas of American Strategic Primacy,*

eds., McDonough and Ross (Toronto, ON: Royal Canadian Military Institute, 2005), 9–11, 28–30; and Ross, "American Missile Defence, Grand Strategy and Global Security" (2005), 35–43.

50. Michael Den Tandt, "Continental Missile Shield Still an Option, O'Connor says," *Globe and Mail* (February 24, 2006).

51. Doug Saunders and Brian Laghi, "Missile Dispute Threatens to Throw G8 Off Course," *Globe and Mail* (June 6, 2007).

52. Lieber and Press, "The Rise of U.S. Nuclear Primacy."

53. Luke Harding, "Russia Claims New Missile Can Thwart U.S. Defences," *Globe and Mail* (May 30, 2007).

54. Chivers, C.J., "Putin Proposes Alternatives for Missile Defense System," *New York Times* (June 9, 2007).

55. Adrian Blomfield, "Russia Suspends Arms Pact," *National Post* (April 27, 2007).

56. On UK flights, see Anonymous, "For the first time...," *Aviation Week and Space Technology* (July 23, 2007); regarding Guam and Arctic flights, see Andrew E. Kramer, "Recalling Cold War, Russia Resumes Long-range Sorties," *New York Times* (August 18, 2007).

57. Adrian Blomfield, "Russia to Aim Missiles at City 'Targets'," *National Post* (June 4, 2007).

58. Graham Allison, *Nuclear Terrorism: The Ultimate Preventable Catastrophe* (New York, NY: Times Books/Holt, 2004).

59. On the progress toward first-strike nuclear dominance over Russia, see Lieber and Press, "The Rise of U.S. Nuclear Primacy."

60. Adrian Blomfield, "Russia, China Flex Military Muscle," *National Post* (August 18, 2007).

61. For test details, technical commentary and helpful explanatory graphics, see Carl Hoffman, "Battlefield Space," *Popular Mechanics* (July 2007).

62. Hoffman, "Battlefield Space."

63. United States Department of Homeland Security, *Securing Our Homeland: US Dept. of Homeland Security Strategic Plan* (Washington, DC: Government Printing Office, 2004).

64. Kent Roach, *September 11: Consequences for Canada* (Kingston, ON: McGill-Queen's University Press, 2003).

65. Don Martin, "No Time to Relax on Terrorism Threats," *National Post* (February 14, 2007).

66. Clifford Krauss, "Evidence Grows that Canada Aided in Having Terrorism Suspects Interrogated in Syria," *New York Times* (September 17, 2005).

67. James Gordon, "Post 9/11 Security Measures Cost $2.6 billion," *National Post* (July 9, 2007).

68. Andrew Mayeda, "Double Forces in Afghanistan, Think-tank Says" (November 22, 2007).

69. Editorial/GM, "Auditor General's Report: The Gaps at the Border," *Globe and Mail* (October 31, 2007).

70. Standing Senate Committee on National Security and Defence, *The Myth of Security at Canada's Airports* (Ottawa, ON: Government of Canada, 2003), 112.

71. Standing Senate Committee on National Security and Defence, *Canadian Security Guide Book: 2005 Edition, An Update of Security Problems in Search of Solutions* (Ottawa, ON: Government of Canada, 2004), 184–86.

72. Senate of Canada, *Canadian Security Guide Book, 2007 Edition: Airports,* Report of the Standing Senate Committee on National Security and Defence, March 2007, 67.

73. Kim Bolan, "Airport Staff Screening Insufficient, Inquiry Told," *National Post* (June 2, 2007).

74. Senate of Canada, *Canadian Security Guide Book, 2007 Edition: Seaports,* Report of the Standing Senate Committee on National Security and Defence, March 2007.

75. *Defence,* 2004, 134.

76. Senate of Canada, *Canadian Security Guide Book,* 29.

77. Ibid., 31.

78. Senate of Canada, *Canada's Coastlines: The Longest Under-Defended Borders in the World.* 2 vols, Report of the Standing Senate Committee on National Security and Defence. Senator Colin Kenny, Committee Chair, October 2003, 81.

79. Standing Senate Committee on National Security and Defence, *Canadian Security Guide Book: 2005 Edition, An Update of Security Problems in Search of Solutions* (Ottawa, ON: Government of Canada, 2004), 41.

80. Ibid., 3.

81. Senate of Canada, *Canadian Security Guide Book, 2007 Edition: Coasts,* Report of the Standing Committee on National Security and Defence, Senator Colin Kenny, Chair, March 2007, 1–2.

82. Ibid., 8–10.

83. Ibid., 11.

84. Ibid., 15.

85. David Pugliese, "$3 billion for Arctic ships, PM," *National Post* (July 10, 2007).

86. For details and maps see the *Canadian–American Strategic Review* website: www.sfu.ca/casr.

87. Martin Lubin, "Strings Between Governments at the Top, Hands Across the Border at the Base: The role of Subnational Governments During the Bush–Chretien Era and Beyond," in *Perspectives on US–Canada Relations Since 9/11: Four Essays,* eds., H. Cody, Martin Lubin, Donald Caccioletta, and Marie Christine Therrien (Orono, ME: The Canadian–American Center, 2003), 21–43.

88. Statistics Canada, 2000, "Brain Drain and Brain Gain...," *The Daily* (May 24, 2000), http://www.statcan.ca/Daily/English/000524/d000524a.htm (accessed May 2, 2006).

89. Maureen Appel Molot and Norman Hillmer, "The Diplomacy of Decline," in *A Fading Power,* eds., Hilmer and Molot (Don Mills, ON: Oxford University Press, 2002).

90. DAMF Consultants, Inc., with L.P. Tardif and Associates, *The Cumulative Impact of U.S. Import Compliance Programs at the Canada/U.S. Land Border on the Canadian Trucking Industry* (Ottawa, ON: Transport Canada, 2005).

91. Rachel L. Swarns, "Capitol's Pariah on Immigration is Now a Power," *New York Times* (December 24, 2005).

92. Ibbitson, "Homeland Security" (August 16, 2007).

93. "Senator Fires Back at U.S. Family Upset with Seal Hunt," (March 17, 2006), www.cbc.ca (accessed September 17, 2007).

94. Robert Fulford, "Canada's Emotional Necessity," *National Post* (December 17, 2005).

95. Mel Hurtig, *The Vanishing Country: Is It Too Late to Save Canada?* (Toronto, ON: M&S., 2002).

96. Stephane Roussel, "The Blueprint for 'Fortress North America'," *Fortress North America? What 'continental security' means for Canada,* eds., D.R. Furneaux and N. Furneaux (Toronto, ON: The Canadian Institute of Strategic Studies, 2002).

97. Canada, House of Commons, *Getting Back to Business* (Ottawa, ON: Standing Committee on Industry, Science, and Technology Susan Whelan, Chair, 2001).

98. Christopher Sands, *Canada and the War on Terrorism: The US Challenge on the North American Front, Canada Focus* (Washington, DC: Center for Strategic and International Studies, 2001).

99. Standing Senate Committee on National Security and Defence, *Canadian Security Guide Book,* 2005 Edition, 97–8.

100. Ibid., 117–8.

101. Standing Senate Committee on National Security and Defence, *Borderline Insecure: Canada's Land Border Crossings as Key to Canada's Security and Prosperity. Why the Lack of Urgency to Fix Them? What Will Happen if we Don't?* (Ottawa, ON: Government of Canada, 2005), 19, 37.

102. Peter Andreas, "A Tale of Two Borders: The U.S.–Canada and U.S.–Mexico Lines after 9-11," in *The Rebordering of North American: Integration and Exclusion in a New Security Context,* eds., Andreas and T.J. Bierstecker (New York, NY: Routledge, 2003), 9.

103. *Defence,* 2005, 47.

104. Andreas and Athanasios Hristoulas, "Trading Places: Canada, Mexico, and North American Security," in *The Rebordering of North America: Integration and Exclusion in a New Security Context,* eds., Andreas and T.J. Bierstecker (New York, NY: Routledge, 2003), 24–45.

105. Ibid.

106. Howard Cody, "US–Canada Trade, Defense and Border Issues Since September 11: The View From Canada," in *Perspectives on US–Canada Relations Since 9/11: Four Essays,* eds., Cody, Martin Lubin, Donald Caccioletta, and Marie Christine Therrien (Orono, ME: The Canadian–American Center, 2003), 3–15.

107. Clarkson, *Uncle Sam and Us: Globalization, Neoconservatism and the Canadian State* (Toronto, ON: University of Toronto Press, 2003)

108. Pratt, Anna, *Securing Borders: Detention and Deportation in Canada.* Vancouver, BC: University of British Columbia Press, 2005.

109. *Defence,* 2003, 120.

110. *Defence,* 2005, 7.

111. Hristoulas, "Trading Places," 2003.

112. Jenifer Welsh, *At Home in the World: Canada's Global Vision for the 21st Century* (Toronto, ON: HarperCollins, 2004).

113. Anthony Campbell, "Canada–United States Intelligence Relations and 'information sovereignty'," *Coping with the American Colossus,* eds., D. Carment, Fen Osler Hampson, and Hillmer (Toronto, ON: Oxford University Press, 2003).

114. Executives 2003.

115. Jan Nicholls, "Canadian–Mexican Military Relations: A Reflections Piece," in *Canadian and Mexican Security in the New North America: Challenges and Prospects,* ed., Jordi Díez (London, ON: McGill-Queen's University Press, 2006), 101–6.

116. Graeme Smith, "Insurgents' Intelligence Improving, Experts say," *Globe and Mail* (November 7, 2007).

117. Paul Koring, "Tories Plan New Defence Pact with U.S.," *Globe and Mail* (February 20, 2006).

118. Privy Council Office, *Securing an Open Society: One Year Later, Progress Report on the Implementation of Canada's National Security Policy* (Ottawa, ON: Government of Canada, 2005), Preface.

119. David Pulgliese, "'High-risk' Military Projects Over Budget, Behind Schedule," *National Post* (October 29, 2007).

120. For potential energy reserves at issue, see: Doug Saunders, "Beefing Up Arctic Claim Leaves Canada on Thin Ice," *Globe and Mail* (October 20, 2007).

121. Senate of Canada, Standing Committee on National Security and Defence, *Borderline Insecure: Canada's Land Border Crossings are Key to Canada's Security and Prosperity. Why the Lack of Urgency to Fix Them? What Will Happen If We Don't?* (Ottawa: Government of Canada, June 2005).

122. Senate of Canada, *Canadian Security Guide Book, 2007 Edition: Seaports,* 1.

123. Ashton B. Carter, Michael M. May and William J. Perry, "The Day After: Action Following A Nuclear Blast in a U.S. City," *Washington Quarterly* 30, no. 4, (Autumn 2007): 19–32.

CHAPTER 4

1. Much of the fieldwork for this chapter was done along two Mexico–U.S. border points, and in a variety of U.S. libraries, with intermittent interviews at different locations. The two Mexico–U.S. borders were Matamoros-Brownsville and Reynosa-McAllen. Interviews were less useful here, in Tamaulipas-Texas, than presumed, in part owing to the huge routine traffic demanding extra post–9/11 attention, in part due to the shortage of officials versed in scholarly exchanges, in part because of the general reluctance of officials to engage in scholarly parleys, and so forth. Low-level officials who volunteered their time did so more to break their routine workload than to shed any new light, and could be approached only sporadically and informally rather than officially. Especially the investigative questions were left largely unanswered, or fetched unreliable responses: We could not quote or refer to any specific official, and no documents not available in large libraries could be attributed to the agencies visited or cited. Fortunately, plenty of materials were available in several central libraries near the border: University of Texas at Brownsville, University of Houston, Rice University, the University of Texas at Edinburg, and the University of Texas at Austin. In addition were materials available at the University of Pennsylvania main library. Interview questions asked are reproduced in the book's appendix. Also see note 56.

2. Yet, the issue divided Republicans. Richard N. Bond, a former Republican National Committee member, feared so in a piece he wrote for the *Los Angeles Times,* "Weed out immigrant-bashing: U.S. Republicans should follow Bush's constructive agenda," published in Mexico City's only English daily newspaper (which briefly went out of circulation between 2004 and 2007), *News* (March 27, 2002): 12. Henceforth just *News.*

3. Robert A. Pastor and Rafael Fernandez de Castro, eds., *The Controversial Pivot: The U.S. Congress and North America* (Washington, DC: Brookings Institution, 1998).

4. *Cinco Mayo* commemoration of the eviction of the French Emperor Maximilian in 1867 was ironic after 9/11: That the United States participated in this celebration, no less inside the White House, not only echoed U.S. sympathy for Mexico against Maximilian (even then barely 15 years after the Treaty of Guadalupe-Hidalgo took away huge chunks of Mexican territory in Polk's War); it also anticipated the huge post–9/11 France-U.S. discord over the Iraq war. See Jaime Suchlicki, *Mexico: From Montezuma to the Fall of the PRI,* 2nd ed. (Washington, DC: Brasseys, 2001), 87–94; and Imtiaz Hussain, "Doggone Diplomacy? The Iraq war, North American Bilateralism and Beyond," *Canada and the New American Empire,* ed., George Melnyk (Calgary, AB: University of Calgary, 2004), 213–30.

5. Ginger Thompson, "Little Progress on Agenda for Mexico–U.S. Relations," *News* (March 25, 2002): 5.

6. Figure from "Bush Announces Goal of Single NAFTA Frontier: Border to be Opened for Trade, Closed to Drugs, Terrorists," *News* (March 24, 2004): 2.

7. To be sure, NAFTA is a collection of three bilateral agreements in its origins; though trilateralization remains a tendency, bilateralism rules the day.

8. See a more cynical assessment by Michael Kleinberg, "Out of Bounds? The Response Fox Received from the United States and Canada on his Open-immigration Proposal was Clear: Don't Covet Thy Neighbor's Border," *Business Mexico* (October 2000): 26–28.

9. An anticipatory study highlights the pros and cons. See "The Issue of Voting by Residents Abroad," *Review of the Economic Situation in Mexico* 74, no. 876 (November 1998): 428–33.

10. Tessie Border, "Mexican Citizens Living Abroad Seek Voting Rights," *News* (March 28, 2002): 2.

11. Celeste Tarricone, "Citizens Abroad May Get to Vote in 2006," *News* (March 15, 2002): 2.

12. Stevenson Jacobs, "Fox Recruits Fiscal Help from U.S. Giants: Aims to Slow Exodus of Rural Emigration," *News* (January 23, 2002): 3.

13. For example, see Richard E. Neustadt, *Presidential Powers: The Politics of Leadership,* With an Afterword on JFK (New York, NY: John Wiley and Sons, 1960).

14. The party breakdown was: In the Senate, PRI controlled 60 seats, PAN 46, PRD 15, PVEM 5, others 2, for a total of 128; and in the Chamber, PRI controlled 211, PAN 207, PRD 51, PVEM 16, others 15, for a total of 500. See Andrew Hurst, "Many in Mexico Ask: Who Really Runs Country?" *News* (January 5, 2002): 3; and "Fox: Tough Lessons have been Learned," ibid.

15. Traci Carl, "Senate Defies President, Says He Cannot Travel: Fox Blames Intransigent Opposition," *News* (April 10, 2002): 2; and "Castañeda, Fox Hit Back at Senate 'vengefulness': govt [*sic*] Prepares for Fight with Congress," *News* (April 11, 2002): 2.

16. Jason Lange, "Opposition Unites Against U.N. Vote: PAN Stands Alone in Congress Debate," *News* (April 19, 2002): 2.

17. Stevenson Jacobs, "Fox Laments Failure of Ambitious Fiscal Reform: Funds 'insufficient' for Government Needs," *News* (January 3, 2002): 2; and "Cantankerous Congress shows its teeth," ibid.

18. http://www.ins.usdoj.gov/graphics/aboutins/statistics/illegalalien/index.htm.

19. From Michael C. LeMay, "U.S. Immigration: A Reference Handbook," in *ABC-CLIO Contemporary World Issues Series* (Santa Barbara, CA: ABC-CLIO, 2004), 54–56.

20. For a profile, see Hussain, "Canadian Immigration, Mexican Emigration, and a North American Regional Interpretation," *Journal of International Migration and Integration* 6, no. 1 (Winter 2005): 81–92.

21. Marta Tienda traces the expansion of illegal immigration to roughly this period and event. See "Looking to the 1990s: Mexican Immigration in Sociological Perspective," in *Mexican Migration to the United States Origins, Consequences and Policy Options,* eds., Wayne A. Cornelius and Jorge A. Bustamante (San Diego, CA: University of California, San Diego, Center for Mexico-U.S. Studies, 1989), 115, but see 109–47.

22. LeMay, *U.S. Immigration: A Reference Handbook,* 3–21.

23. For a Snapshot, see Julie Watson, "Remote Río Bravo Crossing Still Open, Despite Worries," *News* (March 21, 2002): 3; and "US Border Fence Plan 'shameful'," *BBC News* (December 19, 2005), http://news.bbc.co.uk/2/hi/americas/4541606.stm. For Calderon's quote, see Mary Milliken, "Calderón , in L.A., Seeks Greater 'co-responsibility':

President Calls U.S. Elections' Singular Opportunity' to Strengthen Ties," *News* (February 15, 2008): 1.

24. On what that campaign produced, see Jim Gilchrist and Jerome R. Corsi, *Minutemen: The Battle to Secure America's Borders* (New York, NY: World Ahead Publishing, 2006).

25. Includes *Mara Salvatrucha* and 18th St. Gang. See Ana Ariana, "How the Street Gangs Took Central America," *Foreign Affairs* (May/June 2005): 98–110.

26. See Hussain, "Knocking on Mexico's Doors: Central America's Unholy Trinity," *Dialogo Iberoamericano,* no. 2 (August–December 2005): 14–18.

27. With apology to Strobe Talbott, whose book of the same name chronicled the US–Soviet nuclear arms race of the 1970s–1980s. See *Deadly Gambits: The Reagan Administration and the Stalemate in Nuclear Arms Control* (New York, NY: Knopf, 1984).

28. Scott Lindlaw, "Bush Seeks Amnesty Bill for Illegal Immigrants," *News* (March 20, 2002): 9; and Ruben Nararrette, "Cross-border Confusion," *News* (March 21, 2002): 12.

29. Samuel P. Huntington, "The Hispanic Challenge," *Foreign Policy* no. 141 (March/April 2004): 30–45.

30. Wayne A. Cornelius, "Impacts of NAFTA on Mexico–U.S. Migration," *NAFTA in the New Millennium,* eds., Edward J. Chambers and Peter H. Smith (La Jolla, CA, and Edmonton, Alberta: Center for U.S.–Mexico Studies, University of California, San Diego, and University of Alberta Press, 2002), 287–304. Quotation from p. 293.

31. Tito Alegria, "Demand and Supply of Mexican Cross-border Workers," *Journal of Borderland Studies* 17, no. 1 (Spring 2002): 37–55.

32. Six types exist: Visa E1 for real estate and services corporation employees if at least 50 percent of investments are Mexican; E2 for those interested in investing in the US with at least 50 percent Mexican ownership; Visa H1B for professionals seeking specialized temporary work; H2B for companies with temporary needs; L1 for companies with subsidiaries in the other country; and TN, also called the NAFTA visa, permitting certain professionals employment. See "U.S. Provides Six Pptions For Guest Workers," *News* (March 10, 2002): 5.

33. One Arellano brother was killed in Mazatlan, another arrested in Puebla, and a third arrested on a yacht in the Pacific Ocean, thus ingloriously ending the fearsome Tijuana gang of the same name.

34. Bruce M. Bagley and William O. Walker III, "Introduction," in *Drug Trafficking in the Americas,* eds., Bagley and Walker (New Brunswick, NJ: Transactions Publishers, 1994), ix, but see entire chapter for overview.

35. Peter H. Smith, "Drug Trafficking in Mexico," in *Coming Together? Mexico–U.S. Relations,* eds., Barry P. Bosworth, Susan M. Collins, and Nora Lustig (Washington, DC: Brookings Institution, 1997), 126, but see 125–54.

36. Smith, "Drug Trafficking in Mexico," 140.

37. Gabriela D. Lemus, "U.S.–Mexican Border Drug Control: Operation Alliance as a Case Study," *Drug Trafficking in the Americas* 434–35.

38. More on this by Smith, "Drug Trafficking in Mexico," 134–40.

39. Jorge Dominguez and Rafael Fernandez de Castro, *The United States and Mexico: Between Partnership and Conflict* (New York, NY: Routledge, 2001), 37–51.

40. Term applied by David Mares in "Strategic Interests in the US–Mexican Relationship," in *Strategy and Security in U.S.–Mexican Relations Beyond the Cold War,* ed., John Bailey and Sergio Aguayo Quezada (La Jolla, CA: Center for US–Mexican Studies, University of California, San Diego, 1996), chap. 2.

41. Domínguez and Castro, *The United States and Mexico,* 49.

42. Guadalupe González González and Stephan Haggard, "The United States and Mexico: A Pluralistic Security Community," in *Security Communities,* eds., Emanuel Adler and Michael Barnett (Cambridge, UK: Cambridge University Press, 1998), 298–99, but see chap. 9.

43. Vivien Lowndes sees similar distinctions but dubs them "traditional" and "new" institutionalism, respectively. See "Institutionalism," in *Theory and Methods in Political Science,* eds., David Marsh and Gerry Stoker, 2nd ed. (Houndsmills, Basingtoke, Hampshire, UK: Palgrave 2002), chap. 4.

44. Denise Dresser, "Castro Angered—That's Ok," *News* (April 11, 2002): 12; Jose Antonio O'Farrill Avila, "It's Pathetic That We're Forgetting Our Tradition of Friendship, Hospitality," *News* (March 27, 2002): 3; Kieran Murray, "Dispute Sends Cuba–Mexico Ties to All-time Low," *News* (March 28, 2002): 3; and Roger E. Hernandez, "Mexico and a New Cuba," *News* (April 5, 2002): 12.

45. Marc Frank, "Cuba Blasts Mexico Over Castro Tiff at U.N. Summit," *News* (March 25, 2002): 2; "Cuban Paper Lambastes 'Machiavelli' Castañeda," *News* (March 27, 2002): 2; and Jason Lange, "Opposition Unite Against U.N. Vote: PAN Stands Alone in Congress Debate," *News* (April 19, 2002): 2.

46. On this point, see Hussain "Doggone diplomacy?"

47. Christopher Leroy, "Mexican Intelligence At a Crossroad," *SAIS Review* 24, no. 1 (Winter–Spring 2004): 108.

48. Ibid., 117.

49. John Bailey, "Law Enforcement and Intelligence in the Bilateral Security Context: U.S. Bureaucratic Dynamics," in *Strategy and Security in U.S.–Mexican Relations Beyond the Cold War,* eds., Bailey and Sergio Aguayo Quezada (La Jolla, CA: Center for U.S.–Mexican Studies, University of California, San Diege, 1996), 176, but see chap. 9.

50. See Stevenson Jacobs, "Ridge Says New Border Agreement Close: Neighbors Seeking 'shared approach'," *News* (March 6, 2002): 2.

51. US Department of Homeland Security, "The Mexico–US Border Partnership: Progress Report, 2002-2004" (January 17, 2005).

52. "Mexico–U.S. Seal Border Security Plan: "Partnership for Prosperity" also Gets Presidential Boost," *News* (March 23, 2002): 2.

53. The existing six were at Tijuana-SanYsidro (two), Mesa de Otay-Otay Mesa (two), and Ciudad Juárez-El Paso (including Lerdo-Stanton); while the new seven were at Tijuana Puerta-San Ysidro (two), Mexicali-Calexico, Nogales-Nogales, Ciudad Juárez-El Paso at Ysletta/ Zaragoza, Nuevo Laredo-Laredo, and Matamoros-Brownsville. All seven new ones are for vehicles except one of the two at Tijuana Puerta-San Isidro.

54. The breakdown: two at Juarez/El Paso, one at Nuevo Laredo/Laredo, Reynosa/Pharr, Matamoros/Brownsville, Mexicali/Calexico, and Mesa de Otay/Otay Mesa.

55. These are at Nogales, Arizona/Nogales, Sonora, Santa Teresa/Ciudad Juárez, Rio Grande City/Camargo, Tagle Pass/Piedras Negras, Del Rio/Ciudad Acuña, Tecate, CA/ Tecate, BC, Douglas, AZ/Agua Prieta, Sonora, San Luis, AZ/San Luis Río Colorado, Sonora.

56. My own case illustrates. Holding a Bangladesh passport, a U.S. residence permit, a Mexican work permit, and a last name Hussain, after 9/11, I am invariably called for an interview at every U.S. border-crossing port. Almost always, the interview starts late, one major reason being finding an officer for the task. It is not that officers are in short supply or too swamped by other "customers." On the contrary, there are many of them at any time of the day or night (with fewer night staff than daytime). They simply run around on other errands,

often unrelated to the interview tasks; and sometimes with interviews, too many other officials need to be consulted before any single interviewer begins the job. My cases have always been with Mexican–American officials, either experienced first generation immigrants who still betray their cultural origins by resorting to loaded personal, nonessential questions or comments, or fluent second generation counterparts who play more by the "book", that is, the pre-oriented questions given them. When, finally, an officer arrives, the questions that matter remain more ritual than personal, as if reading off a memorized list of what questions must be asked: "What brings you to Mexico?" "Where are you headed in the United States?" "What do you do?" When told I teach/research international relations, the follow-ups come as close to an idiosyncratic exchange as any: "Is NAFTA working?" "How is the Mexico–US relationship?" The questions were simple but protracted; and the answers were equally straightforward in all cases—never less than an hour in duration, often more than two hours (much of the time waiting). Topping such sessions come some cream questions: "Which other countries have you visited recently?" And, of course, what I call the give-away question: "Have you been to France?" Border and airport treatments differ. After all the routine check-in and customs/immigration inspections in airports, my travel is generally routine. Only once in a while am I asked for an extra interview in a separate room, but these are by officials whom I dub "bad apples": One can usually tell by glancing through the multiple immigration officials at the various windows while waiting to be called who these bad apples may be. Yet, just as these are few and far in between, at the border there are no exceptions: I am asked to pull over every time, and very courteously at that, then interviewed by officers with the vaguest of international relations consciousness/knowledge. Out of 275 million Mexico–U.S. border crossers each year, I can understand why stopping a third nationality passerby becomes headlines news, but if the questions, attitudes, and efficiency were more competent, as a U.S. green-card holder, I would feel much more confident of institutional rules flowing smoothly at the local level—even if the waiting is three hours long, that too after driving 13 hours from Mexico City. Experiences with Mexican officials, by contrast, tend to be fret-free, but without necessarily enhancing confidence in the institutions.

57. U.S. Department of State, "Smart Border: 22 Point Agreement—US–Mexico Border Partnership Action Plan" (March 21, 2002), Factsheet, available at http://www.state.gov/p/wha/rls/fs/8969.htm.

58. Julie Watson, "Arrests of Illegal Border Crossers Plummets: Once-busy Centers for Undocumented Migrants Deserted," *News* (June 8, 2002): 3.

59. International Monetary Fund, *Direction of Trade Statistics Yearbook, 2004* (Washington, DC: IMF, 2005), various pages.

60. International Monetary Fund, *Direction of Trade Statistics* (Washington, DC: IMF, 2004), 120–21.

61. David Shields, "Remittances from U.S. Are Set to Rise Again," *News* (May 13, 2002): 26.

62. On this last point, Mexico–U.S. borderland relations reflect the general case made by Ronald L. Jepperson, Alexander Wendt, and Peter J. Katzenstein, "[I]t is clear that the security domain has become less exclusively an *interstate* realm: states' hegemony over security by allowing (or promoting) a vast unregulated market in arms sales, feeding myriad groups, and ethno-religious camps have proliferated and have attained regional and even global reach." See "Norms, identity, and culture in national security," *The Culture of National Security: Norms and Identity in World Politics* (New York: Columbia University Press, 1996), 75, but see chap. 2.

CHAPTER 5

1. "Focus Shifts North Among Terror Fears," *USA Today* (December 18, 2006): 4a; Mexican border figures from "Keep Out: Voters Like The Idea of Tougher Borders But the Cost is High and the Benefits are Limited," *Economist* special migration section, "Open up" (January 5, 2008): 10.

2. See Roy Pateman, *Residual Uncertainty: Trying to Avoid Intelligence and Policy Mistakes in the Modern World* (Lanham, MD: University Press of America, 2003), 9–10.

3. http://www.pbs.org/wgbh/pages/frontline/shows/trail/etc/canada.html.

4. "Focus Shifts North Among Terror Fears," *USA Today* (December 18, 2006): 4a.

5. Peter Andreas, "The Mexicanization of the US–Canada Border: Asymmetric Interdependence in a Changing Security Context," *International Journal* 60, no. 2 (Spring 2005): 449–62.

6. Dawn Kopeki, "Boeing's Border Patrol," *Business Week* no. 4006 (October 23, 2006).

7. Maude Barlow, "Dinosaurs and Deep Integration: Standing up to the American Nightmare," *Our Times* 24, no. 5 (2005): 29–33.

8. Conference of Defence Associations Institute, "Understanding the Crisis in Canadian Security and Defence" (Ottawa: CDAI, March. 2005).

9. Joel J. Sokolsky and Phillipe Lagasse, "Suspenders and Belt: Perimeter and Border Security in U.S.–Canada Relations," *Canadian Foreign Policy* 12, no. 3 (2005/06): 15–29.

10. Frank P. Harvey, "Canada's Addiction to American Security: The Illusion of Choice in the War on Terrorism," *The American Review of Canadian Studies* 35, no. 2 (2005): 265–95.

11. Ian Fergusson, *United States–Canada Trade and Economic Relationship: Prospects and Challenges* (Washington, DC: Congressional Research Service, Library of Congress, 2006), 20.

12. Jill L. Hochman, "Border Planning for the 21st Century," *Public Roads* 68, no. 4 (January/February 2005).

13. http://www.locationcanada.com/2005/art_2.htm, 1.

14. Ibid.

15. http://www.locationcanada.com/2005/art_2.htm, 2.

16. Ibid.

17. Peter Andreas, "A Tale of Two Borders: The US–Canada and US–Mexico Lines After 9-11," in *The Re-bordering of North America,* ed., Peter Andreas and Thomas Bierstaker (New York, NY: Routledge, 2003), 7-8.

18. Heather Nicol and James Townsend, *Holding the Line: Borders in a Global World* (Vancouver, BC: University of British Columbia Press, 2005), 124–27.

19. See information on the United States Visitor and Immigrant Status Indicator Technology (US-VISIT). Available at http://www.locationcanada.com/2005/art_2.htm.

20. "Clogged Border? The Border: How Bad Is It?" *The Bar-Code Border* 2, no. 34 (June 15, 2003).

21. Jason Ackleson, "Navigating the Northern Line: Discourses of the US–Canadian Borderlands," Paper presented at International Studies Association, Annual Convention, Los Angeles, March 2000.

22. Victor Konrad and Heather Nicol, "Boundaries and Corridors: Rethinking the Canada–United States Borderlands in the post–9/11 Era," Canadian–American Center, Occasional Paper Series (Maine, 2004).

23. Ian Fergusson, *United States–Canada Trade and Economic Relationship* (Washington, DC: Congressional Research Office, The Library of Congress, 2005), 3.

24. Ibid., 4.

25. All calculations are from the absolute dollar figures illustrated in table 5.1.

26. Border Policy Research Institute, "Diversity of the Ports-of-Entry along the 49th parallel," *Border Policy Brief* 2, no. 5 (September 2007): 1.

27. The post-9/11 securitization includes tripling the number of border agents, commission of the national guard to help with patrols and inspections at the border ports of entry. Two of the new U.S. air and marine bases have been established in Bellingham, WA and Plattsburgh, NY. Three others are scheduled for Detroit, MI, Grand Forks, ND, and Great Falls, MO. See in this regard, Andreas, "Mexicanization of the U.S–Canada border," 455–56.

28. *Border Policy Brief* 2, no. 5 (September 2007): 4.

29. http://www.locationcanada.com/2005/art_2.htm, 2

30. Steven Globerman, "The Impact of 9/11 on Canada–US Trade," Working Paper, Center for International Business Working Group, Western Washington University. The paper cites other factors, such as price changes of the commodities, demand swings, foreign competition, and dollar exchange rate troubles with other major currencies may have played a role as well.

31. Ibid.

32. Alan D. MacPherson, James E. McConnell, Anneliese Vance, and Vida Vanchan, "The Impact of US Antiterrorism Policies on Canada–US Cross-border Commerce: An Exploratory Study From Western New York and southern Ontario," *The Professional Geographer* 58, no. 3 (2006): 266–77.

33. The Whatcom Council of Governments in the Seattle-Vancouver Area, which includes the local and regional governmental representatives from both Canada and the United States, is precisely hoping for ways to best combine enhanced border security collaboration and partial policy convergence in both countries. Interviewees questioned the presence of two sets of customs agents and immigration officials at the border check-points. They hoped that someday soon only one set of agents would be necessary if both countries share the will to cooperate with the increased securitization to the same degree. The term used to describe such possibilities was "cross-accredition/designation," implying at some point the United States and Canadian customs agents would act as each other's perfect substitutes, and that there would be a single process of clearance for all crossing the border from both sides.

34. For example, the then-leader of the Opposition Canadian Alliance, Stokwell Day, asked the Canadian government to change its laws so that suspected terrorists can be apprehended and deported from the Canadian soil. See Government of Canada, Hansard, selected discussion concerning the Canada–US border, from www.1410Eham099.htm.

35. Joseph Nunez, "Canada's Global Role: A Strategic Assessment of Its Military Power," *Parameters* (Autumn 2004): 75–93.

36. Brian MacDonald, "The Capital and the Future Force Crisis," in *Canada Without Armed Forces,* ed., Douglas Bland (Kingston, ON: Queen's University, 2003), 27–29.

37. Mark Odell, "Canada Calls for Greater Commitment from NATO Countries to Mission in Afghanistan," *Financial Times* (December 4, 2003): 2.

38. Government of Canada, Department of National Defence, "Canadian Army Hosts Conference of American Armies," November 14, 2003, http://www.army.dnd.ca/.

39. Nunez, "Canada's Global Role," 86.

40. Andrew Cohen, *While Canada Slept: How we Lost our Place in the World* (Toronto, ON: McLelland and Stewart, 2003), 22–23.

41. See Robert Kagan, *Of Paradise and Power* (New York, NY: Alfred A. Knopf, 2003).

42. All calculations are made by the author based on the data provided in *The World Bank, World Development Report 2006* (Washington DC: The World Bank and Oxford University Press, 2006), 234–39.

43. "Security Assessment—North America," *Jane's Sentinel* (October 7, 2003).

44. http://www.fas.org/asmp/fast_facts.htm, 1–8.

45. For example, Canadian Alliance leader Stephen Harper, the current prime minister, and others, have repeatedly stated that Canada should support U.S. plans for military strikes against Iraq with or without UN support. These tensions have strong economic undertones. Available at http://www.globeandmail.com/servlet/ArticleNews/front/RTGAM/20021002/schr1001/fr.

46. From Thomas Hughes, *The Fate of Facts in a World of Men: Foreign Policy and Intelligence-making,* Foreign Policy Association, Headlines Series #233 (New York, NY: Foreign Policy Association, 1976).

47. In this regard, interesting comments were made by many of the interviewees. For example, although they agreed in a general sense that the US-Canadian values originate from the same cultural milieu, yet they insisted that differences of perception on specific issues have appeared because of differences in socialization. Canadians have been socialized in a more social democratic view of the world, while the U.S. citizens are more exposed to the libertarian ways of managing societal affairs.

48. In addition to Hughes, *The Fate of Facts in a World of Men,* see Glenn Hastedt, "Controlling Intelligence: The Role of the D.C.I.," *International Journal of Intelligence and Counterintelligence* 1, no. 4 (1986): 28.

49. Winn L. Taplin, "Six General Principles of Intelligence," *International Journal of Intelligence and Counterintelligence* 3, no. 4 (1989): 475–91.

50. Peter Gill popularizes this term in *Policing Politics: Security Intelligence and the Liberal Democratic State* (London: Frank Cass, 1994).

51. Steve Hewitt, "Reforming the Canadian Security State: The Royal Canadian Mounted Police Security Service and the 'key sectors' program," *Intelligence and National Security* 17, no. 4 (Winter 2002): 166, but see 165–84.

52. From W. Raymond Wannall, "The FBI's Domestic Intelligence Operations: Domestic Security in limbo," *International Journal of Intelligence and Counterintelligence* 4, no. 4 (1990): 443.

53. Athan Theoharis, *Spying on Americans: Political Surveillance from Hoover to the Huston Plan* (Philadelphia, PA: Temple University Press, 1978); and Jim Vander Wall, *The COINTELPRO Papers: Documents from the FBI's Secret Wars Against Dissent in the United States* (Boston, MA: South End Press, 1990).

54. Frederick P. Hitz and Brian J. Weiss, "Helping the CIA and FBI Connect the Dots in the War on Terrorism," *International Journal of Intelligence and Counterintelligence* 17, no. 1 (2004): 4–6, but see 1–41.

55. Stuart Farson, "Parliament and Its Servants: Their Role in Scrutinizing Canadian Intelligence," in *American–British–Canadian Intelligence Relations, 1939–2000,* ed., David Stafford (Toronto, ON: Routledge, 2000), 226, but see chap. 11.

56. Roy Rempel, "Canada's Parliamentary Oversight of Security and Intelligence," *International Journal of Intelligence and Counterintelligence* 17, no. 4 (2004): 641–3, but see 634–54.

57. Melvyn A. Goodman, "9/11: The Failure of Strategic Intelligence," *Intelligence and National Security* 18, no. 4 (Winter 2003): 59, but see 59–71.

58. Geoffrey R. Weller, "Assessing Canadian Intelligence Literature: 1980–2000," *International Journal of Intelligence and Counterintelligence* 14, no. 1 (2001): 51, but see 49–61.

59. Donald M. Snow adds a second questionable rationale for the U.S. invasion: Ties to Terrorism, *al-Qaeda* specifically. He does not go as far as to call these rationales false, only as being "essentially discredited," though "policymakers were generally given the benefit of doubt." See Snow, *National Security for a New Era: Globalization and Geopolitics,* 2nd ed. (New York, NY: Pearson Education, Inc., and Longman, 2007), 57. That is not the message coming across in the 2006 media, nor consistent with election messages and follow-up congressional investigations. Richard L. Russell is more blatant, calling these rationales "a catastrophic intelligence failure. . . arguably one of the greatest intelligence failures since the CIA's inception in 1947." See Russell, "A Weak Pillar for America's National Security: The CIA's Dismal Performance Against WMD Threats," *Intelligence and National Security* 20, no. 3 (September 2005): 468, but see 466–85.

60. Weller, "Assessing Canadian Intelligence Literature," 54.

61. Reg Whitaker, "Spies Who Might Have Been: Canada and the Myth of Cold War Counterintelligence," *Intelligence and National Security* 12, no. 4 (October 1997): 25-43.

62. The picture-puzzle analogy brings together what Lt. General Hoyt Sanford Vandenberg called the "overall picture" as seen by troops in their corners of the world, and what Admiral Roscoe H. Hillenkoetter described as a "gigantic jigsaw," necessitating "a researcher, engaged in hard, painstaking work, poring over foreign newspapers and magazines, reference works and similar materials, endlessly putting fact upon fact, until the whole outline appears and the details begin to fill in." Vandenberg was formerly head of the army's G2 until appointed the second DCI (Director of Central Intelligence), from July 1946; Hillenkoetter became the first director of the CIA after the National Security Act was enacted in July 1947. See Roger Hilsman, Jr., "Intelligence and Policy-making in Foreign Affairs," *International Politics and Foreign Policy: A Reader in Research and Theory,* ed., James N. Rosenau (New York, NY: The Free Press of Glencoe, 1969), 210, but see chap. 22. Also see Richard Immerman, "A Brief History of the CIA," *The Central Intelligence Agency: Security Under Scrutiny,* eds, Athan Theoharis, et al., *Understanding our Government Series* (Westport, CT: Greenwood Press, 2006), chap. 1.

63. Snow, *National Security: Defense Policy for a New International Era* (New York, NY: St. Martin's Press, 1995), 42–65.

64. The Constitutional Convention placed intelligence in civilian hands, and Congress authorized the first secret service fund, the Contingent Fund on Foreign Intercourse, on July 1, 1790. See Edwards F. Sayle, "The Historical Underpinnings of the U.S. Intelligence Community," *International Journal of Intelligence and Counterintelligence* 1, no. 1 (1986): 9, but see 1-27.

65. Wesley K. Wark, "Canada and the Intelligence Revolution," in *Secret Intelligence in the Twentieth Century,* eds., Heike Bungert, Jan G. Heitmann, and Michael Wala (London: Frank Cass, 2003), 184–85, but see chap. 13.

66. See his classic, *Democracy in America,* trans., Arthur Goldhammer (New York, NY: Library for America for Penguin Putnam, 2004).

67. Mark Phythian, "Still a Matter of Trust: Post-9/11 British Intelligence and Political Culture," *International Journal of Intelligence and Counterintelligence* 18, no. 4 (2005): 654–56, but see 653–581.

68. Bradley F. Smith traces Anglo-American cooperation "to the extremely close and warm relations which prevailed between American civil and military authorities on one hand, and those of Great Britain on the other," even pointing to a 1906 Admiralty memorandum

indicating Britain to be "on the best of terms" with the United States. See Smith, "The American Road to Central Intelligence," *Intelligence and National Security* 12, no. 1 (January 1997): 1–21. Also of interest is Colin MacKinnon, "William Friedman's Bletchley Park Diary: A New Source for the History of Anglo-American Intelligence Cooperation," *Intelligence and National Security* 20, no. 4 (December 2005): 654–69.

69. Mr. X, "Sources of Soviet foreign policy," *Foreign Affairs,* no. 25 (July 1947): 575.

70. From Bruce Maxwell, *Homeland Security: A Documentary History* (Washington, DC: Congressional Quarterly Press, 2004), 258. Full speech accessed for this study was in Cynthia A. Watson's resourceful *U.S. National Security* (Santa Barbara, CA: ABC-CLIO, 2002), 200–6.

71. Michael A. Turner, "A Distinctive U.S. Intelligence Identity," *International Journal of Intelligence and Counterintelligence* 17, no. 1 (2004): 42–43.

72. He is not the only one. Acknowledging nuances, Snow also sees this paradigm as "the dominant organizational device" for purposes of intelligence and security. See Snow, *National Security for a New Era,* 70, but broadly 50–72.

73. On consociationalism, see Arend Lijphart, "Consociational Democracy," *World Politics* 21, no. 1 (October 1968): 216, but see 207–221. Also see Lijphart, "Typologies of Democratic Systems," *Comparative Political Studies* 1, no. 1 (April 1968): 3–44; and Peter Lange and Hudson Meadwell, "Typologies of Democratic Systems: From Political Inputs to Political Economy," in *New Directions in Comparative Politics,* ed., Howard J. Wiarda (Boulder, CO: Westview Press, for the Center for International Affairs, Harvard University, 2002), chap. 5.

74. Canadian competitiveness involves as many actors as, though perhaps makes less noise than, in the US. On the actors, see Farson, "Parliament and Its Servants," 252–3; and Martin Rudner, "The Future of Canadian's Defense Intelligence," *International Journal of Intelligence and Counterintelligence* 15, no. 1 (2002): 540–64.

75. For a useful diagram and discussions, see Jeffrey T. Richelson and Desmond Ball, *The Ties That Bind: Intelligence Cooperation Between the UKUSA Countries: The United Kingdom, the United States of America, Canada, Australia and New Zealand* (Boston, MA: Allen & Unwin, 1985), 85 for RCMA Secret Service and 95 for CSIS, but see chap. 5 in general.

76. Thomas F. Troy, "The Quaintness of the U.S. Intelligence Community: Its Origin, Theory, and Problems," *International Journal of Intelligence and Counterintelligence* 2, no. 2 (1988): 253, but see 245–66.

77. Ibid., 156–58.

78. See Douglas M. Charles, "'Before the Colonel arrived': Hoover, Donovan, Roosevelt, and The Origins of American Central Intelligence," *Intelligence and National Security* 20, no. 2 (June 2005): 225–37.

79. See Peter Jackson, "Historical Reflections on the Uses and Limits of Intelligence," in *Intelligence and Statecraft,* eds., Jackson and Jennifer Siegal (New York, NY: Praeger, 2005), 32–35, but see chap. 1.

80. Troy, "The Quaintness of the U.S. Intelligence Community," 247.

81. Harry Truman's middle name is not an initial.

82. From Larry Valero, "'We need our new OSS, our new General Donovan, now. . .': The Public Discourse Over American Intelligence, 1944–53," *Intelligence and National Security* 18, no. 1 (Spring 2003): 91–118.

83. Figure from Rempel, "Canada's Parliamentary Oversight of Security and Intelligence," 637–8. Compare to U.S. OSS having over 13,000 in 1944. See Jackson, "Historical Reflections on the Uses and Limits of Intelligence," 33.

84. Farson, "Parliament and Its Servants," 230–31.

85. Farson, "Canada's Long Road From Model Law to Effective Oversight of Security and Intelligence," in *Who's Watching the Spies? Establishing Intelligence Service Accountability,* eds., Hans Born, Loch K. Jonson, and Ian Leigh (Washington, DC: Potomac Books, 2005), 110–14, but see 99–119.

86. Troy, "The Quaintness of the U.S. Intelligence Community," 256–57.

87. Cecil V. Crabb, Jr., and Kevin V. Mulcahy, "The National Security Council and the Shaping of U.S. Foreign Policy," *Journal of Intelligence and Counterintelligence* 3, no. 2 (1989): 153–68.

88. Hastedt, "Controlling Intelligence," 29–30.

89. Post–Cold War modifications of the paradigm have not been included since the objective is to check security community relevance rather than security community improvisations.

90. Council on Foreign Relations, *Building a North American Community,* Independent Task Force Report No. 53 (New York, NY: Council on Foreign Relations, 2005).

CHAPTER 6

1. The third was environmental protection, which we omit as it is less related to 9/11 imperatives. See Guadalupe González González and Stephan Haggard, "The USA and Mexico: A Pluralistic Community," in *Security Communities,* eds., Emanuel Adler and Michael Barnet (Cambridge, UK: Cambridge University Press, 1998). Other externalities accredited as and when needed.

2. From Paul Todd and Jonathan Bloch, *Services Today* (London: Zed Books, 2003), 96.

3. Representing "the collection, analysis, evaluation, and dissemination of information for 'positive' intelligence and counterintelligence and the conduct of Special Activities (covert action)." See Winn L. Taplin, "Six General Principles of Intelligence," *International Journal of Intelligence and Counterintelligence* 3, no. 4 (1989): 475–91.

4. As Caesar D. Sereseres argues, however, "Mexico's leaders have generally denied that Mexico has security interests at stake in Central America . . ." This was true until the 1980s, when his comments were made, during the Central American wars. Those wars, he further posits, compounded "the traditional dynamics of Chiapas" with "new factors": guerrillas and refugees. Accordingly, "the Mexican military has assumed a more significant presence," with the following innovations in the 1980s: intelligence gathering, security coordination with other Mexican agencies, military reorganization, and new deployments. See Caesar D. Sereseres, "The Mexican military looks south," in *Modern Mexican Military: A Reassessment,* ed., David Ronfeldt, Center for U.S.–Mexican Studies, Monograph #15 (La Jolla, CA: Center for U.S.–Mexican Studies, university of California, San Diego, 1984), 201–13. Quotes from 201, 204, 211–12, respectively. We generally agree with this assessment, but would add his "traditional dynamics" operated independent of Central American dynamics during the 1994–97 *Zapatista* uprisings, and 20 years after his writing, gangs and drugs fuel the migrants more than war.

5. Donald M. Snow adds a second questionable rationale for the U.S. invasion: ties to terrorism, *al-Qaeda* specifically. He does not go as far as to call the rationale false, only as being "essentially discredited," though "policymakers were generally given the benefit of doubt." That is not the message coming across in the 2006 media, nor consistent with election messages and follow-up congressional investigations. See Snow, *National Security for a New Era: Globalization and Geopolitics,* 2nd ed. (New York, NY: Pearson Education, Inc., and Longman, 2007), 57. Richard L. Russell is more blatant, calling the rationale "a catastrophic intelligence failure. . .arguably one of the greatest intelligence failures since the CIA's inception in 1947."

See Russell, "A Weak Pillar for America's National Security: The CIA's Dismal Performance Against WMD Threats," *National Security* 20, no. 3 (September 2005): 468, but see 466–85.

6. See John Lewis Gaddis, *Strategies of Containment: A Critical Appraisal of Postwar American National Security Policy* (New York, NY: Oxford University Press, 1982), chaps. 7–8.

7. See his classic, *Democracy in America,* trans., Arthur Goldhammer (New York, NY: Library for America for Penguin Putnam, 2004).

8. Historian Lorenzo Meyer put the predicament in very succinct terms: "Has democracy—any kind of democracy—a place in Mexico's present political system? The answer is at best uncertain." See Meyer, "Historical roots of the authoritarian state in Mexico," *Authoritarianism in Mexico,* eds., José Luis Reyna and Richard S. Weinert (Philadelphia, PA: Institute for the Study of Human Issues, 1977), 20. Vargas Llosa's *perfect dictatorship* comment was made in a dialogue with Mexican Nobel Laureate, Octavio Páz, in 1990.

9. Bradley F. Smith traces Anglo-American cooperation "to the extremely close and warm relations which prevailed between American civil and military authorities on one hand, and those of Great Britain on the other," even pointing to a 1906 Admiralty memorandum indicating Britain to be "on the best of terms" with the United States. See Smith, "The American Road to Central Intelligence," *Intelligence and National Security* 12, no. 1 (January 1997): 1–21. Also of interest is Colin MacKinnon, "William Friedman's Bletchley Park Diary: A New Source for the History of Anglo-American Intelligence Cooperation," *Intelligence and National Security* 20, no. 4 (December 2005): 654–69.

10. Britain's rise and decline are discussed by Robert Gilpin, *U.S. Power and the Multinational Corporation: The Political Economy of Foreign Direct Investment* (New York, NY: Basic Books, 1975).

11. See, for example, Daniel C. Levy and Kathleen Bruhn, *Mexico: The Struggle for Democratic Development* (Berkeley, CA: University of California Press, 2006).

12. From Bruce Maxwell, *Homeland Security: A Documentary History* (Washington, DC: Congressional Quarterly Press, 2004), 258. Full speech accessed for this study was in Cynthia A. Watson's resourceful *U.S. National Security* (Santa Barbara, CA: ABC-CLIO, 2002), 200–6.

13. Michael A. Turner, "A Distinctive U.S. Intelligence Identity," *International Journal of Intelligence and Counterintelligence* 17, no. 1 (2004): 42–43.

14. Roderic Ai Camp, *Generals in the Palacio: The Military in Modern Mexico* (New York, NY: Oxford University Press, 1992), chap. 4.

15. He is not the only one. Acknowledging nuances, Snow also sees this paradigm as "the dominant organizational device" for purposes of intelligence and security. See Snow, *National Security for a New Era,* 70, but broadly 50–72.

16. As "the collection of those entities loosely knitted together by a number of committees." See Thomas F. Troy, "The Quaintness of the U.S. Intelligence Community: Its Origin, Theory, and Problems," *International Journal of Intelligence and Counterintelligence* 2, no. 2 (1988): 253, but see 245–66.

17. James C. McKinley, Jr., "Assault on Drug Cartels Feels Like War: In spite of Success Against Narcos, Peace Still Elusive," *News* (January 27, 2008): 4–5; and Lauris Freeman, "Déjà vu: la política antidrogas en la relación México-Estados Unidos," *Foreign Affairs en Español* 8, no. 1 (enero-marzo 2008): 16–18.

18. Stephan Haggard and Guadalupe González González, "The United States and Mexico: A Pluralistic Security Community?" in *Security Communities,* eds., Emanuel Adler and Michael Barnett (Cambridge, UK: Cambridge University Press, 1998), 317–22; and

James F. Rochlin, *Redefining Mexican "Security": Society, State, and Region Under NAFTA* (Boulder, CO: Lynne Rienner, 1997).

19. Robert A. Dahl, *Pluralist Democracy in the United States: Conflict and Consent* (Chicago, IL: Rand McNally, 1967); ———, *Democracy in the United States: Promise and Performance* (Chicago: Rand McNally, 1976); and David B. Truman, *Governmental Process: Political Interest and Public Opinion* (New York: Knopf, 1951); among others.

20. A. Paul Pross, *Group Politics and Public Policy,* 2nd ed. (Toronto, ON: Oxford University Press, 1992), chap. 9.

21. Harold L. Wilensky, *The "New Corporatism", Centralization, and the Welfare State* (London: SAGE Publications, 1976).

22. Reginald J. Harrison, *Pluralism and Corporatism: The Political Evolution of Modern Democracies* (London: Allen & Unwin, 1980).

23. Roderic Ai Camp, *Politics in Mexico: The Democratic Consolidation,* 5th ed. (New York, NY: Oxford University Press, 2007), 10, 12–13, 145, and 154–55.

24. Judgment is still open, but that corporatism is under strain comes across in Nikki Craske, "Dismantling or Retrenchment? Salinas and Corporatism," in *Dismantling the Mexican State?* eds., Rob Aitken, Craske, Gareth A. Jones, and David E. Stansfield (Houndsmills, Basingstoke, Hampshire, UK: Macmillan Press Ltd., 1996), 78–92.

25. Gerard S. Vano, *Canada: The Strategic and Military Pawn* (New York, NY: Praeger, 1988), 143.

26. Term first used by Dwight David Eisenhower in his farewell address to Congress, January 17, 1961. More on what he meant in Moer L. Carey, ed., *The Military Industrial Complex and U.S. Foreign Policy* (Pullman, WA: Washington State University Press, 1969). Contemporary relevance on what is dubbed "new military industrial complex," and debate stemming from it, in Rachel Weber, *Swords Into Dow Shares: Governing the Decline of the Military Industrial Complex* (Boulder, CO: Westview Press, 2001); and Helen Cadicott, *The New Nuclear Danger: George W. Bush's Military-Industrial Complex* (New York, NY: The New Press, 2002).

27. Roderic Ai Camp, *Generals in the Palacio: The Military in Modern Mexico* (New York, NY: Oxford University Press, 1992), 67–68.

28. Aptly illustrated in Michael Isikoff and David Corn, *Hubris: The Inside Story of Spin, Scandal, and the Selling of the Iraqi War* (New York, NY: Crown Publishers, 2006).

29. See, for example, Stephen D. Morris, *Corruption and Politics in Contemporary Mexico* (Tuscaloosa, AL: University of Alabama Press, 1991).

30. Joseph Marguiles, *Guantánamo and the Abuse of Presidential Power* (New York, NY: Simon and Schuster, 2006); and Victoria Brittan and Gillian Slovo, *Guantánamo: 'Honor Bound to Defend Freedom'* (London: Oberon, 2004).

31. "Manual lays out rules for Guantanamo trials *CNN* (January 18, 2007), http://www.cnn.com/2007/LAW/01/18/detainee.trials/index.html.

32. "New US Rules on Terror Detainees," *BBC News* (January 19, 2007), available at http://news.bbc.co.uk/2/hi/americas/6276989.stm.

33. See George Melnyk, ed., *Canada and the New American Empire: War and Anti-war* (Calgary, AB: University of Calgary Press, 2004).

34. Or take the form of suicide bombing. See Daniel B. Kennedy, "A Précis of Suicide Terrorism," *Journal of Homeland Security and Emergency Management* 3, no. 4, art. 2 (2006), from Berkeley Electronic Press: www.bepress.com.

35. Ana Arana, "How the Street Gangs Took Central America," *Foreign Affairs* 85, no. 3 (May/June 2005): 104.

36. The GDP and population data from *World Development Report,* 1992 and 2006.

37. Taken from Gary Gereffi and Martha Martinez, "Mexico's Economic Transformation under NAFTA," in *Mexico's Democracy at Work,* eds., Russell Crandall, Guadalupe Paz, and Riordan Roett (Boulder, CO: Lynne Rienner, 2005), 136.

38. Migration Information Source, *The US–Mexico Border* (June 1, 2006), www.migrationinformation.org.

39. Percentages are calculated from table 6.9.

40. Bureau of Transportation Statistics, *Issue Brief* no. 13 (December 2005).

41. According to Bureau of Transportation statistics, in July 2004, the total number of monthly airline passengers surpassed the peak number of 65.4m registered in the month of July of 2001. By July of 2005, the monthly total of airline passengers had reached 74m. See Bureau of Transportation Statistics, *Issue Brief* no. 13 (December 2005).

42. Jill Hochman, "Border Planning for the 21st Century," *Public Roads* 68, no. 4, (January/February 2005): 1.

43. "Keep Out: Voters Like the Idea of Tougher Borders, But the Cost is High and the Benefits are Limited," *Economist* special migration section, "Open up," January 5, 2008, 101.

44. "Fresh Thought, Authoritative Data, and Global Reach: The US–Mexico Border," *Migration Information Source* (June 1, 2006), available at http://www.migrationinformation.org/Feature/print.cfm?ID=407.

45. Jason Ackleson, "Fencing in Failure: Effective Border Control is Not Achieved by Building More Fences," *Migration Policy in Focus* 4, no. 2 (April 2005): 1–2.

46. Fact Sheet, *US Customs and Border Protection Actions Taken Since 9/11,* DHS Press Release, September 17, 2004.

47. Ackleson, "Fencing in Failure...", 1.

48. DHS Press Release, "Fact sheet: ICE accomplishments in fiscal year 2006," available at http://www.dhs.gov/xnews/releases/pr_1162228690102.shtm.

49. Presidential Determination No. 2005-36, White House Press Release, "Statement of president authorizing secretary of state to transmit to Congress Annual report listing major illicit drug-producing and drug-transit countries" (September 15, 2005), available at http://www.state.gov/p/inl/rls/prsrl/ps/53326.htm.

50. See for example, Michael Shifter, "Latin America's Drug Problem," *Current History* (February 2007): 58–59.

51. Ibid., 61.

52. *El Universal,* Mexico City (January 2, 2007): 1.

53. Ibid.

54. *El Heraldo,* Mexico City (December 30, 2006): 7.

55. *Reforma,* Mexico City (January 3, 2007): 1.

56. "Seven Dead in Acapúlco Ambushes," available at http://news.bbc.co.uk/2/hi/americas/6337201.stm.

57. *El Heraldo,* Mexico City (January 3, 2007): 1.

58. *La Jornada,* Mexico City (December 26, 2006): 12.

59. *La Jornada,* Mexico City (December 31, 2006): 13.

60. *El Heraldo,* Mexico City (December 30, 2006): 3.

61. *La Jornada,* Mexico City (January 5, 2007): 4.

62. *Reforma,* Mexico City (January 1, 2007): 2

63. http://www.northcom.mil/about_us/about_us.htm, 1.

64. http://usinfo.state.gov/wh/Archive/2005/Mar/16-51355.html.

65. Peter Zirnite, "Militarization of the US Drug Control Program," *Foreign Policy in Focus* 3, no. 27 (1998): 1–4.

66. "US Crackdown Sends Meth Labs South of the Border," *Los Angeles Times* (November 26, 2007): 4.

67. Ibid.

68. Report of the Independent Task Force on Immigration and America's Future, *Immigration and America's Future: A New Chapter* (Washington DC: Migration Policy Institute, September 2006), in particular chaps. II, VII, and IX.

69. Christopher Rudolph, "Security and the Political Economy of International Migration," *American Political Science Review* 97, no. 4 (2003): 609–610.

70. Ibid., 609.

71. John Torpey, "States and the Regulation of Migration in the Twentieth-century North Atlantic World," in *The World Around the West,* eds., Peter Andreas and Thomas Snyder (Lanham, MD: Rowan and Littlefield, 2000).

72. Elizabeth Rolph, *Immigration Policies: Legacy from the 1980s and Issues for the 1990s* (Santa Monica, CA: RAND, 1992).

73. Rudolph, "Security and the Political Economy of International Migration," (2003).

74. Ibid., 615.

75. Peter Andreas, "Politics on Edge: Managing the US–Mexico Border," *Current History* (February 2006): 64–68.

76. "The State of US–Mexico Border," *Congressional Report,* 2006.

77. *El Heraldo,* Mexico City (December 26, 2006): 7.

78. Jorge Nowalski, "Human Security and Sustainable Livelihoods: The 'maras' in Central America," in *National Human Security Issues in Latin America,* eds., Satya Pattnayak and Lowell Gustafson (Lewiston, NY: Edwin Mellen, 2006), 218–19.

79. Arana, "How the Street Gangs Took Central America."

80. Ibid., 3.

81. The White House, "President Bush Addresses the Nation on Immigration Reform," *Press Release* (May 15, 2006).

82. White House SPP, "Fact Sheet: Security and Prosperity Partnership of North America," March 31, 2006, 1–2.

83. Jill L. Hochman, "Border Planning for the 21st Century," *Public Roads* 68, no. 4 (January/February 2005): 1–2.

84. Stephen Flynn and Jeanne Kirkpatrick, "Rethinking the Role of the U.S.–Mexican border in the post–9/11 World," *Written Testimony before a hearing of the Committee on Foreign Relations,* United States Senate, March 23, 2004.

85. Lee Rosenberg, "Immigration Policy Must Tilt to Security," Public Affairs Report, Institute of Governmental Studies, University of California, Berkeley, 1–3, http://igs.berkeley.edu/publications/par/summer2002.pdf.

86. Fact Sheet: HHS in 2001, available at http://www.hhs.gov/news/press/2001pres/20011231.html.

87. The White House, *The National Security Strategy of the United States of America,* (March 2006), 47–48.

88. News Release: Secretary Veneman and Ambassador Zoellick announce formation of U.S.–Mexico Consultative Committee on Agriculture, available at www.usda.gov/news/releases/2002/04/0131.htm.

89. See an argument to that effect in Robert A. Pastor, "North America's Second Decade," *Foreign Affairs* 83, no. 1 (2004): 124–25.

90. See "The Bi-national Sustainability Laboratory," available at www.sandia.gov/ACG/BNSL/.

91. See http://www.ins.usdoj.gov/graphics/lawenfor/bmgmt/inspect/bciint.htm.

92. See http://www.state.gov/topical/global/develop/02032204.htm.

93. "The U.S.–Mexico Border," *Migration Information Source* (June 1, 2006), available at http://www.migrationinformation.org/feature/print.cfm?ID=407.

94. Ibid.

95. Migration Policy Institute, Department of Homeland Security, MIP Terrorism data base.

96. White House SPP Fact Sheet, March 31, 2006.

97. Ibid.

98. The White House, "Security and Prosperity Partnership of North America Agenda," 2005.

99. See Border Infrastructure Program, available at http://www.fhwa.dot.gov/.

100. The State Department Report on Terrorism, 2006, the Section on Mexico.

101. All interviewees maintained that although Mexico has not faced a 9/11 type event yet, it has since experienced a surge in personal terrorism and aggregate crime, which increases its perception of threat to Mexican society.

102. For example, see Daniel S. Hamilton, "Societal Security and Homeland Security," in *Protecting the Homeland: European Approaches to Societal Security,* eds., Hamilton, B. Sundelius, and J. Gronvall (Washington, DC: The Johns Hopkins University Press, Center for Transatlantic Relations, 2005), 2–3.

103. Hamilton, "Societal Security: Implications for the United States," in *Protecting the Homeland: European Approaches to Societal Security,* 150–52.

104. See for example, Wayne Cornelius, "Controlling 'unwanted immigration': Lessons from the United States, 1993–2004," *Journal of Ethnic and Migration Studies* 31, no. 4, 775–94; and Douglas S. Massey, Jorge Durand, Nolan J. Malone, *Beyond Smoke and Mirrors: Mexican Immigration in an Era of Economic Integration* (New York, NY: Sage, 2002), 3–7.

105. Wayne Cornelius, T. Tsuda, P. Martin, and J. Hollifield, *Controlling Immigration: A Global Perspective* (Stanford, CA: Stanford University Press, 2004).

106. Also see Paul Ganster and David Lorey, *Borders and Border Politics in a Globalizing World* (Lanham, MD: S.R. Books, 2004).

107. Council on Foreign Relations, "Building a North American Community," *Independent Task Force Report,* no. 53 (New York, NY: Council on Foreign Relations, 2005).

108. Michael d'Arcy, Michael O'Hanlon, Peter Orszag, Jeremy Shapiro, and James Steinberg, *Protecting the Homeland 2006/2007* (Washington, DC: Brookings Institution Press, 2006). In particular, chaps. 1, 4, 5, and 7.

109. Ibid.

110. Although the original mandate of NAFTA did not mean to handle politics nor security, the tremendous progress in the economic front has made it imperative that a collaborative approach be extended to these areas in the aftermath of 9/11. See Monica Serrano, "Integration and Security in North America" *International Journal* 61, no. 3 (Summer 2006): 611–32.

111. Two interviewees speculated that there is a possibility of regional elites disagreeing with the leaders at the national level in terms of how to deal with illegal immigration. If nourished properly, the four U.S. border states may develop a concerted approach that is different from the national political approach to illegal immigration. We must admit that not much evidence points to this particular possibility as of yet.

CHAPTER 7

1. What culture means within the military context is not far different from what it means generically. Allan D. English sees culture "as the collection of values, attitudes, and beliefs which provide people with a common way of interpreting events. . . . as a learned way of coping with the challenges of life." "Socialization," he goes on to add, "is a key method of cultural communication in an organization." See *Understanding Military Culture: A Canadian Perspective* (Montréal and Kingston, Canada: McGill-Queen's University Press, 2004), 15 and 23, but see chaps. 2 and 3. My usage is similar. Although of Canadian authorship, the definition is very consistent with what Mexican scholars mean by military culture. See, for example, Roderic Ai Camp's sixth, seventh, eighth, and ninth hypotheses, all based on the notion of military professionalism, in *Generals in the Palacio: The Military in Modern Mexico* (New York: Oxford University Press, 1992), 11–13.

2. Andrew Cohen, "Canadian–American Relations: Does Canada Matter in Washington? Does it matter if Canada doesn't matter?" *Canada Among Nations 2002: A Fading Power* (Toronto: Oxford University Press, 2002), 34–48.

3. This was a congressional *quid pro quo* to accepting Bush's proposal to exempt terrorist detainees from a wide variety of rights.

4. Stéphane Roussel, "Honey are you still mad at me? I've changed, you know. . . Canada–US relations in a post-Saddam/post-Chrétien era," *International Journal* 58, no. 4 (Autumn 2003): 571–90.

5. See "Don't Dictate to me, Canadian Leader tells US," *CNN* (December 14, 2005), http://edition.cnn.com/2005/WORLD/americas/12/14/canada.martin.reut.index.html.

6. See Lee Carter, "Canada in Protest Over Rendition," *BBC News* (October 7, 2006), available at http://news.bbc.co.uk/2/hi/americas/5415320.stm.

7. For a contrary viewpoint, see "University instructor likens Bush to Hitler," *CNN* (October 11, 2006), available at http://www.cnn.com/EDUCATION/10/11/instructor.sept.11.ap/index.html.

8. Several works show the resilience of the Canadian–U.S. relations. See David A. Baldwin, "Canadian–American relations: Myth and Reality," in *Canadian–American Relations: The Politics and Economics of Interdependence: A Conference Report,* eds., Baldwin and Frank Smallwood (Dartmouth, NH: The Public Affairs Center, 1967), 19–44; Robert Gilpin, "The Politics of Transnational Economic Relations," in *Transnational Relations and World Politics,* eds., Robert O. Keohane and Joseph S. Nye (Cambridge, MA: Harvard University Press, 1972), sporadically through 48–69; Keohane and Nye, *Power and Interdependence* (New York, NY: Longman, 2001, 145–69); and Denis Stairs, "Change in Management of Canada–United States Relations in the Post-war Era," in *Toward a North American Community: Canada, the United States, and Mexico,* eds., Donald Barry, Mark O. Dickerson, and James D. Gaisford (Boulder, CO: Westview Press, 1995), 53–74.

9. David B. Billar, "Canada and the United States: Defense Cooperation in U.S. Northern Command," in *The Homeland Security Papers: Stemming the Tide of Terror,* eds., Michael W. Ritz, Ralph G. Hensley, Jr., and James C. "Chris" Whitmore (Maxwell, AL: US Counterproliferation Center, 2004), 224, but see 223–24 specifically, chap. 10 generally.

10. See the collection of articles in George Melnyk, ed., *Canada and the New American Empire* (Calgary, AL: University of Calgary Press, 2004).

11. Elaborated in Imtiaz Hussain's "Doggone Diplomacy? The Iraq War, North American Bilateralism, and Beyond," *Canada and the New American Empire,* 213–30.

12. After the U.S. civil war was won and the 1854 Reciprocity Agreement with Canada was terminated by the United States in December 1865, groups of Irish settlers in the United States vowed to liberate Ireland from Britain by holding Canada hostage. On May 31, 1866, more than fifteen hundred of them defeated small contingents of Canadian troops in and around Fort Erie. See, among others, Desmond Morton, *A Short History of Canada* (Toronto: McClelland and Stewart, Inc., 1994), 91–93.

13. Roderic Ai Camp traces the country's civil–military relations to Díaz's administration. See *Mexico's Military on the Democratic Stage* (Westport, CT: Praeger Security International, 2005), 16–17.

14. From Gregory S. Kealey, "The Surveillance State: The Origins of Domestic Intelligence and Counter-subversion in Canada, 1914–21," *Intelligence and National Security* 7, no. 3 (July 1992): 184, but see 179–210.

15. Reg Whitaker, "Cold War Alchemy: How America, Britain and Canada Transformed Espionage into Subversion," *Intelligence and National Security* 15, no. 2 (Summer 2000): 177–210.

16. Scott Anderson, "The Evolution of the Canadian Intelligence Establishment, 1945–1950," *Intelligence and National Security* 9, no. 3 (July 1994): 448–71.

17. Whitaker's Argument. See "The Politics of Security Intelligence Policy-making in Canada, I: 1970–84," *Intelligence and National Security* 6, no. 4 (October 1991): 652–3.

18. But it was on the road toward those goals. See J.J. Blais, "The Political Accountability of Intelligence Agencies—Canada," *Intelligence and National Security* 4, no. 1 (January 1989): 108–18.

19. Stuart Farson "Parliament and its Servants: Their role in Scrutinizing Canadian Intelligence," *Intelligence and National Security* 15, no. 2 (Summer 2000): 225–58.

20. Ibid., 230–31.

21. On Canadian values, see Denis Stairs, "Myths, Morals, and Reality in Canadian Foreign Policy," *International Journal* 58, no. 2 (Spring 2003): 239–56; and Steve Lee, "Canadian Values in Canadian Foreign Policy," *Canadian Foreign Policy* 10, no. 1 (Fall 2002): 1–10.

22. English, *Understanding Military Culture,* 89–97.

23. Ibid., 115.

24. Kenneth G. Robertson, "Canadian Intelligence Policy: The Role and Future of CSIS," *International Journal of Intelligence and Counterintelligence* 3, no. 2 (1989): 234–37.

25. This is not a conspiratorial identity, since ideologically different parties create more suspicion than collaboration, but by and large there seems to be an instinctual togetherness after World War I, and increasingly so during conflicts. See Christopher Andrew, "The Growth of the Australian Intelligence Community and the Anglo-American Connection," *Intelligence and National Security* 4, no. 2 (April 1989): 213–56; and Reg Whitaker, "Cold War Alchemy: How America, Britain, and Canada Transformed Espionage into Subversion," *Intelligence and National Security* 15, no. 2 (Summer 2000): 177–210.

26. Not everyone agrees to these specific issues. Roger Bartra, for instance, emphasizes the Central American war of the 1980s, economic crisis, and increasing domestic opposition. See "Revolutionary Nationalism and National Security in Mexico," in *Mexico in Search of Security,* eds., Bruce Michael Bagley and Sergio Aguayo Quezada (New Brunswick, NJ: Transaction Publishers for the North-South Center, 1993), 142, but see 142–43.

27. Camp, *Military on the Democratic Stage,* 14–16.

28. Michael Bonser and Marshall Conley, "Canada, International Organization, and Human Rights," in *Canada and the New World Order: Facing the New Millennium,* eds., Michael Tucker, Raymond B. Blake, and P.E. Bryden (Toronto, ON: Irwin Publishing, 2000), 55–70. Also see

Andrew F. Cooper and Leslie A. Pal, "Human Rights and Security Policy," in *Border Crossings: The Internationalization of Canadian Public Policy,* eds., G. Bruce Doern, Leslie A. Pal, and Brian W. Tomlin (Toronto: Oxford University Press, 1996), 207–36.

29. Philippe C. Schmitter defines corporatism "as a system of interest intermediation in which the constituent units are organized into a limited number of similar, compulsory, non-competitive, hierarchically ordered and functionally differentiated categories, recognized or licensed (if not created) by the state and granted a deliberative representational monopoly within their respective categories in exchange for observing certain controls on their selection of leaders and articulation of demands and supports." See "Still the century of corporatism?" *The Review of Politics* 36, no. 1 (1974): 93–94, but broadly 85–131; on Latin variations, see Howard J. Wiarda, "Corporatism and Development in the Iberic–Latin World: Persistent Strains and New Variations," ibid., 3–33.

30. Emphasizing elite collaboration across various sectors in ethnically divided countries, consociationalism leads to grand coalitions, a mutual veto among constituting groups, representation and proportionality in elections and appointments, and autonomy for each segments in the group. See L.J. Boulle, *Constitutional Reform and the Apartheid State: Legitimacy, Consociationalism, and Control in South Africa* (New York, NY: St. Martin's Press, 1984), 46–51. The term was coined from the Latin, *consociare,* to join together; and utilized to describe interest intermediation first by David Apter, *The Political Kingdom in Uganda: A Study in Bureaucratic Nationalism* (Princeton, NJ: Princeton University Press, 1967); Arend Lijphart, "Typologies of Democratic Systems," *Comparative Political Studies* 1, no. 1 (April 1968): 3–44; ———, "Consociational Democracy," *World Politics* 21, no. 2 (January 1969): 207–25; and K. McRae, ed., *Consociational Democracy: Political Accommodation in Segmented Societies* (Toronto, ON: McClelland and Stewart, 1974). From Boulle, "Constitutional Reform and the Apartheid State," 66.

31. Francisco Madero, who led the revolutionaries, became president until 1913. See Camp, *Military on the Democratic Stage,* 15–18.

32. Ibid., 25.

33. Alicia Hernández Chávez, "Mexican Presidentialism: A Historical and Institutional Overview," *Mexican Studies/Estudios Mexicanos* 10, no. 1 (Winter 1994): 220–25.

34. Sergio Aguayo Quezada, "Revolutionary Nationalism and National Security in Mexico," 107–8.

35. Whitaker, "Politics of Security Intelligence, I," 653–59.

36. Ibid., 659–65.

37. On the evaporation of resistant corporatism, see Judith Teichman, "Neoliberalism and The Transformation of Mexican Authoritarianism," *Mexican Studies/Estudios Mexicanos* 13, no. 1 (Winter 1997): 121–47.

38. For a sense of how other Canadian groups operate in consociationalist ways, see Abigail Eisenberg, "Two Types of Pluralism," in *How Canadians Connect,* eds., Harvey Lazar and Tom McIntosh, *The Canada: The State of the Federation, 1998–99 Series* (Montreal and Kingston: McGill-Queen's University Press, 1999), chap. 3; and Margaret Prang, "Networks and Associations and the Nationalizing of Sentiment in English Canada," eds., R. Kenneth Carty and W. Peter Ward (Vancouver, BC: University of British Columbia Press, 1986), chap. 3.

39. Royal North West Mounted Police, established in 1873.

40. Steve Hewitt, "Royal Canadian Mounted Spy: The Secret Life of John Leopold/Jack Esselwein," *Intelligence and National Security* 15, no. 1 (Spring 2000): 146–47, but see 144–68.

41. Bruce Craig tells us of the September 5 defection. He was a cipher clerk in the Soviet embassy in Ottawa, worked under the embassy military attaché Colonel Nicolai Zabotin

who served the Soviet Military Intelligence (GRU), and "stole an impressive cache documentation that established the existence of several espionage rings in Canada." See "A Matter of Espionage: Alger Hiss, Harry Dexter White, and Igor Gouzenko—the Canadian connection reassessed," *Intelligence and National Security* 15, no. 2 (Summer 2000): 213–14.

42. "Security Intelligence Making in Canada, I," 653.

43. Geoffrey R. Weller, "Assessing Canadian Intelligence Literature: 1980–2000," *International Journal of Intelligence and Counterintelligence* 14, no. 3 (Fall 2001): 51, but see 49–61.

44. See Larry Hanan's "Access to the Inside: An Assessment of 'Canada's Security Service: A History'," *Intelligence and National Security* 8, no. 3 (July 1993): 152–53.

45. Martin Rudner, "The Future of Canada's Defence Intelligence," *International Journal of Intelligence and Counterintelligence* 15, no. 4 (Winter 2002–2003): 542–43, but see 540–64.

46. Elinor C. Sloan, *Security and Defence in the Terrorist Era: Canada and North America* (Montreal and Kingston, Canada: McGill-Queen's University Press, 2005), 140. She erroneously ascribes the agreement to Theodore Roosevelt.

47. Personal observations of a participant, Escott Reid, "Forming the north Atlantic Alliance, 1949," in *Canadian Foreign Policy: Selected Cases,* eds., Don Munton and John Kirton (Scarborough, ON: Prentice-Hall, 1991), 27–42.

48. At least this is Ann Denholm Crosby's argument. See *Dilemmas in Defence Decision-making: Constructing Canada's Role in NORAD, 1958–96* (London: Macmillan Press, 1998), 23–25. Also see Andrew Richter, *Avoiding Armageddon: Canadian Military Strategy and Nuclear Weapons, 1950–63* (Vancouver: University of British Columbia, 2002), esp. chap. 2.

49. Peter Gill gives a thumbs-up SIRC assessment in "Symbolic or Real? The Impact of the Canadian Security Intelligence Review Committee, 1984–88," *Intelligence and National Security* 4, no. 3 (July 1989): 55–75.

50. Steve Hewitt, "Reforming the Canadian Security State: The Royal Canadian Mounted Police Security State and the 'Key Sectors' Program," *Intelligence and National Security* 17, no. 4 (Winter 2002): 166, but see 165–84.

51. The former circumscribing activities within the public interest, the latter in terms of agency efficiency and effectiveness, thus producing a potentially inconsistent and self-contradictory intelligence framework. See Whitaker, "Security Intelligence Making in Canada, I," 650.

52. Whitaker, "The Politics of Security Intelligence Policy Making in Canada: II, 1984–91," *Intelligence and National Security* 7, no. 2 (April 1992): 53–76.

53. Roy Rempel, "Canada's Parliamentary Oversight of Security and Intelligence," *International Journal of Intelligence and Counterintelligence* 17, no. 4 (Winter 2004–05): 635–36, but see 634–54.

54. See Peter Chalk and William Rosenau, *Confronting the "Enemy Within": Security Intelligence, the Policy, and Counterterrorism in Four Democracies* (Santa Monica, CA: RAND Corporation, 2004), 26–27.

55. Chalk and Rosenau, *Confronting the "Enemy Within,"* 27–28.

56. Ibid., 637 for the first quote, and 652 for the last two.

57. Farson, "Parliament and its Servants: Their Roles in Scrutinizing Canadian Intelligence," 226, the two OAG deficiencies from 235 and 240.

58. Borrowing from Thomas Kuhn and Alexander George, James J. Wirtz proposes a post–Cold War counterpart. See "The Intelligence Paradigm," *Intelligence and National Security* 4, no. 4 (October 1989): 829–37.

59. On this point, see Hugh Segal, "Geopolitical Integrity for Canada," in *Geopolitical Integrity,* ed., Segal (Montreal: Institute for Research on Public Policy, 2005), 31. He points out at least one tension in Canadian–U.S. *interoperability:* Canada's inclination toward peacekeeping, United States toward military engagement. Douglas L. Bland and Sean M. Maloney elaborate more on this tension. See *Campaigns for International Security: Canada's Defence Policy at the Turn of the Century* (Montreal-Kingston, Canada: McGill-Queen's University Press, 2004).

60. See Ronald J. Daniels, "Introduction," in *The Security of Freedom: Essays on Canada's Anti-Terrorism Bill,* eds., Daniels, Patrick Macklem, and Kent Roach (Toronto, ON: University of Toronto Press, 2001), chap. 1; quote from 3, bill, provisions from 4.

61. Ibid., 48–53.

62. Reference to the *Charter of Rights and Freedom.* Also see Gary T. Trotter, "The Anti-Terrorism Bill and Preventative Restraints on Liberty," *Security of Freedom,* 239, quote from 246–47.

63. Even as this is being drafted, the entire police force of Tijuana, the key metropolitan across the San Diego border, is being fired for alleged drug connections. See Duncan Kennedy, "Mexican Police 'probed on drugs'," *BBC News* (October 6, 2006), http://news.bbc.co.uk/2/hi/americas/5415018.stm.

64. He told the *Washington Post* correspondent, "We are Seeing the Beginning [of the] Iraqification of Afghanistan." See Glen Kessler and Michael Abramowitz, "Bush Brings Afghanistan, Pakistan to the Table: President is Pushing Karzai and Musharraf Toward Commonalities," *Washington Post* (September 27, 2006): A22. Also see Jim Lobe, "'War on Terror' Returning to its Cradle," *Asia Times* (October 5, 2006), available at http://www.atimes.com/atimes/South_Asia/JJO5Df02.html.

65. See Jorge Chabat for a different conclusion from a study of economic integration, "Mexico's Foreign Policy and NAFTA: The Tools of Interdependence," in *Bridging the Border: Transforming Mexico–U.S. Relations,* eds., Rodolfo O. de la Garza and Jesús Velasco (Lanham, MD: Rowman and Littlefield, 1997), chap. 2. Almost a decade earlier, before NAFTA talks began, other authors discussed how to overcome interdependence, obviously proposing economic integration. See the collection of Works in Report of the Bilateral Commission on the Future of United States–Mexican Relations, *The Challenge of Interdependence: Mexico and the United States* (Lanham, MD: Rowman and Littlefield, 1989).

66. Richard Feinberg, "The Political Economy of United States' Free Trade Arrangements," Paper, Berkeley APEC Study Center (BASC), University of California, Berkeley, March 21–22, 2003.

CHAPTER 8

1. This is the original and classic work on neofunctionalism, by Ernst B. Haas, *The Uniting of Europe: Political, Social, and Economic Forces, 1950–1957* (Stanford, CA: Stanford University Press, 1958).

2. Leon Lindberg, *The Political Dynamics of European Integration* (Stanford, CA: Stanford University Press, 1963).

3. Louis Tsoukalis, ed., *Europe, America, and the World Economy* (Oxford, UK: Basil Blackwell, for the College of Europe, 1986).

4. Barbara Hogenboom, *Mexico and the NAFTA Environmental Debate* (Utrecth, The Netherlands: International Books, 1998); Pierre Marc Johnson and André Beaulieu, *The Environment and NAFTA: Understanding and Implementing the New Continental Law* (Washington,

DC: Island Press, 1965), and Christopher Thomas and Gregory A. Tereposky, "The NAFTA and The Side Agreement on Environmental Cooperation—Addressing Environmental Concerns in a North American Regime," *Journal of World Trade* 27, no. 6; and for labor see Joaquin F. Otero, "The North American Agreement on Labor Cooperation: An Assessment of its First Year's Implementation," *Columbia Journal of Transnational Law* 33 (1995): 637–62.

5. On differences, see Andrew Moravcsik, "Negotiating the Single European Act." In *The European Community: Decision-Making and Institutional Change,* eds., Robert O. Keohane and Stanley Hoffmann (Boulder, CO: Westview Press, 1991), 41–84.

6. This came out mostly in U.S. relations. Michael Tucker and others document the internationalism highlighted by Trudeau with the rest of the world. See *Canadian Foreign Policy: Contemporary Issues and Themes* (Toronto, ON: McGraw-Hill Ryerson Ltd., 1980).

7. Congress of the United States, Office of Technological Assessment, "Two Traditions, One Continent: Labor Relations and Labor Markets in Mexico and the United States," in *U.S.–Mexico Trade: Pulling Together or Pulling Apart?* (Washington, DC: US Government Printing Office, 1992).

8. On punitive U.S. trade policies, see Jagdish Bhagwati and Hugh Patrick, eds., *Aggressive Unilateralism: America's 301 Trade Policy and the World Trading System* (Ann Arbor, MI: University of Michigan, 1990); and Greg Mastel, *American Trade Policy After the Uruguay Round* (Armonk, NY: M.E. Sharpe, 1996).

9. Terms from Richard E. Feinberg, *Summitry in the Americas: A Report* (Washington, DC: Institute of International Economics, 1997), chap. 1.

10. Illustrated by Kenneth N. Waltz, *Theory of International Politics* (Menlo Park, CA: Addison-Wesley, 1979).

11. Forcefully brought out by Hans J. Morgenthau, *Politics Among Nations: The Struggle for Power and Peace* (New York, NY: Alfred Knopf, 1948).

12. See Michael Doyle's discussion, "Liberalism and World Politics," *American Political Science Review* 80, no. 4 (December 1986): 1150–69.

CHAPTER 9

1. Council on Foreign Relations, *Building a North American Community, Independent Task Force Report #53* (New York, NY: Council on Foreign Relations, 2005).

2. Purposeful analogy with Strobe Talbot's *Deadly Gambits:The Reagan Admninistration and the Stalemate in Nuclear Arms Control* (New York, NY: Knopf, 1984).

3. In turn prompting the same old remedial proposals he offered time after time. Even as this piece is being written, the local newspaper raises the same subject for the umpteenth time. See Victor Davis Hanson, "With Help and Tough Love," *Philadelphia Inquirer* (January 30, 2007): A15.

4. James Rosenau, *Along the Domestic-Foreign Frontier: Exploring Governance in a Turbulent World* (Cambridge, UK: Cambridge University Press, 1997).

5. Samuel P. Huntington comes closest to dramatizing the central value incompatibilities. See Samuel P. Huntington, "The Hispanic Challenge," *Foreign Policy* no. 141 (March/April 2004): 30–45; and *Who are We? The Challenges of American Identity* (New York, NY: Simon and Schuster, 2004).

6. This is the central theme in Imtiaz Hussain, "Canadian Immigration, Mexican Emigration and a North American Regional Interpretation," *Journal of International Migration and Integration* 6, no. 1 (Winter 2005): 81–92.

Appendix: Investigative Questions

QUESTIONS

1. How would you characterize the current bilateral relations?
2. What are the two main issues characterizing this relationship?
3. How has Homeland Security affected this bilateral relationship since 9/11, if at all?
4. Do you see visible security-related changes in this bilateral relationship? If so, in what way?
5. In your opinion, have economic ties suffered from the post–9/11 security emphasis? If yes, how?
6. Is NAFTA compatible with the new security priorities? Please justify answer.
7. Have there been disagreements with the Canadian/Mexican/U.S. authorities over the interpretation of DHS regulations? Please elaborate.
8. Have there been disagreements with the Canadian/Mexican/U.S. authorities over the implementation of the DHS regulations? Please elaborate.
9. How can the bilateral relations be improved to your satisfaction? In other words, what steps must the two sides take (that have not yet been taken) to enhance bilateral economic relations?
10. How can the third partner affect this bilateral relationship?
11. Where do you see this bilateral relationship headed in five years?
12. Will bilateral economic relations flourish under the security umbrella? Please justify.
13. Taking all into account, are you satisfied with current bilateral relations? Please justify.
14. How would you characterize the other two North American bilateral relations?
15. What in your view are the two main issues characterizing these other bilateral relationship?
16. How has U.S. Homeland Security affected these other bilateral relationships since 9/11?
17. Are there visible changes in the other bilateral relations given the security priority since 9/11?
18. Have economic ties suffered from the security emphasis since 9/11? If yes, in what ways?

19. How do you see economic and security interests adjusting in this specific bilateral relation?
20. How do you see a similar adjustment in the other two North American bilateral relations?
21. Where do you see these other bilateral relationships headed five years from now?
22. Will these other economic relations flourish given the new security emphasis? Please justify.
23. Are you satisfied with the state of the other bilateral relations currently? Please justify.
24. How do you see the trilateral NAFTA relationship presently?
25. Is your view more or less optimistic after 9/11?
26. If you see problems in this partnership, what would be the top few sources of these problem?
27. If you see such problems, do you also see resolutions for them? Please elaborate the modalities.
28. How symmetrical do you see the nature (not substance) of the trilateral negotiations to be?
29. Did 9/11 alter this in any way?
30. Is asymmetry a problem in the first place?
31. Do you believe your country can do more for this trilateral relationship?
32. What in your opinion could the other two countries do to enhance this trilateral partnership?
33. How does DHS impact security policy in each neighboring country?
34. Does DHS influence the harmonization of immigration, border policing, and legal practices between the United States and the other neighbor?
35. Is DHS-based security a bilateral or trilateral phenomenon, or a mixture of both?
36. Are there any economic-political trade-offs within either of the U.S. neighbors in pursuing trilateral relations?
37. What strategies may lessen the asymmetrical bent across North America?

Bibliography

Ackleson, Jason. "Fencing in Failure: Effective Border Control is not Achieved by Building More Fences." *Migration Policy in Focus* 4, no. 2 (April 2005).

Anderson, Scott. "The Evolution of the Canadian Intelligence Establishment, 1945–1950." *Intelligence and National Security* 9, no. 3 (July 1994): 448–71.

Andreas, Peter. "A Tale of Two Borders: The US–Canada and US–Mexico Lines After 9-11." In *The Rebordering of North America: Integration and Exclusion in a New Security Context.* Edited by Peter Andreas and Thomas J. Bierstecker, 1–23. New York: Routledge, 2003.

———. "Redrawing the Line: Borders and Security in the Twenty-first Century." *International Security* 28, no. 2 (2003): 78–111.

———. "The Mexicanization of the U.S.–Canada Border." *International Journal* 60, no. 2 (Spring 2005): 449–62.

———. "Politics on Edge: Managing the US–Mexico Border." *Current History* 105, no. 688 (February 2006): 64–68.

Andrew, Christopher. "The Growth of the Australian Intelligence Community and the Anglo American Connection." *Intelligence and National Security* 4, no. 2 (April 1989): 213–56.

Apter, David. *The Political Kingdom in Uganda: A Study in Bureaucratic Nationalism.* Princeton, NJ: Princeton University Press, 1967.

Ariana, Ana. "How the Street Gangs Took Central America." *Foreign Affairs* 84, no. 3 (May/June 2005): 98–110.

Associated Press. "Memos Detail 74 CIA Landings in Canada" (February 23, 2006).

Avis, Captain Peter C. *Comparing National Security Approaches to Maritime Security in the Post–9/11 Era.* Halifax: Centre for Foreign Policy Studies, Dalhousie University, 2005.

Bacevich, Andrew. *American Empire: The Realities and Consequences of U.S. Diplomacy.* Cambridge, MA: Harvard University Press, 2002.

Baker III, James, and Lee H. Hamilton. *The Iraq Study Group Report: The Way Forward, A New Approach.* New York, NY: Vintage Books, 2006.

Baldwin, David A. "Canadian–American Relations: Myth and Reality." In *Canadian American Relations: The Politics and Economics of Interdependence: A Conference Report.* Edited by David A. Baldwin and Frank Smallwood, 19–44. Dartmouth, NH: The Public Affairs Center, 1967.

Barger, Deborah C. "It is Time to Transform, Not Reform, US Intelligence." *SAIS Review* 24, no. 1 (Winter–Spring 2004): 26–30.

Barlow, Maude. "Dinosaurs and Deep Integration: Standing up to the American Nightmare." *Our Times* 24, no. 5 (2005): 29–33.

Bartra, Roger. "Revolutionary Nationalism and National Security in Mexico," In *Mexico in Search of Security.* Edited by Bruce Michael Bagley and Sergio Aguayo Quezada. New Brunswick, NJ: Transaction Publishers for the North-South Center, 1993.

Benjamin, Daniel, Steven Simon, and Richjard Falkenrath. "The War of Intended Consequences." *Foreign Affairs* 85, no. 2 (March/April 2006).

Berkowitz, Bruce. "Intelligence For the Homeland." *SAIS Review* 24, no. 1 (Winter–Spring 2004): 1–6.

Bhagwati, Jagdish, and Hugh Patrick., eds. *Aggressive Unilateralism: America's 301 Trade Policy and the World Trading System.* Ann Arbor, MI: University of Michigan, 1990.

Billar, David B. "Canada and the United States: Defense Cooperation in U.S. Northern Command." In *The Homeland Security Papers: Stemming the Tide of Terror.* Edited by Michael W. Ritz, Ralph G. Hensley, Jr., and James C. "Chris" Whitmore, chap. 10. Maxwell, AL: US Counterproliferation Center, 2004.

Blair, Bruce G. *Global Zero Alert for Nuclear Forces.* Washington, DC: Brookings Institution, 1995.

Blais, J.J. "The Political Accountability of Intelligence Agencies–Canada." *Intelligence and National Security* 4, no. 1 (January 1989): 108–18.

Blanchfield, Mike. "Government, Not Generals, Will Decide Mission: Harper." *National Post* (March 8, 2006).

———. "52% of Canadians Support Operation." *National Post* (March 4, 2006).

Bland, Douglas, ed. *Canada Without Armed Forces.* Kingston, ON: Queen's University Press, 2003.

Blomfield, Adrian. "Russia Suspends Arms Pact." *National Post* (April 27, 2007a).

———. "Russia to Aim Missiles at City 'Targets.'" *National Post* (June 4, 2007b).

———. "Russia, China Flex Military Muscle." *National Post* (August 18, 2007c).

Boag, Peter. "Restore Unity Along the U.S.–Canada Border." *Aviation Week and Space Technology* (January 23, 2006).

Bohrnstedt, George W. "A Quick Method of Determining the Reliability and Validity of Multiple Item Scales." *American Sociological Review* 34 (1969): 542–48.

Bolan, Kim. "Airport Staff Screening Insufficient, Inquiry Told." *National Post* (June 2, 2007).

Bonser, Michael, and Marshall Conley. "Canada, International Organization, and Human Rights." In *Canada and the New World Order: Facing the New Millennium.* Edited by Michael Tucker, Raymond B. Blake, and P.E. Bryden, 55–70. Toronto, ON: Irwin Publishing, 2000.

Boot, Max. "The Case For an American Empire." *Weekly Standard* (October 15, 2001): 4.

Border Policy Research Institute. "Diversity of the Ports-of-Entry Along the 49th Parallel." *Border Policy Brief* 2, no. 5, (September 1–5, 2007).

Boulle, L.J. *Constitutional Reform and the Apartheid State: Legitimacy, Consociationalism, and Control in South Africa.* New York, NY: St. Martin's Press, 1984.

Brittan, Victoria, and Gillian Slovo. *Guantánamo: 'Honor Bound to Defend Freedom'.* London: Oberon, 2004.

Brookes, Adam. "US Military Plans for 'Long War.'" *BBC News* (February 4, 2006). Available at http://news.bbc.co.uk/2/hi/americas/4678942.stm.

Bureau of Transportation Statistics. *Issue Brief* no. 13 (December 2005).

Burns, Roberts. "Combat Death Tolls at a High: Worst 4 Months for US; Shift to Urban Fight Cited." *Philadelphia Inquirer* (February 8, 2007): A1–A2. Bush, George. The National Security Strategy of the United States of America. Washington, DC: The White House, September 2002.

Cadicott, Helen. *The New Nuclear Danger: George W. Bush's Military-Industrial Complex.* New York, NY: The New Press, 2002.

Camp, Roderic Ai. *Generals in the Palacio: The Military in Modern Mexico.* New York, NY: Oxford University Press, 1992.

———. *Mexico's Military on the Democratic Stage.* Westport, CT: Praeger Security International, 2005.

———. *Politics in Mexico: The Democratic Consolidation.* 5th ed. New York, NY: Oxford University Press, 2007.

Campbell, Anthony. "Canada–United States Intelligence Relations and 'Information Sovereignty.'" In *Coping With the American Colossus.* Edited by D. Carment, Fen Osler Hampson, and Norman Hillmer. Toronto, ON: Oxford University Press, 2003.

Canadian Council of Chief Executives. *Building a 21st Century Canada–United States Partnership in North America.* Ottawa, 2004.

Canadian Press. "Cdn. General Resigns Over Afghan Deployment." Available at www.ctv.ca/servlet/ArticleNews/story/CTVnews/1045260261742_40669461// (accessed May 2, 2006).

CanWest News Service. "Quebecers Want Canadian Troops Brought Home." *Vancouver Province* (August 24, 2007).

CBC News. "Senator Fires Back at U.S. Family Upset with Seal Hunt" (March 17, 2006). www.cbc.ca (accessed September 17, 2007).

Carter, Lee. "Canada in Protest Over Rendition." *BBC News* (October 7, 2006). Available at http://news.bbc.co.uk/2/hi/americas/5415320.stm.

Carey, Moer L., ed. *The Military Industrial Complex and U.S. Foreign Policy.* Pullman, WA: Washington State University Press, 1969.

Chabat, Jorge. "Mexico's Foreign Policy and NAFTA: The Tools of Interdependence." In *Bridging the Border: Transforming Mexico–U.S. Relations.* Edited by Rodolfo O. de la Garza and Jesús Velasco, chap. 2. Lanham, MD: Rowman and Littlefield, 1997.

Chalk, Peter, and William Roseanau. *Confronting The 'Enemy Within': Security Intelligence, the Policy, and Counterterrorism in Four Democracies.* Santa Monica, CA: RAND Corporation, 2004.

Chambers, Edward J., and Peter H. Smith., eds. *NAFTA in the New Millennium.* La Jolla, CA: Center for U.S. Mexican Studies, University of California, San Diego, and Edmonton, AB: The University of Alberta Press, 2002.

Charles, Douglas M. "'Before the Colonel Arrived': Hoover, Donovan, Roosevelt, and the Origins of American Central Intelligence." *Intelligence and National Security* 20, no. 2 (June 2005): 225–37.

"China 'to dwarf G7 states by 2050.'" *BBC News* (March 6, 2006). Available at http://news.bbc.co.uk/2/hi/business/4770590.stm.

Chivers, C.J. "Putin Proposes Alternatives for Missile Defense System." *New York Times* 9 (2007).

Choudhry, Sujit. "Protecting Equality in the Face of Terror: Ethnic and Racial Profiling and s.15 of the Charter." In *The Security of Freedom: Essays on Canada's Anti-Terrorism Bill.*

Edited by Ronald J. Daniels, Patrick Macklem, and Kent Roach, 367–82. Toronto, ON: University of Toronto Press, 2001.

Clarkson, Stephen. *Uncle Sam and Us: Globalization, Neoconservatism and the Canadian State.* Toronto, ON: University of Toronto Press, 2004.

———. "Smart Borders and the Rise of Bilateralism." *International Journal* 61, no. 3 (Summer 2006): 588–609.

"Clogged Border? The Border: How Bad is it?" *The Bar-Code Border* 2, no. 34 (June 15, 2003).

Cody, Howard. "US–Canada Trade, Defense and Border Issues Since September 11: The View from Canada." In *Perspectives on US–Canada Relations Since 9/11: Four Essays.* Edited by Cody, Martin Lubin, Donald Caccioletta, and Marie Christine Therrien, 3–15. Orono, ME: The Canadian–American Center, 2003.

Cohen, Andrew. "Canadian–American Relations: Does Canada Matter in Washington? Does it Matter if Canada doesn't Matter?" *Canada Among Nations 2002: A Fading Power,* 34–48. Toronto, ON: Oxford University Press, 2002.

———. *While Canada Slept: How we Lost our Place in the World.* Toronto, ON: McLelland and Stewart, 2003.

Conference of Defence Associations Institute. "Understanding the Crisis in Canadian Security and Defence." Ottawa: CDAI, March 2005.

Cooper, Andrew F., and Leslie A. Pal. "Human Rights and Security Policy." In *Border Crossings: The Internationalization of Canadian Public Policy.* Edited by G. Bruce Doern, Leslie A. Pal, and Brian W. Tomlin, 207–36. Toronto: Oxford University Press, 1996.

Cornelius, Wayne. "Controlling 'Unwanted Immigration': Lessons from the United States, 1993–2004." *Journal of Ethnic and Migration Studies* 31, no. 4 (2005): 775–94.

Cornelius, Wayne, T. Tsuda, P. Martin, and J. Hollifield. *Controlling Immigration: A Global Perspective.* Stanford, CA: Stanford University Press, 2004.

Council on Foreign Relations. "Building a North American Community." *Independent Task force Report No. 53.* New York, NY: Council on Foreign Relations, 2005.

Crabb, Cecil V., Jr., and Kevin V. Mulcahy. "The National Security Council and the Shaping of US Foreign Policy." *Journal of Intelligence and Counter Intelligence* 3, no. 2 (1989): 153–68.

Craig, Bruce. "A Matter of Espionage: Alger Hiss, Harry Dexter White, and Igor Gouzenko—the Canadian Connection Reassessed." *Intelligence and National Security* 15, no. 2 (Summer 2000): 213–14.

Craske, Nikki. "Dismantling or Retrenchment? Salinas and Corporatism." In *Dismantling the Mexican State?* Edited by Rob Aitken, Craske, Gareth A. Jones, and David E. Stansfield, 78–92. Houndsmills, Basingstoke, Hampshire, UK: St. Martin's Press, 1996.

Crosby, Ann Denholm. *Dilemmas in Defence Decision-making: Constructing Canada's Role in NORAD, 1958–96.* London: Macmillan Press, 1998.

Curtis, Richard F., and Elton F. Jackson. "Multiple Indicators of Survey Research." *American Journal of Sociology* 68 (1962): 195–204.

Dahl, Robert A. *Pluralist Democracy in the United States: Conflict and Consent.* Chicago, IL: Rand McNally, 1967.

———. *Democracy in the United States: Promise and Performance.* Chicago, IL: Rand McNally, 1976.

DAMF Consultants Inc., with L-P Tardif and Associates. *The Cumulative Impact of U.S. Import Compliance Programs at the Canada/U.S. Land Border on the Canadian Trucking Industry.* Ottawa: Transport Canada, 2005.

Daniel, Donald C.F., Peter Dombrowski, and Rodger A. Payne. "The Bush Doctrine is Dead: Long Live the Bush Doctrine." *Orbis* 49, no. 2 (Spring 2005): 199–212.

Daniels, Ronald J. "Introduction." In *The Security of Freedom: Essays on Canada's Anti-Terrorism Bill.* Edited by Daniels, Patrick Macklem, and Kent Roach, chap. 1. Toronto, ON: University of Toronto Press, 2001.

d'Arcy, Michael, Michael O'Hanlon, Peter Orszag, Jeremy Shapiro, and James Steinberg. *Protecting the Homeland 2006/2007.* Washington, DC: Brookings Institution Press, 2006.

Den Tandt, Michael. "Continental Missile Shield Still An Option, O'Connor Says." *Globe and Mail. Toronto Daily* (February 24, 2006).

Den Tandt, Michael, and Clark Campbell. "Canadian Takes Charge of Coalition in Kandahar." *Globe and Mail* (March 1, 2006).

Deutsch, Karl, et al. *Political Community and the North American Area: International Organization in the Light of Historical Experience.* Princeton, NJ: Princeton University Press, 1957.

Domínguez, Jorge, and Rafael Fernandez de Castro. *The United States and Mexico: Between Partnership and Conflict.* New York, NY: Routledge, 2001.

Donnelly, Sally B. "When can the U.S. go?" *Time* (February 27, 2006): 15.

"Don't dictate to me, Canadian leader tells US." *CNN* (December 14, 2005). Available at http://edition.cnn.com/2005/WORLD/americas/12/14/canada.martin.reut.index.html.

Dougherty, James E., and Robert L. Pfaltzgraff, Jr., eds. "Theories of International Integration, Regionalism, and Alliance Cohesion." In *Contending Theories of International Relations: A Comprehensive Survey.* Edited by Dougherty and Pfaltzgraff, 431–59. New York, NY: Harper and Row, 1990.

Doyle, Michael. "Liberalism and World Politics." *American Political Science Review* 80, no. 4 (December 1986): 1151–1170.

Eisenberg, Abigail. "Two Types of Pluralism: How Canadians Connect." In *Canada: The State of the Federation, 1998–99 Series.* Edited by Harvey Lazar and Tom McIntosh, chap. 3. Montreal and Kingston: McGill-Queen's University Press, 1999.

English, Allan D. *Understanding Military Culture: A Canadian Perspective.* Montréal and Kingston, Canada: McGill-Queen's University Press, 2004.

Fact Sheet. "HHS in 2001." Available at http://www.hhs.gov/news/press/2001pres/20011231.html.

Fact Sheet. "US Customs and Border Protection Actions Taken Since 9/11." *DHS Press Release* (September 17, 2004).

Farson, Stuart. "Parliament and Its Servants: Their Role in Scrutinizing Canadian Intelligence." *Intelligence and National Security* 15, no. 2 (Summer 2000): 225–58.

———. "From '49th Parallel' to 'Security Perimeter': Changing Conceptions, Values and Structures Along the U.S.–Canada Border." In *Homeland Security: Protecting America's Targets.* Edited by John F. Forest, 44–59. Westport, CT: Praeger Security International, 2006.

Feinberg, Richard. *Summitry in the Americas: A Progress Report.* Washington, DC: International Institute of Economics, 1997.

———. "The Political Economy of United States' Free Trade Arrangements." Paper, Berkeley APEC Study Center (BASC), University of California, Berkeley. March 21–22, 2003.

Fergusson, Ian. *United States–Canada Trade and Economic Relationship: Prospects and Challenges.* Washington, DC: Congressional Research Service, Library of Congress, 2006.

Fergusson, James. "A Strange Decision in a Strange Land: The Irrelevance of Ottawa's Missile Defence 'no'." In *The Dilemmas of American Strategic Primacy.* Edited by David S. McDonough and Douglas A. Ross, 9–34. Toronto, ON: Royal Canadian Military Institute, 2005.

Flynn, Stephen, and Jeanne Kirkpatrick. "Rethinking The Role of The US Mexican Border in the Post–9/11 World." *Written Testimony before a hearing of the Committee on Foreign Relations.* United States Senate, March 23, 2004.

"Focus Shifts North Among Terror Fears." *USA Today* (December 18, 2006): 4a.

Freeman, Lauris. "Déjà vu:la política antidrogas en la relación México–Estados Unidos." *Foreign Affairs en Español* 8, no. 1 (enero-marzo, 2008): 16–8.

"Fresh Thought, Authoritative Data, and Global Reach: The US–Mexico Border." *Migration Information Source* (June 1, 2006). Available at http://www.migrationinformation.org/Feature/print.cfm?ID=407.

Frey, Frederick. "The Problem of Actor Designation in Political Analysis." *Comparative Politics* 17, no. 2 (January 1985): 127–52.

Fulford, Robert. "Canada's Emotional Necessity." *National Post Canadian Newspaper* (December 17, 2005).

Gaddis, John Lewis. *Strategies of Containment: A Critical Appraisal of Postwar National Security Policy.* Oxford, UK: Oxford University Press, 1982.

———. "A Grand Strategy of Transformation." *Foreign Policy* no. 133 (November–December 2002): 50–57.

Galloway, Gloria, and Ingrid Peritz. "Troops Won't Stay Unless All Parties Agree, PM says." *Globe and Mail* (June 23, 2007).

Ganster, Paul, and Alan Sweedler. "The United States–Mexican Border Region: Security and Interdependence." *United States–Mexico Border Statistics Since 1900.* Edited by David Lovey. Los Angeles: University of California Los Angeles, Latin American Center Publications, 1990.

Ganster, Paul, and David Loret. *Borders and Border Politics in a Globalizing World.* Lanham, MD: S.R. Books, 2004.

Gereffi, Gary, and Martha Martinez. "Mexico's Economic Transformation Under NAFTA." *Mexico's Democracy at Work.* Edited by Russell Crandall, Guadalupe Páz, and Riordan Roett. Boulder, CO: Lynne Rienner, 2005.

Gibbins, Roger. "Meaning and Significance of the Canadian–American Border." *Borders and Border Politics in a Globalizing World.* Edited by Paul Ganster and David E. Lovey, chap. 10. Lanham, MD: S.R. Books, 2004.

Gill, Peter. "Symbolic or Real? The Impact of the Canadian Security Intelligence Review Committee, 1984–88." *Intelligence and National Security* 4, no. 3 (July 1989): 55–75.

———. *Policing Politics: Security Intelligence and the Liberal Democratic State.* London: Frank Cass, 1994.

Gilpin, Robert. "The Politics of Transnational Economic Relations." *Transnational Relations and World Politics.* Edited by Robert O. Keohane and Joseph S. Nye, 48–69. Cambridge, MA: Harvard University Press, 1972.

———. "Integration and Disintegration on the North American Continent." *International Organization* 28, no. 4 (Autumn 1974): 851–74.

———. *U.S. Power and the Multinational Corporation: The Political Economy of Foreign Direct Investment.* New York, NY: Basic Books, 1975.

Globerman, Steven. "The Impact of 9/11 on Canada–US Trade." Working Paper, Center for International Business Working Group. Western Washington University, 2005.

Goodman, Melvyn A. "9/11: The Failure of Strategic Intelligence." *Intelligence and National Security* 18, no. 4 (2003): 59–71.

Gordon, James. "Post 9/11 Security Measures Cost $2.6b." *National Post* (July 9, 2007).

Government of Canada. Department of Foreign Affairs. Government Response to the Recommendations of the Standing Committee on Foreign Affairs and International Trade on Canada's Nuclear Disarmament and Non-Proliferation Policy, 1999. As at www.dfait-maeci.gc.ca/nucchallenge/ANNEXB-en.asp (accessed May 2, 2006).

Government of Canada. Department of Foreign Affairs. Canada's Approach to the 2005 NPT Review Conference, 2005. From www.dfait-maeci.gc.ca/arms/2005NPTclosing-en.asp (accessed May 2, 2006).

Government of Canada. Government of. Department of National Defence. "Canadian army hosts conference of American Armies," November 14, 2003. Available at http://www.army.dnd.ca/.

Government of Canada. House of Commons. *Getting Back to Business.* Eds., S. and T. Standing Committee on Industry, Susan Whelan, Chair. Ottawa, 2001.

Government of Canada. Senate. *Canada's Coastlines: The Longest Under-defended Borders in The World.* 2 vols. Report of the Standing Senate Committee on National Security and Defence. Sen. Colin Kenny, Chair. October 2003.

Government of Canada. Senate. "Borderline insecure." Report of the Standing Senate Committee on National Security and Defence. Senator Colin Kenny, Chair. June 2005.

Government of Canada. Senate. Standing Senate Committee on National Security and Defence. *The Myth of Security at Canada's Airports.* Ottawa, 2003.

Government of Canada. Senate. Standing Senate Committee on National Security and Defence. *Canadian Security Guide Book: An Update of Security Problems in Search of Solutions.* Ottawa: Government of Canada, 2004.

Government of Canada. Senate. Standing Senate Committee on National Security and Defence. *Borderline Insecure: Canada's Land Border Crossings are Key to Canada's Security and Prosperity. Why the Lack of Urgency to Fix Them? What Will Happen if We Don't?* Ottawa: Government of Canada, 2005.

Grabo, Cynthia M. *Anticipating Surprise: Analysis for Strategic Warning.* Washington, DC: Joint Military Intelligence, 2002.

Granatstein, J.L. *The Importance of Being Less Earnest: Promoting Canada's National Interests Through Tighter Ties with the US.* Toronto, ON: CD Howe Institute, 2003.

———. *Whose War is it? How Canada Can Survive in the post–9/11 World.* Toronto, ON: A Phyllis Bruce Book, HarperCollins Publishers Ltd, 2007.

Grinspun, Ricardo, and Maxwell A. Cameron., eds. *The Political Economy of North American Free Trade.* New York, NY: St. Martin's Press, 1993.

Haas, Ernst B. *The Uniting of Europe: Political Economical, and Social Forces, 1950–1957.* Stanford, CA: Stanford University Press, 1958.

Haggard, Stephen, and Guadalupe González González. "The United States and Mexico: A Pluralistic Security Community?" In *Security Communities.* Edited by Emanuel Adler and Michael Barnett, 295–332. Cambridge, UK: Cambridge University Press, 1998.

Hamilton, Daniel. "Societal Security: Implications for the United States." *Protecting the Homeland: European Approaches to Societal Security.* Edited by D. Hamilton, et al. Washington, DC: Transatlantic Relations, 2005.

Hamilton, Daniel S., Bengt Sundelius, and Jesper Gronvall. *Protecting the Homeland: European Approaches to Societal Security.* Washington, DC: Center for Transatlantic Relations, 2005.

Hanant, Larry. "Access to the Inside: An Assessment of 'Canada's Security Service: A History'." *Intelligence and National Security* 8, no. 3 (July 1993): 149–59.

Hanson, Victor Davis. Hanson. "With help and tough love." *Philadelphia Inquirer* (January 30, 2007): A15.

Harding, Luke. "Russia Claims New Missile Can Thwart U.S. Defences." *Globe and Mail* (May 30, 2007).

Hardy, Quentin. "Inside Dope." *Forbes* (2003): 10.

Harrison, Reginald J. *Pluralism and Corporatism: The Political Evolution of Modern Democracies.* London: Allen and Unwin, 1980.

Harvey, Frank P. "Canada's Addiction to American Security: The Illusion of Choice in the War on Terrorism." *The American Review of Canadian Studies* 35, no. 2 (2005): 265–95.

Hastedt, Gelnn. "Controlling Intelligence: The Role of the D.C.I." *Journal of Intelligence and Counter Intelligence* 1, no. 4 (1986): 25–40.

Hernández Chávez, Alicia. "Mexican Presidentialism: A Historical and Institutional Overview." *Mexican Studies/Estudios Mexicanos* 10, no. 1 (Winter 1994): 220–25.

Hewitt, Steve. "Royal Canadian Mounted Spy: The Secret Life of John Leopold/Jack Esselwein." *Intelligence and National Security* 15, no. 1 (Spring 2000): 144–68.

———. "Reforming the Canadian Security State: The Royal Canadian Mounted Police Security State and the 'Key Sectors' Program." *Intelligence and National Security* 17, no. 4 (Winter 2002): 165–84.

Heymann, Philip. *Terrorism and America: A Common Sense Strategy for a Democratic Society.* Cambridge, MA: MIT Press, 1998.

Hilsman, Jr., Roger. "Intelligence and Policy-making in Foreign Affairs." In *International Politics and Foreign Policy: A Reader in Research and Theory.* Edited by James N. Rosenau, chap. 22. New York, NY: The Free Press of Glencoe, 1969.

Hitz, Frederick P. and Brian J. Weiss. "Helping the CIA and FBI Connect the Dots in the War on Terror." *International Journal of Intelligence and Counter Intelligence* 17, no. 1 (2004): 1–41.

Hochman, Jill L. "Border Planning for the 21st Century." *Public Roads* 68, no. 4 (January/February 2005).

Hoffman, Carl. "Battlefield Space." *Popular Mechanics* (July 2007).

Hogenboom, Barbara. *Mexico and the NAFTA Environmental Debate.* Utrecth, The Netherlands: International Books, 1998.

Hristoulas, Athanasios. "Trading Places: Canada, Mexico, and North American Security." In *The Rebordering of North America: Integration and Exclusion in a New Security Context.* Edited by Peter Andreas and T.J. Bierstecker, 24–45. New York, NY: Routledge, 2003.

Hughes, Thomas. *The Fate of Facts in a World of Men: Foreign Policy and Intelligence-making. Foreign Policy Association, Headlines Series, #233.* New York, NY: Foreign Policy Association, 1976.

Hulnick, Arthur S. "Does the U.S. Intelligence Community need a DNI?" *International Journal of Intelligence and Counter Intelligence* 17, no. 5 (2004): 710–30.

———. "Indications and Warning for Homeland Security: Seeking a New Paradigm." *International Journal of Intelligence and Counter Intelligence* 18, no. 4 (2005): 593–608.

Huntington, Samuel P. "The Hispanic Challenge." *Foreign Policy* (March/April 2004): 30–45.

———. *Who are We? The Challenges of American Identity.* New York, NY: Simon and Schuster, 2004.

Hurtig, Mel. *The Vanishing Country: Is It Too Late to Save Canada?* Toronto, ON: Mitchell and Sharpe, 2002.

Hussain, A. Imtiaz. "Doggone Diplomacy? The Iraq War, North American Bilateralism and Beyond." In *Canada and the New American Empire.* Edited by George Melnyk, 213–30. Calgary, AL: University of Calgary, 2004.

———. "Canadian Immigration, Mexican Emigration and a North American Regional Interpretation." *Journal of International Migration and Integration* 6, no. 1 (Winter 2005): 81–92.

———. "Knocking on Mexico's Doors: Central America's Unholy Trinity." *Dialogo Iberoamericano* no. 2 (August–December 2005): 14–18.

Ignatieff, Michael. "Canada in the Age of Terror: Multilateralism Meets a Moment of Truth." In *Independence in An Age of Empire: Assessing Unilateralism and Multilateralism.* Edited by G.F. Walker, 31–41. Halifax: The Centre for Foreign Policy Studies, 2004.

Immerman, Richard. "A Brief History of the CIA." In *The Central Intelligence Agency: Security Under Scrutiny.* Edited by Athan Theoharis, et al., chap. 1. *Understanding our Government Series.* Westport, CT: Greenwood Press, 2006.

Independent Task Force on Immigration and America's Future, Report of. 2006. "Immigration and America's future: A New Chapter." Washington DC: Migration Policy Institute, September.

Isikoff, Michael, and David Corn. *Hubris: The Inside Story of Spin, Scandal, and the Selling of the Iraqi War.* New York, NY: Crown Publishers, 2006.

Jackson, Peter. "Historical Reflections on the Uses and Limits of Intelligence." In *Intelligence and Statecraft.* Edited by Jackson and Jennifer Siegal, chap. 1. New York, NY: Praeger, 2005.

Jamieson, Ruth, Nigel South, and Ian Taylor. "Economic Liberalization and Cross Border Crime: The North American Free Trade Area and Canada's Border with USA." *International Journal of the Sociology of Law* 26 (1998): 256–58.

Jepperson, Ronald L., Alexander Wendt, and Peter J. Katzenstein. "Norms, Identity, and Culture in National Security." In *The Culture of National Security: Norms and Identity in World Politics.* Edited by Peter J. Katzenstein. New York, NY: Columbia University Press, 1996.

Jervis, Robert. "Understanding the Bush Doctrine." *Political Science Quarterly* 118, no. 3 (2003): 365–88.

Jonson, Pierre Marc, and André Beaulieu. *The Environment and NAFTA: Understanding and Implementing the New Continental Law.* Washington, DC: Island Press, 1995.

Kagan, Robert. *Of Paradise and Power.* New York: Alfred A. Knopf, 2003.

Kaplan, Robert. "Islam vs. The West." *Rolling Stones* 7 (August 2003): 38.

Kealey, Gregory S. "The Surveillance State: The Origins of Domestic Intelligence and Countersubversion in Canada, 1914–21." *Intelligence and National Security* 7, no. 3 (July 1992): 179–210.

Keating, Tom. *Canada and World Order: The Multilateralist Tradition in Canadian Foreign Policy.* New York, NY: Don Mills; and Oxford, UK: Oxford University Press, 2006.

"Keep Out: Voters Like the Idea of Tougher Borders But the Cost is High and the Benefits are Limited." *Economist.* Special migration section, "Open up." January 5, 2008, 10.

Kennedy, Daniel B. "A Précis of Suicide Terrorism." *Journal of Homeland Security and Emergency Management* 3, no. 4, art. 2 (2006). From Berkeley Electronic Press: www.bepress.com.

Kennedy, Duncan. "Mexican Police 'probed on drugs.'" *BBC News* (October 6, 2006). Available at http://news.bbc.co.uk/2/hi/americas/5415018.stm.

Keohane, Robert O. "International Liberalism Reconsidered." *The Economic Limits to Modern Politics.* Edited by John Dunn. Cambridge, UK: Cambridge University Press, 1990.

———, and Joseph S. Nye. *Power and Interdependence: World Politics in Transition.* Boston, MA: Little, Brown, 1977.

Kessler, Glen, and Michael Abramowitz. "Bush Brings Afghanistan, Pakistan to the Table: President is Pushing Karzai and Musharraf Toward Commonalities." *Washington Post* (September 27, 2006): A22.

Kindleberger, Charles P. *The World in Depression, 1929–1939.* Berkeley, CA: University of California Press, 1973.

Konrad, Victor, and Heather Nicol. "Boundaries and Corridors: Rethinking the Canada–United States Borderlands in the Post–9/11 Era." *Canadian–American Center, Occasional Paper Series* (Maine), 2004.

Kopeki, Dawn. "Boeing's Border Patrol." *Business Week.* October 23, no. 4006 (2006).

Koring, Paul. "Tories Plan New Defence Pact with US." *Globe and Mail* February 20 (2006a).

———. "Citing 'Liberal' Immigration Laws, US Blasts Canada on Terrorism." *Globe and Mail* (April 29, 2006b).

Kramer, Andrew E. "Recalling Cold War, Russia Resumes Long-Range Sorties." *New York Times* (August 18, 2007).

Krasner, Stepen D. "Structural Causes and Regime Consequences: Regimes as Intervening Variables." *International Organization* 36, no. 2 (Spring 1982): 185–206.

Krauss, Clifford. "Evidence Grows that Canada Aided in Having Terrorism Suspects Interrogated in Syria." *New York Times* (September 17, 2005).

Kresl, Peter Karl. "NAFTA and its Discontents." *International Journal* 60, no. 2 (Spring 2005): 417–28.

Kristol, William. "A Classicist's Legacy: Empire Builders." *New York Times Week in Review* (May 4, 2003): 4.

Laghi, Brian. "Majority Opposed to Afghan Mission." *Globe and Mail* (February 24, 2006).

Lange, Peter, and Hudson Meadwell. "Typologies of Democratic Systems: From Political Inputs to Political Economy." In *New Directions in Comparative Politics.* Edited by Howard J. Wiarda, chap. 5. Boulder, CO: Westview Press, for the Center for International Affairs, Harvard University, 2002.

Lee, Steve. "Canadian Values in Canadian Foreign Policy." *Canadian Foreign Policy* 10, no. 1 (Fall 2002): 1–10.

Levy, Daniel C., and Kathleen Bruhn. *Mexico: The Struggle for Democratic Development.* Berkeley, CA: University of California Press, 2006.

Lieber, Keir A., and Daryl G. Press. "The Rise of U.S. Nuclear Primacy." *Foreign Affairs* 85 no. 2 (March/April 2006): 42–54.

Leroy, Christopher. "Mexican Intelligence at a Crossroad." *SAIS Review* 24, no. 1 (Winter/Spring 2004): 111–18.

Levy, Daniel C., and Kathleen Bruhn. *Mexico: The Struggle for Democratic Development.* Berkeley, CA: University of California Press, 2006.

Lijphart, Arend. "Typologies of Democratic Systems." *Comparative Political Studies* 1, no. 1 (April 1968): 3–44.

———. "Consociational Democracy." *World Politics* 21, no. 2 (January 1969): 207–25.

Lindberg, Leon. *The Political Dynamics of European Economic Integration.* Stanford, CA: Stanford University Press, 1963.

Lobe, Jim. "'War on Terror' Returning to its Cradle." *Asia Times* (October 5, 2006). Available at http://www.atimes.com/atimes/South_Asia/HJ05Df02.html.

Lubin, Martin. "Strings Between Governments at the Top, Hands Across the Border at the Base: The Role of Subnational Governments During the Bush-Chrétien Era and Beyond." In *Perspectives on US–Canada Relations Since 9/11: Four Essays.* Edited by H. Cody, Martin Lubin, Donald Caccioletta, and Marie Christine Therrien, 21–43. Orono, ME: The Canadian–American Center, 2003.

Lucas, Alastair. "National Approaches: Canada." In *Energy Security: Managing Risk in a Dynamic, Legal, and Regulatory Environment.* Edited by Barry Barton, Catherine Redgewell, Anita Ronne, and Donald N. Zillman, 171–202. New York, NY: Oxford University Press, 2004.

Lustig, Nora, Barry P. Bosworth, and Robert Z. Lawrence., eds. *North American Free Trade: Assessing the Impact.* Washington, DC: Brookings, 1992.

MacKinnon, Colin. "William Friedman's Bletchley Park Diary: A New Source for the History of Anglo-American Intelligence Cooperation." *Intelligence and National Security* 20, no. 4 (December 2005): 654–69.

Macklin, Audrey. "Borderline Security." In *Essays on Canada's Anti-Terrorism Bill.* Edited by Ronald J. Daniels, Patrick Macklem, and Kent Roach, 383–404. *Security of Freedom.* Toronto, ON: University of Toronto, 2001.

Macnamara, W.D., and Ann Fitzgerald. "A National Security Framework for Canada." In *Geopolitical Security.* Edited by H. Segal, 81–104. Montreal: Institute for Research on Public Policy, 2005.

MacPherson, Alan D., James E. McConnell, Annelise Vance, and Vida Vanchan. "The Impact of US Antiterrorism Policies on Canada–US Cross-border Commerce: An Exploratory Study from Western New York and Southern Ontario." *The Professional Geographer* 58, no. 3 (2006): 266–77.

Mahant, Edelgard, and Graeme S. Mount. *Invisible and Inaudible in Washington: American Policies Toward Canada.* Vancouver, BC: University of British Columbia Press, 1999.

"Manual lays out rules for Guantanamo trials," *CNN* (January 18, 2007). Available at http://www.cnn.com/2007/LAW/01/18/detainee.trials/index.html.

Mares, David. "Strategic Interests in the U.S.–Mexico Relationship." *Strategy and Security in U.S.–Mexico Relations: Beyond the Cold War.* Edited by John Bailey and Sergio Aguayo Quesada, chap. 2. La Jolla, CA: University of California Press for Center for U.S.–Mexico Studies, 1995.

Marguiles, Joseph. *Guantánamo and the Abuse of Presidential Power.* New York, NY: Simon and Schuster, 2006.

Martin, Don. "No Time to Relax on Terrorism Threats." *National Post* (February 14, 2007).

Martin, Kate. "Domestic Intelligence and Civil Liberties." *SAIS Review* 24, no. 1 (Winter–Spring 2004): 7–22.

Massey, Douglas, et al. *Beyond Smoke and Mirrors: Mexican Immigration in an Era of Economic Integration.* New York, NY: Sage, 2002.

Mastanduno, Michael. "Preserving the Unipolar Moment: Realist Theories and US Grand Strategy After the Cold War." In *Unipolar Politics: Realism and State Strategies After the Cold War.* Edited by B. Kapstein and Michael Mastanduno, 138–81. New York, NY: Columbia University Press, 1999.

Mastel, Greg. *American Trade Policy After the Uruguay Round.* Armonk, NY: M.E. Sharpe, 1996.

Maxwell, Bruce. *Homeland Security: A Documentary History.* Washington, DC: Congressional Quarterly Press, 2004.

Mayer, Frederick C. *Interpreting NAFTA: The Art and Science of Political Analysis.* New York: Columbia University Press, 1998.

Maynard Ghent, Jocelyn. "Did He Fall or Was he Pushed? The Kennedy Administration and the Collapse of the Diefenbaker Government." *International History Review* 1, no. 2 (April 1979): 246–70.

McDonough, David S. "The New Triad, Bunker Busters and 'Counterproliferation Wars': Nuclear Primacy and its Implications for Canadian Security Policy." In *The Dilemmas of American Strategic Primacy: Implications for the Future of Canadian–American Cooperation.* Edited by David S. McDonough and Douglas A. Ross. Toronto, ON: Royal Canadian Military Institute, 2005.

McKinley, Jr., James C. "Assault on Drug Cartels Feels like War: In spite of Success Against Narcos, Peace Still Elusive." *News* (January 27, 2008): 4–5.

McRae, K., ed. *Consociational Democracy: Political Accommodation in Segmented Societies.* Toronto, ON: McClelland and Stewart, 1974.

Melnyk, George., ed. *Canada and the New American Empire: War and Anti-war.* Calgary, AB: University of Calgary Press, 2004.

Meyer, Lorenzo. "Historical Roots of the Authoritarian State in Mexico." In *Authoritarianism in Mexico.* Edited by José Luis Reyna and Richard S. Weinert. Philadelphia, PA: Institute for the Study of Human Issues, 1977.

Migdal, Joel S., Atul Kohli, and Vivienne Shue. *State Power and Social Forces.* New York, NY: Cambridge University Press, 1994.

Migration Information Source. *The US–Mexico Border* (June 1, 2006). Available at www.migrationinformation.org.

Mitrany, David. "The Functional Approach to World Organization." *International Affairs* 24, no. 3 (July 1948): 350–63.

———. *A Working Peace System.* Chicago, IL: Quadrangle Books, 1966. Originally 1943.

Molot, Maureen Appel and Norman Hillmer. "The Diplomacy of Decline." In *A Fading Power.* Edited by N.H. and M. A. Molot. Don Mills, Ontario: Oxford University Press, 2002.

Moravcsik, Andrew. "Negotiating the Single European Act." In *The European Community: Decision-Making and Institutional Change.* Edited by Robert O. Keohane and Stanley Hoffmann, 41–84. Boulder, CO: Westview Press, 1991.

Morgenthau, Hans. J. *Politics Among Nations: The Struggle for Power and Peace.* New York, NY: Alfred Knopf, 1948.

Morris, Stephen D. *Corruption and Politics in Contemporary Mexico.* Tuscaloosa, AL: University of Alabama Press, 1991.

Morton, Desmond. *A Short History of Canada.* Toronto: McClelland and Stewart, Inc., 1994.

National Commission on Terrorist Attacks Upon the United States. *The 9/11 Report.* New York, NY: St. Martin's, 2004.

Nau, Henry. "From Integration to Interdependence: Gains, Losses, and Continuing Gaps." *International Organization* 33, no. 1 (Winter 1979): 119–47.

Netherton, Alexander, Allen Seager, and Karl Froschauer, eds. *In/security: Canada in the post–9/11 World.* Burnaby, BC: Centre for Canadian Studies, Simon Fraser University, 2005.

"New US Rules on Terror Detainees." *BBC News* (January 19, 2007). Available at http://news.bbc.co.uk/2/hi/americas/6276989.stm.

Nicholls, Jan. "Canadian–Mexican Military Relations: A Reflections Piece." In *Canadian and Mexican Security in the New North America: Challenges and Prospects.* Edited by Jordi Díez, 101–106. London, ON: McGill-Queen's University Press, 2006.

Nicol, Heather, and James Townsend. *Holding the Line: Borders in a Global World.* Vancouver, BC: University of British Columbia Press, 2005.

Nowalski, Jorge. "Human Security and Sustainable Livelihoods: The 'maras' in Central America." In *National Human Security Issues in Latin America.* Edited by Satya Pattnayak and Lowell Gustafson. Lewiston, NY: Edwin Mellen, 2006.

Nunez, Joseph R. "Canada's Global Role: A Strategic Assessment of its Military Power." *Parameters,* vol. 34 (Autumn 2004): 75–93.

Nye, Joseph S. "Soft Power and American Foreign Policy." *Political Science Quarterly* 119, no. 2 (2004): 255–70.

O'Brien, Robert. "North American Integration and International Relations Theory." *Canadian Journal of Political Science* 28, no. 4 (December 1995): 693–724.

Odell, Mark. "Canada Calls for Greater Commitment from NATO Countries to Mission in Afghanistan." *Financial Times* (December 4, 2003): 2.

Office, Privy Council. *Securing an Open Society: One Year Later, Progress Report on the Implementation of Canada's National Security Policy.* Ottawa: Government of Canada, 2005.

Orvik, Nils. "Canadian Security and 'Defence against help'." *Survival* (January–February 1984): 26–31.

Osiewicz, Estanislao. "Poll Finds Support Soft for Iraq War." *Globe and Mail* (March 1, 2006).

Otero, Joaquin F. "The North American Agreement on Labor Cooperation: An Assessment of its First Year's Implementation." *Columbia Journal of Transnational Law* 33 (1995): 637–62.

Pastor, Robert A. *Towards a North American Community: Lessons from the Old World for the New.* Washington, DC: The Petersen Institute, 2001.

———. "North America's Second Decade." *Foreign Affairs* 83, no. 1 (January–February 2004): 124–25.

Pastor, Robert A., and Rafael Fernandez de Castro, eds. *The U.S. Congress and North America: The Controversial Pivot.* Washington, DC: Brookings, 1998.

Pateman, Roy. *Residual Uncertainty: Trying to Avoid Intelligence and Policy Mistakes in the Modern World.* Lanham, MD: University Press of America, 2003.

Pentland, Charles. *International Theory and European Integration.* New York, NY: Free Press, 1973.

Phythian, Mark. "Still a Matter of Trust: Post–9/11 British Intelligence and Political Culture." *International Journal of Intelligence and Counter Intelligence* 18, no. 4 (2005): 653–81.

Prang, Margaret. "Networks and Associations and the Nationalizing of Sentiment in English Canada." In *National Politics and Community in Canada.* Edited by R. Kenneth Carty and W. Peter Ward, chap. 3. Vancouver, BC: University of British Columbia Press, 1986.

Pratt, Anna. *Securing Borders: Detention and Deportation in Canada.* Vancouver, BC: University of British Columbia Press, 2005.

"Presidential Determination No. 2005-36." *White House Press Release* (2005). "Statement of President Authorizing Secretary of State to Transmit to Congress Annual Report Listing Major Illicit Drug-Producing and Drug-Transit Countries." September 15. Available at http://www.state.gov/p/inl/rls/prsrl/ps/53326.htm.

Pross, Paul A. *Group Politics and Public Policy.* 2nd ed. Toronto, ON: Oxford University Press, 1992.

Pugliese, David. "$3b for Arctic Ships, PM." *National Post* (July 10, 2007).

Reid, Escott. "Forming the North Atlantic Alliance, 1949." In *Canadian Foreign Policy: Selected Cases.* Edited by Don Munton and John Kirton, 27–42. Scarborough, ON: Prentice-Hall, 1991.

Relyea, Harold C. "Organizing for Homeland Security." *Presidential Studies Quarterly* 33, no. 3 (September 2003): 602–24.

Rempel, Roy. "Canada's Parliamentary Oversight of Security and Intelligence." *International Journal of Intelligence and Counter Intelligence* 17, no. 4 (Winter 2004–05): 634–54.

Richelson, Jeffrey T., and Desmond Ball. *The Ties That Bind: Intelligence Cooperation Between the UKUSA Countries: The United Kingdom, the United States of America, Canada, Australia and New Zealand.* chap. 5. Boston, MA: Allen & Unwin, 1985.

Richter, Andrew. *Avoiding Armageddon: Canadian Military Strategy and Nuclear Weapons, 1950–63.* Vancouver, BC: University of British Columbia, 2002.

———. "A Question of Defense: How American Allies Are Responding to the US Missile Defense Program." *Comparative Strategy* 23, no. 2 (April–June 2004): 143–72.

Rittberger, Volker, ed. *Regime Theory and International Relations.* Oxford, UK: Clarendon Press, 1993.

Roach, Kent. "The Dangers of a Charter-Proof and Crime-based Response to Terrorism." In *The Security of Freedom: Essays on Canada's Anti-Terrorism Bill.* Edited by Ronald J. Daniels, Patrick Macklem, and Kent Roach, 131–50. Toronto, ON: University of Toronto Press, 2001.

———. *September 11: Consequences for Canada.* Kingston, ON: McGill-Queen's University Press, 2003.

Robertson, Kenneth G. "Canadian Intelligence Policy: The Role and Future of CSIS." *International Journal of Intelligence and Counter Intelligence* 3, no. 2 (Summer 1989): 234–37.

Rochlin, James F. *Redefining Mexican "Security": Society, State, and Region Under NAFTA.* Boulder, CO: Lynne Rienner, 1997.

Rolph, Elizabeth. *Immigration Policies: Legacy from the 1980s and Issues for the 1990s.* Santa Monica, CA: RAND, 1992.

Rosenau, James. *Along the Domestic-Foreign Frontier: Exploring Governance in a Turbulent World.* Cambridge, UK: Cambridge University Press, 1997.

Rosenberg, Lee. "Immigration Policy Must Tilt to Security." *Public Affairs Report* (Summer 2002). Berkeley: Institute of Governmental Studies, University of California.

Ross, Douglas A. *In the Interests of Peace: Canada, the United States and Vietnam, 1954–1973.* Toronto, ON: University of Toronto Press, 1984.

———. "Canada's Functional Isolationism and the Future of Weapons of Mass Destruction." *International Journal* 53, no. 1 (Winter 1998–99): 120–42.

———. "Foreign Policy Challenges for Paul Martin: Canada's International Security Policy in an Era of American Hyperpower and Continental Vulnerability." *International Journal* 58, no. 4 (Autumn 2003): 533–70.

———. "American Missile Defence, Grand Strategy and Global Security." In *The Dilemmas of American Strategic Primacy: Implications for the Future of Canadian–American Cooperation.* Edited by David S. McDonough and Ross, 35–66. Toronto, ON: Royal Canadian Military Institute, 2005.

Rossi, Peter H., James D. Wright, and Andy B. Anderson. *Handbook of Survey Research.* New York, NY: Academic Press, 1983.

Roussel, Stéphane. "The Blueprint for Fortress North America." In *Fortress North America? What 'Continental Security' Means for Canada.* Edited by David Rudd and N. Furneaux. Toronto, ON: The Canadian Institute for Strategic Studies, 2002.

———. "Honey, are you still mad at me? I've changed, you know..." *International Journal* 58, no. 4 (Autumn 2003): 571–90.

Rovner, Joshua, and Austin Long. "The Perils of Shallow Theory: Intelligence Reform and the 9/11 Commission." *International Journal of Intelligence and Counter Intelligence* 18, no. 4 (2005): 609–37.

Rudner, Martin. "The Future of Canada's Defence Intelligence." *International Journal of Intelligence and Counter Intelligence* 15, no. 4 (Winter 2002–03): 540–64.

Rudolph, Christopher. "Security and the Political Economy of International Migration." *American Political Science Review* 97, no. 4 (November 2003): 603–20.

Russell, Richard L. "A Weak Pillar for America's National Security: The CIA's Dismal Performance Against WMD Threats." *Intelligence and National Security* 20, no. 3 (September 2005): 466–85.

Sallot, Jeff. "War Could Spawn Terrorists, CSIS Chief Says." *Globe and Mail* (October 21, 2005).

Sands, Christopher. *Canada and the War on Terrorism: The US Challenge on the North American Front, Canada Focus.* Washington, DC: Center for Strategic and International Studies, 2001.

Saunders, Doug, and Brian Laghi. "Missile Dispute Threatens to Throw G8 Off Course." *Globe and Mail* (June 6, 2007).

Schmitter, Philippe C. "Still the Century of Corporatism?" *The Review of Politics* 36, no. 1 (January 1974): 85–131.

"Security Assessment—North America." *Jane's Sentinel* (October 7, 2003).

Segal, Hugh, ed. "Geopolitical Integrity for Canada." In *Geopolitical Integrity.* Montreal: Institute for Research on Public Policy, 2005.

Senate of Canada. Canadian Security Guide Book, 2007 Edition: Coasts. Report of the Standing Committee on National Security and Defence. Sen. Colin Kenny, Chair, March 2007.

Senate of Canada. Canadian Security Guide Book, 2007 Edition: Airports. Report of the Standing Senate Committee on National Security and Defence, March 2007a.

Senate of Canada. Canadian Security Guide Book, 2007 Edition: Seaports. Report of the Standing Senate Committee on National Security and Defence, March 2007b.

Serrano, Monica. "Integration and Security in North America." *International Journal* 61, no. 3 (Summer 2006): 611–32.

Sereseres, Caesar D. "The Mexican Military Looks South." In *The Modern Mexican Military: A Reassessment.* Edited by David Ronfeldt, Center for U.S.–Mexican Studies, Monograph #15, 201–13. La Jolla, CA: Center for U.S.–Mexican Studies, University of California, San Diego, 1984.

"Seven Dead in Acapúlco Ambushes." Available at http://news.bbc.co.uk/2/hi/americas/6337201.stm.

Shifter, Michael. "Latin America's Drug Problem." *Current History* 106, no. 697 (February 2007): 58–63.

Sinclair, Jill. "Canada's International Security Policy." In *Natural Allies? Canadian And Mexican Perspectives on International Security.* Edited by Hal P. Klepak, chap. 8. *Changing American Series* no. 2. Ottawa: Carleton University Press and Canadian Foundation for the Americas–FOCAL, 1996.

Sloan, Elinor C. *Security and Defence in the Terrorist Era: Canada and North America.* Montreal & Kingston, Canada: McGill-Queen's University Press, 2005.

Smith, Bradley F. "The American Road to Central Intelligence." *Intelligence and National Security* 12, no. 1 (1997): 1–21.

Snow, Donald M. *National Security: Defense Policy for a New International Era.* New York, NY: St. Martin's Press, 1995.

———. *National Security for a New Era: Globalization and Geopolitics.* New York, NY: Pearson Education, Inc., 2007

Sokolsky, Joel J. "Northern Exposure? America's Homeland Security and Canada." *International Journal* 60, no. 1 (Winter 2004/05): 36–44.

Sokolsky, Joel J., and Phillipe Lagasse. "Suspenders and Belt: Perimeter and Border Security in US–Canadian Relations." *Canadian Foreign Policy* 12, no. 3 (2005/06): 15–29.

Stairs, Denis. *The Diplomacy of Constraint: Canada, the Korean War and the United States.* Toronto: University of Toronto Press, 1974.

———. "Change in Management of Canada–United States Relations in the Post war Era." In *Toward a North American Community: Canada, the United States, and Mexico.* Edited by Donald Barry, Mark O. Dickerson, and James D. Gaisford, 53–74. Boulder, CO: Westview Press, 1995.

———. "Myths, Morals, and Reality in Canadian Foreign Policy." *International Journal* 58, no. 2(Spring 2003): 239–56.

Standing Senate Committee on National Security and Defence. *The Myth of Security at Canada's Airports.* Ottawa, 2003.

Standing Senate Committee on National Security and Defence. *Canadian Security Guide Book: An Update of Security Problems in Search of Solutions,* 2005 Edition, Ottawa: Government of Canada, 2004.

Standing Senate Committee on National Security and Defence. *Borderline Insecure: Canada's Land Border Crossings as Key to Canada's Security and Prosperity. Why the Lack of Urgency to Fix Them? What Will Happen if We Don't?* Ottawa: Government of Canada, 2005.

Statistics Canada. "Brain Drain and Brain Gain..." *The Daily* (May 24, 2000), www.statcan.ca/Daily/English/000524a.htm? (accessed May 2, 2006).

Swarnes, Rachel L. "Capitol's Pariah on Immigration is Now a Power." *New York Times* (December 24, 2005).

Talbott, Strobe. *Deadly Gambits: The Reagan Administration and the Stalemate in Nuclear Arms Control.* New York, NY: Knopf, 1984.

Taplin, Winn L. "Six General Principles of Intelligence." *International Journal of Intelligence and Counter Intelligence* 3, no. 4 (Winter 1989): 475–91.

Teichman, Judith. "Neoliberalism and the Transformation of Mexican Authoritarianism." *Mexican Studies/Estudios Mexicanos* 13, no. 1 (Winter 1997): 121–47.

"The Bi-national Sustainability Laboratory." Available at www.sandia.gov/ACG/BNSL/.

"The State of US–Mexico Border." *Congressional Report* 2006.

"The US–Mexico Border." *Migration Information Source* (June 1, 2006). Available at http://www.migrationinformation.org/feature/print.cfm?ID=407.

Theoharis, Alan. *Spying on Americans: Political Surveillance from Hoover to the Huston Plan.* Philadelphia, PA: Temple University Press, 1978.

Thomas, Christopher, and Gregory A. Tereposky. "The NAFTA and the Side Agreement on Environmental Cooperation—Addressing Environmental Concerns in a North American Regime." *Journal of World Trade* 27, no. 6 (December 1993): 5–34.

Tocqueville, Alexis de. *Democracy in America.* Translated by Arthur Goldhammer. New York, NY: Library for America for Penguin Putnam, 2004.

Todd, Paul, and Jonathan Bloch. *Global Intelligence: The World's Secret Services Today.* London: Zed Books, 2003.

Torpey, John. "States and the Regulation of Migration in the Twentieth-Century North Atlantic World." In *The World Around the West.* Edited by Peter Andreas and Thomas Zinder. Lanham, MD: Rowan and Littlefield, 2000.

Treverton, Gregory F. "Intelligence, Law Enforcement and Homeland Security." *The Century Foundation.* (August 2002). Available at www.homelandsec.org.

Trotter, Gary T. "The Anti-terrorism Bill and Preventative Restraints on Liberty." In *The Security of Freedom: Essays on Canada's Anti-Terrorism Bill.* Edited by Ronald J. Daniels, Patrick Macklem, and Kent Roach. Toronto, ON: University of Toronto Press, 2001.

Troy, Thomas F. "The Quaintness of the U.S. Intelligence Community: Its Origin, Theory, and Problems." *International Journal of Intelligence and Counter Intelligence* 2, no. 2 (Summer 1988): 245–66.

Truman, David B. *Governmental Process: Political Interest and Public Opinion.* New York, NY: Knopf, 1951.

Tsoukalis, Loukalis, ed. *Europe, America, and the World Economy.* Oxford, UK: Basil Blackwell, for the College of Europe, 1986.

Turner, Michael A. "A Distinctive U.S. Intelligence Identity." *International Journal of Intelligence and Counter Intelligence* 17, no. 1 (Spring 2004): 42–43.

United States Congress "PATRIOT Act of 2001." HR 3162, 107th Congress, 1st Session. October 24 (2001). Available at http://www.epic.org/privacy/terrorism/hr3162.html.

United States Department of Homeland Security. *Securing Our Homeland: US Department of Homeland Security Strategic Plan.* Washington, DC, 2004.

United States Department of Homeland Security. *Fact Sheet: ICE Accomplishments in Fiscal year 2006.* Press release. Available at http://www.dhs.gov/xnews/releases/pr_1162228690102.shtm.

"University Instructor Likens Bush to Hitler." *CNN* (October 11, 2006). Available at http://www.cnn.com/EDUCATION/10/11/instructor.sept.11.ap/index.html.

"US Crackdown Sends Meth Labs South of the Border." *Los Angeles Times* (November 26, 2007): 4.

Valero, Larry. "'We need our new OSS, our new General Donovan, now...': The Public Discourse over American Intelligence, 1944–53." *Intelligence and National Security* 18, no. 1 (Spring 2003): 91–118.

Vano, Gerardo S. *Canada: The Strategic and Military Pawn.* New York, NY: Praeger, 1988.

von Reikhoff, Harald. "The Impact of Prime Minister Trudeau on Foreign Policy." *Canadian Foreign Policy: Historical Readings.* Edited by Granatstein, 286–99. Toronto, ON: Copp Clark Pitman, Ltd., a Longman Co., 1993.

Mr. X. 1947. "The Sources of Soviet conduct." *Foreign Affairs* 25, no. 4 (July 1947): 566–82.

Walt, Stephen M. "Rigor or Rigor Mortis? Rational Choice and Security Studies." *International Security* 23, no. 4 (Spring 1999): 5–48.

Waltz, Kenneth N. *Theory of International Politics.* Menlo Park, CA: Addison Wesley, 1979.

Wannall, W. Raymond. "The FBI's Domestic Intelligence Operations: Domestic Security in limbo." *International Journal of Intelligence and Counter Intelligence* 4, no. 4 (1990).

Wark, Wesley K. "Canada and the Intelligence Revolution." In *Secret Intelligence in the Twentieth Century.* Edited by Heike Bungert, Jan G. Heitmann, and Michael Wala, chap. 13. London: Frank Cass, 2003.

Watson, Cynthia A. *U.S. National Security.* Santa Barbara, CA: ABC-CLIO, 2002.

Weber, Max. *The Protestant Ethic and the Spirit of Capitalism.* Edited by Talcott Parsons and R.H. Tawney. Dover, UK: Dover Publications, 2003.

Weber, Rachel. *Swords Into Dow Shares: Governing the Decline of the Military Industrial Complex.* Boulder, CO: Westview Press, 2001.

Weller, Geoffrey. "Assessing Canadian Intelligence Literature: 1980–2000." *International Journal of Intelligence and Counter Intelligence* 14, no. 3 (Fall 2001): 49–61.

Welsh, Jennifer. *At Home in the World: Canada's Global Vision for the 21st Century.* Toronto, ON: HarperCollins, 2004.

Whitaker, Reg. "The Politics of Security Intelligence Policy-making in Canada, I: 1970–84." *Intelligence and National Security* 6, no. 4 (October 1991): 652–53.

———. "The Politics of Security Intelligence Policy-making in Canada, II, 1984–91." *Intelligence and National Security* 7, no. 2 (April 1992): 53–76.

———. "Spies who Might Have Been: Canada and the Myth of Cold War Counterintelligence." *Intelligence and National Security* 12, no. 4 (October 1997): 25–43.

———. "Cold War Alchemy: How America, Britain, and Canada Transformed Espionage into Subversion." *Intelligence and National Security* 15, no. 2 (Summer 2000): 177–210.

White House, The. "Fact Sheet: Security and Prosperity Partnership of North America." (March 31, 2006).

——— "President Bush Addresses the Nation on Immigration Reform." *Press Release* (May 15, 2006).

———. *The National Security Strategy of the United States of America.* (March 2006).

Wiarda, Howard J. "Corporatism and Development in the Iberic–Latin world: Persistent Strains and New Variations." *The Review of Politics* 36, no. 1 (1974): 3–33.

Wilensky, Harold L. *The "New Corporatism", Centralization, and the Welfare State.* London: SAGE Publications, 1976.

Winham, Gilbert R. *Trading With Canada: The Canada–U.S. Free Trade Agreement.* New York, NY: Priority Press Publications for Twentieth Century Fund, 1988.

Wirtz, James J. "The Intelligence Paradigm." *Intelligence and National Security* 4, no. 4 (October 1989): 829–37.

Wise, Carol, ed. *The Post-NAFTA Political Economy: Mexico and the Western Hemisphere.* College Park, PA: The Penn State University Press, 1998.

Works in Report of the Bilateral Commission on the Future of United States–Mexican Relations. *The Challenge of Interdependence: Mexico and the United States.* Lanham, MD: Littlefield and Rowman, 1989.

Zirnite, Peter. "Militarization of the US Drug Control Program." *Foreign Policy in Focus* 3, no. 27 (1998): 1–4.

ADDITIONAL INTERNET SOURCES

http://www.ins.usdoj.gov/graphics/lawenfor/bmgmt/inspect/bciint.htm.

http://www.state.gov/topical/global/develop/02032204.htm.

http://www.northcom.mil/about_us/about_us.htm.

http://usinfo.state.gov/wh/Archive/2005/Mar/16-51355.html.

http://www.ins.usdoj.gov/graphics/aboutins/statistics/illegalalien/index.htm.

http://www.dhs.gov/xabout/structure/index.shtm.

http://www.ccr-ny.org/v2/print_page.asp.

http://opendoors.iienetwork.org/?p=89207.

http://www.cric.ca/en_html/guide/border/border.html#smart.

http://www.aflcio.org/aboutus/thisistheaflcio/ecouncil/ec02272006e.cfm.

https://www.cia.gov/csi/studies/vol46no3/article01.html.

http://www.pbs.org/wgbh/pages/frontline/shows/trail/etc/canada.html.

http://www.locationcanada.com/2005/art_2.htm.

http://www.globeandmail.com/servlet/ArticleNews/front/RTGAM/20021002/schr1001/fr.

http://www.international.gc.ca/anti-terrorism/declaration-en.asp.

Index

ABM Defence Cooperation, 67, 69, 94; radar site related to, 70; as treaty, 59, 68, 70–71
abnegation, as policy approach, 113
Abwehr, 205
Achilles Heel, human rights as, 169; Canada's intelligence institutions as, 213; as Mexico's, 108
ACLU (American Civil Liberties Union), 50
Adjutant's Office, United States, 150
Advance Passenger Information System. *See* APIS
Afghanistan, 57–58, 64, 66, 156, 161, 243; and Canada, 78, 155, 219; *iraqification* of, 214
AFL-CIO (American Federation of Labor-Congress of Industrial Organizations), 51
Afro-Americans, as U.S. minority, 107
Ahmedinajad, President (Iranian), 71
Air-India explosion (1985), 72, 204, 211; inquiry of, 75
Alaska, 70, 226
Alemán, Miguel, 207
al Qaeda, 142, 188–89, 243
amalgamated security community. *See* ASC
Ambassador Bridge, 89
American Civil Liberties Union. *See* ACLU
americanization, 203, 205
Andean countries, 186
Anglo-Saxon, 3, 148; ties, 147; values, 143, 157, 207, 229, 232, 235, 237, 242, 247
anti-Americanism, 31
Anti-Terrorism Act, 72. *See* Bill C-23
APEC (Asia-Pacific Economic Cooperation), 102, 234
APIS (Advance Passenger Information System), 191
Arar, Maher, 73, 145, 200
Arizona, 106, 117, 183; desert of, 247
Arctic, 70; basin, 95; Canadian, 192
Arctic Ocean, 8, 53, 59
Arctic Offshore Patrol Ships, 95
ASAT (anti-satellite) weapons system, 70–71
ASC (amalgamated security community), 13 passim, 124 passim, 232
Asia Pacific Gateway, 95
asymmetrical context, 7
asymmetry, economic, 49, 177; security, 216
Australia, 247
Avian and Human Pandemic Influenza, 93
Axworthy, Lloyd, 65; his successors, 66
Azerbaijan, 70

Bailey, John, 116
balancing, as policy approach, 113
bandwagoning, as policy approach, 113
Barger, Deborah C., 6
Berkowitz, Bruce, 6
Berlin Wall, 106
biculturalism, 88
Big Three, 150
bilateralism (and bilateralizing), 103, 196, 224, 227, 232, 241, 247, 249
bilingualism, 88
binational constituency, 105
binationalism, 108
BIP (Border Industrialization Program), United States, 106
Bill 245 (United States), 107
Bill C-9 (Canadian), 8
Bill C-23 (Canadian), 73
Bill C-36 (Canadian), 9–10, 151, 204, 212 passim, 220
Blaine, as mega port, 139
Blair, Tony, 103
Bloch, Jonathan, 160
Bloc Québecois (Canadian), 64
Board of Economic Warfare, United States, 150
Boeing (aircraft company), 132
Bolshevik revolution, 205
Borden, Robert, 205; his Union Government, 207
Border Action Plan (2002), or 22-point plan, 117, 188, 198, 215
Border Anti-Smuggling Coalition, 191
Border Coordination Initiative, Mexico-United States, 190
border crossings, Canada-United States, 138–40
Border Industrialization Program. *See* BIP
Border Infrastructure Fund, 136
Border Management System, 116
border militarization, with Mexico, 51
Border Patrol, United States, 131; agents of, 183
Border Patrol's Search and Rescue Teams. *See* BORSTAR
Border Vision, INS-CIC, 136
born-free upbringing, 26
BORSTAR (Border Patrol's Search and Rescue Teams), 116
Bracero program, United States, 187
Bretton Woods (conference), 27
Britain, Great, 162
British empire, 207
British North American Confederation, 147
Broken Promise, Plan, 117
Brookings Institution, United States, 192
BSI (Border Safety Initiative), 116
Buffalo, NY, as megaport, 139–40
Bureau of the Budget, United States, 5
Bureau of Navigation, United States, 150
Bureau of Transportation, United States, 138; statistics from, 179 passim
Bush Administration (George. W.), 34, 50, 57, 61 passim, 92
Bush Doctrine, 13, 143
Bush, George H. W., 2; ideological position of, 8
Bush, George W., 6, 121, 149, 154, 219; his competitive liberalism policy, 2; on Mexican immigration, 103; preference for political realism, 32; proposing OHS, 5; on strained relations with Chrétien, 199
butcher, baker, policy-maker categories, 143 passim

CAFTA (Central American Free Trade Agreement), 200
Cahan, C. H., 205, 208
Calderón Hinojosa, Felipe, 49, 51, 111–13, 116, 165, 185–6, 194, 200, 218
California, 179, 184, 187; southern, 183
Camacho, Vila, General, 168
Camarena, Enrique, 111
Cambodia, 62
Camp, Roderic Ai, 168, 207
Camp X., 205
Canada/Canadian: Canadian Afghani mission/commitments, 58; Canadian Air Transport Security Authority. *See* CATSA; Canadian Border Services Agency. *See* CBSA; Canadian

Conference Board, 82; Canadian Council of Chief Executives, 66, 82; Canadian Criminal Code, 8, 211; "Canada First," policy approach, 77; Canadian Food Inspection Agency. *See* CFIA; Canadian immigration, 92; Canada-Mexico relations, 27, 121, 198, 222; Canadian Police Information Centre, 211; Canadian policy-making, 113; Canadian Security and Intelligence Service. *See* CSIS; Canadian Security Investigation Division, 211; Canadian trade, 82, 121; Canada-U.S. border, 96, 134–35, 189, 191–2, 206, 222; Canada-U.S. comparisons, 149; Canada-U.S. Free Trade Agreement, 63, 81, 118; Canada-U.S. partnership, 136; Canada-U.S. relations, 7–8, 27, 46, 82, 131, 160, 226 passim, 237, 246 passim; Canada-U.S. security relations, 58, 232; Canada-U.S. trade, 136 passim, 177 passim; Canadian-U.S. Auto Pact, 25; Canada-U.S. Transportation Border Working Group, 134; special forces of, 57
Cárdenas, Lazaro, General, 207
Caribbean, the, 48, 62
Carranzo, Venustiano, 168
Casey, William, 152
Castañeda, Jorge, 114
Castro, Fidel, 114
CATSA (Canadian Air Transport Security Authority), 75
CBNRC (Communications Branch of the National Research Council), Canadian, 208, 210
CBP (Customs and Border Protection), United States, 36, 134
CBSA (Canadian Border Services Agency), 60, 74, 76, 91, 134
Centinela, Mexican operation, 190
Central America/ns, 27, 62, 107, 164, 174, 226; Free Trade Agreement. *See* CUFTA; gangsters, 108, 174, 186, 194; over emigrants, 111, 129
Central Canada-Western Ontario-Michigan-Great Lakes Corridor, 135
Central Intelligence Agency, United States. *See* CIA
Central Intelligence Group, United States. *See* CIG
CF (Canadian Forces), 58, 67–68, 79, 94
CFE (Conventional Forces in Europe), Treaty, 70
CFIA (Canadian Food Inspection Agency), 91, 134
CFR (Council on Foreign Relations), New York, 157, 192, 214, 247
Council on Foreign Relations, New York. *See* CFR
Chabat, Jorge, 25
Chalabi, Ahmad, 145
Chalk, Peter, 9
Charter of Freedoms, Canadian, 213; related discussions on, 221
checks and balances, 11
Chertoff, Michael, 6
Chiápas, 161
Chile, 63
China, 62, 69, 242; as possible great power, 32; in terms of its economic growth, 2; over immigration, 27; as trading partner, 202
Choudhry, Sujit, 9
Chrétien, Jean, 8, 57, 62–63, 68, 121, 154, 157, 212, 246; decade of, 67; government of, 58, 67; his resignation, 151; sparring with George W. Bush, 156, 199 passim, 206
CIA (Central Intelligence Agency), United States, 3, 5, 6, 10, 19, 164, 166, 236; creation of, 144; deficiencies of, 38–39; terrorism coordination with, 72, 188; tussle with FBI, 149
CIB (Criminal Investigation Branch), Canadian), 205
CIC (Citizenship and Immigration Department, Canada), 74, 91
CIG (Central Intelligence Group), United States, 150
CINCNORAD (Commander-in-chief of NORAD), 59
CINCNORTHCOM

(Commander-in-Chief of NORTH-COM), 59
cinco de mayo, Mexican celebration, 103
CIPAC (Critical Infrastructure Partnership Advisory Council), United States, 36–37
CISEN (*Centro de Inteligencia y Seguridad Nacional*), Mexican, 3, 9, 114, 167, 198, 204, 207, 209 passim, 220
Citizenship and Immigration Services, United States, 34
Ciudad Juárez, 108
civil law, traditions of, 113
Civil Rights Act, 1964, United States, 40
CJIC (Canadian Joint Intelligence Committee), 208
Clarkson, Stephen, 51, 66, 91
Clinton, William (Bill), United States, 199; his administration, 68
CMR (civil-military relations) in Mexico, 205 passim, 214, 216
Coalition for Secure and Trade-efficient Borders, Canadian. *See* CSTB
Coast Guard, United States, 5, 36, 60, 134, 190; Canadian, 76, 78, 94, 96
Cohen, Andrew, 7
Cold War, 8, 38, 103, 145, 152, 171, 191, 204–5, 226; paradigm, 212; post–Cold War, 204, 233; thaw, 2, 53in trade-off, 1
collective security, 7
COMINT (communications intelligence), 10, 210
Commission Report, 9/11, United States, 38
Committee on Organization of Government Work, United States, 4
Commonwealth, British, 65
Communications Branch of the National Research Council, Canada. *See* CBNRC
communications intelligence. *See* COMINT
Communications Security Establishment. *See* CSE
concentration, trade, 121
Conference Board of Canada, 66
Congress, United States, 34, 66; Mexican, 191
Conservative Party (Canadian), 68, 80, 93, 212; "Canada First" Defence Strategy of, 77
consociationalism/ist, 151; Canadian version, 154, 207
constitution, United States, 5
constructivism, school of, 149, 165
Container Security Initiative, 191
containment of Soviet communism, 61
Conventional Forces in Europe. *See* CFE
cooperative security, 7
Coordinated Border Infrastructure Program, 191
Cornelius, Wayne A., 107
corporatism/corporatist, 167, 207
corridors, border, 136
Council on Foreign Relations. *See* CFR
counterintelligence, 8
counterterrorism, 8
Counter Terrorism Center. *See* CTC
coyotes, 2, 107, 116
Crabb, Cecil V., 152
Creel, Santiago, 116
Criminal Investigation Branch, Canadian. *See* CIB
Cross-Border Crime Forum, 136
cross-border externalities, 1, 112, 165; air travel, 179; trade, 188
Cross-Cultural Roundtable on Security, Canadian, 94
CSE (Communications Security Establishment), Canadian, 74, 211
CSIS (Canadian Security and Intelligence Service), 8–10, 19, 60, 62, 74, 207, 209 passim; in public debate, 150–51
CSTB (Coalition for Secure and Trade-efficient Borders), Canadian, 81
CTC (Counter Terrorism Center), United States, 38
C-TPAT (Customs-Trade Partnership Against Terrorism), 87, 191
Cuba, 63, 106, 114
CUFTA. *See* Canada-U.S. Free Trade Agreement
culture. *See* strategic culture
Customs and Border Protection, United States. *See* CBP

Customs and Excise (Canadian), 76
Customs-Trade Partnership Against Terrorism. *See* C-TPAT
Czech Republic, 69

Dallas, Secretariat of NAFTA's environmental secretariat in, 226
Damoclean sword, 113
Daniels, Ronald, J., 9
Davos World Economic Forum, congregation at (1990), 229
DC (*Departamento Confidencial*), 208
DCI (Department of Citizens and Immigration), Canadian, 74
DCI, United States (Director of Central Intelligence, United States), 150, 164
DEA (Drug Enforcement Agency), United States, 186
Dean, Howard, 48
dedazo, Mexican traditional gesture, 172
deep integration (as cliché), 66
Defence Intelligence Agency, United States *See* DIA
Defence Ministerial of the Americas, 141
Defence Production Sharing Agreements, 69
de la Madrid, Miguel, 209
demand-side, as Mexico-U.S. immigration problem, 110
Democratic National Committee, United States, 48
Democratic Party, United States, 49; leadership of, 50; left-wing of, 54
Departamento de Investigación Política y Social. See DIPS
Department of Agriculture, United States, 189
Department of Commerce and Labor, United States (from 1903), 4
Department of Defense, United States. *See* DOD
Department of Energy, United States, 189
Department of External Affairs, Canada, 207
Department of Fisheries and Oceans (Canadian), 76
Department of Foreign Affairs, Canadian, 58
Department of Justice, United States, 190
Department of National Defense, Canadian, 58
Department of State, United States, 134, 184
dependency theory, 157
Derbez, Luis Ernesto, 114
de Tocqueville, Alexis, 26, 148, 161
Detroit, as mega port, 139; border with Windsor, 135
Deutsch, Karl W., 13 passim, 123 passim
DFA (Department of Foreign Affairs), Canada, 58, 69; and International Trade, 91
DGIPS (*Dirección General de Investigaciones Políticas y Sociales*), 208
DGISN (*Dirección General de Investigación y Seguridad Nacional*), 208
DGS (*Dirección General de Seguridad*), 208
DHS (Department of Homeland Services), United States, 2, 6, 9, 37, 247; Canada and, 78, 131; Mexico and, 164, 166–67
DIA (Defense Intelligence Agency), United States, 150
Díaz, Porfirio, 168, 204, 207
Diefenbaker, John G., 65
DIPS (*Departamento de Investigación Política y Social*), 208
Dion, Stéphane, 64
Dirección General de Investigaciones Políticas y Sociales. See DGIPS
Dirección General de Investigación y Seguridad Nacional. See DGISN
Dirección General de Seguridad. See DGS
Directorate of Management, 35; Office of Operations Coordination under, 36; Office of Policy Directorate under, 36; organizational structure of, 30, 34–35 passim; strategic plan of, 72
Director of National Intelligence, United States, 37
Director of Central Intelligence, United States. *See* DCI

DND (Department of National Defence), Canada, 58, 69, 74, 78
DNI (Director of National Intelligence), United States, Office of, 37, 39
DOD (Department of Defense), United States, 5, 34; intelligence apparatus of, 39, 150, 188; forward operating locations of, 186
Domestic Nuclear Detection Office, United States, 36
Dominguéz, Jorge, 13 passim, 111
domino theory, 62
Donovan, William J, "Wild Bill," 150
Dorgan, Byron (North Democrat Democrat), 132
Doyle, Kate, 206
DP (Dominion Police), Canadian, 148, 205
drug cartels, 46,
Drug Enforcement Agency, United States, *See* DEA
drug-trafficking, 32, 103, 185, 197
Dubai Port World, 54
Duceppe, Gilles, 64
Dulles, Allen, 152

EAI (Enterprise of the Americas), 2
ECSC (European Coal and Steel Community), 25, 246
EDIG (Executive Directorate of the Inspector General), Canadian, 8
EII (Enforcement Information Index), Canadian, 8, 211
elites (as theoretical variable), 171–2
emigration: Mexico-United States, 104
Empty Chair crisis (European Community), 226
English, Allan D., 206
English (as a language), 229, 232
English Enlightenment, 157
Enhanced Border Security and Visa Entry Reform Act (2002), 188
environmental degradation, 32
EO (Executive Order) 13228, United States, 5–6
Executive Office of the President, United States, 4
expatriates, externalities: Mexicans in United States, 105; negative, 46, 196. *See also* "cross-border externalities"
Eurobarometer Poll, 31
European Community, 230
European Union, 7

Farson, Stuart, 144, 151, 205, 211
FAST (Free and Secure Trade), 87, 116–17, 134
FBI (Federal Bureau of Investigation), United States, 6, 72, 144, 149, 164; deficiencies of, 38; terrorism related discussions of, 188
FDA (Food and Drug Administration), United States, 87, 189
Federalist Papers, 4
Federal Emergency Management Directorate, United States. *See* FEMD
Federal Emergency Measures Act, United States. *See* FEMA
Federal Highway Works Administration, United States, 134
Federal Law Enforcement Training Center, United States, 36
Federal Law for Information Access, Mexican, 205
FEMA (Federal Emergency Measures Act), United States, 5
FEMD (Federal Emergency Management Directorate), United States, 36
Fenian Brotherhood, United States, 147
Fernandez de Castro, Rafael, 13 passim, 103, 111
FIRA (Foreign Investment Review Agency), Canadian, 25
FISA (Foreign Intelligence Surveillance Act), United States, 6
FLQ (*Front de Liberación du Québec*), 210
foedus pacificum, Kantian, 239
FOLs (forward operating locations), 186
Food and Drug Administration, United States. *See* FDA
Foreign Affairs, Canada, 134
Foreign Intelligence Surveillance Act, United States. *See* FISA

Foreign Investment Review Agency, Canadian. *See* FIRA
Foreign Terrorist Tracking Task Force, United States, 90
Fort Williams, Canada, 205
Fox, Vicente Quesada, 7, 10, 54, 121, 164, 172, 188, 194; common currency proposal, 92; his administration, 104, 184, 188; migration proposal, 103; post-Fox, 201; relationship with George W. Bush, 199, 206
FPP, 10
Francaphone, la, 65
free trade agreement. *See* FTA
Free Trade Area of the Americas. *See* FTAA
Freedom of American Scientists, 79
French, as language, 232; as people, 235
Front de Liberación du Québec. See FLQ
FTAA (Free Trade Area of the Americas), 2, 87, 157, 200, 222, 234, 243, 247 passim
FTAs (free trade agreements), 2, 25, 198, 241; bilateral, 87; Canadian, 211
functionalism, theory of, 216

gangs, Central American, 111–12, 188. *See maras*
Ganster, Paul, 8
Gates, Robert (U.S. Defense Secretary), 169
Gibbins, Roger, 8
globalism, 234
globalization, 104, 176
González González, Guadalupe, 1, 112, 159
Goodman, Melvyn A., 145
Gore, Albert, 68
Gottlieb, Allan, 91
Granatstein, J. L., 57, 66
Great Lakes Saint Lawrence Seaway system, 134
Green Berets, U.S. force, 161
Grupo Betas, 117
Guadalupe-Hidalgo, Treaty of, 1848, 163
Guantánamo, 167; camp, 169
Guatemala, 53, 62, 161
guest workers, 106
Guévara, Ché, 114
Guezenko, Igor, 145, 209
Gulf Cartel, 111
Gulf of Mexico, 186
Gulf War, Persian: first, 39, 142
Guns-butter exchange, 122

Haas, Ernst, 175
Haas, Richard, 214
Haggard, Stephen, 1, 112, 159
Haiti, 66, 95
Hamilton, Alexander, 4
hard power, 31
Harper, Steve, 8, 49, 51, 64, 71, 121, 156, 172, 212; government of, 58, 66, 76–77, 93–94, 101, 132, 136; his era, 59; his party, 152; his policies, 73; his relations with United States, 200
Hastedt, Glenn, 152
Helms, Richard, 152
Hernández, Juan, 105
Hewitt, Steve, 143, 210
Hiller, Rick, General (Canadian), 64
Hilsman, Roger, Jr., 146
hispanic(s): as challenge, 3, 107, 229, 242; as U.S. minority group, 107, 245; values of, 232
Hitz, Frederick P., 144
homeland defense, 4–5
homeland security, 4–5, 191, 224
Homeland Security Act, United States. *See* HSA
Homeland Security Order, United States. *See* HSO
Homeland Security Science and Technology Advisory Committee, United States. *See* HSSTAC
Hong Kong style, 96
Hoover, J. Edgar (FBI director), 143, 150
HSA (Homeland Security Act), United States, 4, 34
HSAC (Homeland Security Advisory Council), United States, 36
HSO (Homeland Security Order), United States, 5
HSSTAC (Homeland Security Science and Technology Advisory Committee), United States, 36

hub-and-spoke argument, 219
Hughes, Thomas, 143, 150
human intelligence. *See* HUMINT
human security, 65
human trafficking, 32, 188
HUMINT (human intelligence), 10, 80, 175, 208, 210
Huntington, Samuel P., 107
Hussein, Saddam, 22, 67

IAEA (International Atomic Energy Administration), United Nations, 61
IANC (Inter-American Naval Conference), 93
IC (intelligence community), 143, 149–50; United States, 150, 164–65
ICC (Immigration and Customs Canada), 8, 211
ICBMs (intercontinental ballistic missiles), 70
ICE (Immigration and Customs Enforcement), of DHS, United States, 36, 184
IG (Inspector General), Canadian, 211
Ignatieff, Michael, 67
immigration, 47, 72, 113; United States, 88; illegal United States, 103, 129, 187, 244
Immigration Act, 1976, Canada, 91
Immigration Act Amendment (1994), United States, 187
Immigration and Nationality Act (1976), United States, amendments to, 187
Immigration Reform and Control Act, United States. *See* IRCA
import substitution industrialization. *See* ISI
INAC (Inter-American Naval Conference), 93
India: over immigration, 27; over remittances, 122; in terms of its economic growth, 2; trade with Mexico, 120
Industry Canada, 140
INS (Immigration and Naturalization Service), United States, 5
institutional-procedural trade-offs, 1, 11
institutional tendencies/behavior, 11, 196, 206
integration, as theory, 23, 155–6, 169, 175 passim, 223; regional economic, 125, 227, 241; security, 52, 227, 241
Integration Threat Assessment Center (Canadian), 94
intelligence, as paradigm, 13 passim, 236 passim. *See also* COMINT; HUMINT; SIGINT
Intelligence Producers Council, United States, 151
Intelligence Reform and Terrorism Prevention Act (Canadian, 2004), 135
"intelligence-without-policy," 160
Interagency Coordinating Council on Emergency Preparedness, 37
Inter-American Defence Board, 141
interdependence: as theory, 4, 13, 52, 127–8, 155–6, 169, 175 passim, 192 passim, 218 passim, 223, 227 passim, 236, 241 passim
intergovernmentalism (as a theoretical tenet), 51, 174, 193, 223, 232
Inter-IANC Conference of the Armies of the Americas, 141
Inter-American Naval Conference. *See* IANC
International Convention for the Suppression of the Financing of Terrorism, 9, 212
International Convention for the Suppression of Terrorist Bombings, 9, 212
internationalism, 32
International Atomic Energy Administration. *See* IAEA
International Monetary Fund, 118
International Port Facility Security Code. *See* IPFSC
International Reform and Terrorism Prevention Act, United States. *See* IRTPA
International Security and Assistance Force. *See* ISAF
International Trade Canada, 74
International Traffic in Arms. *See* ITAR

IPFSC (International Port Facility Security Code), 134
Iran, 50, 54, 152; nuclear facilities of, 61
Iraq, 58, 93, 95, 142, 161, 170, 225, 232, 243; war in, 200
IRCA (Immigration and Reform Control Act, 1986), 106, 187
IRTPA (Intelligence Reform and Terrorism Prevention Act, 2004), United States, 37, 39
ISAF (International Security and Assistance Force), in Afghanistan, 93, 217
ISI (import substitution industrialization), 25, 229
Islamic-Christian relations, 157, 247
Islamists, 60
ITAR (International Traffic in Arms), United States, 58

Jay, John, 4
JCB (Joint Coordination Board), Canadian, 208
jihad (or *jihadi/jihadists*), 2, 107
Jintao, Hu (Chinese), 71
Joint Coordination Branch, Canadian. *See* JCB
Joint Terrorism Task Forces. *See* JTTF
JTTF (Joint Terrorism Task Forces), United States, 39
Judd, Jim, 63

Kabul, 63–64, 80
Kandahar, 58, 64
Kaplan, Robert, 32
Karzai, Hamed, 63, 80; government of, 79
Katrina, Hurricane, 35, 50, 192
Kean Commission United States, 6
Keating, Admiral (Canadian), 59
Keohane, Robert O., 23
Kennan, George F., 2, 148
Kenny, Colin (Canadian Senator), 66, 97
King, MacKenzie, 210
Kissinger, Henry, 152
Korea, 62
Kristol, William, 32
Kyoto Protocol, 59

La-18 (Central American gang), 188
Laos, 62
La Raza, 50, 52
Latin America, 47, 52, 108, 245; immigration from, 92, 111
Laurier, Wilfrid, Sir, 25
LAWs (legalized agricultural workers), 106–7
Layton, Jack, 64
Lemus, Gabriela D., 108
Leroy, Christopher, 9, 114
liberalization, 104
Liberal Party (Canadian), 59, 132; government of, 60, 67–68, 80, 242
Lincoln, Abraham, 4
Lindberg, Leon N., 126 passim
Lindert effect, 84

MacDonald Report (Canadian), 25
MacKenzie Royal Commission, Canadian. *See* MRC
MacPherson, Alan D., 140
Manifest Destiny (United States), 26
Manley, John (Canadian), 74
maquiladoras, 8, 106, 129, 178, 202, 234
Mara Salvatrucha, Central American gang, 188
maras, Central American, 111
Marchio, James, 39
marijuana, 186
Marine Corp, United States, 150
Marine Security Operations (Canadian), 76
Martin, Kate, 6
Martin, Paul, 8, 121; his finance minister tenure, 66; his government, 59, 68–69, 89, 152, 211; his party, 200
MaRVed (maneuvering re-entry vehicles) missiles, 70
Matamoros, 186
MC (McDonald Commission), Canadian, 145, 204, 209 passim
McClellan, Anne, 9, 212
McCone, John, 152
McDonald Commission, Canadian. *See* MC
McFarlane, Robert, Canadian, 152

methamphetamine, 186
Mexico/Mexican: city, 97, 99, 105; Mexico-Canada relations, 246 passim; decision-making, 105; Mexico-U.S. borders, 106, 116, 129, 184, 189–90, 245; Mexico-U.S. Consultative Committee, 189; Mexico-U.S. Critical Infrastructure Protection Framework for Cooperation, 116; Mexico-U.S. Defense Commission (1942), 111; Mexico-U.S. intelligence, 146 passim; Mexico-U.S. relations, 7, 27, 46, 104, 120, 129, 160 passim, 173 passim, 222, 226, 246 passim; in terms of clash of cultures, 108
Middle East, 87; government, 108
Military Commissions Manual, United States, 169
military culture, 170, 196
"millennium bomber," 132. *See also* Ressam, Ahmed
Ministry of Agriculture, Mexico, 189
Ministry of Economic Development, 189
Minutemen Project, 187
MIRVed (multiple, independent re-entry vehicles), missiles, 70
Mitrany, David, 175
Montréal, 226; port of, 90, 134
Morales, Candido, 105
Morgenthau, Hans J., 25
MRC (MacKenzie Royal Commission), Canadian, 145, 204, 209 passim
Mulcahy, Kevin V., 152
Mulroney, Brian, 25, 63, 66, 68, 210; government of, 81; pro-U.S. government of, 133
multiculturalism, 46, 48, 88, 133
multilateralism, 62
Musharraf, Pervez, General, 79
Muslims in Canada, 73

NACC (North American Competitiveness Council), 93, 190
NAFTA (North American Free Trade Agreement), 1, 17, 45, 81, 87, 95, 102, 108, 118, 136, 172 passim, 244; as basis of transactions, 6, 54–55, 63, 121, 129, 153; side-agreements of, 226; as source of complaints, 92; as source of trilateralism, 231, 242
narcotrafficking, 47, 104, 122; Mexico and United States, 10, 213, 244; plus, 92. *See also deep* integration
National Corridor Planning, 191
National Counter Terrorist Center, United States, 39
National Defense Department, Canadian, 212
National Foreign Intelligence Board, United States, 151
National Infrastructure Advisory Council, United States. *See* NIAC
National Intelligence Authority, United States. *See* NIA
National Resources Planning Board, United States, 5
nationalism, 176, 234
National Security Advisor. *See* NSA
National Security Agency, 150
National Security Council. *See* NSC
National Security Resources Board. *See* NSRB
National Security Strategy. *See* NSS
NATO (North Atlantic Treaty Organization), 20, 67, 78–80, 141, 153, 155, 158, 171, 206–7 passim; 220, 234, 244
Nau, Henry, 23
NCTC (National Counter Terrorist Center), 39
NEP (National Energy Policy), Canadian, 25
neofunctionalism: in testing tenets, 48 passim, 126, 216 passimas theory, 4, 13, 125 passim, 154, 156, 169 passim, 192 passim, 227 passim
neorealism: as theory, 4, 13 passim, 127 passim, 156, 169, 175 passim, 218 passim, 227 passim
Neustadt, Richard E., 105
New Deal, 5, 166–67
New Democrats (Canadian), 64
New Mexico, 183
NEXUS, 90, 134

NGOs (nongovernmental organizations), 127
NIA (National Intelligence Authority), United States, 150
NIAC (National Infrastructure Advisory Council), United States, 36
Niagara Falls, 135
Nogales, 186
nongovernmental organizations. *See* NGOs
Non-Proliferation Treaty, nuclear. *See* NPT
NORAD (North American Defense, 1958), 59, 65, 68, 90, 94, 133, 206, 208; Canada's membership of, 141
Norma, E. Herbert, 145
North American Defense. *See* NORAD
north americanization, 196
North Atlantic Treaty Organization. *See* NATO
North America/n, 13, 191; asymmetry, 189; community, 99; Competitive Council. *See* NACC; Economic and Security Community, 192, 247; as an integrating region, 1, 26, 45; over trade, 119 passim; playing field, 237; security, 55; Security Perimeter, 91, 157; Transportation Statistics data base, 139
North Atlantic Community, 65
NORTHCOM (Northern Command), 59, 68, 78, 142, 186
Northern Command. *See* NORTHCOM
North Korea, 50, 54, 152
North U.S. Energy Security, 93
North U.S. Smart and Secure Borders, 93
Northwest Passage, 59, 77, 80
NPT (Non-Proliferation Treaty), nuclear, 59, 62
NSA (National Security Advisor), Mexican, 10; United States, 152
NSC (also National Security Council): Mexican, 164–65, 191; United States, 1, 34, 150, 152
NSRB (National Security Resources Board), United States, 5
NSS (National Security Strategy), United States, 2, 30; NSS 2002, 33; NSS 2006, 33
Nuevo Laredo, 186
Nye, Joseph S., 23, 31, 65, 126–27

OAG (Office of the Auditor General), Canadian, 151, 211
OAS (Organization of American States), 142, 234
OASSIS (Operation Against Smugglers and Traffickers in the Safety and Security Initiative), 190
OEM (Office of Emergency Management), United States, 5
Office of the Auditor General, Canadian. *See* OAG
Office of Civil Rights and Civil Liberties, United States, 34
Office of Facts and Figures, United States, 5
Office of the Federal Coordinator for Recovery and Rebuilding of the Gulf Coast Region, United States, 35
Office of Homeland Security. *See* OHS
Office of Inspector General, United States, 34
Office of Legislative and Intergovernmental Affairs, United States, 34
Office of Lend-Lease Administration, United States, 5
Office for Mexicans Living Abroad, 105
Office of Naval Intelligence, United States, 150
Office for Personnel Management, United States, 5
Office of Price Administration and Civilian Supply, United States, 5
Office of Production Management, United States, 5
Office of Scientific Research and Development, United States, 5
Office of Strategic Services, United States, *See* OSS
Office of War Administration, 150
Ogdensburg Agreement (1940), 210
OHS (Office of Homeland Security), United States, 5, 6, 34, 149
Oklahoma City bombings, 132
Ontario border, 135
Operation Against Smugglers and Traffickers in the Safety and Security

Initiative, Mexico-United States. *See* OASSIS
Operation Alliance, 111
Operation Carlos Loyola, 117
Operation Casablanca, 110–11
Operation Gatekeeper, 106
Operation Ice Storm, 117
Operation Rescue, 117
Operation Samaniego-Valenzuela, 117
Operation Supersonic, 117
Operation Victoria, 117
Organization of American States. *See* OAS
OSS (Office of Strategic Services), 143, 150
Ottawa, 57, 61–62, 64, 89, 97–99, 154 passim, 246
Ottawa Land Mines Convention, 66

Pakistan, 70, 79, 219
PAN (*Partido Acción Nacional*), Mexican party, 114, 242
paradigms, 250 passim
Partido Acción Nacional, Mexican. *See* PAN
Partido de la Revolución Democrática. See PRD
Partido Revolucionario Institucional. See PRI
Partido Revolucionario Mexicano. See PRM
Partido Revolucionario Nacional. See PRN
PATRIOT (Providing Appropriate Tools Required to Intercept and Obstruct Terror) Act, United States, 6, 39; functions of, 40, 73, 105, 188
PCO (Privy Council Office): Canadian, 74
peacekeeping, as activity or agenda, 133
Pearl Harbor, 5, 30, 31, 145
Pearson, Lester (Canadian Prime Minister), 145, 210
Pentagon, 78
"perfect dictatorship," as cliché, 105
perimeter defense, 77; as concept, 89
petroleum, 122
Pew Global Attitude Poll(s), 31
PHF (Personal History Files), in Canada, 205
Phythian, Mark, 147
Pike, John, 71
pluralism (theoretical tenet), 50, 166, 172, 193
pluralistic tendencies, 235; security community. *See* PSC
Poland, 69
"policy-without-intelligence," 160
porfiriatos, in Central America, 111
Port Huron, as mega port, 139
Portillo, José López, 209
post-pluralism (theoretical approach), 166
Powell, Colin, 116, 153
PRD (*Partido de la Revolución Democrática*), Mexican, 11, 209, 242
Prébisch, Raúl, 250
PRI (*Partido Revolucionario Institucional*), Mexican, 11, 168, 209
procedural tendencies/behavior, 11, 113, 196
Privy Council (Canadian), 91
Privy Council Office. *See* PCO
PRM (*Partido Revolucionario Mexicano*), 207
PRN (*Partido Revolucionario Nacional*), 207
Providing Appropriate Tools Required to Intercept and Obstruct Terror Act. *See* PATRIOT Act
PSC (pluralistic security community), 13 passim, 113, 124 passim, 158, 232, 236
PSEPC (Public Safety and Emergency Preparedness, Canada), 74, 78–79, 90, 131
PSB (Public Safety Branch), Canadian, 208
Public Safety and Emergency Preparedness, Canada. *See* PSEPC
Public Safety Branch, Canada. *See* PSB
Purdy, Margaret, 94
Putin, Vladimir, 70, 71

Québec, 68, 78; Francophone, 87; people of, 88
quid pro quo policy approach, 204, 218, 222

rancho politics, 7
rail crossings, United States, 135
Rapid Response Team, 189

RAWs (replenished agricultural workers), 106–7
RCMP (Royal Canadian Mounted Police), 8, 10, 19 passim, 60, 73 passim, 136, 143, 151, 204, 208 passim; officers of, 90
Reagan, Ronald, 5, 25, 68; administration of, 63; revolution, 5, 152
realism, political (theory), 53, 149, 192
refugees, Cuban, 1
regional economic integration. *See* REI
regionalism, 127, 176, 234
REI (regional economic integration), 129 passim
Relyea, Howard C., 4–5
remittances, 122
Rempel, Roy, 145, 211
Renuart, Gene, General (Canadian), 59
Republican Party, United States, 48, 242; leadership of, 50; Libertarian wing of, 54; presidential primary campaign, 60
Ressam, Ahmed, 61, 132. *See also* "millennium bomber"
revolution in intelligence affairs. *See* RIA
revolution in military affairs. *See* RMA
RIA (revolution in intelligence affairs), 210
Rice, Condoleezza, 51
Rideau Centre (Canada), 95
Ridge-Manley Accord, 89
Ridge, Tom, 6, 115
Río Grande, River, 174
Rita, Hurricane, 35
RMA (revolution in military affairs), 6, 210
RNWMP (Royal Northwest Mounted Police), Canadian, 148, 205, 209
Roach, Kent, 9, 73
Robertson, Kenneth G., 207
Rochlin, James F., 165
rogue states, 67, 69
roll-back, policy (against communists), 62
Roosevelt, Franklin D., 4, 143, 145, 210
Rosenau, James, 249
Ross, Cam, General (Canadian), 67
Rostow, Walt Whitman, 152
Roussel, Stéphane, 89
Royal Canadian Mounted Police. *See* RCMP
Royal Northwest Mounted Police, Canadian. *See* RNWMP
Rudner, Martin, 210
Russia, 32, 69–70

Saddam. *See* Hussein, Saddam
SAGARPA (*La Secretaria de Agricultura, Ganaderia, Desarrollo Rural, Pesca y Alimentación*), Mexican, 189
Salinas de Gortari, Carlos, 108, 112, 209
SAWs (Specialized agricultural workers), 106–7
Sayle, Edward F., Sir, 146
SBP (Shared Border Process), 136
Schiengold, Stuart, 126 passim
Scowcroft, Brent, 152
SDI (Strategic Defense Initiative), United States, 68
Secretariat de Gobernación, Mexican, 207
Secretariat de Salud, Mexican, 189
Secure Electronic Network for Travelers Rapid Inspection. *See* SENTRI
security community/integration, 227, 239, 241; as theory, 4, 13 passim, 152, 156, 169, 175, 215 passim, 230 passim
Security and Intelligence Review Board, Canadian. *See* SIRC
security intelligence. *See* SIGINT
security perimeter, 47; United States, 133; North American, 192
Security and Prosperity Partnership. *See* SPP
SEDENA (*Secretaría de Defensa Nacional*), Mexican, 10
SEMAR (Mexican), 10
Senlis Council, 61
SENTRI (Secure Electronic Network for Travelers Rapid Inspection), 116, 188
SEVIS, 135
SG (Solicitor General), Canadian, 91, 211
Shamrock Summit, 25
Shanghai Cooperation Organization, 71
Shared Border Process. *See* SBP
SIGINT (security intelligence), 10, 208
Simpson-Mazzoli immigration bills, 106

Sinclair, Jill, 7
sine qua non, policy approach/option, 234
SIRC (Security and Intelligence Review Committee), Canadian, 8, 151, 210 passim
sleeper cells, terrorist, 38
Sloan, Elinor, 210
smart border(s), 47, 89, 134, 152, 213
smart cards, 116
Smith, Peter H., 108
Snider, Brito (CIA Inspector General), 145
Snow, Donald, 146, 160–62
SOA (Summit of the Americas), in Miami, 2; in Québec, 102
soft power, 31, 65, 187
softwood lumber (trade dispute), 69, 87
Solicitor General, Canada. *See* SG
Sonora, 117
South America, 62
Southern Command, United States, 186
Southwest Border Initiative, Mexico-United States, 190
Soviet Union, 176
Spain, 162
Spanish, as language, 232
special activities (covert action), 143
specialized agricultural workers. *See* SAWs
spillover (as theoretical tenet), 49, 172, 193, 216, 228
SPP (Security and Prosperity Partnership), 93, 100, 133, 190
SSP (Mexican), 9
Standing Senate Committee on National Security and Defence, Canada, 76
START (Strategic Arms Reduction Talks), 70
state-society fissures, 27
St. Lawrence Seaway, system of, 90
strategic culture, 238
Strategic Arms Reduction Talks. *See* START
Strategic Defense Initiative. *See* SDI
Strategic Highway Infrastructure Program, 136
Supply Chain and Logistics Canada, 140
supply-side, as Mexico-U.S. immigration problem, 110
supranational tendencies, 193, 232, 249
Sweedler, Alan, 8
symmetry, economic, 48, 229
Syria, 73, 145

TAU (Threat Assessment Unit), Canadian, 8, 211
Taiwan, 71
Taliban, 63, 142, 225; foreign fighters of, 57
Tamaulipas, 185
Taplin, Winn L., 143, 160
Task Force on Immigration, U.S. Report, 188
TC (Transport Canada), 74–75
Tenet, George (CIA Director), 145
terrorism, 22, 31, 34, 74, 98, 120, 236; soft on, 46, 196, 220
terrorist(s), 166, 224; cells, 34; homegrown types, 97
Terrorist Threat Integration Center, United States. *See* TTIC
Texas, 106, 179, 183–184
Thomas, Ginger, 103
Threat and Assessment Unit, Canada. *See* TAU
three-strikes-and-you-are-out, California legislation, 107
Tijuana, 108, 185; border with San Diego, 106–7, 247
Tocqueville, Alexis de. *See* de Tocqueville, Alexis
Todd, Paul, 160
Toronto, June 2006 arrest in, 214, 216
trans-border, as area, 108
Transportation Canada. *See* TC
Transportation Security Administration, United States. *See* TSA
travel and tourism, after 9/11, 42–45
triage, 9
trilateralism/trilateralist, 196, 229, 232, 236 passim, 240 passim
Trotter, Gary T., 9
Troy, Thomas F., 150–51, 165
Trudeau, Pierre E., 25, 206; on intelligence agencies, 145, 210 passim; his NEP, 63; his Vietnam approach, 64–65;

truck-crossing (Canada-United States), 86
Truman, Harry S., 150; administration of, 34
TSA (Transportation Security Administration), United States, 5, 36
TTIC (Terrorist Threat Integration Center), United States, 6
Turner, Michael A., 20, 147–8, 160–61, 163

UN (United Nations), 61, 155, 157; Monterrey, Mexico summit, 103, 114, 116; peacekeeping forces, 67, 141; Resolution 1441, 202, 230Security Council of, 67
UNCTAD (U.N. Conference on Trade and Development), 27
undocumented migrants, 183. See also *immigration,* and *cross-border externalities*
unilateralism, 196, 239 passim
United Nations. *See* UN
United Nations Conference on Trade and Development. *See* UNCTAD
United Province of Central America, 161
United States. *See* U.S.
Universal, El, Mexican daily, 114
undocumented Mexican migrants, 51
U.S. (United States): U.S.-Canada borders, 60; U.S.-Canadian relations, 27, 153, 157, 247; U.S. Congress, 168; U.S. -Latin relations, 160; U.S. leadership, 237; U.S.-Mexican Action Plan for Cooperation, 117; U.S.-Mexican borders, 114, 187; U.S.-Mexican Partnership Treaty for Prosperity, 190; U.S.-Mexican relations, 28; U.S. Military Assistance Advisory Group (Cold War), 111; U.S. policy-making, 113; U.S. security free riders, 242; U.S. Southern Command, 186; U.S.-VISIT (Visitor and Immigrant Status Indicator System), 116, 135

VACIS (Vehicle and Cargo Inspection Systems), 76, 134
values, 224, 249
Vancouver Winter Olympics, 80
Vano, Gerard S., 168
Vargas Llosa, Mario, 105, 161
Vehicle and Cargo Inspection Systems. *See* VACIS
Vietnam, 62, 65; war in, 161
"virtual security fence," 132
VISIT. *See* U.S.-VISIT
Visitor and Immigrant Status Indicator System (VISIT). *See* U.S.-VISIT

Walls, between Mexico and United States, 106, 114
Waltz, Kenneth, 26, 128
"war on terror," 40; United States, 57, 61, 67, 200
War Powers Act, United States, 5
Warsaw Pact Two, 71
Washington, 57, 59, 67, 98, 175, 237
Washington Consensus, 120–21, 214, 229, 245
Washington, George, 147
Weber, Max, 3
Weiss, Brian J., 144
"western alienation," claim of, 80
Western hemisphere, 27, 47, 162
Whitaker, Reg, 145, 210
White House Office, 4, 34, 87
WHTI (Western Hemisphere Travel Initiative), 60, 88, 133, 135
"with-us or against-us" dictum, 20, 154, 171
WMD (weapons of mass destruction), 2, 32, 67; rationale of, 145; U.S. argument based on, 161
World Bank, 142
"world in depression," 4
World Trade Organization. *See* WTO
World War I, 150–51, 203
World War II, 19, 144, 148, 150, 162, 195, 203; post–, 165, 168, 243
WTO (World Trade Organization), 65, 157, 247

Zapatista uprisings, 111, 161, 249
Zedillo Ponce de León, Ernesto, 105, 172, 209; his security policy approach, 111
Zetas, 111, 165, 185
Zinser, Adolfo Aguilar, 10

ABOUT THE AUTHORS

THE AUTHORS

IMTIAZ HUSSAIN is Professor of International Relations at the Department of International Studies, *Universidad Iberoamericana,* Mexico City. His research and teaching interests range across the international relations spectrum, as have his publications. Originally from Bangladesh, he graduated from the University of Pennsylvania in Political Science, and has been at *Universidad Iberoamericana* since 1998. For more, see www.imtiazhussain.net.

SATYA R. PATTNAYAK is Professor of Sociology and Political Science and Director of Latin American Studies at Villanova University. Most recently, he has authored "India as an Emerging Power" (*India Quarterly,* 2007) and *The Return of the State: Globalization, Capital, Coercion, and Development* (2006).

ANIL HIRA is cross-appointed with Latin American Studies, and taught at the American University in Cairo and Tulane University before coming to Simon Fraser University. His research interests include international political economy, economic integration, energy deregulation, participatory governance, and fair trade. His geographical focus is on the MERCOSUR countries of South America. He is author of the books *Ideas and Economic Policy in Latin America* (1998) and *Political Economy of Energy in the Southern Cone* (2003).

THE CONTRIBUTOR

DOUGLAS A. ROSS has been Professor of Political Science at Simon Fraser University since 1988, with major research interests in Canadian foreign and defense policies, strategic studies and arms control, and approaches to grand strategy. He has authored a study on Canada's involvement in the Vietnam War and many other works on Canadian international security relations and has published in *International Journal, Canadian Foreign Policy,* and the *Bulletin of the Atomic Scientists.*